The Edward Snowden Affair

EXPOSING THE POLITICS AND MEDIA BEHIND THE NSA SCANDAL

Michael Gurnow

Blue River Press
Indianapolis

www.brpressbooks.com

The Edward Snowden Affair © 2014 Michael Gurnow
ISBN: 9781935628361
Library of Congress Control Number: 2014930448

Cover designed by Phil Velikan
Editorial assistance provided by Dorothy Chambers
Packaged by Wish Publishing

Printed in the United States of America
10 9 8 7 6 5 4 3 2 1

Distributed in the United States by
Cardinal Publishers Group
www.cardinalpub.com

For my wife, may your watchful eye remain ever-present

ACKNOWLEDGMENTS

Though there were many hands that crafted my ability and willingness to undertake this endeavor, I am obligated to pay my respects to a handful in particular.

Before I met Tom Doherty, I didn't believe laughter within the publication industry could be bilateral. This project might have stagnated if it wasn't for his humorous reprieves, pragmatic sensibility and level-headed judgment.

To my editors, Dorothy Chambers and Holly Kondras, who are living proof literary alchemists walk among us.

Kelly McDaniel not only taught me how government functioned in theory and actuality, he continues to do so with equal amounts of patience and courage.

My IT knowledge and understanding of technopolitics would be nonexistent if it weren't for Floyd Lockhart. Our understated, muffled conversations prove endlessly rewarding.

Without the devoted efforts of my IT team—Daniel Ellinghouse, Latham Hunter and the Bushido Chemist—this project would have come to a premature end.

I owe a debt to Timothy Chism for being a very timely second set of eyes.

I would also like to tip my hat to Philip Dorling, author of one of the Snowden disclosure reports, whose willingness to provide a vital puzzle piece helped maintain the consistency of the narrative.

And my wife, who manipulated me into believing I could do this.

Table of Contents

Prologue:
A Busy Day for Washington

WASHINGTON HAD ITS HANDS FULL. The day before, June 5, a British daily newspaper *The Guardian* revealed that the FBI, with the power of the United States Foreign Intelligence Surveillance Court behind it, was actively utilizing a provision within the PATRIOT Act. A highly secretive order had been issued requiring one of the world's largest telecommunication providers, Verizon, to hand over all domestic call records between the dates of April 25 to July 19, 2013. The government was quick to respond as it reassured everyone the content of Verizon users' calls were not included, merely when and where a call was made, to what number, and on what phones. What the White House conveniently failed to include in its briefing was that the three-month window was not an exception but an ongoing rule: Consecutive extensions had been occurring for the past seven years and, though only hinted at in *The Guardian*'s report, included culled customer information of Verizon's competitors, AT&T and Sprint. The government was also in the process of accommodating the massive amount of incoming data. It was putting the finishing touches on a $1.5 billion top secret building located in the middle of the Utah desert.

A day later as the American capital attempted to quell the flames which were being fanned by the ACLU, Fourth Amendment advocates and enraged Verizon users, not one but two bombs were dropped. Pulitzer-winning journalist Barton Gellman and Oscar-nominated filmmaker Laura Poitras presented another, albeit much grander, revelation about the U.S. government's surveillance methods. In a *Washington Post* article titled, "U.S. intelligence mining data from nine U.S.

Internet companies in broad secret program," the duo disclosed classified information obtained from an anonymous source which had been extracted from the most enigmatic and secretive organization in America and perhaps the world: the National Security Agency. A few minutes later, an American attorney living in Brazil and the man partially responsible for the Verizon story, Glenn Greenwald, seconded the claim in *The Guardian*'s "NSA Prism program taps in to user data of Apple, Google and others." As the same groups who were up in arms about the previous day's shocking headlines lunged forward in protest while gaining international support and sympathy from countries around the world, many anticipated this was the tip of the proverbial iceberg and much, much more was taking place behind the security curtain in Fort Meade, Maryland. Yet, as the White House steadfastly backpedaled amid the incessant barrage of questions, one remained unanswered: Where had Greenwald, Gellman and Poitras gotten their information? If history was any guide, the public might never know unless the person responsible was caught, killed or opted to make a deathbed confession.

Three days later, the world would meet Edward Snowden, a former CIA and NSA contractor who had orchestrated the information dump not months but years prior, who had already fled the country and was now holed up in a hotel room in Hong Kong. This was the person responsible for, in *The New York Times*' approximation, "The most significant security breach in American history."

In the months ahead, a worldwide manhunt would ensue as the press continued to dispense piecemeal information about other covert surveillance programs. Democrats and Republicans would find themselves in uneasy agreement. Global demonstrations would take place. World leaders would learn America had been spying on them. A foreign president's plane would be forbidden safe passage for fear it contained the fugitive. Congress would consider demolishing the foundation upon which democracy was built. In less than two months, after three nations had offered Snowden asylum before the whistleblower accepted temporary sanctuary in Russia, President Barack Obama would appear on national television and unrepentantly announce the former Soviet Union had "slip[ped] back into Cold War thinking and a Cold War mentality." Amid public discussion on whether Snowden's actions might become analogous to Archduke Franz Ferdinand of Austria's assassination leading to the First World War, desperate to dilute the positive public opinion of the American exile and with the aid of the world's leading news source, the Capitol would stage a faux global terror threat. It would order bombings half a world away in hopes of wagging the dog.

Washington had its hands very, very full.

Introduction

IT IS NO SIMPLE MATTER to write a book about a trained spy. It is more difficult when that spy goes to great lengths to cover his tracks. It is a whole different monster to attempt to pin down a spy that was so good at keeping in the shadows, he collectively duped the greatest intelligence agencies the world has ever known. To make matters worse, a lot of what could be known about Edward Snowden will remain locked in olive drab filing cabinets. The U.S. government will make sure of that. It will use the excuse his information must remain classified because he worked for the CIA and NSA. However true, his records will also stay tightly sealed because Washington wants the public to know as little as possible about the embarrassing particulars. Needless to say, when I first approached the project, there were a lot of holes and a monumental amount of questions that needed to be answered. Hopefully I have filled some of those gaps, but many remain.

But this is not just a book about Edward Snowden. It is also about the debates his actions created. Though I devote a portion of time explaining the legal, political and technological aspects of the Snowden affair, my primary agenda is to provide the reader with a transcription of the argumentative evolution between the media, U.S. intelligence, the Capitol, corporations and various world leaders and nations. As can be expected, the discussions are often inadvertently—as well as deliberately—vague. This manifested in many conflicting reports and statements made about the whistleblower and the events surrounding him.

I approached divergent evidence with mental due diligence and benefit of the doubt. When deductive reasoning followed by cross-referenced sources and reverse-engineered data failed to produce a satisfactory answer, I reluctantly kowtowed to majority opinion, meaning I relied on the editorial integrity of disassociated fact-checkers in newsrooms across the globe. An example of reverse engineering can be seen in the attempt to determine when Snowden had broken both of his legs during military training. No press report tried to pinpoint when this had taken place, but all the information was there, all a person had to do was count backward. The results of this technique were often rewarding but consistently revealed other unasked questions. Some cases of reconciling opposing data were met with simple solutions. A *South China Morning Post* report fell outside the periodical's publication pattern. Upon closer examination I realized it housed an erroneous timestamp because a multitude of responses to the report were dated three weeks prior. The same occurred with *The Guardian*'s Boundless Informant exposé. These situations are probably the product of an edit updating an article's origination date. Automatic updates are the bane of a documentarian and a perpetual problem in the digital age. *SCMP* rectified its error shortly before this work went to press. To the best of my knowledge, at the time of publication all listed and cited dates are consistent with those posted by their representative sources.

Many riddles were solved by placing two books side-by-side. When a foreign president's flight crew reported it didn't have enough fuel to reach their destination, I called their bluff after conducting a little research on particular airplanes' fuel capacities while staring at a map. Other instances of irreconcilable information were more demanding because the only available sources were the conflicting reports. This is a frequent dilemma when dealing with newly revealed classified materials whose authors and representatives deny even exist. All one can do is hope additional information will one day be released, but there is no guarantee. Until that time, inductive reasoning is the only compass. For example, an article about a clandestine file stated 2.3 million bits of spy data had been corralled over the course of a decade. Another exposé claimed the same surveillance records had been gathered in a single month. There was no third party to consult, and the primary document was nondescript. I resolved the issue by looking at technological capabilities a decade prior and considering similar numbers in a German report dealing with a comparable espionage method. As always, I discuss how I came to certain conclusions and the methodology used.

However, if an incongruity doggedly persisted and the press's divide was 70/30 or less, I made the conscientious decision to include and discuss the divergent viewpoints. Also, if a reliable source was the only dissenter, especially if an argument was crafted by those who worked directly with Snowden or his stolen files, I include and annotate the fact. In a few instances, a dependable source contradicted itself. Snowden's father reported three different timelines for when his son started working in intelligence. Despite two dates being implausible because I could account for Snowden being elsewhere at that time, I nonetheless include the information so others can consider the possibility and, in the event I overlooked or misinterpreted something along the way, rectify my error.

Another challenge in writing this book was, unlike most historical studies, the Snowden Affair has no natural stopping point. It is one of the rare instances in which the conversation may exhaust itself before the events which initiated the debate come to a close. There are two reasons for continuing the discussion after the titular character steps offstage. One, as mentioned, the work is a study of Snowden, the media and the NSA. It would deprive the reader if the book ended with Snowden's biographical epilogue. Two, Snowden rightfully stated he wants the debate to focus upon modern surveillance policies and practices and not the person who brought them to light. From the present look of things, unless the U.S. government collapses or society suddenly abandons technology, the book—like most—will be a single chapter in a dialogue that spans many volumes. With that said, I chose to end on a thematic high note. For any reader skeptical about whether the surveillance debate should be taken seriously, I ask you read page 254 relating to smartphones.

In respect to the various classified disclosures: I had two diametrically-opposed objectives when writing about them. Though any interpretation harbors implicit bias, NSA analysts, surveillance watch groups and IT professionals may say my reading of the disclosures is too conservative. Legal experts, U.S. intelligence administrators and officials in Washington are apt to claim it is too liberal. Corporations, foreign nations and the press are the most likely to state I am close to the mark. I try to appease no particular audience, faction or party and merely attempt to present an examination of the information provided by the press through the government documents issued by Snowden. Because what is being presented is often highly technical and riddled with legal, technological and military jargon, I provide an introduction to the basic ideas and themes being discussed for readers not as acquainted with the fields as they might like. I refused to ignore any logistic warts for the sake of argumentative convenience while denying the urge to pick at others which begged to be inflamed. I save the rhetorical scratching for the Afterword. Conversely, on an equally frequent basis, I dive further into the materials than the original reports. This is not presumption on my behalf.

Though only a select few individuals and news sources were granted access to Snowden's documents, hundreds of reports emerged from them. The journalists entrusted with the materials were consistent in presenting information in a timely manner that not only steadily progressed the public debate while frequently relating to (con)current events but exhausted the available knowledge at the time of publication. Most of the editorials, especially the early ones, had to be published at a breakneck pace and at an exact time. It is obvious in the tone and organization of the early disclosures that the journalists wanted to say more. I simply try to extend these conversations. However, like any long-term discussion, the contents of many reports overlap. Some are continuations of previous editorials that nonetheless afford new insight. In these cases I offer an overview of a program, policy or law when it is first cited and try not to betray the development of the surveillance argument. However, if a topic is introduced, but a forthcoming discussion will grant the reader a better understanding of the subject matter, I postpone inclusion until the appropriate time. An example of this is SIGADs. Though passing reference is made to Signals Intelligence Activity Designators in numerous preceding reports, in the context of the Snowden affair, their use and purpose only becomes clear in a later disclosure.

I took the liberty of presenting the international edition of *Der Spiegel* exclusives. This admittedly shifts the publication chronology slightly, but the translations nonetheless appeared before thematically related events and never disrupt the progression of discussion. I made this decision because the alternative versions are clearly intended to be the focal exposés. They are more thorough in their coverage and deliberately designed to reach a broader audience.

I preemptively apologize for any vagaries or misreadings found within my analysis of the disclosures, especially those conveyed through a foreign press. These include original editorials in German, Portuguese and French and some tertiary sources in Chinese and Russian. Though my linguistic training took place under an NSA language analyst and I possess an IT and legal background, the Snowden affair extends into many, many fields—often to an exacting degree—which are far abreast of my expertise or even competence. Though no person can be all things all the time, I cannot be faulted for lack of trying; admittedly my ambition exceeds my ability at times. Any and all mistakes have been made in oblivious good faith. For this, I ask the reader to be kind.

I have no doubt the story of the Snowden affair will continue to expand. I hope to one day see entire books devoted to the divisions of his life: Pre-June 5, his time in Hong Kong and the whistleblower in Russia. However unlikely, I am free to dream that one or more of his intelligence colleagues, such as the intern assigned to work alongside him in Switzerland, will write a memoir. Nothing would make me happier than to see enough information float to the surface to generate an extended account of the NSA leaker's 38 days in Sheremetyevo International Airport, the Morales plane incident or the period Snowden spent with his editorial staff while ensconced in the Mira Hotel. I also hope someone will provide a thorough analysis of the Amash Amendment proceedings. Maybe a doctoral student in history or political science will choose to write about Germany or Brazil's response to the disclosures. Intelligence aficionados pray forthcoming Snowden documents will house enough information to fashion volumes, however slim, on the various surveillance programs. And I have no doubt, there will be biographies and autobiographies about and by many of the major players in the Snowden affair, perhaps even one from the whistleblower himself. Until then, I offer this early survey as a starting point for future authors to utilize and rightfully dispute what I read, discovered and learned about the NSA, the media and the one that got away.

Chapter 1
The Man Holding the Rubik's Cube

"If they had taught a class on how to be the kind of citizen Dick Cheney worries about, I would have finished high school."

–Edward Snowden, online chat via *The Guardian*, June 17, 2013[1]

✄ ✄ ✄

EDWARD JOSEPH SNOWDEN ENTERED THE WORLD almost 30 years to the day before it would know his name. He was born on June 21, 1983, in Elizabeth City, North Carolina, to Lon and Elizabeth Snowden. His mother has worked as Chief Deputy Clerk for Administration and Information Technology at the federal court in Baltimore since 1998, while his father is a proud, retired Coast Guard warrant officer of over 30 years who resides in Allentown, Pennsylvania.[2] His older sister, Jessica, is a research associate for the Federal Judicial Center in Washington.[3] It is assumed he has two stepsiblings.[4]

Snowden attended Crofton Woods Elementary in Annapolis, Maryland. Then-classmate Dawn Whitmore, now a professional photographer based in Washington D.C., referred to him as "kind of sweet" but recalled that the articulate nature of his speech captured in *The Guardian* interviews was characteristic of him at an early age: "He was very well thought-out with what he was trying to say." She added his visual trademark was his "nerdy glasses."[5]

He took classes at Anne Arundel Community College (AACC) in Arnold, Maryland, from 1999-2001. He did so not

1

as a premature college student but in hopes of earning enough credits to merit a high school diploma.[6] His father, a stout but by no means fat man who lends the impression of stern deliberation and intense focus and who shares the same clear speech patterns as his son, reported that Edward had contracted mononucleosis[7] during the 1998-1999 academic year.[8] His illness lasted "four or five months"[9] and forced him out of high school as a sophomore. Rather than return to Arundel High School in Gambrills, Maryland, Snowden elected to study for the GED at AACC. Contrary to popular belief, he dropped out before receiving a diploma, which he would confirm on an online message board after having been hired to work for the CIA: "I don't have a degree of ANY type. I don't even have a high school diploma."[10]

There is the possibility Lon is covering up for his son because Snowden would voice harsh disdain for educational institutions throughout his life. As he remarked on an online profile page in 2001, "[...] the public education system turned it's (sic) wretched, spiked back on me."[11] However, if he had been expelled from Arundel High due to disciplinary reasons, few took notice. When his former teachers were asked about Snowden's time in the classroom, none could remember him.[12]

In 2001, the Snowdens relocated to Ellicott City, located within the Baltimore-Washington metropolitan region. After leaving AACC, Edward moved away from his parents and into a gray clapboard-sided, family-owned condo.[13] Then-neighbor Joyce Kinsey remembered Snowden, who stayed in the condo only a few years. "He was a quiet guy," she recalled, "kept to himself. He always dressed nice, was clean cut. He just reminded me of a brainiac." She admitted Snowden "wasn't really personable. He didn't say much at all. He would say 'Hi' but he'd be looking down."[14] Kinsey remembered her neighbor cohabitated with a roommate and then a "kind of artsy" young woman with eccentrically dyed hair whose license plates read "ARTIST."[15] Snowden would later lament leaving this mysterious woman once he'd started his CIA training.[16]

When Snowden moved out of the condo circa 2004, Elizabeth—but not Lon—took up residence. Her only roommate was her dog. Kinsey commented the canine "knows how to get her [Elizabeth] help," perhaps implying the dog served an emotional need for Elizabeth after her divorce three years prior. Kinsey added Elizabeth's furry companion was never out of its owner's sight and even accompanied her to work.[17] Little else is known about Elizabeth.

Public records show Lon lived in Crofton, Maryland, from the early 1990s until 2007.[18] Whether he was dividing time between career and family or had already separated from Elizabeth is unclear.[19] Like many broken marriages involving children, it appears as if Lon and Elizabeth might have waited out their marriage until the kids were grown. What is certain is sometime after 2007, probably upon his retirement in 2009, he moved to the Lehigh Valley and married a 48-year-old woman named Karen Haberbosch.[20]

Interestingly, Snowden would cite having attended Catonsville Community College during this period, February to May 2002. However, the school changed its title to Community College of Baltimore County Catonsville in 1998 and has no record of a student by Snowden's name. Ironically, negligible attendance at another name-changing educational institution followed.[21] Snowden purportedly enrolled in a Windows systems engineering class at the Computer Career Institute at Johns Hopkins University in Columbia, Maryland. At the supposed time of his attendance, the name of the for-profit affiliated entity was Advanced Career Technologies, but the university shut down the facility in 2012 after ending its relationship with the business three years before. The admissions office has no record of an Edward J. Snowden having ever gone to school at Johns Hopkins.[22]

The synchronicity of the two schools denying Snowden's enrollment meant either Snowden was lying about his education in an attempt to compensate for his lack of having the minimal high school diploma, or in the midst of controversy the educational facilities were merely avoiding the limelight.

It is hard to say; many of Snowden's confidants and colleagues would repeat that he would downplay and overcompensate for his lack of formal education.[23]

With such little early information, constructing a psychological profile of young Snowden is difficult, yet it is arguable that his thin physicality, sickly nature and intelligence distanced him from people at an early age. As is often the case with such individuals, he retreated into a realm where social inadequacy was more readily accepted and tolerated. Somewhat stereotypically, he thrust himself into the world of computers, video games and Japanese popular culture.

It was during this time Snowden began appearing online. He and a group of friends tried their hand at creating a business rooted in love: Japanese comics and animation, commonly referred to as "manga" and "anime" respectively. Ryuhana Press was founded in 2001, and Snowden served as its web designer.[24] Snowden's Ryuhanan profile listed him as a 37-year-old father of two, "Lashawnda and Tamiqua; Ages 11 and 12 respectively."[25] He went by the handles "Edowaado," "Phish" and "True HOOHA."[26] His commentary reveals something about his attitude and mindset at the time. Of himself he stated, "I really am a nice guy. You see, I act arrogant and cruel because I was not hugged enough as a child."[27] Obviously Snowden's sense of wit and sarcasm was already being used to veil his true as well as subconscious nature. But even at this formative stage, he was evidencing, however sardonically, an apprehension for authority: "I like Japanese, I like food, I like martial arts, I like ponies, I like guns, I like food, I like girls, I like my girlish figure that attracts girls, and I like my lamer friends. That's the best biography you'll get out of me, coppers!" Yet amid all the grandstanding, he never attempts to hide his interest in computers and technology, "I always wanted to write RPG [Role-Playing (video) Game] campaigns with my spare time, but I'll get about three missions in and scrap the world for my next, better, powergamin' build."[28] Snowden was already aware of his propensity to grow easily bored, even with something as complex as computer programming. He not only housed an interest in designing games but was an apt player. If the anonymous report by one of his former Ryuhana partners can be believed, Snowden reveled in the 1994 video game Tekken and was good enough to garner a crowd at the 2002 Anime USA Convention.[29] Ryuhana ceased operations in 2004, but the website remained online until shortly after Snowden's confidential government disclosures started appearing.[30]

Though there is no manner to confirm their authenticity, there exist hundreds of online posts under the pseudonym "The TrueHOOHA." An account under that name on the Ars Technica message board matches Snowden's age, and when the profile was updated five years after it was created, it listed its owner's occupation as being a government information technology (IT) employee after having previously read "Ryuhana Press." In a post dated August 14, 2006, the account holder relays, "I have no degree, nor even a high school diploma."[31] Most would state that the capstone to the argument that the account was undeniably held by Snowden is pictures of a person who looks remarkably like him were downloaded to the site by The TrueHOOHA in 2006. However, in a world where online predation and identity theft is extremely common, especially with computer-savvy individuals such as those who would frequent a technology-themed website like Ars Technica, it is only best to assume.[32] Yet the chronology of the posts and their content maintain a striking consistency with Snowden's life.

For example, on May 19, 2006, in semi-sardonic reference to a strange clicking heard within another forum member's Xbox360 gaming console, The TrueHOOHA commented, "NSA's [National Security Agency] new surveillance program. That's the sound of freedom, citizen!"[33] If this is Snowden, what is perhaps most interesting is at the age of 20, he was already probing into the intricacies of Internet security. Under a thread titled, "In-depth thoery (sic) questions: How proxies WORK. (Difficulty: Guru)," he inquired, "Is it possible to reroute -all- traffic through a remote proxy? By all, I mean traffic such as SMTP [email] as opposed to the standard HTTP/FTP/SSH/Socks. How could you go about doing this (Is special software required)?" When asked why he wanted this fairly technical knowledge about how to surf the Internet anonymously, he responded, "I want to be protected, but I'm not sure where to draw the line" because of "[the] Patriot Act. If they misinterpret that (sic) actions I perform, I could be a cyb4r terrorist and that would be very fucking bad."[34]

During this time, Snowden left the condo and did something characteristically atypical: He joined the military. He would report almost a decade later that he chose to enlist "[...] to fight in the Iraq war because I felt like I had an obligation as a human being to help free people from oppression"[35] and "I enlisted in the army shortly after the invasion of Iraq and I believed in the goodness of what we were doing, I believed in the nobility of our intentions to free oppressed people overseas."[36] His justification for action would remain consistent throughout his life. History proves he was not fabricating the existence of a youthful patriotism. In a September 2003 Ars discussion about recently released French playing cards whose faces parodied the Bush administration, Snowden's opinion was short and pithy, "Fuck the [F]rench and their bitchy little cards. They can't even come up with decent rules for pronunciation. I certainly couldn't care less what they think of our country's politics."[37] However, the underlying motive for enlisting might have been unemployment. "Waiting for hiring to pick back up," he would comment on Ars during this time, while announcing he spent "eight hours a day surfing [on the Internet], four doing Kung Fu (Tues-Sat), and two playing Tekken at [the dojo where he studied] Kung Fu."[38]

From May 7 to September 28, 2004[39] he was part of the 198th Infantry Brigade in the Army Reserve's 18-X program at Fort Benning, Georgia.[40] The program is designed to fast-track recruits into the Special Forces. This is where Snowden reveals his agnosticism, because he was obligated to list Buddhism as his religion on his military paperwork in the wake of his true belief.[41] (The TrueHOOHA discussed agnosticism a year before on the Ars message board with one of the website's writers, Peter Bright, and its editor-in-chief, Ken Fisher.)[42] But he didn't make it very far in the military. Army spokesman Col. David H. Patterson Jr. stated, "He [Snowden] attempted to qualify to become a Special Forces soldier but did not complete the requisite training and was administratively discharged from the Army." Snowden would later inform *The Guardian* he had been let go after suffering two broken legs in an advanced infantry training[43] accident. This occurred in late July or early August.[44] Since the 18-X program is comprised of 14 weeks of basic training, then airborne skills, followed by another month of training, given his release date, it is likely Snowden broke his legs in a parachuting mishap.

Considering Snowden would later rise through the highest ranks of America's most secretive government agencies with no formal education, it is tempting to hypothesize whether this vague period in the military was early detection and subsequent espionage training by the government, especially since his discharge was inexplicably delayed for over a month. Moreover, to be admitted into the 18-X program, recruits have to pass a vocational aptitude test. Thus the military would have been privy to Snowden's mental capabilities and might have sought to capitalize upon them. To add weight to this theory, Snowden did not post once on his beloved Ars message board during the whole of 2004. The next time such a comparable online absence would take place is after he'd begun work overseas for the CIA. Yet, since Snowden was willing to sacrifice a six-figure salary at a job located in a location getaway all for the sake of earnestness, it is unlikely he would continue to cloak this facet of his life if indeed his intelligence career had begun in 2004. It is more likely because of his temporary incapacitation and rehabilitation that he elected to return to AACC later that year. He took classes until 2005.[45] Surprisingly, his AACC transcript does not cite him having enrolled in a single computer science course.[46]

As much as his academic record is a vague mirage cast in a foggy haze, many of the particulars of his life from this period until June 6, 2013 often fall under the same veil of uncertainty, especially what he did during the second half of 2005 until his employment with the CIA in November 2006. It leaves much to speculation.

A majority of press releases and exposés cites Snowden as having assumed the role of security guard for the NSA during the next six months. This is somewhat of a misnomer, because he worked at the University of Maryland Center for Advanced Study of Language (CASL) in College Park, Maryland.[47] The reason most media report his first professional government position as being with the NSA is that the CASL, founded in 2003, is a joint enterprise between the U.S. government and the University of Maryland. It is the largest language research institute in America and is funded through the Department of Defense. It is tempting to humor whether his title of "security guard" was a cover, because when asked, University of Maryland spokesman Brian Ulmann listed Snowden's official position as having been "security specialist."[48] Snowden himself does not help the situation. At one turn he reported via an April 2006 Ars post that he was "making twice the average income" before later announcing his CIA position "double[d] my salary."[49] Unless security guards at the CASL earn a lot more than the national average or the CIA hires computer technicians at pennies on the dollar, something is amiss. Further deepening the plot, a month later Snowden would be leading an Ars discussion on how to enter the IT industry. In the process he brags, "I make $70k, I just had to turn down offers for $83k and $180k,"[50] yet, frustrating in its contradiction, in 2006 he would reflect, "I was unemployed for a full year and then had to work in a non-IT field for six months before I was able to *get back in IT* [my emphasis] and double my salary."[51]

Even if his time at the CASL is credited as being with the NSA, a presumed biographical typo took place in June 2013 which went largely unnoticed. In a letter addressed to the president penned by Lon Snowden's attorney, it is reported, "Since 2005, Mr. Snowden had been employed by the intelligence community."[52] Lon could have his dates incorrect, but 2005 predates Snowden's CASL employment and follows his military discharge. To Lon's discredit, he would later state his son started working in American intelligence in 2003.[53]

The most intriguing mystery about Snowden is how—regardless of whether he did so first for the CASL, NSA or CIA—he was hired to conduct classified IT work without being enlisted or having a college degree. By reverse engineering Snowden's timeline from his November 2006 start date with the CIA, this would mean he held the position of security "guard" from April/May until almost the end of the year. Given his curiosity and the basic requisite skills required to even get a foot in the door with any national security agency, it is reasonable to assume Snowden devoted the preceding 12 months to computer study. Later, another individual with a government cover who worked alongside Snowden would indirectly second this notion, stating she thought Snowden was "an IT whiz [...] who came by most of his skill and knowledge on his own."[54] Turning the biographical thumbscrews even more, though unemployed for almost a full year by that time, Snowden reported in July 2006 on Ars that he had "spen[t] some time in Ireland in February [of 2006]."[55]

Regardless of the how or why, by early 2007 he was stationed in Geneva, Switzerland. He was living in a four-bedroom apartment[56] and working for the CIA as, in Snowden's own words, a senior adviser.[57] The Swiss foreign ministry confirmed he was in residence from March 2007 to February 2009, not as an intelligence officer but as a U.S. mission employee. This means he was given a cover or, in spy terms, a secret identity by the American government.[58] Many in the press interpret this to mean he was conducting espionage work, and his job of "maintain[ing] computer network security"[59] might not have been as benevolent as it sounds. Snowden confirmed he had received "classified technical training"[60] before being deployed.

A fellow contractor who also possessed high-level clearance was stationed in Geneva with Snowden from 2007-2009.

Mavanee Anderson, a Vanderbilt Law School graduate, worked as an intern alongside, in her words, "Ed." She referred to him as an "incredibly smart, kind and sincere person," a skilled martial artist and someone who, like herself, reveled in Chinese New Year parades. She also noted the moral weight of his position was apparent even at this time: "He was already experiencing a crisis of conscience of sorts."[61] Snowden would prove her right. He later informed *The Guardian*, "Much of what I saw in Geneva really disillusioned me about how my government functions and what its impact is in the world." Snowden added, "I realized that I was part of something that was doing far more harm than good."[62] These statements were made in (partial) reference to Snowden being privy to CIA operatives who were assigned to extract financial information concerning pending transparency legislation from a Swiss banker. The mission was accomplished by taking the banker out drinking, goading him to attempt to drive home in his impaired condition and waiting until he got pulled over before offering him understated legal assistance for a *quid pro quo*.[63] The operation was in direct violation of the Vienna Convention on Diplomatic Relations.[64]

Some found Snowden's story dubious, namely Swiss President Ueli Maurer. "This would mean that the CIA successfully bribed the Geneva police and judiciary. With all due respect, I just can't imagine it," he told the Zurich-based German newspaper *SonntagsBlick*.[65] However, aside from subtly defending the capability and integrity of his own security forces by doubting the veracity of Snowden's claim, Maurer is basing his assessment on the assumption that CIA agents—who were very likely, like Snowden, recognized by the Swiss government as being in the country for diplomatic purposes—would break cover by formally introducing themselves and divulging their agenda to a foreign police force and various judiciary boards before attempting to pay them off. It is much more feasible that one team of operatives treated the banker to dinner while another set of agents posing as Swiss police officers awaited the banker's drunken departure. Aside from being trained professionals, their ruse would have been all the more convincing to someone who was intoxicated.

Critics of Snowden's report where quick to ask why the United States would have an interest in keeping tabs on the Swiss. It is well known that many American entrepreneurs hold offshore accounts to evade taxes, and a handful of Swiss banks have a reputation for being sympathetic to these interests because of their profitability. As time would tell, the most powerful nation in the world was not content to merely monitor American tax dodgers. In January 2013, Switzerland's oldest bank, Wegelin & Co., was for all intents and purposes closed by U.S. authorities. This was after Swiss banking executives failed to appear in court once it was confirmed that from 2002 to 2010 the bank had made agreements with American clients to hide funds and aid in submitting false tax returns. The cumulative loss was $1.2 billion in U.S. revenue.[66] Others questioned the plausibility of Snowden's assertion on the grounds of how someone contracted to work in IT would learn of other highly classified, non-IT-related CIA assignments. Yet closer examination doesn't necessarily remedy an already-puzzling storyline but convolutes it.

What is undeniable and equally remarkable is that Snowden's latent mental abilities lunge forward during this time, probably because his 140 IQ[67] was finally being engaged and challenged. This is clear by his writing at the time. In all truth, the largest bulk of his 773 Ars posts relates to video games, with various IT and personal exchanges sprinkled in along the way.[68] After five months of Ars silence, which had been, barring the whole of 2004, preceded by a steady stream of chatter since he began posting in 2001, Snowden appeared online once again. He avidly and almost exclusively engaged in highly involved stock market discussions. For example, on November 18, 2008, he posted, "Holy [J]esus, have you guys started using the new triple levered long/short Russell 1000/2000 index etfs? BGZ/BGU & TNA/TZA are the tickers, I believe. Puts the 2x ultra etfs to shame."[69] Two days later, he announced he'd invested $4,000 in TZA stock. He had bought it at $127.90 a share. By the end of the day, it was trading at $141.37.[70]

An "etf" is an exchanged-trade fund. It functions as a normal stock but is actually a security that tracks an index, commodity or basket of assets as an index fund does. Because of its duel-sided nature, expense ratios of an ETF are lower than regular stock. The owner gets the benefit of the diversification an index fund provides but with the malleability of selling short if desired. As irony would have it, the best known ETF is the Spider, whose stock exchange symbol is "SPY." An "ultrashort," "inverse" or "bear" ETF is a type of fund designed specifically to profit from loses. It is a component of the highly complex derivative market. Some share holders invest in inverse ETFs in order to hedge their portfolios.

It is always possible Snowden had absorbed some of the economic and political atmosphere around him and, in much the same manner that he perpetually overcompensated for his lack of a formal education, fabricated the numbers to impress Ars board members. If this is the case, he went to great lengths to create and sustain the ruse. By December 4, he was citing 1930s economic theory.[71]

It is also feasible, yet not probable, Snowden had taught himself the intricacies of the modern stock market. However, considering his disclosure concerning the Swiss banker atop exhibiting a functional knowledge on an online forum of economic principle put into practice, it is not outside of reason that Snowden had been trained in this field. Where he would have found the time to tutor himself to such a professional degree is another logistic issue because, as previously noted, his position with the CIA had kept him from steadily posting on Ars for the first time in over five months. Instead of viewing justification for Snowden's European activities necessitating a monumental leap in cognitive application and exercise, the most reasonable explanation is he was stationed in Geneva, in part, as the IT component of a financial investigation. This is a polite way of saying he was sent to Switzerland to hack into personal and financial databases, a skill which he would later explicitly and specifically be hired to do for the NSA. Advanced economic training would allow him to better understand his targets. Moreover, he was in an indisputable position of power. He would later list on his résumé he had been "called upon repeatedly for temporary duty" [...] "including support of the U.S. president" while working for the CIA.[72] In other words, Snowden was responsible for the president's IT security when the commander-in-chief arrived in Europe. Though portions of his résumé would later be questioned, this citation was not. Years later, in a letter of gratitude to a former Senator, he would also admit he had once worked for the Defense Intelligence Agency.[73] This is one of the most clandestine branches of American government intelligence. It specializes in espionage. The organization recruits and trains agents, moles and spies who, in part, collect human intelligence such as pending financial policies from foreign bankers. It is also the bureau that former vice president Dick Cheney assigned to design and execute more drastic interrogation measures.[74] Regardless of the particulars, Snowden's moral objection to what he had witnessed was not a disagreement with the U.S. government's seeking information about suspected financial crimes but the manner and method by which the data was being obtained.

Snowden admitted it was during this time that he first considered exposing government secrets. His motive for not going public was twofold: "Most of the secrets the CIA has are about people, not machines and systems, so I didn't feel comfortable with disclosures that I thought could endanger anyone." His second reason rested on the recent election of Barack Obama. Though he did not vote for the politician, it nonetheless gave him hope there might be policy reforms upon the Bush administration's invasive intelligence and surveillance doctrines which Snowden, as part of his job, was currently obligated to abide by and therefore support.[75] Anderson also insinuated Snowden left the CIA in order to distance himself from his troubled conscience.[76]

What Anderson did not know is that the apprehension she saw in her colleague was not just theoretical reservation.

"How do you launch a VM from a LiveCD?" Snowden queried on the Ars board on February 14. "The goal here is to be able to bring a LiveCD (Virus/Malware/Keylogger-free VM-launching platform) and a USB drive (VM Image) to any given computer and be able to [do] your work through the VM without leaving anything behind on the physical host machine."[77] Snowden was asking how to extract data from a computer without leaving a trace. Thus, on Valentine's Day 2009, the month he would leave the CIA, Snowden took the first steps which would later manifest into one of the largest intelligence leaks in history. It remains a curiosity why—given it would be four years in the making—this rather bold yet seemingly naïve question available to anyone with a computer went undetected. The answer is manifold. One, Snowden only vaguely hinted at what he did for a living on the Ars boards. Two, IT questions are a dime a dozen on a techie forum like Ars. Three, given he was a senior advisor, the CIA probably didn't feel the need to surveil Snowden, and even if it did, covert IT work was what he had been hired to do. (Perhaps not to personally conduct data extraction but, as senior advisor, the ability to instruct field agents in how to do so.) Snowden was clever in this aspect. He probably assumed no one would think twice about the post. For the query to arouse suspicion, a person would need to have all the Snowden puzzle pieces. An individual would have to know who "TrueHOOHA" was, what the Ars account holder did for a living, what the question meant, as well as know he was disgruntled.

The problem was he had been caught trying to access highly classified files. It is not known if Snowden was merely challenging his IT abilities, seeking to steal highly incriminating documents or trying to get a better understanding of the system in an effort to calm his emotional nerves. Once he was found out, his superior wrote a "derogatory" note. It was not sent further up the administrative ladder. Snowden had merely been told to take the rest of the day off.[78] The CIA would later dispute this claim. Because the two anonymous officials who came forward with the information refused to redact the statement, the agency's denial is indicative of not wanting to be further implicated in the Snowden debacle. Snowden would later refute the allegation.[79]

His tenure with the CIA would come to a close by the end of February. He submitted his resignation after an internal investigation was ordered as a consequence of the write-up.[80] However, if Anderson's intuition is correct that he left the CIA in an attempt to turn a blind eye to the U.S. government's questionable intelligence tactics and remove himself from personal and moral culpability, he did not journey far. Another intelligence organization was impressed with Snowden's work and offered him a position which permitted him to continue doing what he loved in a place he had dreamed about since he was a teenager. The temptation to take a vastly higher-paying job in a mystical foreign land was too great to resist. It also afforded Snowden the opportunity to see how other intelligence agencies functioned.[81]

He was hired as a contractor for the NSA through the Columbia, Maryland, branch of the Texas-based computer firm Dell Computers. The computer giant asked him to move to Japan. He'd listed on Ars this was his most sought-after country. In hopeful preparation of one day arriving there, he had taken three semesters of Japanese.[82] It is unclear how long he was in Japan before the company transferred him—in what would later be a stroke of excessively bad luck for the U.S. government—to Hawaii.

What is known about Snowden's time in the Far East is limited. During his first summer there, he entered the Tokyo campus of University of Maryland University College, which is located on an American military outpost, and undertook Asian Studies. He was only enrolled for a semester.[83] In another stroke of ironic synchronicity, Japan is where Snowden met fellow Marylandian, Lindsay Mills.

Mills would pose a paradoxical challenge for the press years later. It had difficulty reconciling how the introverted nature and formal appearance of Snowden had aligned with the Maryland Institute College of Art graduate.[84] She appeared to be the philosophical opposite of her boyfriend. Mills ran a blog,

"L's Journey,"[85] and possessed Twitter, Pinterest, Flickr, YouTube and Instagram accounts.[86] The media could not account for the apparent personality conflict due to what many would crassly designate as Mill's flagrant exhibitionism.

Throughout the Internet, Mills has hundreds of photographs of herself, a majority scantily clad, several involving acrobatics and many that include pole dancing as their centerpiece. In them the audience is met by a long-haired, dirty blonde with a slim, athletic build and crystal blue eyes. Yet the focal point of most every self-portrait is the overt playfulness and wry innocence Mills innately espouses. It would be easier for the press to sensationally refer to Mills as Snowden's "pole dancing" girlfriend than take the time to explain that the photographs were Mills' art. A few, such as *The New Yorker*, granted passing lip service to the possibility her online presence was not the average, ego-driven, spur-of-the-moment posting that Snowden was, in part, battling against the government exploiting. For example, in one picture "[Mills] stands just to the right of the center of the frame, wearing black lace underwear and a black bra, holding herself tight in a gesture of despondency, a bright yellow Forever 21 bag covering her face in a way that unfortunately recalls the infamous photos of prisoners in Abu Ghraib."[87] It is debatable whether her political allusion, color juxtaposition and sociological commentary of being unable to see, blinded as it were, due to an icon of consumerism, a shopping bag (which also cleverly critiques the pursuit of immortality through materialism via the brand name) is comparable to Annie Liebovitz's portraits. But it is undeniable an artistic mindset is avidly trying to express itself. Her creative impulse is also apparent in her prose. After Snowden fled the United States, leaving Mills behind, she wrote, "My world has opened and closed all at once. Leaving me alone at sea without a compass. Surely there will be villainous pirates, distracting mermaids, tides change in the new open water chapter of my journey. But at the moment, all I feel is alone … sometimes life doesn't afford proper goodbyes."[88]

The press frustratingly discovered that Mills' colleagues and co-workers liked and were devoted to her. Four days after the world learned Snowden's face, reporters were met by a vacant performance hall, Studio 4, in Hawaii, where Mills was part of the Waikiki Acrobatic Troupe. Its owner, Karl Vorwek, told reporters, "The pole people are definitely not coming back as long as you're [the press] here." He is referring to Mills, not being a stripper as the press's cursory label would suggest, but "a beginner at acrobatics" by Vorwek's professional assessment. Yet, as numerous former neighbors of the couple would confirm, Mills and Snowden kept their private lives private. Fellow co-worker Billy Bellew was oblivious to the fact Mills had been in an extended relationship with a live-in boyfriend.[89] Mills even admits this in a blog post, "I was able to finally introduce E to my skeptical friends (they weren't quite sure E existed)."[90]

Something that was known during this time in Snowden's life was that he had expert hacking capabilities. On a revised résumé, Snowden cited he had received his Ethical Hacker Certification, or CEH, in 2010.[91] This is an official title, earned after passing a 125-question multiple-choice test issued by the International Council of E-Commerce Consultants. To take the exam, a person must have either taken a five-day course at an accredited training center or have a minimal of two years professional IT security experience.

To reconcile the seeming paradox of the phrase "ethical hacker," one must first understand the common label for the three types of hackers: white, gray and black hat. Following the iconography established in American Western cinema, a black hat is what most people think of when hearing the word *hacker*, a bad guy. A black hat attempts to penetrate computer systems and networks in order to insert malicious computer code. These individuals are typically self-serving because the program financially benefits them through a click-for-profit scheme or by revealing sensitive financial data. By contrast the "good guy" white hat targets a system in order to reveal its weaknesses so a person or business can better fortify their property. This is called a "security audit." As the title suggests, a gray hat is a mixture of the two and an ethical fence-sitter. The latter does not make IT decisions based upon personal gain or the welfare of a paying client but is swayed by the moral demands of the situation. An example of a gray hat is the underground Anonymous coalition. At one turn the group targeted websites hosting child pornography.[92] Later in the same year Anonymous attacked Sony after the company attempted to install hacking defenses on its PlayStation 3 game system.[93] In theory a CEH is a white hat hacker. The government wanted Snowden to wear a white hat. Instead, he donned a gray one.

A professional security technician who had worked for two of the most clandestine intelligence agencies in the world did not need a third party to verify his ability. He sought certification because the U.S. government unapologetically required he be acknowledged as a hacker. CEH certification is mandated for government IT employees as outlined by Department of Defense Directive 8570.[94] Snowden was also certified by and held membership in (ISC)², the International Information Systems Security Certification Consortium. Unlike catch-all CEH- validation, the (ISC)² has levels of certification. When queried, the (ISC)² refused to disclose what type of (ISC)² certification Snowden possesses.[95]

Midway through his time with Dell, somewhat perplexingly because an undergraduate degree is a mandatory prerequisite, Snowden enrolled in a graduate program at one of the top 200 universities in the world.[96] In 2011, he commenced online work for a master's degree in computer security at the University of Liverpool. He was not auditing the program, because his graduation date was scheduled for 2013.[97] A university representative stated that Snowden was not active in his studies, probably because he went from being the supervisor of a team assigned to modernize backup computer infrastructures to a "cyberstrategist" and "cyber counterintelligence" agent for Dell. The latter two self-described roles were assumed after he arrived back on American soil.[98]

During this time Snowden was subjected to a five-year "periodic [background] reinvestigation."[99] Required of any government employee with top secret clearance, the inquiry was conducted by the firm which holds over 100 federal contracts and oversees background checks for more than 95 government agencies: U.S. Investigations Services (USIS).[100] The same year, the company would become involved in an extended criminal investigation for its "systemic failure to adequately conduct investigations under its contract."[101] USIS gave Snowden a green light in 2011 despite an inconclusive internal investigation involving claims of attempting to access and possibly steal classified materials. USIS also failed to examine a facet of his résumé another government contractor would look at very closely.

If Snowden's thoughts of whistleblowing had not already gone from being a germ of an idea alongside a juvenile attempt to peek behind the surveillance curtain when he was in Geneva to resolute intentions gradually being put into action, they were certainly starting to congeal. He was again growing disenchanted with the government's actions. One of the reasons he hadn't already gone public was starting to dissipate. Snowden said it was at this time he "watched as Obama advanced the very policies that I thought would be reined in." As a consequence, Snowden said he "got hardened."[102] He would reiterate this during an online chat on June 17, 2013: "Obama's campaign promises and election gave me faith that he would lead us toward fixing the problems he outlined in his quest for votes. Many Americans felt similarly. Unfortunately, shortly after assuming power, he closed the door on investigating systemic violations of law, deepened and expanded several abusive programs, and refused to spend the political capital to end the kind of human rights violations like we see in Guantanamo, where men still sit without charge."[103]

Snowden was back in the States no later than March 2012 because, obviously having given up hope Obama would reform intelligence legislation, he made a donation to Ron Paul's 2012 presidential bid from a residence in Columbia, Maryland.[104] (On July 12 during a Moscow meeting with Russian officials, attorneys and human rights groups, he could label himself a Libertarian.)[105] He traveled throughout the U.S. for Dell before taking time off to spend with his family, although he remained on the computer company's payroll. He had already begun executing his plan. Though Snowden's going all but silent on his beloved Ars boards in February 2010 could have been due to increased responsibility at Dell, it was likely he had done so as one of the preliminary steps in his intention to blow the whistle: He was reducing his digital footprint. During his last month at Dell he extracted data from its systems which related to eavesdropping programs of the NSA and Britain's Government Communications Headquarters. Snowden had made a novice mistake, but he didn't get caught. Dell would later confirm Snowden had left an electronic footprint.[106] (Shortly after the press debuted the story of Snowden receiving a written CIA reprimand, he quickly issued a statement refuting the assertion he'd tried to steal CIA files. However, Dell's report remained uncontested months after it was made. Therefore, his testimony that the "derogatory" note was the result of administrative backlash after Snowden had proved his supervisor wrong about a security flaw is suspect, especially since the event took place the month of the Valentine's Day query on Ars.)[107] One of the most vital stages came next. He applied to work for another government intelligence contractor.

Booz Allen Hamilton (BAH) is a technology consulting firm which holds government contracts alongside Dell in Hawaii.[108] Snowden wanted to switch employers for one simple reason and that was where BAH would have him working: Kunia Regional SIGINT Operations, which is part of the NSA's Threat Operations Center. The outpost's focus is China's classified programs. This segment of the NSA is an infiltration target for Chinese spies, both private and for the Chinese equivalent of the NSA, the Ministry of State Security of the People's Republic of China, or MSS, as well as for the Second Department of the People's Liberation Army, known as 2PLA. Snowden wanted information about American surveillance of China because he already had incriminating evidence about the American government's activities domestically as well as in Europe. He was aware of what Kunia did due to his proximity on the island when he was with Dell and had suspicions of what Kunia might contain. He was not disappointed.

The location was pivotal but the job he'd applied for was vital. As an infrastructure analyst Snowden would be given the ability to accomplish what he wanted. By BAH's own definition, an infrastructure analyst provides the ability for "organizations to process, interpret, and use massive data stores in weeks or months."[109] His job would be to move and reorganize files but he was hired as a professional hacker who could locate and exploit vulnerabilities in signal communication systems ("SIGINT" in Kunia's title is the military acronym for "signals intelligence"). Kunia hacks Chinese telephone and Internet networks. With its over one billion users primarily divided between three carriers, China is the world's largest mobile network carrier. Furthermore, the NSA provided Snowden with an unguarded, open door. He was part of the team expected to monitor whether other countries were attempting to do the same to America. In cyberintelligence terms, this is referred to as moving from offense, cyberwarfare, to defense, cybersecurity or counterintelligence. It is standard operating procedure to have analysts try their hand at both roles in order to determine their greatest strengths, propensities and preferences. It was a perfect situation. If Snowden triggered an alarm after extracting or moving data while working defense, he could easily account for it using the alibi that he was merely testing a system's integrity.[110]

Snowden didn't ease into a position at BAH. The firm expressed reservations about his résumé. It did not know about his CIA reprimand. The contractor's concern was his claim he had been a student at John Hopkins.[111] After explaining the institution's name change, though no university representative could confirm his enrollment, Snowden was given the job.

Snowden wouldn't start for BAH until late March or early April 2013, but he moved into a blue, 1,559-square-foot rental house which sat on the corner of the street in Waipahu, Hawaii, in May 2012.[112] This is where he made a second donation to the Libertarian presidential candidate.[113] Mills joined him the next month.[114] Little attention has been paid to Snowden's second "dark year" and how he occupied his time during this furlough. American Director of National Security Lieutenant General Keith Alexander stated Snowden had held a position at the NSA a year before assuming his position at BAH. It is not clear whether the general is referring to the analyst's tenure at Dell, which was much longer, or if there was yet another job the whistleblower once had in the Department of Defense.[115]

He knew he'd gotten the job with BAH by December, because this is when he first attempted to make anonymous contact with *The Guardian*'s Glenn Greenwald. Not receiving a response, a month later he tried Oscar-nominated documentarian Laura Poitras. Though non-committal at the time, she redirected him to Pulitzer-winning journalist Bart Gellman of the *The Washington Post*. Snowden emailed him the following month to mixed results. Time was of the essence, because though it would be several months before he would flee the country and almost three weeks hence when newspapers would release their famed first exposés, Snowden had yet to complete his last data reconnaissance mission.

He stayed with his family in Maryland while undergoing two weeks of training for BAH at Fort Meade.[116] He told his father he had changed jobs due to budget cuts.[117] After saying goodbye, he left for Kunia on April 4.[118] He would confirm during a one-hour interview in June with the *South China Morning Post* that the documentation he was providing the newspaper had been gathered two months before.[119] Many published disclosures would bear the end date of April 2013.

There was much speculation as to how the stolen data was physically transported out of Kunia. Two parties quickly formed: those who believed he had nonchalantly walked out of the building with the four laptops he was seen with when he arrived in Hong Kong,[120] and people who argued Snowden used the less conspicuous removable flash/junk/thumb drive.

The second faction stated the obviousness of removing entire computers from the intelligence compound was impossible given security protocols. This observation was met by the counterargument that a security system's greatest weakness is the people who run it because they can be socially engineered. Social engineering is psychology in motion. It is the direct and indirect emotional, intellectual and political manipulation of people. In most any other scenario, the argument might be a convincing one. A person bold enough to be freely seen removing laptops from a secure area is assumed to be doing so with express, permitted purpose and freedom. However, an NSA campus is not any secure facility. It is the NSA. Those who argued Snowden had used thumb drives to extract the data had to defend against the NSA policy forbidding any portable recording device on the premises.[121] However, Snowden's job title permitted him to be one of the select few exceptions. It was his job to transport data. Yet even as an infrastructure analyst working defense, Snowden could only set off so many alarms for unauthorized downloads before serious questions were asked. Months later, the NSA would still be unable to provide an accurate assessment of the quantity and quality of the materials stolen, no less the method(s) used. It would even be some time before it was clear his pilfering wasn't limited to Kunia.

By May 1, the house he and Mills were renting was empty. This was not because Snowden was about to flee the country; the property owner wanted to put it on the market.[122] The couple moved a few blocks away into a home which housed a two-story living room. They had received the keys for their new residence two weeks prior.[123] Mills had no clue what was about to take place. Less than a month into his role as infrastructure analyst, Snowden requested a two-week reprieve in order to seek medical treatment for his epilepsy which, he stated, had manifested the year before. He was granted the time off.[124]

Early on Monday, May 20, in a very risky move since all NSA personnel are required to file for international travel at least 30 days in advance, Snowden boarded a plane for Hong

Kong.[125] He told Mills, who had just returned from visiting her family in Laurel, Maryland, he would return shortly. By noon he had checked into the 429-room Mira Hotel located in Tsim Sha Tsui. It cost him $330 per night.[126] He had, in his terms, a "basic understanding" of Mandarin from at least seven years prior.[127] Unfortunately the predominant language in Hong Kong is Cantonese.

Greenwald and Poitras arrived in Hong Kong on June 1. They had no idea what Snowden looked like. He told them to go to the third floor of the Mira and look for a man holding a Rubik's Cube. To ensure Murphy's Law was not in effect should another person be in coincidental possession of the puzzle toy, they were to ask him when the restaurant would open and he would advise against the establishment.[128]

The government had already been informed it had a leak.

On Wednesday, June 5, *The Guardian* debuted "NSA collecting phone records of millions of Verizon customers daily."

On Thursday, June 6, *The Washington Post* presented "U.S. intelligence mining data from nine U.S. Internet companies in broad secret program" twenty minutes before the *The Guardian* published "NSA Prism program taps in to user data of Apple, Google and others." The newspapers' source is anonymous. All three editorials included top secret, classified government documents.

On Saturday, June 9, *The Guardian* released the first part of a video interview of the man purportedly responsible for the previously announced NSA leaks. The world got to see its first glimpse of Edward Snowden.

Chapter 2
How to Blow a Whistle

"The consent of the governed is not consent if it is not informed."

–Edward Snowden, online chat via *The Guardian*, June 17, 2013[1]

❧ ❧ ❧

THE WORLD MIGHT NOT HAVE EVER HEARD of Edward Snowden if it hadn't been for Thomas Drake.[2]

Thomas Andrews Drake is the son of a World War II veteran and the secretary of famed American novelist Pearl S. Buck.[3] His first encounter with U.S. intelligence was as an airborne voice processing specialist for the Air Force from 1979 to 1989.[4] In civilian terms, he listened to communications as he flew reconnaissance over the Eastern bloc of Germany.[5] From there he would meet Bill Clinton during his presidency when Drake worked at the National Military Joint Intelligence Center for the U.S. Navy.[6] A lifelong academe, he then did contract work for the NSA evaluating software before being hired by the agency in SIGINT.[7] His first day with the NSA was September 11, 2001.[8] Within three years, he had been promoted from technical director of software engineering implementation to process portfolio manager. His rising star was shot down after he reported to Congress the NSA's post-9/11 surveillance programs were wasteful and ineffective. Because he told Capitol Hill what the NSA was doing, Drake was reassigned to a professorship at the National Defense University where he would eventually become chair, yet in 2008 he was forced to resign from the NSA.[9]

Drake's contention was that then-NSA director General Michael Hayden had chosen a program called "Trailblazer" over another, titled "ThinThread." Both programs were designed to contend with monitoring the new and exponentially expanding World Wide Web and the advent and increased use of cell phones. Drake was part of a small but well-versed minority that believed ThinThread might have been able to detect and stop the 9/11 attacks had it not been discontinued three weeks prior (some reports claim it was never implemented). Remarkably Trailblazer was still theoretical on September 11, whereas ThinThread had been fully operational since the beginning of the year.[10] Drake and his coalition outlined that ThinThread was more effective in processing gross amounts of data, and unlike Trailblazer, it was mindful of Americans' pocketbooks and Fourth Amendment privacy rights.[11] ThinThread cost $3 million; Trailblazer had a $1.2 billion price tag.[12]

Following government protocol, Drake worked his way up the administrative grievance ladder. He appealed to his superiors, the NSA inspector general, the Defense Department inspector general, then the House and Senate. As a last resort, Drake—along with the Republican's staff expert on NSA's budget for the House Intelligence Committee, Diane Roark, and the lead designers of ThinThread, William Binney, Ed Loomis and J. Kirk Wiebe—presented a book-length complaint to the Department of Defense in 2002. Roark even went as far as contacting Dick Cheney's attorney, David Addington.[13] What Roark didn't know was Addington had been the pen behind the Bush administration's warrantless wiretapping program.[14] Though the Defense Department would eventually internally acknowledge that Drake and Co. had been correct in their assessment, the wasteful, ineffective and invasive programs continued.

There are three motivating factors that permitted the flawed system to persist. One, the government was reluctant to end any security project for fear of appearing unpatriotic. Two, the intelligence agency wanted the illicit data. These two are not mutually exclusive, because any politician labeled unpatriotic during this time risked reelection, and the biggest political donors were corporations who had a vested interest in personal data for marketing and advertising purposes. Three, Hayden was a lieutenant general closing in on retirement. He had only been director of the NSA for a few years and wanted to make a name for himself. He was made a full general a year before retiring in 2006.

Having played by the rules and even getting those responsible to admit fault yet unable to induce them to change their ways, Drake decided to go to the press. Between February 2006 and November 2007, *The Baltimore Sun* published a series of exposés on various aspects of the NSA, including the Trailblazer program.

Eight months later, the FBI stormed the homes of every author of the Department of Defense report except Drake. Binney, having been caught in the shower and still fully nude, was held at gunpoint.[15] The FBI was hoping it could elicit through intimidation incriminating evidence against Drake.[16] Not a single person was charged, but various items including computers and personal records were confiscated. Then in November, the FBI arrived at Drake's home.[17]

He was charged under the Espionage Act. A team of attorneys led by Steven Tyrrell worked on the case. The goal was to indict all involved. Two years into the investigation, Tyrell was replaced by William Welch,[18] who dropped all efforts to implicate co-conspirators and focused solely upon Drake. The government wanted to make a single and very harsh example.

Drake was brought up on multiple offenses by three divisions within the Department of Justice, the FBI and the NSA. The most serious was "Willful Retention of National Defense Information." This referred to five documents found inside Drake's residence.[19] All materials had been declassified. A kangaroo court ensued. Led by Welch, the prosecution sought to withhold exhibits, restrict cross-examinations, bar jurors from reading evidence and prohibit the defense from incorporating whistleblower argumentation.

Then on May 22, 2011, the television program *60 Minutes* aired an exposé about Drake's circumstance.[20] Eighteen days later, all charges were dropped.

Snowden learned three lessons from Drake.[21] Playing by the rules and keeping questionable information in-house accomplishes one thing: personal persecution. The intelligence community as well as the American government demanded absolute conformity and cohesion, and nothing was left up to debate. Two, because The Drake Report had already revealed what Snowden had to say yet no one paid attention, he needed a new format. *The Baltimore Sun*'s sources had been kept anonymous. It allowed the government to imply and explicitly state there was no manner or method to validate what it considered exaggerated and fabricated claims, and any supplemental documentation could be and was forged or had been taken out of context. It did not matter that Drake would later reveal himself as the source of the leaks; the government had already successfully executed damage control. It had convinced the American public everything was in order and the people responsible were disgruntled workers crying sour grapes because their project had not been chosen. If the story had ended here, Snowden might have left the intelligence community and said nothing. He would have viewed any effort to make matters known as futile and personally dangerous. Yet the third lesson made all the difference. Snowden had witnessed the impact the media could have on such affairs.

Snowden realized a disclosure of classified information required three things in order to raise the necessary eyebrows: a face so that credentials could not be doubted, documentation for support and the proper venue. He approached the selection of media channels through which he would filter thousands upon thousands of classified government intelligence documents in much the same manner he had extracted the purloined data, with great patience and meticulousness.

If a person wanted to bring an issue to the public's attention, most would seek the largest possible audience so it would have the greatest potential impact. However, the two largest news outlets were not an option for Snowden. Neither the news station with the greatest number of viewers, Fox News, nor the daily newspaper with the most readers, *The Wall Street Journal*, would have been sympathetic to Snowden's information due to their conservative platforms. Snowden was also sociologically astute enough to know he needed to legitimize and humanize the information with a face but knew an exclusively televised premier of the story would trivialize many of the pertinent details in favor of sensationalism and the opportunity for sound bites. His next, and best, venue was *The Wall Street Journal*'s rival, *The New York Times*. There was only one problem. Snowden didn't trust the *Times*.

James Risen and Eric Lichtblau wrote a story about the NSA's warrantless wiretapping program for the *Times* in November 2004.[22] It did not appear until December 2005 because the White House had caught wind of it. The Bush administration had requested it not be published during the election year on grounds that it might jeopardize ongoing investigations. When the article finally premiered, the *Times* obliged the government's request to omit various portions of the original report. Risen and Lichblau won the Pulitzer Prize for National Reporting the following year. The day after the exposé made headlines, the *Times* Executive Editor, Bill Keller, admitted this was not the first occasion the newspaper had withheld a story due to federal pressure.[23]

When asked by the *Times* on August 13 why he hadn't brought his information to the famed periodical, Snowden was polite but honest, "After 9/11, many of the most important news outlets in America abdicated their role as a check to power—the journalistic responsibility to challenge the excesses of government—for fear of being seen as unpatriotic and punished in the market during a period of heightened nationalism. From a business perspective, this was the obvious strategy, but what benefited the institutions ended up costing the public dearly. The major outlets are still only beginning to recover from this cold period."[24]

Snowden needed sympathetic ears whose owners had a strong, if not impeccable, track record for journalistic integrity. Though it wouldn't be obvious for several months, he also wanted people who lived in strategic locations: Europe and South America. Ironically the newspaper with the second-largest distribution in the nation provided him with his second contact after his first refused to respond. On August 8, 2012, the *Times* ran a doc-op piece on William Binney by filmmaker Laura Poitras.[25]

Born in 1964 and raised in Boston, Poitras studied at the San Francisco Art Institute under experimental filmmaker Ernie Gehr, whose 1970 *Serene Velocity* is preserved in the United States National Film Registry.[26] She received a graduate degree from The New School for Public Engagement in 1996. It wasn't *Flag Wars*, her first feature-length documentary which examines gentrification in America, which would garner the government's attention, but her sophomore effort, *My Country, My Country*. Ostensibly *My Country, My Country* is a portrait of Dr. Riyadh al-Adhadh and his work as a doctor and Sunni political candidate. The heart of the film is the daily life of American soldiers and those living in occupied Iraq. Though her narrative would merit an Academy Award nomination, it would also place Poitras on the Department of Homeland Security's watch list. Her "threat rating" is the highest the agency assigns, 400 out of 400.[27] Instead of allowing herself to be spooked, Poitras sallied forth. Her next documentary, *The Oath*, is a tale divided between Salim Ahmed Hamdan and Nasser al-Bahri, one of Osama bin Laden's drivers and bodyguards respectively. It was shot on location in Yemen and Cuba. The documentary is as much an exposé on the two individuals as it is a critical look into where a portion of the production was filmed, Guantánamo Bay.[28] In 2012, Poitras was awarded the most coveted, prestigious award for artists after the Nobel Prize, a MacArthur Fellowship.[29]

Snowden saw something not just in Poitras' subject matter but in her perseverance and refusal to be intimidated. Homeland Security's fetish for Poitras has manifested in what appears to be the hobby of border detainment. Beginning in Vienna in 2006,[30] she has been held in transit over 40 times. Her cameras, phones, notes, baggage and computers are perpetually seized without a warrant and delayed return. It is a sticky legal situation. The government claims since such altercations take place at international zones, constitutional rights aren't applicable. During an interrogation in Newark, she was instructed to quit taking notes lest she be handcuffed because her pen could be construed as a weapon. Given the government's reaction to Poitras, there is little doubt it is metaphorically right. She complied. What would appear to be a flippant request, she then asked for a crayon.[31] Not only does this follow United States interrogation protocol but implied how she perceived the proceedings. Chilling in its historical import, her airplane tickets are imprinted with "SSSS," Secondary Security Screening Selection. This signals to security the ticket holder is to be detained upon arrival.[32] To accelerate her perpetually delayed alighting time, Poitras started having fellow passengers check her bags. Unfortunately Homeland Security recently became privy to this technique. This method of baggage evasion would later backfire on one of her colleagues reporting on Snowden. Poitras became so exhausted by the perpetual harassment, she took an apartment in East Berlin in order to do her work in peace.[33]

Though Poitras was the first journalist to connect with Snowden, she was the last of the trio to speak about her experiences of communicating with the then-mysterious voice behind the screen.[34] In January 2013, three months before he would start working for his last NSA contactor, Snowden contacted Poitras anonymously and asked for her encryption key.[35]

There are two types of email encryption: symmetrical and asymmetrical. The easiest way to understand the difference is to imagine a box. Within the box is a rotating partition. It also has locks on the front and back. In symmetric encryption, one key opens both sides and the divider can be freely rotated from either side, exposing the box's contents to anyone who has access. A person who puts something in the box can also take it out of the box. With asymmetric encryption, the two locks are different and require two different keys. Also, when something is placed in the box, the sender must rotate the partition, which then locks into place. The person who made the deposit can open the box again but cannot retrieve whatever was originally put inside. Only the individual with the other key can. Symmetric encryption is understandably faster but less secure than asymmetrical encoding.

Due to the nature of her work, Snowden knew Poitras would already have encryption programs in place. She sent him the key. She received instructions on how to download extremely secure programs and was told to establish a very long passphrase. By definition, a passphrase is longer than a password, and therefore the possible permutations are exponentially increased and consequently harder to crack. The standard method for gaining unauthorized password access is called a "brute force attack." To save time, a brute force attack program will not progress alphabetically but instead tries the most statistically probable variations first. For example, in the English language, there is a 26 percent likelihood a word beginning with the letter "s" will be immediately followed by a "t." (This is why the NSA hires professional linguists to work in cryptology.) Frighteningly, Snowden told her to "[a]ssume that your adversary is capable of a trillion guesses per second."[36]

Snowden then began filling her inbox with outlines of government surveillance programs. She had only heard of one. Alarmed at the obvious legal implications of possessing the information, she disconnected from the Internet after deleting the messages.[37] She at first believed this was the government attempting to get her to incriminate herself and her sources. (She had just returned from interviewing the founder of the anti-secrecy website WikiLeaks, Julian Assange.) After giving thought to the situation, she decided to try to get Snowden to call his own bluff. She said she "[...] called him out. I said either you have this information and you are taking huge risks or you are trying to entrap me and the people I know, or you're crazy."[38]

Snowden was in a predicament. He made himself more susceptible to discovery with each keystroke. Semantic analysis is a detection method wherein a person can be traced back via word choice and sentence structure patterns. Every line he sent made his linguistic fingerprint more distinct.[39] He needed to get Poitras to agree to a personal meeting so a face would accompany the story. Instead of providing more evidence which could flesh out an article without the need to meet its source, he wisely told Poitras his reasons for choosing her. He discussed her history of border abuses and documentary on Binney.[40] She remained dubious, but her suspicions eased when Snowden didn't press her for information as a government agent would. He informed her she would need someone else's assistance in the story and advised the American attorney-turned-journalist Glenn Greenwald. Snowden recommended Greenwald for an express reason. He needed someone who knew the Constitution inside and out. He also happened to live in Brazil. She in turn suggested he contact Bart Gellman of the *The Washington Post*. She offered Gellman because she trusted him, having worked alongside the journalist at The Center on Law and Security at New York University.[41] He would be the one whose word she would value most on whether to proceed with the anonymous emailer.[42]

Glenn Greenwald was born in New York City in 1967 but raised in south Florida. Before graduating from New York University Law School in 1994, he earned his bachelor's from George Washington University. He was hired into the litigation department at Wachtell, Lipton, Rosen & Katz in New York City but within two years would open Greenwald, Christoph & Holland. This permitted him to focus on constitutional law and civil rights. He left the firm nine years later to pursue a writing career.

He'd started his own political blog, "Unclaimed Territory," a year before leaving his firm. His early writing dealt with the CIA, Lewis "Scooter" Libby and America's warrantless wiretapping program. By February 2007 he was a contributor for *Salon*. Due in part to Greenwald's work for the website, John

Brennan withdrew his candidacy for CIA director and director of national intelligence.[43] In hopes of reaching a different, broader audience, Greenwald accepted a position at the 191-year-old British periodical *The Guardian* in 2012. He lives in Rio de Janeiro because of what he claims is The Defense of Marriage Act preventing his partner, David Miranda, from acquiring immigration rights.[44]

Greenwald's first book was published in 2006, *How Would a Patriot Act?* It explores post-9/11 executive power abuses and was ranked #1 on Amazon.com before becoming a *New York Times* bestseller. Shortly after joining the *Salon* staff, Greenwald's second book hit shelves, *A Tragic Legacy*. The book-length character study of George W. Bush brought Greenwald back to the bestseller lists. Two more books followed: *Great American Hypocrites* in 2008 and *With Liberty and Justice for Some* in 2011. The former focuses upon the incongruities between the marketing and branding strategies of Republican candidates and the politicians' real lives. The latter examines the American court system since Watergate and the judicial double standard it uses to protect the elite.

In much the same manner that the intelligence community stacked the deck against itself by transferring Snowden to Hawaii, enabling him to become privy to BAH and Kunia where he might not have otherwise, it was the U.S. government's fault Greenwald personally knew Poitras. Poitras met Greenwald in 2010 after reading his work on WikiLeaks for *Salon*. Having been patient with the border harassment, after Newark she gave Greenwald permission to write about her transit tribulations.[45]

Snowden had emailed Greenwald in December 2012. Eliciting no response, he followed with a guide to encryption; when no answer came, he submitted an instructional video. Greenwald remained silent.[46] Snowden decided to take Poitras' advice.

Born in 1960, Barton "Bart" Gellman would be the senior and most decorated journalist among the trio Snowden contacted. He graduated *summa cum laude* from Woodrow Wilson

School of Public and International Affairs at Princeton University where he would later be lecturer and author in residence. As a Rhodes Scholar, he studied and received his master's in politics at Oxford. He would work for *The Washington Post* for 21 years. Though he covered the Washington D.C. superior court system early in his career, he is known for having been the Pentagon's Gulf War correspondent. He became an expert on the military. Gellman reported on Somalia, the Iraq War, women in combat, al Qaeda and gay military rights. By 1994 he was bureau chief for Jerusalem. Nominated in 1999 and 2004 in the category of Explanatory Reporting, he won the Pulitzer Prize for National Reporting in 2002. He officially retired in 2010 to focus on his book writing and teaching.[47]

Even if Snowden wasn't familiar with Gellman's work and approached him upon Poitras' recommendation, he obviously researched Gellman beforehand. He knew Gellman would be politically sympathetic because of the writer's decade-long criticism of the Bush administration. Gellman largely focused on the transient nature of Iraq's weapons of mass destruction before shifting to the topic of national security. The journalist's background in intelligence also includes his work as contributing editor-at-large for *Time* magazine, where he has written on FBI Director Robert Mueller, and his blog titled "CounterSpy."[48] In Hong Kong Gellman's 2008 bestseller, *Angler*, was sitting on Snowden's nightstand.[49] The book is a novelistic telling of how then-vice president Dick Cheney deliberately lied to his party concerning the degree of threat posed by Iraq to garner greater support for war.

Snowden's communications with Gellman progressed much more rapidly and smoothly than they had with Poitras and eventually would with Greenwald. Given the speed of the Gellman/Snowden discourse, Poitras had undoubtedly mentioned to Gellman she'd referred him to Snowden while conferring with the veteran journalist in February about whether she should humor the overly cautious email requests.

In Gellman's own ambiguous words, "A series of indirect contacts preceded our first direct exchange May 16."[50] It is unclear what Gellman means by "indirect" since the writer admits that even after May 16, Snowden had not disclosed his name. The contextual meaning would seem to imply Gellman is referring to the preliminary exchanges Snowden had with all his journalists: encryption instructions, installation and testing before transmission of any subject matter. Yet Gellman notes, "[H]e [Snowden] wrote in early May, 'I understand that I will be made to suffer for my actions, and that the return of this information to the public marks my end,' before we had our first direct contact."[51]

Snowden had assumed the pseudonym "Verax," which is Latin for "truth teller." He'd given Gellman the somewhat coy alias "BRASSBANNER." The historic import of Snowden's chosen *non de plume* was not lost on Gellman. The journalist noted in October 1651, Clement Walker died in the Tower of London for having been an outspoken critic of Parliament. Conversely, the publicly lauded Henry Dunckley died without incident in June 1869 after spending a lifetime expressing his disdain for parliament in local newspapers. Both British dissenters had adopted the title "Verax." Vainly, Gellman tried goading Snowden into prophesizing which of the antipodal histories might eventually reflect his own.[52]

Snowden prohibited Gellman from direct quotation for fear of semantic analysis and unequivocally informed him that the U.S. intelligence community "will most certainly kill you if they think you are the single point of failure that could stop this disclosure and make them the sole owner of this information." On May 24 Snowden told Gellman he intended to make his identity public and sought asylum in Iceland.[53] Snowden then pitched his idea of how the *Post* should unveil the intelligence secrets.

Snowden wanted the newspaper to publish all 41 PowerPoint slides he had relating to a program called PRISM atop a cryptographic key in order to prove he was the source of the leaks and therefore reliable due to his employment history. All of this was to be done within a 72-hour timeframe.

When Gellman said he could not guarantee the *Post* could meet Snowden's terms, the former NSA contractor replied, "I regret that we weren't able to keep this project unilateral." Snowden was wagering the potential to lose exclusivity might force the *Post*'s hand. The implied ultimatum didn't work. The newspaper felt uneasy about full disclosure and sought government approval of which slides could be made public.[54] Washington reluctantly agreed to permit four slides to be printed. Snowden was disappointed because he had "carefully evaluated every single document I [Snowden] disclosed to ensure that each was legitimately in the public interest. There are all sorts of documents that would have made a big impact that I didn't turn over, because harming people isn't my goal. Transparency is."[55] He added "I don't desire to enable the Bradley Manning argument that these were released recklessly and unreviewed."[56]

Manning was a private assigned to Army Intelligence who was found guilty of leaking classified information to WikiLeaks and sentenced to 35 years. Snowden's citation refers to some of the released documents that purportedly put American soldiers at risk and damaged diplomatic relations. Unlike Snowden, Manning left editors to judge which articles would be withheld in the public's interest. In Snowden's professional assessment, "The unredacted release of cables was due to the failure of a partner journalist to control a passphrase."[57]

Desperate, distraught and now running out of time, Snowden had no other choice but to play his trump card. He had wanted Greenwald to cover his story from the start and had merely settled for Gellman. Snowden cleverly nudged the person whose attention he did have—Poitras—in order to get his desired journalist's attention. Snowden knew it was reasonable to suggest Poitras contact Greenwald as opposed to seeking out another journalist because it was public knowledge the two were Freedom of the Press Foundation board members.[58] Snowden also admitted he was familiar with Greenwald's border harassment article which appeared on April 8. But it was still a risky move. Greenwald had adamantly ignored his requests, and continuing down this road could waste even more time. Where Snowden's gambit with the *Post* failed to pay off, it worked like a charm on Poitras. She set out to talk to Greenwald because Snowden had shown he was willing to stand on principle with Gellman and already told her she would need a journalist alongside her. She had to do something in order to stay involved.

There is a debate about when Greenwald first communicated with Snowden. On June 10 via Twitter, Greenwald claimed he and Poitras had started "working with" Snowden in February.[59] The statement is technically true, but the implication leaves a lot to be desired. Freelance reporter Peter Maass relays a different account in the *Times* from interviews he'd conducted with Poitras only a few weeks after she and Greenwald had visited Snowden in Hong Kong.[60] The only person aside from Snowden who can offer legitimate discussion to the order in which the communications might have transpired is Poitras, yet she remained solemnly professional in her refusal to get into the middle of the debate. The existence of the *Salon* detainment report also makes Greenwald's proclamation much less credible.

Poitras emailed Greenwald in April stating they needed to meet in person. Snowden had provided her documents by this time. They met in a New York City hotel lobby. She instructed Greenwald not to bring his cell phone. She suspected the U.S. government had the ability to remotely listen to conversations even when a phone is turned off.[61] She showed him Snowden's emails. Greenwald took the matter seriously because Poitras had proof in hand and almost certainly informed him the *Post* had expressed interest but also apprehension.

Greenwald and Poitras had met in March to do the *Salon* exposé. It is reasonable to believe since Poitras was willing to violate source confidentiality with Gellman, she would have seized the opportunity to do the same at this time with Greenwald, her "colleague and friend."[62] It was obviously a hot story, and she would make an express effort to bring it to Greenwald's attention a month later. It is also sensible that one of the two journalists would mention the encryption key request if for no other reason than the sender's dogged perseverance. She came to Greenwald because she and Gellman had delivered the story to the editorial board of the *Post* and knew the status of the article was on unstable ground.

Greenwald would attest that it wasn't until he and Poitras were in the air over the Pacific that he realized the person who had contacted him six months prior was the one they were about to meet despite he and Poitras previously congregating at *The Guardian*'s New York City offices to discuss the assignment.[63] His late entry into the communication loop is also signaled by Greenwald's dancing back and forth between the 20 rows separating him and Poitras on the flight to Hong Kong as he repeatedly sought her feedback on the documents recently placed in his possession.[64] His giddiness superseded professional reserve because Poitras was on a watch list and he was holding highly classified materials. Had he been included as early as he implies, though he was not issued solid documentation until later, the basics of the situation would not have been novel by this time.

The most condemning evidence for Greenwald is that Snowden didn't proffer an all-or-nothing ultimatum to *The Guardian* as he had with Gellman. Snowden had learned his lesson and didn't want to risk losing another journalist. As Greenwald would confirm, Snowden "never once made any demands about how we publish and never once complained about what we published."[65] To Greenwald's credit, Snowden had been "working with" him and Poitras since February. As a team this is true. Snowden had been actively talking with Poitras, but he did not have an open dialogue with Greenwald until late May.[66] Of the three journalists, Greenwald was the first to be contacted but the last to communicate with Snowden.

In analogous essence, Snowden had tried calling Greenwald three times, but the phone was left ringing. Snowden then called Poitras and told her he had something urgent to say to Greenwald, with the implication that if Greenwald didn't pick up, he would take his business elsewhere as he had once before. Fearful of losing her commission, Poitras quickly buzzed Greenwald and told him who was on the other line. Only then did Greenwald bother answering. When he finally did, Poitras uttered a sigh of relief.

Greenwald's evidence to the contrary was he was also in possession of the same PRISM documents as Gellman. Greenwald stated this was "because *The Washington Post* dragged its feet for so long."[67] Through this line of reasoning, Snowden's selection of news outlets was predicated upon timing, not full disclosure. If this were the case, Snowden wouldn't have bothered having Poitras contact a person who had exhibited no interest in his story. Also, the complementary PRISM articles debuted twenty minutes apart. Snowden had obviously chosen to play the safety should Poitras be detained and her copies of the information be confiscated. If this happened to the documentarian, it was reasonable to assume the *Guardian* team's materials might meet a similar end since they were on the same flight. Gellman could still break the story if the U.S. government didn't shut down the *Post*'s project.

As a last-minute precautionary measure to help ensure the emailer was authentic, Poitras set up an anonymous online interview between the NSA contractor and former WikiLeaks associate and Internet security expert Jacob Appelbaum. Poitras was satisfied after Snowden deftly addressed a barrage of direct techno-political questions.[68]

Once communication was open with Greenwald, Snowden told the filmmaker and journalist he was preparing to meet with them shortly.[69] Greenwald had received approximately 20 confidential documents, but Poitras had rightfully earned the bulk.[70] Poitras cleverly but necessarily asked if they would be traveling by train or airplane. In late May, he informed them of their destination: Hong Kong. *The Guardian*'s American editor insisted that since the paper's reputation was at stake, they would be accompanied by veteran reporter Ewen MacAskill. They boarded at J.F.K. Sixteen hours later they landed in Hong Kong on Saturday, June 1. Though Poitras had brought Snowden's story to the *Post*, she unofficially joined the *Guardian* team because of Greenwald's legal background. He was more capable of conducting interviews, and having an attorney by her side might dissuade authorities from detaining her.[71]

They met the man with the Rubik's Cube shortly thereafter.

The media entourage was taken aback by Snowden's youth. Snowden was annoyed they had arrived before their prescribed meeting time.[72] He took them back to his hotel room and, confirming Poitras' suspicions, had them remove their cell phone batteries and placed the phones in the refrigerator. Snowden lined the doors with pillows to prevent eavesdropping.[73] When he logged onto his computer, he draped a red hood over his head. If there were hidden cameras—or if Poitras' footage was closely examined should she catch him at the right moment from the proper angle—his passphrases wouldn't be comprised.[74] Poitras immediately started filming.[75]

Because full disclosure could no longer be demanded, Snowden's priority became information dispersal. He was worried he (and those working with him) might be apprehended at any moment. His anxiety was justified. Snowden knew the government would send out the "Q Group,"[76] the internal police force of the associate directorate for security and counterintelligence, even before he failed to return to work if intelligence suspected he'd left the country.[77] It did not help that, having no other choice, he'd purchased tickets under his own name using his own credit cards. An electronic dragnet would be cast which would attempt triangulation through his recent purchases, online activity and his phone's GPS. Snowden was racing against this contingency alongside a threat he himself had created.

The *Post* began production upon its whistleblowing report no later than May 16. Confirmation with the government over the authenticity of the documentation followed. Snowden had either acknowledged the inevitable necessity and asked that cross-referencing take place after he took flight on May 20, or he withheld full document submission until he was on the ground in Hong Kong. Snowden's trademark discretion makes the latter scenario more plausible. He was still communicating anonymously in mid-May while on medical leave. Even if the U.S. government became aware of a leak while Snowden was still on American soil, he knew he had a flawless, extended reputation with the intelligence community and numerous people had access to the classified PRISM information. On the afternoon of May 23 and two weeks before *The Guardian*'s Verizon report would go live, Obama delivered a speech on the government's intelligence gathering methods at the National Defense University. This implies the *Post* requested its data check between the afternoon of May 20 and the morning of May 23.

If Snowden had been in control, the Verizon exposé would have debuted earlier. The delay in publication was not due to any laxity on Greenwald's behalf. The journalist worked around the clock. When Greenwald wasn't interviewing, he was writing, studying and researching. Snowden would commend Greenwald on his ability to remain focused after consecutive days without sleep.[78] It was *The Guardian* that postponed the first article, probably because it, too, was seeking governmental validation of the source material. It might have taken even longer for the first story to premier had Greenwald not threatened to send a draft to another publisher or place it, along with all other reports, on a website titled "NSADisclosures."[79] Greenwald was obviously fearful that Gellman would break the story.

As with Gellman, Snowden informed Greenwald before they met that he wanted to go public. He said his primary motive for putting a face with the documents was to keep the government from harassing his family and placing undue pressure on his colleagues. Greenwald and Gellman's articles appeared Thursday evening while Poitras was still shooting. The first 12 minutes of Poitras' video footage aired three days later, the same day Snowden would chat with Gellman over the Internet. Interviews had continued non-stop for almost a full week.

A little over 10 minutes of footage was all the people of Hong Kong needed in order to figure out where Edward Snowden was hiding.

Chapter 3
The Whistle Blows

"Truth is coming, and it cannot be stopped."

–Edward Snowden, online chat via *The Guardian*, June 17, 2013[1]

❊ ❊ ❊

AT THE START OF THE DAY on Wednesday, June 5, Washington was met with a typical bill of fare. The day's headlines included oil concerns, a vacant Senate seat, IRS corruption and military abuse allegations.[2] Yet the White House, intelligence community, Capitol Hill, multinational corporations, civil liberty groups, China and the American populace were about to be treated to a five-day production by Glenn Greenwald. Its star had yet to be named, but cameos included a Pulitzer-winning journalist and an Oscar-nominated filmmaker. By the time the sun crept over the horizon the following Monday, it would be one of the longest weekends in Washington's recent memory.

Behind the headlines the U.S. government was already in a mad scramble. Greenwald had been clever. He was aware the American government knew there was a leak, be it due to the *The Washington Post* having yet published anything relating to the Snowden files, the coincidental nature of Obama's National Defense University speech or Snowden's failure to return from sabbatical on June 4. (FBI agents had spoken to Kerri Jo Heim, the real estate agent overseeing the sale of Snowden's former rent house, Wednesday morning.[3]) Knowing the White House would be bracing for the worst, Greenwald judiciously threw a vicious curve ball.

It is obvious Greenwald was aware Snowden had contacted Gellman, because the adjoining *Guardian/Post* PRISM articles appeared within 20 minutes of one another.[4] Since Greenwald now had documents in hand, the story was no longer exclusive. Yet he was in no rush; there was a reason the *Post* was sitting on the material. It was very likely the U.S. government was either dragging its feet validating the documents for the *Post* or it was explicitly blocking publication as it had with *The New York Times* in 2004. Greenwald knew this because he had already been denied comment from the White House, the NSA and the Department of Justice about another leak no one knew about.[5] Washington promptly responded to what it considered the lesser of the two leaks because it was unable to fathom the scope of what was to come.

Most novice journalists in Greenwald's position would select the most condemning exposé to debut. The two award-winning journalists would later prove which document in their mutual possession was deemed the most jaw-dropping. But because Washington expected PRISM, Greenwald presented Verizon.

On Wednesday, June 5, *The Guardian* published "NSA collecting phone records of millions of Verizon customers daily."[6] Greenwald paints a small portion of a collage which his readers anxiously complete. His strategy is to suggest then goad his audience. For example, his title forces readers to immediately wonder, "If Verizon is doing this ... ?" but as a safety later adds, "It is not known whether Verizon is the only cellphone provider to be targeted with such a[n] [court] order" and, almost as an aside, briefly alludes to AT&T, Verizon and BellSouth having been caught doing the same in 2006. Greenwald doesn't need to bother exploring the mirror situations of Verizon's competitors. His readers—but more importantly the press[7]—were quick to satiate their curiosity.

With equal brevity, Greenwald highlights that the U.S. government's bulk telecommunications (telecoms) data collection had been occurring since April 25 and was slated to end on July 19. This was the result of the FBI being given the authority by the Foreign Intelligence Surveillance Court (FISC) to force Verizon to submit the information to the NSA. The classified FISC order informs the telecommunications provider it will submit "[a]ll call detail records or 'telephony metadata' created by Verizon for communications (i) between the United States and abroad; or (ii) wholly within the United States, including local telephone calls."[8] As he had with the AT&T, Verizon and BellSouth tip-off, Greenwald later includes, "It is also unclear from the leaked document whether the three-month order was a one-off, or the latest in a series of similar orders." He then summarily proceeds to what is being recorded by the NSA, thereby nudging inquisitive readers to research the covert edict. Without having to devote a single word toward an answer, Greenwald let the world discover for itself that the three-month surveillance window was not a singular incidence. Consecutive extensions of 50 U.S.C. §1861 within Section 215 of the PATRIOT Act had been occurring since 2006. Greenwald left his audience to connect the political dots and let history unravel itself.

In 2006 *USA Today* picked up where Risen and Lichtblau had left off five months prior.[9] It questioned American telecoms' role in wiretapping. Shortly after 9/11, then-President George W. Bush signed a top secret executive order permitting the NSA to wiretap without a warrant. His administration later justified the directive by arguing the process of obtaining warrants was too time-consuming. As a result of the *Times* article, the FISC ruled in 2007 that warrants must be obtained if an NSA-desired communication passes through an American network. The Bush administration bought itself time by rebutting with a stopgap that permitted the NSA to continue wiretapping. The stopgap expired in 2008. By then everything was in place. Five years later it would be revealed that the U.S. government had merely placated the public. It had restricted one clandestine order, thereby insinuating wiretapping had come to an end shortly thereafter, all while gradually implementing a covert clone directive. As with the executive order, the public wasn't privy to these machinations because they had taken place behind closed doors before being classified as top secret.

The NSA's power underwent a paradigm shift after 9/11. It was granted access to information which it did not have legal right to act upon. Before, the NSA's domestic domain was restricted to American embassies and missions. (The FBI deals with domestic issues, while the CIA contends with foreign matters of security.) After 9/11, it was allowed to eavesdrop upon foreigners, then permitted to involve itself in communications between foreigners and Americans, all before obtaining the carte blanche ability to wiretap anyone.

The irony is that in 1975 the NSA was subject to a congressional investigation. The inquiry revealed that the agency had been intercepting domestic communications without a warrant since its creation in 1952. The NSA was found guilty of abusing its power after spying on peaceful antiwar protests and civil rights activists.[10] The Foreign Intelligence Surveillance Act (FISA) was chartered in 1978 as a result. The representative secret court which was created to uphold the FISA laws and prohibit warrantless wiretapping was now rubberstamping one order after another. Americans had been watched by the NSA for almost 60 years.[11]

Greenwald's report is pithy. Aside from publishing the top secret four-page order alongside the story, he bluntly contrasts blanket collection to what most would consider sensible surveillance terms: an individual who is targeted due to reasonable suspicion. The FISC order does not require probable cause before search and seizure, thereby violating Americans' Fourth Amendment rights. Greenwald makes sure to raise even more eyebrows by noting that the law expressly forbids the telecom provider from publicly acknowledging the government directive or, in other words, Verizon was under a gag order, "It is further ordered that no person shall disclose to any other person that the FBI or NSA has sought or obtained tangible things under this Order [...]." (Greenwald nevertheless sardonically reports Verizon refused to comment.) He continues to hit hard by outlining the linguistic dexterity involved in the controversial legislation. The data being collected is labeled "metadata" instead of "communications" because individual warrants must be issued before "communications" can be confiscated.

Greenwald soundly establishes that the NSA wasn't acting alone and Congress was privy to and implicated in the
surveillance dragnet. He tells the tale of two senators, Ron
Wyden and Mark Udall, both members of the Intelligence
Committee, and their two-year history of cryptically alluding
to the government's current surveillance policies and practices.
Despite being unable to openly discuss the covert directive, it
was nonetheless admitted that the American public would be
"stunned" if it were made aware of the "secret legal interpre-
tations" which had led to current spying tactics. Perhaps
intentionally, Greenwald fails to comment upon the paradox
involved in a domestic surveillance directive coming from a
court which oversees foreign intelligence. Though the order
explicitly states that Verizon calls which originate and end in
a foreign land are exempt, it shrewdly includes the clause "[tele-
communications] between the United States and abroad" so
the court's authority is applicable.

Greenwald's ruse worked. From daybreak on Thursday
until approximately 6:00 that evening, the world was consumed
by *The Guardian*'s claims. Capitol Hill, Verizon and privacy
advocates frantically responded.

Dianne Feinstein, chair of the Senate Intelligence Committee and Vice Chair Saxby Chambliss defended the order. The
former contended the directive was a product of the FISC and
was therefore lawful. The latter freely admitted the order had
been consistently renewed for seven years but dubiously added,
"Every member of the United States Senate has been advised
of this." (Five days later, as they left a congressional briefing
concerning the headline surveillance, Representative Elijah
Cummings sardonically stated, "We learned a lot [...]," and
his peer, Bill Pascrell said, "People should know what's going
on in their name but we need to start with Congress knowing
what the heck is going on.")[12] Feinstein interjected that Second (sic) Amendment concerns had been humored on the
Senate floor during related discussions. Chambliss ironically
implied popular consent by observing that in all its years of
operation, no citizen had filed a complaint about the top se-

cret order.[13] The White House assured Americans their conversations were not being recorded. The government as a whole rested upon the defense that metadata is cast into the public domain and also shared with one's service provider. As such, metadata cannot be considered private. Instead of quelling concerns, this line of reasoning placed the privacy of calls' contents into immediate question.

Verizon preoccupied itself with redirecting the blame. The company rebutted that its hand had been forced by law. What took time for the press to relay was however true, telecommunication companies had lobbied for impunity after the 2006 AT&T et al. uproar resulted in numerous civil lawsuits.[14] Providers agreed to comply if they were indemnified. In other words, they agreed to turn over all data if the government would take the public relations and legal fall should the public ever find out. Technically the threat of a lawsuit should have been greater from the federal government. Section 222 of The Communications Act of 1934 forbids telephone companies from issuing the exact same information the intelligence community was now demanding be turned over: numbers engaged, duration and transmission routes. The fine is $130,000 per day per violation.[15] The U.S. government viewed this as fair and lawful for 62 years. Large segments of the legislation were appealed or amended with the Telecommunications Act of 1996.[16] The collection of "aggregate information" or bulk data collection became fair game once the federal government saw the opportunities emerging that technology now provided. Not only was the fear of the government's monetary penalties no longer a concern, but the communication providers wanted to provide the service. The NSA could not expect the businesses to provide the labor, material and time-intensive information for free. Taxpayers were unknowingly paying their government to spy on them. When the White House was questioned about this, it justified its actions on financial grounds: The agreement shielded telecommunication providers from bankruptcy.[17]

In essence, because the government had already fallen under strict scrutiny for wiretapping, it had the telephone companies do it for them. However, to evade lawsuits the providers required the government to "force" them to hand over the information. This method of data extraction was a lot less expensive than if the intelligence community purchased the records outright. Verizon charges $775 per tap the first month and $500 each additional month. AT&T's fee is $325 for a single activation followed by a $10 per day, per line fee.[18] With 249 million American cell phone subscribers, the government had no choice if it wanted the data.

Privacy advocates feared social network analysis. They acknowledged the retrieved information did not include the contents of a conversation or users' names. They claimed it didn't because there was no need. A subscriber's identity could be gleaned by cross-referring telephone numbers with consumer data. Another concern was when signal strength and receiving tower location is placed alongside duration, a location and time stamp is logged. It can be determined whether a caller is engaging someone at a strip club for an hour twice a week or five minutes for the first time in 10 years. The NSA could therefore track where an individual goes, how frequently and at what times. A profile of a telephone user's habits quickly forms and reveals if a person is a homebody, traveler, sports nut, barfly, health enthusiast, psychiatric client or churchgoer.[19]

Beautifully orchestrated in its understatement, the brevity of Greenwald's article served other purposes. It preoccupied Washington and permitted him to direct his time and energy to a bigger, more revelatory editorial. What Snowden might not have informed Greenwald was that the Verizon disclosure also left the U.S. government scratching its head.

If Snowden was already a suspect after not returning to work the previous day, this tossed a monkey wrench in the intelligence community's theories of who its mole might be. The directive's storage had no relevance to Snowden's job with BAH. Technically there was no method or manner by which he could have accessed the form. Washington fretted over the implications. The crippling possibility of multiple persons[20] or a very skilled hacker now existed since the *Post* had sought government comment on its PRISM documentation. Only after Snowden went public was the U.S. government able to breathe a little easier. Once American intelligence knew the identity of its leaks, it could reverse engineer how the FISC order had been obtained. Though Snowden had no direct access to the document while employed as an infrastructure analyst, the NSA naively waved it in front of him during his BAH training. Knowing the location of the data he needed, Snowden proceeded to find a way to get it.[21]

As the U.S. government's chaotic day was finally coming to a close, right when many Americans were preparing to get off work and others were sitting down to dinner, Gellman and Greenwald got on either side of the lid and opened Pandora's Box. At 5:43, *The Washington Post* released "U.S. intelligence mining data from nine U.S. Internet companies in broad secret program."[22] Twenty minutes later *The Guardian* seconded the *Post*'s documented claims with "NSA Prism program taps in to user data of Apple, Google and others."[23] If Washington believed a whistle had been blown the day before, it was about to realize the previous day's revelation was a toot by comparison.

While the non-Verizon subscriber could issue a cursory glance at Greenwald's June 5 headline and walk away without realizing the article's implications, only a minuscule percentage of readers were immune to the bookend PRISM articles.

The *Post* editorial opens by capsizing any reassurances the government wasn't just listening in on America, but watching its every move. Gellman reports that the NSA and FBI are extracting audio, video, photographs, emails, documents and connection logs from the central servers of nine major Internet companies: Microsoft, Yahoo, Google, Facebook, PalTalk, AOL, Skype, YouTube and Apple (listed in the order of entry into the spy program with Dropbox "coming soon"). The popular email service Hotmail is owned by Microsoft, as is Skype. Due to their "exponential growth," Facebook and Skype are frequent hosts to NSA spying. Facebook's favoritism is due to its "extensive search and surveillance capabilities against the variety of online social networking services." The irony would soon be apparent that U.S. citizens were making it even easier for the government to spy on them because nearly every American was freely volunteering their personal information through one or more of these companies' websites.

The program used to collect the data is called Planning Tool for Resource Integration, Synchronization, and Management or "PRISM" and has been in operation since 2007. It is so effective that it is the "most prolific contributor to the President's Daily Brief." PRISM data was included in the president's memo an average of four times a day during 2012. One in seven intelligence reports contain PRISM information.

Admittedly, though the NSA has a constant data stream from its nine current providers, it does not review everything. Analysts use search terms to pull up desired information. Occasionally when filling a search request, PRISM gathers "incidental" data an analyst doesn't want and shouldn't see. As a PRISM training slide instructs, when this happens the analyst is to report the error. Yet if the NSA technician fails to do so, the omission is "nothing to worry about."

What is considered of interest to an analyst has mind-numbing implications. When a person is cited as a target of suspicion, the NSA starts "contact chaining" at a minimal distance of "two hops." For example, Bob is an American foreign exchange student spending a semester abroad at the University of Oxford in England. He wants feedback on his paper comparing suicide bombers in Iraq to acts of domestic terror in the United States. He sends it to his Harvard advisor for review. The essay includes the keywords "al Qaeda," "White House," "jihad," "bomb," "Iraq," "Koran" and "Obama administration." This throws up a red flag, and the NSA designates Bob as a person of interest. Intelligence will then investigate anyone found in his email account or whom he has "friended" on Facebook. This is the "first hop." The NSA then proceeds to the second hop. It looks into anyone electronically associated with the people now under the radar after the first hop. In other words, Mary has emailed Bob and Susan has "friended" Mary. Even though Bob has never met and does not know Susan, she is now being investigated by the NSA. (Six days after Gellman's article debuted, NSA Deputy Director John Inglis informed Congress that analysts were permitted three hops.)[24] Scientific studies of social networks show at three hops, roughly half the American population can be permissibly surveilled. For Facebook and Twitter account holders, the likelihood is greatly increased. The average degree of separation between random users is only 4.74[25] and 3.43[26] respectively. Statistically, someone utilizing Facebook has an 84 percent chance of being "targeted by association." A person posting on Twitter runs an 87 percent risk. Before 9/11, the Justice Department had deemed American contact chaining illegal.[27]

Perhaps the only thing more frightening than "friending" a person who "liked" something which a government target also listed as a Facebook hobby,[28] thereby placing an innocent websurfer under federal suspicion, is the NSA can access real-time data, i.e., live surveillance. This means an analyst has the ability to watch people as they casually surf the Internet.

Gellman highlights one of the primary differences between the participating Internet businesses and the NSA-mined telecoms: The Internet firms didn't have to be ordered to submit their data. They merely acknowledged a "directive" from the attorney general and director of national intelligence in exchange for legal impunity. In the event a developing Internet enterprise refuses to play along, 2008 legislation permits the FISC to make a company "comply."

Suggestive of a gag order being in place, a Google representative speaking on condition of anonymity stated, "From time to time, people allege that we have created a government 'backdoor' into our systems, but Google does not have a 'backdoor' for the government to access private user data." Gellman specifies that the few congressional members privy to PRISM, such as Wyden and Udall, are also not allowed to express their opinions because they are "bound by oaths of office to hold their tongues."

The U.S. government did not detain the *Post* article as it had the 2004 *Times* exposé and even permitted four PRISM slides to serve as irrefutable proof. It reluctantly did so because Snowden had been judicious with his choice of sources. Greenwald worked for a foreign publisher and had based his writing career around the issue of civil liberties and overreaching intelligence programs and agencies. The domestic *Post* was famous for having reported the Pentagon Papers and Watergate. The White House knew that if it didn't meet the writers halfway, they would have invariably issued all 41 slides. Though the same four slides accompany both articles, Gellman and *The Guardian* gradually released others.[29]

Whereas Gellman states that the NSA and FBI are "tapping directly into" servers, Greenwald elects to open his broadside with the more caustic and aggressive phrase "obtained direct access." His opening bell is promptly followed by a user's "search history, the content of emails, file transfers and live chats" being compromised by PRISM. But Greenwald loses speed early in the article. Hoping to display the depth of the program's clandestine nature via the reluctance of government officials and industry spokespersons to comment or even acknowledge PRISM—"[a]lthough the presentation claims the program is run with the assistance of the companies"—Greenwald betrays the topic's sense of urgency. Fortunately he quickly regains focus.

He makes clear that if an individual communicates with anyone outside the United States, the person is automatically targeted, but "[u]nlike the collection of [telecommunication providers'] call records, this surveillance can include the content of communications and not just the metadata." This means a person's static documents as well as live communications will be surveilled. Still going for the throat, Greenwald unequivocally relays PRISM's lack of political and judicial oversight: "The Prism program allows the NSA, the world's largest surveillance organisation, to obtain targeted communications without having to request them from the service providers and without having to obtain individual court orders."

Because Washington wouldn't consent to full disclosure of the slideshow, Greenwald satisfies himself with discussing the withheld data. He successfully paints a picture of an NSA at odds with Capitol Hill's supervision. One restricted slide provides a PRISM trainee with the NSA's perspective on intelligence legislation, "Fisa was broken because it provided privacy protections to people who were not entitled to them. It took a Fisa court order to collect on foreigners overseas who were communicating with other foreigners overseas simply because the government was collecting off a wire in the United States. There were too many email accounts to be practical to seek Fisas for all." Greenwald explains that the FISA Amendment Act (FAA) redefined what "electronic surveillance" meant. Under previous rules, an NSA analyst was not permitted to spy upon anyone in the United States. Current legislation considers a lawful target to be anyone "reasonably believed" to be outside of America at the time of transmission. If Frank uses his Canadian-based Hushmail account to discuss something that took place in Quebec earlier in the day, it could be argued he was on-site at the time. He is now the subject of an investigation. All of his (and his primary, secondary and tertiary associations') live and collected data will be requested and reviewed.

Toward the end of the article, Greenwald makes a point using implied hyperbole. If the U.S. is not spying on Americans, then an average of 65 foreigners per day—2,000 per month—are making plans to harm the nation. That is the number of PRISM reports filed in 2012.

The exposés accomplished what they were designed to do. Yet it is obvious the PRISM twins' impact would have been much greater if their authors hadn't been racing to a headline and instead worked together to fashion complementary bookends. Other news sources would successfully combine forces to produce buttressed, simultaneous reports of classified data that Snowden had nabbed.

Gellman's report is strong in its presentation, well organized, but too skeletal. Its weakness is juxtaposed by Greenwald's nervous verbosity and pacing fueled by moral outrage. It is retrospectively obvious Greenwald was preoccupied during its research and composition. Most likely due to the stress of attempting to write, interview and research amid jetlag and sleep deprivation while in Hong Kong, salient points are made but in such a hectic, disjointed manner; it feels less like being led through a topic than being dragged by it. Whereas Gellman is professionally removed and patient, Greenwald's rapid pulse is felt through his pen. His unbridled prose desperately needs an editor. It introduces political and technical jargon with little or no explanation, is prey to redundancy, surrenders to the temptation to sardonically comment upon its subject and wastes time transcribing information which an accompanying slide makes unequivocally clear. Conversely, Gellman's work requires a contributor to provide his reader with a more complete picture and understanding of the topic. Due to his tone, readers consent to Gellman's apprehensions. They have no other choice because they cannot visualize the completed puzzle. Greenwald's audience expresses the same discontent but must first attempt to organize their inflamed thoughts. Only then can they begin to understand exactly why they are ticked off.

The strongest immediate reaction to the adjoining articles came from the named companies. Seven explicitly stated free access had not been given to the government (AOL and PalTalk remained silent). As they did so, Gellman quietly revised and expanded his work. His motivations for doing so were suspect but would soon become clear.

With the aid of four contributors—Julie Tate, Robert O'Harrow, Cecilia Kang and Ellen Nakashima—Gellman's article would double its size by 8:51 the next morning. Its title now implicated the United Kingdom in the domestic spying game: "U.S., British intelligence mining data from nine U.S. Internet companies in broad secret program."[30] Readers learn *The Guardian* had just revealed the U.S. government had given the British equivalent to the NSA, Government Communications Headquarters (GCHQ), copies of PRISM.[31*] Use of the

---

* Friday, June 7, "UK gathering secret intelligence via covert NSA operation."

American technology grants GCHQ the legal loophole necessary to gather domestic information. Furthermore, the revision reveals how important Microsoft, Yahoo and Google are to the American government. The trio account for an outstanding 98% of PRISM data intake. Gellman reiterates that participating companies are "immunized" from legal fallout but adds Congress consented via the Protect America Act of 2007 and FISA Amendments Act of 2008.

Aside from the pivotal whitewashing—no longer was "a person's movements and contacts over time" monitored, only "foreign targets'" activities, and technology companies didn't "participate knowingly" but instead were merely "essential to PRISM operations"—the most noticeable change in the article is the amount of direct quotes. It is evident that most whom Gellman initially attempted to contact had become willing to be put on hold in order to provide an official statement to the *Post*.

For the sake of customer morale, a handful of the listed Internet businesses flatly denied any knowledge of a covert data exchange with the federal government. Others blatantly proclaimed no such program was in place. Speaking on behalf of Apple, Steve Dowling announced, "We have never heard of PRISM"[32] while the chief security officer for Facebook, Joe Sullivan, declared, "We do not provide any government organization with direct access to Facebook servers,"[33] despite the PRISM slide which includes the phrase, "Collection directly from the servers of." Judiciously and highly intuitively, Gellman accepts some of the company spokespeople's claims to ignorance. Innocuously inserted in his newest revision is the addendum, "In another classified report obtained by the *Post*, the arrangement is described as allowing 'collection managers [to send] content tasking instructions directly to equipment installed at company-controlled locations,' rather than directly to company servers." Gellman expected violent reactions from the article and kept some documents in reserve to have a counterargument readily available. He admits the Internet representatives might not know their servers were open to the FBI's Data Intercept Technology Unit. The information is then relayed to the NSA through a contracted intermediary such as BAH.

Gellman also makes another distinction between the two enterprises. FISC-ordered telecoms filter their data prior to submission. They do not submit subscriber names or the contents of the conversations. By leaving a backdoor open for the NSA, the Internet companies' captured data is unedited. Senator Udall calls attention to this distinction: "As it is written, there is nothing to prohibit the intelligence community from searching through a pile of communications, which may have been incidentally or accidentally been collected without a warrant, to deliberately search for the phone calls or e-mails of specific Americans." Ironically when Senator Wyden asked how many people this affected, Inspector General Charles McCullough III stated that reporting the figure would constitute a privacy violation.[34]

Even Director of National Intelligence James Clapper had something to say to Gellman. In a statement issued "late Thursday," Clapper informed the *Post* that "numerous inaccuracies" resided in the parallel PRISM reports but "did not specify" what they were. Clapper was already at the end of his tether in the midst of what was becoming a strenuous time for the NSA.

Greenwald was met with the same pressures but refused to retract his steadfast assertions of direct access. It appeared Greenwald was standing on principle or being stubborn. It seemed *The Washington Post* had gone the way of *The New York Times* by willfully redacting claims made less than 24 hours before. Gellman's quiet and therefore implied admission of guilt created more questions than it answered. Does domestic spying in fact occur? After June 5, the answer seemed to be an irrefutable "yes," and therefore it does not follow that the American intelligence community would settle for only a portion of the available data. It was unclear why telecoms were being forced to submit while the Internet companies were not. This ambiguity allowed for the possibility that the online businesses' assertions of ignorance about PRISM were true. Perhaps these public entities were unaware they were providing information because, in fact, the American government was hacking into U.S. communication lines. Pandora's Box was open. What people didn't know or expect was that it was Gellman's turn to attempt to be clever.

Gellman's motivation for revision was subtly, coyly staring everyone in the face. Greenwald's refusal to change a word and *The Guardian* not publishing a redaction could have been dismissed as orneriness if Gellman had done one thing. A team of *Post* journalists had worked at breakneck speed to issue a major revision in less than 15 hours. Yet, despite the softening of the language and a few retractions that Internet companies were providing direct access, the first half of Gellman's opening sentence remained untouched. The independent clause, "The National Security Agency and the FBI are tapping directly into the central servers of nine leading U.S. Internet companies" continued to sit on the page. It simply refused to budge.

Greenwald and Gellman were aware that even if promised legal impunity, no Internet company would voluntarily agree to hand over data. This would leave the firms liable to public backlash for having freely violated their customer's privacy should it ever become known. Both journalists exploited this simple fact because they needed something in order to definitively prove their claims: the Internet companies' FISC orders.

If Snowden had possessed an FISC blanket order forcing even one Internet company to comply, the news sources would have included it in their reports. Because they didn't have proof, the journalists knew if they deliberately misinterpreted the meaning of the PRISM slides, the firms would be obligated to absolve themselves of responsibility. In so doing, they would simultaneously incriminate the government in the process.

Gellman was trying to force a semantic argument. He admitted in his revision he knew what actually took place. An NSA analyst would submit a data request to the FBI. The FBI in turn would pull the information from servers at contracted locations. He knew this because Snowden knew this but needed the companies to admit it. Gellman anticipated and accepted the claims by the Internet companies' spokespeople that servers were not directly accessed. Facebook said, "We do not provide any government organization with direct access to Facebook servers." Apple's response was almost verbatim: "We do not provide any government agency with direct access to our servers." Yahoo followed the cookie-cutter pattern: "We do not provide the government with direct access to our servers, systems, or network."[35] This was true. Greenwald pointed out that the PRISM program is run with the *assistance* of the companies. After FISC orders were distributed, analogous to AT&T's Room 641A in San Francisco where beam splitters provide the NSA open access to the telecoms' fiber-optic lines, Internet firms had set up dropboxes to which the government has access.[36] In the *Times'* words, "[T]he companies were essentially asked to erect a locked mailbox and give the government the key."[37] It came down to the definition of terms. The access in question wasn't technically direct, but it was unequivocally free. In the event the NSA wanted a live feed, all it had to do was ask. Greenwald's choice of "obtained direct access" was the most accurate assessment of the situation.

Having perhaps learned their lesson the day before, members of Congress were notably silent. This may have been due to a White House directive. The surveillance issue had attracted enough attention for the president to formally address it. He did so on June 7 at the Fairmont Hotel in San Jose, California, hours before entering a summit with China's president. Obama stated the PRISM program "does not apply to U.S. citizens and it does not apply to people living in the United States" before paradoxically adding, "I think it's important to recognize that you can't have 100 percent security and also then have 100 percent privacy and zero inconvenience."[38] He echoes the legislation within Section 702 of FISA (which was reauthorized under the Obama administration in December 2012 after having been expanded by Bush four years before). The statute refuses any data request of an American citizen in or outside the United States. Under this law, an application is brought before FISC judges to determine if "targeting" and "minimization" requirements have been met (the latter process ensures there is a 51 percent or greater likelihood the target is not American). Upon approval, an order is then issued.

If the Internet companies were merely submitting data upon receipt of a subpoena, there would have been no story to report. It was logical for Greenwald and Gellman to assume that since the government went to great lengths to gerrymander access to telecommunications providers' call data, it had done the same with the treasure trove of information the Internet offered. This idea had its own validity but PRISM's existence all but declared this was taking place. What made the notion even more plausible were the dropboxes. If court orders demanded data, the Internet providers could merely extract and present it. There would be no need for the U.S. government to pay the companies millions of dollars to set up "secure portals."[39] Microsoft, Facebook and Yahoo affirmed they had built the requested data facilities.[40] This indicated a blanket FISC order existed. Yet it was still unclear whether the Internet providers were depositing data after receiving individual FISC orders—in the firms' terms, National Security Letters (NSL)—or whether the intelligence community had full, unfettered access to the dropboxes which were duplicating all incoming data.

Gellman believed he had the U.S. government in a corner. At any moment Washington would bow to the Internet companies' pressure to let them release the paperwork that forced them to turn over data. The message from the companies was clear: "Either let us regain the confidence of the consumer before our stocks plummet, or the next election cycle will be sparsely funded." It was a good plan and almost worked.

NSLs would prove blanket access hadn't been granted and Section 702 was being followed. The next week Microsoft[41] and Facebook[42] presented transparency reports for the second half of 2012, but they were accompanied by an asterisk: The government would only allow the information to be made public if the data lumped together all other requests from local, state and federal law enforcement agencies. To further obfuscate the issue, totals were rounded to the nearest 1,000. Microsoft showed a minimum average of 32 requests per day, affecting user accounts every six minutes. The following week Yahoo[43] and Apple[44] would report the first half of 2013. PalTalk and AOL didn't even bother to appease their clients, because it was futile. The implication was apparent. Without permission to publish the individual court order or letters and no way to prove to customers the aggregated data wasn't fabricated or merely the number of times the government had dipped into a company's dropbox, Greenwald and Gellman's claims could not be successfully refuted. But they had not been conclusively proven either. Though the argument was in their favor, Greenwald and Gellman still needed to establish they were right.

Gellman was no Greenwald when it came to journalistic blackmail. Washington had been unwilling to take another direct hit after the Verizon fiasco. Internet companies adamantly objected. They could only watch as people uninstalled Yahoo toolbars, turned off Skype, deactivated Facebook accounts and transferred Gmail files to email providers with reputations for privacy. Questions continued to linger.

Though The Electronic Privacy Information Center had released data showing applications had indeed been presented to the FISC, the report didn't ease tensions or fill in any blanks. The requests had been rubber stamped. Only two of 8,591 appeals had been rejected between 2008 and 2012.[45] (A single rejection out of 1,789 requests had taken place in 2012.)[46] This does not mean that out of nearly a quarter of a billion American Internet users, only five per day were being investigated. Under 702, once an application has been approved, additional names and Internet services can be added without further authorization. This is undoubtedly when contact chaining commences. An approved order remains open for one year.

Loose ends were abundant. The PRISM slide clearly informs an analyst that data is "[c]ollect[ed] directly from the servers." Yet Gellman included in his revision, "[C]ollection managers [can send] content tasking instructions directly to equipment installed at company-controlled locations." Even more puzzling is that Google admitted compliance with PRISM but, unlike its Internet peers, does not use a dropbox to deliver information. It either transports by hand or transfers data over an encrypted FTP channel.[47] There was no subsequent explanation why the NSA permits this form of electronic (and much less expensive) transport for one company but the other eight firms were bound to dropboxes. The reports either fail to explore or barely mention whether domestic communication providers were being obligated to release data they had access to as a result of business arrangements with foreign providers or if U.S. law applied to an American company's overseas servers. This is important because a Texan's email may travel to Europe to reach a friend in Florida. Servers do not take the shortest route but the cheapest.[48] Google operates in Europe, Asia and South America.[49]

Greenwald didn't have to change a word of his article because he knew he was right. Gellman tried extortion because he lacked something Greenwald had when presenting his Verizon exposé: proof. But Greenwald was aware it had been a trying time for the American government. He opted to give Washington a thematic intermission before producing conclusive evidence the U.S. government was spying on its citizens.

Within hours of the *Post* rewrite and just before President Obama was to host his Chinese equivalent—newly elected Xi Jinping—at Rancho Mirage, California, to discuss alleged cyberattacks emanating out of the People's Republic, *The Guardian* released, "Obama orders US to draw up overseas target list for cyber-attacks."[50]

The article presents an unpublished Presidential Policy Directive issued in October 2012.[51] The document instructs the secretary of defense, director of national intelligence and head of the CIA to create a list of overseas targets of "national importance" for possible cyberattacks. The purpose of the tentative attacks is not heightened defense, retaliatory action or even as a pre-emptive measure. It is to "advance U.S. national objectives around the world with little or no warning to the adversary or target and with potential effects ranging from subtle to severely damaging." Dauntingly the commander in chief also humors domestic targeting but specifies such theoretical operations cannot be carried out unless he has issued his consent or there is a national emergency, whereby various departments are authorized to act autonomously. Likewise the 18-page manuscript states cyberattacks are to conform to U.S. and international law unless they are overridden by presidential approval.

The order tells its recipients to remain mindful of the possible consequences: loss of life, property damage, retaliatory responses, injury to international trade and regressive foreign policy impact. Greenwald acknowledges a history of debate precedes the directive. Security researchers and academes have frequently voiced concern over the possibility that offensive cyber initiatives may result in full-scale warfare if collateral damages are heavy enough.

Greenwald quotes an unnamed intelligence insider as stating that the president's pending cyber grievance with China is hypocritical. A month after the directive's April deadline expired and less than half a year after the Pentagon greenlit expansion of American's Cyber Command Unit, the U.S. government reported on what could easily be interpreted as retaliatory hacking by China into the Pentagon's military programs. Obama was already entering the informal summit with China holding, in the words of the Director of the National Computer Network Emergency Response Technical Team/ Coordination Center of China Huang Chengqing, "mountains of data" documenting previous American attacks.[52] The timeline of American cyber aggression toward the Asian superpower is unspecified, but Obama's order was an update of a 2004 National Security Presidential Directive. In only a few days, Snowden would provide evidence that China's attacks had emanated from the clandestine offices of the American government.

At the end of the two-day conference, pundits criticized Obama for skirting around the subject of international cyberattacks. Though China refused to deny it had hacked combat aircraft and ship designs atop missile defense systems (Huang merely muttered that if the U.S. wanted to keep such documents secret, it shouldn't put them online), America was contending with its Eastern competitor being aware that almost three-million Chinese computers had been hacked by 4,062 U.S.-based computer servers.[53] They deliberately spoke in ambiguous umbrella terms and shied away from particulars. The two leaders agreed they had "similar concerns" over an issue that is a "doubled-edged sword." Jinping let the American president escort the conversation over to mutual disapproval of North Korea's continued nuclear development and the topic of global warming.[54]

Intermission was over. Greenwald didn't have time to see if the American government would take the bait from the Internet companies' demands for transparency. It was time to prove to the American people they were being watched.

On Saturday, June 8, Greenwald hit hard with "Boundless Informant: the NSA's secret tool to track global surveillance data."[55] This exposé is relatively short compared to his previous three articles, because the data speaks for itself. The report opens with the news agency declaring it has irrefutable proof the NSA is recording American communications. Accompanied by a screenshot, four slides and an unclassified but in-house user guide for analysts, Greenwald introduces the top secret program Boundless Informant, a tool that summarizes and reports the NSA's metadata collection records and history.

The crux of the article focuses upon a color-coded heat map of the world produced by Boundless Informant. It shows how much data had been collected from each country during March 2013. Condemningly, the United States is presented in a median color after having nearly three billion pieces of data extracted. The program offers an analyst the option of reviewing a particular nation's recorded volume and can break it down into categorical types of surveilled information.

Greenwald humbly announces that the existence of Boundless Informant makes it extremely difficult for the NSA to declare it doesn't spy on its citizenry. He notes that the month the screenshot was captured, Senator Wyden asked Intelligence Director Clapper, "Does the NSA collect any type of data at all on millions or hundreds of millions of Americans?" Clapper starkly replied, "No sir." (He would later infamously state that his response had been the "least most untruthful.")[56] One of the accompanying slides attests that the program has been in use since at least July 2012. For obvious reasons, the NSA does not want Congress to know it has or is using this type of technology. This is likely the reason one of its slides states that FISA data is not collected by Boundless Informant.

Greenwald makes sure to highlight that the NSA knew it had to quickly change its story. NSA spokesperson Judith Emmel informed *The Guardian* that U.S. intelligence does "not have the ability to determine with certainty the identity or location of *all* [my emphasis] communicants within a given communication." Greenwald relays that Boundless Informant's data breakdown can pinpoint report information to an individual Internet Protocol (IP) address. This means the analyst knows at least what region, if not city, a person is in, if not the exact computer that produced the data. When placed alongside consumer reports or even the social networking information derived from telecoms' metadata, a user's search habits easily confirm who they are. As she desperately tries to validate her claims, Emmel digs the hole even deeper: "Current technology simply does not permit us to positively identify *all* [my emphasis] of the persons or locations associated with a given communication. [...] It is harder to know the ultimate source or destination, or more particularly the identity of the person represented by the TO:, FROM: or CC: field of an e-mail address or the abstraction of an IP address." Aside from the frightening insinuation involved in her use of the term "current," Emmel is careful not to categorically deny that individual identification is impossible, merely "harder."

The existence of Boundless Informant proved surveillance programs like PRISM were capturing American data. The question that remained was whether U.S. intelligence was deliberately seeking its citizens' information. After shifting gears once Boundless Informant was revealed, the official statement became that American data interception was "incidental." What makes this claim immediately suspicious is the previously mentioned requirement that analysts must possess a 51% or greater certainty a slated target isn't a U.S. citizen. No one seemed to know why the federal government had to resort to guessing which of its people were its own. Though Greenwald had cast light on what the U.S. government had been doing behind closed doors, questions remained. But it appeared as if the journalist had run out of answers. Indeed he had for the time being, but he knew someone who did.

After a series of extremely volatile, highly condemning back-to-back exposés, the U.S. government was browbeaten. The requests by news sources for comments concerning top secret classified information had inexplicably stopped. Washington was too tired to wonder why and merely hoped it was a sign the war was over. As the weekend slowly wound down, the Capitol took a deep breath and braced itself for what promised to be a very busy week. Internet companies were frantically putting the finishing touches on their requests for transparency. The American Civil Liberties Union was picking out what tie it would wear when it filed suit against the NSA on Monday. Clapper began debating whether to declassify congressional "telephony metadata" records 21 years before their expiration date. Brokers anxiously hypothesized how the stock market might teeter between online security firms' inevitable boom and what many expected would be the freefalling funds of Verizon and the cited Internet companies.

Then the news broke. *The Guardian* had posted a 12-minute interview with the American whistleblower.[57] The video had been shot by an Academy Award-nominated filmmaker. The person responsible was talking and talking a lot. Everyone flocked to their televisions, and, against their better judgment, those not in close proximity to a television logged onto their computers or phones to get a glimpse of the man behind the leaks. (The video footage of the leaker was so ubiquitous, few noticed that a complementary, near mirror print interview by Greenwald and MacAskill had also been posted online.)[58] It was the U.S. government's worst nightmare. Greenwald was humanizing his reports by putting a face to his stories. The face was polite, well spoken, knowledgeable and worst of all, camera friendly. Washington ground its teeth because Snowden would now have personal, popular support. Bringing him up and convicting him of charges had just become exponentially harder.

The video opens with a sea of black before centered, white letters reading "PRISM" and beneath it "Whistleblower" emerge. Poitras' audiences recognize this as her traditional title screen. The scene cuts to boats at port before "Hong Kong" appears in the bottom left corner of the frame. A thin, young man then appears. He is seated diagonally and facing stage right. His brunette hair with blond highlights is politely parted on the left. Rectangular, perhaps designer, glasses rest high on his aquiline nose. His gray-blue button-up is left open, not at the top, but two buttons down. He harbors a fashionable growth of beard. He introduces himself.

His speech is clear, paced and deliberate. "My name is Ed Snowden. I'm 29 years old. I worked for Booz Allen Hamilton as an infrastructure analyst for NSA in Hawaii." As he does so the words "EDWARD SNOWDEN" fade in above "NSA Whistleblower" in the left, bottom corner of the screen. This brings attention to what appears to be someone in the background. It then becomes clear the speaker is stilling in front of a mirror.

The screen goes black once again as "June 6, 2013" slowly emerges where Snowden's name had been. Below it reads "GLENN GREENWALD, interviewer" and below that "LAURA POITRAS, filmmaker."

In the tradition of whistleblowers, the world did not expect to learn the source of the disclosures until the person was either caught or made a deathbed confession. Viewers were even more surprised when they saw Snowden. Much like Poitras and Greenwald, the intimation was that top secret information would only be available to intelligence personnel who had climbed their way up the administrative ladder after decades of dedicated work. Instead audiences were met by a guy who looked to be a graduate student at best, at worst the assistant manager of a retail outlet.

Greenwald judiciously opens off-screen by asking Snowden his credentials.

"I've been a systems engineer, systems administrator, senior adviser for the Central Intelligence Agency, solutions consultant, and a telecommunications information system officer." Aside from the implication Snowden was very well-versed and well-rounded in IT, his mention of having served as senior advisor for the CIA undoubtedly caught people's attention. Audiences quickly deduced this person was either genuine or delusional because no sensible individual would attempt to lie about holding such a privileged position. For those familiar with the previous days' articles, the immediate inference was that this person hadn't merely grabbed a handful of papers stamped "Top Secret" and run. He knew what he was stealing, what the documents meant, and had a reason for taking them.

Greenwald then asks Snowden to explain when he decided to whistleblow. Instead of reporting, "When I was in Geneva I was witness to ... ," Snowden focuses upon the broader picture and ends on an egalitarian note.

"When you're in positions of privileged access like a systems administrator for these sorts of intelligence community agencies, you're exposed to a *lot* more information on a broader scale than the average employee and because of that, you see things that may be disturbing, but over the course of a normal person's career, you'd only see one or two of these instances. When you see everything, you see them on a more frequent basis and you recognize that some of these things are actually abuses, and when you talk to people about them in a place like this, where this is the normal state of business, people tend not to take them very seriously and move on from them. But over time that awareness of wrongdoing sort of builds up, and you feel compelled to talk about it, and the more you talk about it, the more you're ignored, the more you're told 'It's not a problem' until eventually you realize that these things need to be determined by the public and not by somebody who was simply hired by the government." He later adds, "[...] you have to make a determination about what it is that's important to you, and if living unfreely but comfortably is something you're willing to accept—and I think that many of us are, it's the human nature—you can get up everyday, go to work, you can collect your large paycheck for relatively little work against the public interest, and go to sleep at night after watching your shows. But if you realize that that's the world you helped create and it's going to get worse with the next generation and the next generation who extend the capabilities of this sort of architecture of oppression, you realize that you might be willing to accept any risk, and it doesn't matter what the outcome is so long as the public gets to make their own decisions about how that's applied."

Snowden makes it apparent he did not blow the whistle out of spite, for money, or fame but due to an overbearing sense of moral obligation. If his intention was to deliberately harm the United States, he assures Greenwald he could—and would—have already done so: "Anybody in the positions of access with the technical capabilities that I had could suck out secrets [and] pass them on the open market to Russia. They always have an open door as we do. I had access to the full rosters of everyone working at the NSA, the entire intelligence community, and undercover assets all over the world, the locations of every station; we have what their missions are, and so forth. If I had just wanted to harm the U.S....? You could shut down the surveillance system in an afternoon." In a little over a week, to quell any concerns he was a double agent, Snowden would put to his audience the rhetorical question, "Ask yourself: If I were a Chinese spy, why wouldn't I have flown directly into Beijing? I could be living in a palace petting a phoenix by now."

~~To ensure his intent was benevolent, he poses a question~~ after making clear he had what many would consider an idyllic life: "[I was] living in Hawaii, in paradise, and making a ton of money." With this, he asks, "What would it take [for] *you* to leave everything behind?" As history proved, he was not exaggerating the life he'd been living. He had a six-figure salary, lived in a world-renowned vacation destination and was in a relationship of several years. He remarks that he is now susceptible to being "[...] rendered by the CIA. I could have people come after me or any of their third-party partners. They work closely with a number of other nations or they could pay off the Triads, any of their agents or assets." (The Triads are the most recent incarnation of a centuries-old Chinese crime syndicate.) He readily admits this is "[...] a fear I'll live under for the rest of my life, however long that happens to be." With the concluding statement in which a hint of desperation is evident in his voice, Snowden obviously believes what he told Gellman months before: "[The intelligence community] will most certainly kill you if they think you are the single point of failure that could stop this disclosure and make them the sole owner of this information."

Some might claim Snowden's dramatic response is an inflated cloak-and-dagger fantasy proving his delusions of grandeur, but when Greenwald asked him how he thought the U.S. government might react to his disclosures, Snowden's patient response did not include discussion of media spin, government slander or outright denial. If he didn't truly believe his life was in jeopardy, he would have likely proffered a more modest and therefore believable reply. Interestingly, during an intelligence conference the day before the interview aired, a foreign affairs analyst named Steve Clemons was sitting in Dulle's airport in Washington D.C., when he overheard four intelligence officers discussing Snowden and Greenwald. One remarked that both whistleblower and reporter should be "disappeared."[59] MacAskill asked Snowden his opinion of the matter. "Someone responding to the story said 'real spies do not speak like that.' Well, I am a spy and that is how they talk," Snowden testified. "Whenever we had a debate in the office on how to handle crimes, they do not defend due process—they defend decisive action. They say it is better to kick someone out of a plane than let these people have a day in court. It is an authoritarian mindset in general."[60]

Yet Snowden divulges that his greatest fear is not death but his efforts might ultimately be in vain, "[...] that nothing will change. People will see the media, all of these disclosures [and] they'll know the lengths that the government is going to grant themselves powers unilaterally to create greater control over American society and global society, but they [the American people] won't be willing to take the risks necessary to stand up and fight to change things, to force their representatives to actually take a stand in their interests." He closes the interview with a prediction of where the current state of affairs might ultimately lead: "And the months ahead, the years ahead, it's only going to get worse until eventually there will be a time where policies will change because the only thing that restricts the activities of the surveillance state are *policy*. Even our agreements with other sovereign governments, we consider that to be a stipulation of *policy* rather than a stipulation of *law* and because of that, a new leader will be elected ... they'll find the switch ... say that 'Because of the crisis—because of the dangers we face in the world—some new and unpredicted threat, we need more authority, we need more power' and there will be nothing the people can do at that point to oppose it and it will be turnkey tyranny."

Early in the dialogue, Greenwald bluntly puts to Snowden, "Does it [the intelligence community] target the actions of Americans?" Greenwald wants to have the world hear, directly from the lips of a high-ranking ex-CIA employee and NSA contractor, what is taking place behind the surveillance curtain.

"The NSA, and intelligence community in general, is focused on getting intelligence wherever it can, by any means possible. It believes—on the grounds of sort of a self-certification—that they serve the national interest. Originally we saw that focus very narrowly tailored as foreign intelligence gathered overseas. Now, increasingly, we see that it's happening domestically and to do that they, the NSA specifically, targets the communications of everyone. It ingests them by *default*. It collects them in its system and it filters them and it analyses them and it measures them and it stores them for periods of time simply because that's the easiest, most efficient, and most valuable way to achieve these ends." He continues, "Any analyst at any time can target anyone, any selector, anywhere. Where those communications will be picked up depends on the range of the sensor networks and the authorities that analyst is empowered with. Not all analysts have the ability to target everything, but I, sitting at my desk, certainly had the authorities to wiretap anyone from you or your accountant, to a federal judge, to even the president if I had a personal e-mail." He adds that the American populace should take notice "[b]ecause even if you're not doing anything wrong, you're being watched and recorded, and the storage capability of these systems increases every year consistently by orders of magnitude to where it's getting to the point where you don't have to have done anything wrong. You simply have to eventually fall under suspicion from somebody even by a wrong call, and then they can use this system to go back in time and scrutinize every decision you've ever made, every friend you've ever discussed something with and attack you on that basis to sort of derive suspicion from an innocent life and paint anyone in the context of a wrongdoer."

Aside from affirming with first-hand experience that the intelligence community is "target[ing] the communication of everyone," the most intimidating facet of his narrative is reference to the NSA's propensity to operate under "self-certification." Preceding history confirms this tendency by the agency after Clapper blatantly lied to Congress regarding domestic surveillance and Boundless Informant had been hidden from oversight committees. The day Poitras' video aired, Clapper appeared on NBC[61] to backpedal. He told interviewer Andrea Mitchell, "To me, collection of a U.S. person's data would mean taking the books off the shelf, opening it up, and reading it." Under this semantic designation, an item's purpose must be utilized if the object is to be part of a collection.

Under Clapper's definition coin, stamp or wine collections would be an oxymoronic impossibility.

Hearing this from Snowden, especially when he illustrates a point by including fragments of daily life inside the intelligence community, makes the veracity of his claims difficult to doubt. It is clear he is not attempting to exaggerate the severity of what he has witnessed: "I didn't change these [documents]," he attests. "I didn't modify the story. This is the truth. This is what's happening. You should decide whether we need to be doing this." His earnestness is apparent from the conviction in his voice during the interview, which is perpetually accompanied by the suggestion of stanch disapproval.

Greenwald had accomplished what he set out to do. While the Obama administration scurried over with fire extinguishers to put out one Greenwald-sponsored fire, the attorney-turned-journalist was striking the next match, and the next one, and the next one, all before presenting his towering inferno of a finale.

He had done the unthinkable. Not only had he shattered the illusion that 21st-century America had not caught up to George Orwell's *Nineteen Eighty-Four*, but he also produced the biggest intelligence leak in American history. Greenwald had gotten the American people to doubt the two things it couldn't live without: cell phones and the Internet. He'd even delivered the man behind the Rubik's Cube. Though every bit as exhausted as the American government, Greenwald couldn't afford the luxury of sitting down, because the world was now after a man named Edward Snowden.

It would find him in less than 24 hours.

Chapter 4
Pearl of the Orient

"We hack everyone everywhere."

–Edward Snowden, *The Guardian* interview,
June 9, 2013[1]

❀ ❀ ❀

BY MONDAY MORNING THE WORLD WAS ABUZZ with the man behind the NSA leaks. Perhaps the most remarkable aspect of Snowden's immediate impact was he'd blurred partisan affinities. Shortly after Poitras' video aired, Democratic icon Michael Moore tweeted that Snowden was "Man of the Year."[2] Conservative media personality Glenn Beck followed minutes later with "I think I have just read about the man [in reference to Snowden] for which I have waited. Earmarks of a real hero."[3] The next day former presidential candidate Ron Paul said, "We should be thankful for individuals like Edward Snowden and Glenn Greenwald who see injustice being carried out by their own government and speak out, despite the risk. They have done a great service to the American people by exposing the truth about what our government is doing in secret."[4]

Though Moore's liberal defense of societal freedoms being seconded by Paul's Libertarian belief in liberty was hardly surprising considering their parties' contemporary philosophies, Beck's statement baffled his core audience. Over the years, people had grown accustomed to Beck's steadfast Republican support of national defense. But his Fox network peers, Rush Limbaugh and Bill O'Reilly, would express similar opinions during the upcoming week.

As he informed his radio listeners that Snowden's disclosures shouldn't be surprising because the talk show host assumed "this kind of stuff has been going on a long time,"

Limbaugh was reserved in his initial assessment of Snowden. He nevertheless displayed admiration for Snowden's intelligence, "[...] when I was 29, I wasn't capable of speaking that way. I didn't know anywhere near what this guy knew about the ways of the world. Not just about the CIA but the ways of the world. I don't think I had anywhere near that level or degree of maturity, at least as I read what the guy had to say."[5] Similarly, O'Reilly refused to pass blanket judgment on Snowden during his television program, *The O'Reilly Factor*. He approved of metadata collection but declared the PRISM program was unconstitutional. The television commentator was also apprehensive about the dangers involved in data preservation. He mentioned contemporary cases where retained information had been deliberately leaked in the face of political or economic opposition. Though O'Reilly didn't specifically cite the incident, metadata had revealed Army General and then-CIA director David Petraeus' extramarital affair. The information was leaked by the FBI to various attorneys who proceeded to go public. Petraeus resigned in November 2012.[6] O'Reilly added that Snowden "should be arrested" even if "what he did may ultimately be a good thing."[7]

On the opposite end of the political gamut, former Democratic president Jimmy Carter echoed O'Reilly. He refrained from explicitly endorsing Snowden but conjectured the whistleblower's actions might ultimately prove "beneficial."[8] The night the Verizon article broke, former vice president Al Gore tweeted "[...] secret blanket surveillance [is] obscenely outrageous."[9] The next week he informed *The Guardian*, "[U.S. domestic surveillance] violates the Constitution—the Fourth Amendment and the First Amendment—and the Fourth Amendment's language is crystal clear."[10]

The reason Beck, Limbaugh and O'Reilly's perspectives are confusing is they are typically more akin to those of House Republican and chair of the homeland security subcommittee Peter King. On Monday King called for Snowden's extradition.[11] Likewise, on the Tuesday edition of ABC's *Good Morning America*, Republican House Speaker John Boehner labeled

Snowden a "traitor."[12] This would be the exact term former vice president Dick Cheney would apply the following weekend.[13] Aside from their party affiliation, King and Boehner's condemnation of Snowden was to be somewhat expected given their government roles. Likewise, Democratic senator and chairman of the United States Senate Select Committee on Intelligence Diane Feinstein went on record stating, "I don't look at this as being a whistleblower. I think it's an act of treason."[14] One of the few dissenters on Capitol Hill was Ron Paul's son, Senator Rand Paul.[15]

As government largely condemned Snowden and the media leaned in favor of him, the American populace sat equally divided. The Tuesday following the bulk disclosures, Gallup surveyed 1,008 people via telephone and asked, "Do you think it was right or wrong for him [Snowden] to share that [classified intelligence] information?" Forty-four percent said it was right, and 42 percent said it was wrong. Registered Democrats showed a 10 percent greater disapproval amongst themselves whereas Republicans reported an 11 percent favoritism. Without Snowden in the picture, the populace's difference of opinion widened. When questioned, "Based on what you have heard or read about the program[s], would you say you approve or disapprove of th[ese] government program[s]," 53 percent disapproved, while only 37 percent supported them. Democratic pollsters were 49-40 in favor of surveillance, while a great chasm separated Republican voters, 32-63.[16]

When moving from right to left on the political spectrum, personal freedoms are revoked in favor of state cohesion. Theoretically Democrats should be the proponents of national security as they edge toward socialism, whereas Republicans, and especially Libertarians, ought to exhibit trepidation while nearing anarchism. However, in post-9/11 American politics— due largely to the unrelated platform association—Republicans have traditionally voted to restrict civil liberties to ensure a stronger national defense. Until Snowden, Democrats demanded the converse: greater civil rights and less militarization.

Libertarians had stringently advocated minimal restrictions on either a state or civilian level. This was the reason Snowden had avoided contacting the two largest news outlets, the right-leaning *The Wall Street Journal* and Fox News, and instead looked into the leftist *The Guardian*, *The Washington Post* and *The New York Times*.

Moore, Gore and Carter were in ideological defiance of their political principles and Feinstein remained dogmatically true. Similarly Boehner, King and Cheney ran counter to the tenets of their party as Beck, Limbaugh and O'Reilly returned thematically home, as did the American populace. In respect to modern political practice, it was the converse. Moore, Gore and Carter were true Democrats as Feinstein reneged on her party, much like Beck, Limbaugh and O'Reilly. Boehner, King and Cheney represented the current Republican outlook. The general population was in a state of political contradiction.

The most likely explanation for the contemporary legislative confusion is that the current administration was Democratic. Liberals did not want to appear hypocritical after having avidly protested Bush's wiretapping laws. Republicans had an opportunity to further criticize an already controversial president. Had Snowden gone public during Bush's time in office, it is very probable the popular response would have been flipped and maintained its modern political outlook.

A portion of the 44 percent of Americans who believed Snowden was justified in his actions started a petition on June 9.[17] They asked the White House to issue the former intelligence worker "a full, free, and absolute pardon for any crimes he has committed or may have committed related to blowing the whistle on secret NSA surveillance programs." The White House promises to address any petition that obtains 100,000 signatures in 30 days or less. Snowden's appeal had the requisite number of autographs in half that time. The U.S. government remained silent even though it had responded to numerous other petitions within the same timeframe. Some of the appeals it addressed during this time housed less than the required number of signatures. When questioned about the delay, National Security Council spokesperson Caitlin Hayden stated, "Response times vary" and the obvious, "We're not in a position to comment on the substance of a response before it has been issued."[18] The White House metaphorically informed its people that it was unable to tell everyone how a cake tasted until it had been baked.

Everyone seemed to have an opinion about Snowden. Despite having his reasons for doing what he did, the world wanted to know more about the guy who was too young to have single-handedly hoodwinked the NSA, FBI and CIA. Reporters across the globe banged their heads on their computer terminals. There were no Edward Snowden Facebook, Twitter, Pinterest or Instagram accounts. What made journalistic matters worse is that Snowden had spent his entire adult life in the intelligence community. It was therefore unlikely any government employee could be socially or financially engineered into talking. Midway through their desperate, frantic scramble for a lead, the press and public finally stumbled across Greenwald and MacAskill's interview with Snowden.[19]

The article serves as a rough overview of Snowden. It dispatches piecemeal information with little or no explanation. *The Guardian* team incorrectly relays that Snowden had earned a GED and first worked for the U.S. government as a security guard for the NSA. The journalists subtly blow another whistle by telling the tale of Snowden growing disillusioned with the intelligence community early in his career after having witnessed the CIA's extortion of a Swiss banker. Likewise, Greenwald and Co. expose Dell as a previous employer before referencing the existence of a girlfriend, his childhood in Elizabeth City and throughout Maryland, time spent in Japan and Snowden's Army enlistment. The interview quietly brings to audiences' attention one of the avenues by which Snowden used to anonymously communicate with his journalists: "His allegiance to internet freedom is reflected in the stickers on his laptop: 'I support Online Rights: Electronic Frontier Foundation,' reads one. Another hails the online organisation offering anonymity, the Tor Project." Similarly Greenwald and MacAskill initiated a fund-raising campaign for Snowden[20] by mentioning his daily expenses in Hong Kong. As a slap in the U.S. government's face, the journalists also outline the process by which Snowden fled the country and how he used the ruse of needing a two-week medical leave to treat epilepsy before departing Hawaii on May 20.

Reporters searched for answers anywhere they could. Phones rang at Dell and the Swiss Foreign Ministry. Comments were sought from the Army. FBI agents and news crews traveled to Maryland and Hawaii to conduct interviews with anyone and everyone who might have known, worked or associated with Snowden. The FBI had already darkened the doorway of Lon Snowden's Pennsylvania home before supper on Monday.[21]

The press quickly discovered Mills' online presence and set to sensationalize her "pole dancing." Other reports focused on the real estate agent responsible for the property which Snowden's landlord had him evacuate by May 1 so it could be sold. In typical news-writing fashion, because there was so little to be had about the man behind the leaks and the acronym and jargon-riddled disclosures didn't lend themselves to being transformed into sound bites or condensed into 300-word articles, the press started running with stories.

On Tuesday BAH announced, "Edward Snowden, 29, was an employee of our firm for less than 3 months, assigned to a team in Hawaii. Snowden, who had a salary at the rate of $122,000, was terminated June 10, 2013 for violations of the firm's code of ethics and firm policy."[22] The salary disclosure appears out of place. However, this was a coy jab by BAH to discredit Snowden. In its introduction to the whistleblower, *The Guardian* team had stated, "He has had 'a very comfortable life' that included a salary of roughly $200,000." The press took BAH's cue. Numerous news outlets claimed Snowden's 61 percent reported difference in pay brought his character and intent into question. Since Snowden had exaggerated his salary, people automatically started to wonder what else he might have embellished.

The *Post* contacted Greenwald for comment. Being the ever vigilant attorney, Greenwald highlighted BAH's use of the phrase "rate of $122,000." He conjectured BAH had listed Snowden's prorated pay.[23] If this were the case, his year-end total would have been at least $488,800. Snowden would personally settle the matter six days later during a live Internet chat. When asked point blank, "Did you lie about your salary? What is the issue there? Why did you tell Glenn Greenwald that your salary was $200,000 a year, when it was only $122,000?" He responded, "I was debriefed by Glenn and his peers over a number of days, and not all of those conversations were recorded. The statement I made about earnings was that $200,000 was my 'career high' salary. I had to take pay cuts in the course of pursuing specific work. Booz was not the most I've been paid."[24] When asked by BAH why he was willing to incur such a substantial pay cut, he undoubtedly commented upon how he favored the idyllic locale, that he would be further expanding his résumé atop the job affording him new IT experiences.

As one side of the world vainly grasped at the ghost of Snowden, people a quarter of the way around the globe had already found him.

Shortly after noon the following Monday, Snowden was forced out of the Mira. A mass Twitter effort had identified his location using Poitras' video. The purported giveaway was the particular design of a lamp within the hotel room despite Poitras trying to throw people off with a view of Victoria Harbor from Greenwald's hotel.[25] His whereabouts and activities for the next 13 days were veiled in the fog of ambiguity and rumor. It was presumed he relocated to a safe house.[26] What could not be refuted was that he quickly went back to work. Within the next 48 hours, while the U.S. government began preparing charges against him, Snowden gave an interview to the Chinese English-language periodical, the *South China Morning Post* (*SCMP*).

Theories began to circulate that he was a Chinese double agent. Others believed he was defecting. Though he would later inform the online community that he's chosen China because he required "a country with the cultural and legal framework to allow me to work without being immediately detained,"[27] the intelligence community knew why he was there. He wanted to personally ensure the delivery of SIGINT information which would reinforce Greenwald's June 7 U.S. cyberattack exposé. Conducting the interview was yet another risky move, especially since the world now knew who he was. Instead of contenting himself with gathering the data, delivering it to the press, and refusing further involvement, then seeking personal safety in a country without an American extradition treaty, he continued his mission. He would tell the *SCMP*, "I am not here [in Hong Kong] to hide from justice; I am here to reveal criminality."[28]

Snowden admitted in his interview with Greenwald that most would assume his choice of destinations to be a mistake because "people think 'Oh China, Great [Internet] Firewall.'"[29] But he had done his homework. He was not in China, he was in Hong Kong. Unlike mainland China, where Internet usage and free speech are restricted, Hong Kong mirrored traditional American freedoms of expression.[30] As later witnessed in news coverage, without reservation or impediment from regional authorities, protesters went to the streets of Hong Kong in support of Snowden.[31]

Hong Kong was a British colony until it was returned to China in 1997. Due largely to its English influence and extreme Westernization by Eastern standards, China granted Hong Kong almost exclusive autonomy with the exception of militarization and foreign policy.[32] Though these two components might appear crucial for Snowden, Hong Kong's judiciary system is likewise independent of China. He was aware that surrender proceedings with Hong Kong were lengthy and would buy him time. (Only mainland China could extradite him, and it was not "technically" legally possible for Beijing to remove Snowden from Hong Kong under the latter's "One Country, Two Systems" agreement.)[33] He would buy himself even more time by disclosing data which would further incriminate the U.S. government in China's eyes. It would endear him to the Chinese and give Hong Kong even greater pause in detaining him. Snowden also anticipated that the White House would trip over its own hubris and unintentionally give Hong Kong legitimate reason not to hand him over.

When compared to Gellman and Greenwald's reports, the *SCMP*'s coverage of Snowden's disclosures is extremely short and sparse. This is because the newspaper tried to stretch headlines using a one-hour interview with Snowden.

Remembering China is 13 hours ahead of the U.S., the *SCMP* ran a teaser article, "Whistle-blower Edward Snowden talks to South China Morning Post,"[34] on Wednesday, June 12, at 8:51 p.m. local time. A day later, "Edward Snowden: US government has been hacking Hong Kong and China for years"[35] was published. The article reports Snowden had provided the newspaper with documents containing evidence the NSA had been hacking into Hong Kong and mainland China since 2009. The agency had expressly targeted Hong Kong's civilian population: Chinese University, public officials, various businesses and students. This was not traditional cyberwarfare. None of the Sino-related hacking paperwork showed any evidence of attacks upon Eastern military systems. Snowden added, "We [the U.S.] hack network backbones—like huge Internet routers, basically—that give us access to the communications of hundreds of thousands of computers without having to hack every single one." Chinese University is one of the six major Chinese Internet hubs. It is home of the Hong Kong Internet Exchange, and all of the city's Internet traffic is routed through the university system.

The next day "Edward Snowden: Classified US data shows Hong Kong hacking targets[36]" appeared. It is a follow-up to the previous report and states the documents suggesting American intrusion of civilian networks include specific dates and IP addresses of Hong Kong and mainland computer systems. The data also lists whether a hack assignment had been completed or a particular computer system was perpetually monitored. As Snowden would relay in a later *SCMP* report concerning the evidence, "[T]he specific details of external and internal Internet protocol addresses could only have been obtained by hacking or with physical access to the computers." A 75 percent success rate is noted. Snowden clarifies, "The primary issue of public importance to Hong Kong and mainland China should be that the NSA is illegally seizing the communications of tens of millions of individuals without any individualised suspicion of wrongdoing. They simply steal everything so they can search for any topics of interest." Both whistleblowing articles include the annotation that the confiscated NSA documents could not be independently verified. Clearly the U.S. government was not willing to acknowledge them.

The Chinese government immediately set to finding proof of U.S. intrusion. Security Secretary Lai Tung-kwok quickly assured Hong Kong's Legislative Council there was no evidence the Internet Exchange had been compromised, though it was obvious it had been monitored.[37] Given the constant cyberespionage parlaying between the two countries, the official response was likely a testament to the world of the exchange's integrity, especially since China asked the U.S. government to respond to the claims. Behind the public relations veil, hacking was already known, but mainland China was the suspect.

At Snowden's request, the *SCMP* sat on more confidential information. His motive was manifold because he wanted to keep the fire hot and *The Guardian* had a time-sensitive report the world needed to read without distraction. The subsequent *SCMP* articles also contained personal, incriminating information Snowden wanted known but didn't need considered as the U.S. government processed criminal charges. In the words of the *SCMP*'s editor-in-chief, Xiangwei Wang, the newspaper agreed to let the "dust settle."[38]

In a little over a week, Snowden had set the American populace and Chinese people against the U.S. government. He now had his sights set on Britain. The journalistic barrage would be quick and unrelenting. By the end, several of the world's most powerful countries would be demanding immediate responses from England as well as what was slowly becoming clear was its spying partner, America.

A week after Snowden had gone public and two days after the *SCMP* went into greater, more incriminating detail about American surveillance in China, Ewen MacAskill led a team of *Guardian* journalists with "GCHQ intercepted foreign politicians' communications at G20 summits."[39] Whereas the *SCMP*'s exposés only made reference to unseen, unverified directives and forms, *The Guardian* provided its readers with primary documentation. The article's sources are a top secret January 20, 1999 briefing paper, various classified documents and confidential PowerPoint slides all provided by Snowden. The report debuted a day before the eight wealthiest countries—all of which were potential targets of the headline spying—were to meet in Ireland at the annual G8 Summit.

Started in 1999, the G20 Summit is the once biannual and now annual aggregation of 19 of the world's top financial leaders with the European Union (EU) as the final member. They represent two-thirds of the world's population and 80 percent of its gross product and trading. Its purpose is to discuss and examine international economic policy issues which lie outside the scope and capability of any one particular country or organization to address. Due to the growth of other world nations, in 2009 the G20 replaced the G8—started in 1975—as the main economic forum for wealthy nations.

MacAskill and Co. offer no quarter from the beginning: "Foreign politicians and officials who took part in two G20 summit meetings in London in 2009 had their computers monitored and their phone calls intercepted on the instructions of their British government hosts, according to documents seen by the *Guardian*. Some delegates were tricked into using Internet cafes which had been set up by British intelligence agencies to read their email traffic." GCHQ's stated eavesdropping agenda was to learn each country's negotiating position and leverage so Britain could have tactical advantage during the April and September 2009 meetings. However, Snowden's documents make clear the confiscated user access data, i.e., user names and passwords, was intended to be used to continue spying on various nations' officials after the summit ended: "[We] were able to extract key logging info, providing creds for delegates, meaning we have sustained intelligence options against them even after [the] conference has finished." England's specific targets were its allies South Africa and Turkey. South Africa was a crucial swing vote. With the latter, Britain's objective was to "establish Turkey's position on agreements from the April London summit" and its "willingness (or not) to cooperate with the rest of the G20 nations." The overriding concern was the various countries' positions and attitudes regarding financial reform after the 2008 global banking meltdown.

British intelligence had already hacked into South Africa's foreign affairs network in 2005. It had gathered information by "investigating" the country's telephone lines and compromising diplomats' user accounts. The mission was successful, because South Africa updated its systems shortly thereafter. GCHQ countered by immediately installing electronic backdoors "to increase reliability."[40]

Multiple delegates had been led into Internet cafes that had email filtration and keystroke logging software installed on the diners' computers. For wireless communications, remote relays retrieved the politicians' cell phone data, which was telecast almost live to 45 stand-by GCHQ analysts. The analysts would make their assessments then "provide timely information to UK ministers." Keystroke logging is the recording of what is being typed as it is being typed. This permits the viewer to see the content of any document as it appears on the screen as well as login information, including passwords and phrases, as it is being entered. Over 20 new email "selectors" were obtained by GCHQ.

The Guardian highlights that the covert directives originated at the senior level during then-prime minister Gordon Brown's time in office. Once finalized, orders were issued to various ministers. They were therefore sanctioned by the British government. Like the NSA's data intercepts within Hong Kong and mainland China, none of the G20 targets were under any suspicion of wrongdoing by GCHQ. Britain legally justified its eavesdropping with the 1994 Intelligence Services Act, which states clandestine foreign intelligence is "in the interests of the economic well-being of the United Kingdom in relation to the actions or intentions of persons outside the British Island."[41] Britain had given itself permission to spy if not doing so risked financial loss or inhibited economic growth.

As disclosed in a classified report titled, "Russian Leadership Communications in support of President Dmitry Medvedev at the G20 summit in London—Intercept at Menwith Hill station," the NSA intercepted and decrypted then-Russian president Dmitry Medvedev's telephone calls as they dispatched through satellite links to Moscow starting the day he arrived at the first summit, April 1. Menwith Hill is an NSA outpost located in Harrogate, North Yorkshire in England. Until 2013, it was believed to be the largest intelligence facility in the world. Menwith Hill occupies 560 acres.

Without having to lend a word to the topic, MacAskill made demonstrably clear the United States was in espionage cahoots with England. As Gellman had reported, the NSA had given Britain PRISM and was in possession of classified GCHQ documents. Like Greenwald, MacAskill left the reader to discover that Menwith Hill had been in operation since 1966, is leased to America and suspiciously staffed with both American and British intelligence agents.[42] As of March 2012, there is a one-to-three mix of British to American Menwith employees: 400 to 1,200.[43] Menwith Hill is so productive it was given the NSA's "Station of the Year" award in 1991.[44] The obvious question remained: Why wouldn't Britain be concerned with more powerful attendees' data, such as its former colony, Australia, or America's neighbor, Canada? The answer was coming.

The very next day, South Africa, Russia and Turkey reacted—the latter two violently—to the claims. *The Guardian* reported Turkey demanded nothing short of Britain's ambassador, David Norman Reddaway, arrive at the capital, Ankara, to personally receive the country's official statement on the matter. It was read aloud to him: "If these allegations are true, this is going to be scandalous for the UK. At a time when international co-operation depends on mutual trust, respect and transparency, such behaviour by an allied country is unacceptable."[45] Other British news outlets demurely denied Reddaway was summoned and quoted the U.K. Foreign Office as stating, "No, this was discussed in a phone call."[46] Though the latter seems more probable, given the severity of the accusations, the former circumstance could have taken place and the foreign affairs office was downplaying Britain's apologetic response for public relations purposes. Regardless, *The Guardian*'s report further enflamed tensions between the two nations. Turkey's Prime Minister, Recep Tayyip Erdoðan, specifically cited the BBC as sustaining and advocating civil unrest in Turkey amid nationwide demonstrations and violent protests.[47]

While at the G8 Summit in Ireland, Prime Minister David Cameron refused to attempt to deny, comment upon, or even acknowledge the surveillance allegations: "We never comment on security or intelligence issues and I am not about to start now."[48]

The report did not help U.S.-Russian relations. It appeared amid a heated debate between the two nations on how to address Syrian violence. Eyebrows were raised by Russian officials about America's sincerity in "resetting" the countries' relationship as offered by Obama during a July 7, 2009, speech at Moscow's New Economic School. It was during his first visit to Russia after being elected president that Obama also ironically proclaimed, "In 2009, the great power does not show strength by dominating or demonizing other countries. The days when empires could treat other sovereign states as pieces on a chess board are over."[49]

Greenwald's name is suspiciously absent from the G20 article because he was preparing the unthinkable. The world had been introduced to Snowden through Greenwald's writing as well as his participation in the making of Poitras' video. He was now going to let the world talk to Snowden. As New York was getting ready to take lunch while Hong Kong was going to bed, on Monday, June 17, Snowden gave the world an exclusive interview.

Going "live" online might seem like Snowden was blatantly thumbing his nose at U.S. intelligence, especially since Greenwald issued a two-hour notification before the start of the Q & A session. However, Snowden was on the equivalent of a relay. He was monitoring the questions as they were submitted and sent Greenwald his responses over a secure line. Though a degree of risk was involved because American intelligence knew when he'd be online, it was safer than if he'd posted directly onto the forum.

In the 96-minute interview,[50] Snowden addresses a range of topics: why he chose Hong Kong over Iceland, the public's reaction to the leaks, whether he was working with foreign governments, previous whistleblowers, the Obama administration, WikiLeaks, Internet companies' responses to the PRISM disclosures, the discrepancy in his reported salary and various IT questions. At the commencement of the chat, he makes clear his intent is to make people around the world aware of privacy violations and at no time has he put U.S. citizens at risk: "I did not reveal any US operations against legitimate military targets." He states he did not remain in America because the government "destroyed the possibility of a fair trial" by "openly declaring me guilty" and justifies his decision to flee: "[I]t would be foolish to volunteer yourself to it [an unfair trial] if you can do more good outside of prison than in it." Snowden includes he would not be aiding foreign governments because he "only work[s] with journalists."

The day prior to the chat, Apple and Yahoo responded to claims of allowing U.S. intelligence direct access to their servers. (In a brief aside, Snowden pauses to insinuate FISC orders and NSLs are the companies' alibi for compliance: "If for example Facebook, Google, Microsoft, and Apple refused to provide this cooperation with the intelligence community, what do you think the government would do? Shut them down?" He implicitly acknowledges individual court orders are time consuming but that legality demands their being filed. Snowden is obviously hinting at an ulterior, self-interested motive for the businesses consenting to data submission.) He is asked to clarify the phrase "direct access" and expound upon the implications.

He opens with the assurance that "more detail on how direct NSA's accesses are is (sic) coming" before outlining that an analyst with high enough clearance can query the NSA's databases and "get results for anything they want. Phone number, email, user id, cell phone handset id (IMEI), and so on." The reason the NSA has access to individuals' information who are not targets is because after an investigation is closed, the data that was "incidentally" compiled is not automatically discarded. Snowden relays, "If I target for example an email address, for example under FAA 702, and that email address sent something to you, Joe America, the analyst gets it. All of it. IPs, raw data, content, headers, attachments, everything. And it gets saved for a very long time—and can be extended further with waivers rather than warrants." "Raw" data is collected information which has not been anonymized. It still contains content and identifying markers such as a user's name and location.

This means if Bob is a target and he has emailed Mary, all of Mary's emails will be confiscated. Even if nothing arouses reasonable suspicion, her records are nonetheless kept on file. Though it might appear to be a question of who is lying, Clapper told NBC, "[A]ny of the ill-begotten collection is destroyed." (In the interview transcript on the Office of the Director of National Intelligence's website, Clapper's connotative "collection" is inexplicably replaced by the more innocuous "information.")[51] This could well be true and consistent with Snowden because the director of intelligence does not designate the timeframe of—in his words—the NSA's "retention period" for accidentally gathered data.

Snowden reiterates from his interview with Poitras that there are no technological limitations to what can be gathered and requested. Previewing a forthcoming disclosure, he states, "[T]he intelligence community doesn't always deal with what you would consider a 'real' warrant like a [p]olice department would have to, the 'warrant' is more of a templated form they fill out and send to a reliable judge with a rubber stamp." Policy, which is subject to administrative whim, is the only restraint, but Snowden declares "policy protection is no protection—policy is a one-way ratchet that only loosens and one very weak technical protection—a near-the-front-end filter at our ingestion points. The filter is constantly out of date, is set at what is euphemistically referred to as the 'widest allowable aperture,' and can be stripped out at any time." Like the NSA's reminder to its analysts that accidental intercepts are "nothing to worry about," Britain's system of checks and balances for query protocol is equally lax. "For at least GCHQ," Snowden tells his audience, "the number of audited queries is only 5% of those performed." It is worthy to note Menwith Hill is overseen by a Royal Air Force officer.[52]

Toward the end of the interview, Snowden overtly condemns America's invasive surveillance policies and practices: "Journalists should ask a specific question: [S]ince these programs began operation shortly after September 11th, how many terrorist attacks were prevented SOLELY by information derived from this suspicionless surveillance that could not be gained via any other source?" He assures his audience that regardless of what happens to him or how strict whistleblowing legislation becomes, gray hat leaking will not cease, because "[c]itizens with a conscience are not going to ignore wrongdoing simply because they'll be destroyed for it: the conscience forbids it." He boldly proclaims, "Truth is coming, and it cannot be stopped."

Greenwald charitably gave Washington three days to breathe before heading another barrage of disclosures. On Thursday, June 20, *The Guardian* released, "The top secret rules that allow NSA to use US data without a warrant."[53] With this disclosure, a distinct pattern becomes clear. Snowden was aiding in the order and direction of the various releases. Once the attention-grabbing, nationwide appeal of the Verizon and PRISM information was made public, the publication trajectory was set to incriminate Washington's every step. As witnessed in the timing of the president-directed cyberattack hit list and the G20 leak coinciding within hours of related events, Snowden was also reinforcing his claims each time the nation's capital refuted them. It made for a sweaty-palmed effort by the White House because the intelligence community was still unclear what data had been taken. Even if it did know, it could not preempt the negative impact of future disclosures, because the programs were classified. It had no choice but to attempt to vainly, desperately deny and dodge accusations, hoping Snowden couldn't have the documentation to prove otherwise. In the event a report did appear which undermined a previous official statement, the U.S. government had no choice but to backpedal. Snowden and Greenwald's process was systematic and exact.

Greenwald begins by announcing the publication of accompanying classified documents that prove the U.S. government had passed covert laws through the FISC that permits intelligence to acquire and utilize American communications. Two of the enclosed documents are procedure orders which were signed by Attorney General Eric Holder on July 28, 2009 and put into practice the next day. Greenwald provides a third document, a 2010 one-paragraph umbrella court order, which declares the attorney general's directives "[...] are consistent with the requirements of [...] the fourth amendment to the Constitution of the United States."

The orders allow the NSA to retain "inadvertently acquired" domestic communications for up to five years. Even if a person is not under suspicion, an individual's wholly domestic data can be kept on file because it is encrypted, relates to criminal activity, insinuates potential harm to people or property, or in Greenwald's terms, "[is] believed to contain any information relevant to cybersecurity." Under Holder's directive, attorney-client privilege is suspended if the communication includes "foreign intelligence information." The legislation also permits the gathering of information from "U.S.-based machines[s]" if it is deemed necessary to determine whether a target is located within American borders. As Snowden noted, unlike standard police procedure, where evidence is inadmissible if it was not obtained by a warrant after reasonable suspicion had been established by an external authority, if the NSA "stumbles" across information it deems worthwhile, it can lawfully exploit and act upon the data.

Holder's documents answer a lingering question: "NSA determines whether a person is a non-United States person reasonably believed to be outside the United States in light of the totality of the circumstances based on the information available with respect to that person, including information concerning the communications facility or facilities used by that person." Thus, the U.S. government acknowledges it has alternative means of verifying whether an individual is an American citizen residing within the United States before targeting begins and, within the confines of the documents themselves, incriminates itself further: "[I]n order to prevent the inadvertent targeting of a United States person, NSA maintains records of telephone numbers and electronic communications account/address/identifiers that NSA has reason to believe are being used by United States persons." The intelligence agency admits to keeping files on Americans. Its paradoxical justification is it needs these records to determine who can and cannot be surveilled. It is not disclosed how these records are obtained. The implication is that they consist of "inadvertently" intercepted data and information culled from "U.S.-based machines" used to aid in location verification. It is assumed this data is under a one-year retention license or a five-year extension.

In theory, "domestic" designates any communication that involves a U.S. citizen or takes place on American soil. The disclosures broadly define the term as well as harbor numerous exemptions to supposedly hard-and-fast rules of surveillance.

The decision to extract information begins and ends with the analyst. In the unlikely event an audit questions a retrieval or "task" request, clemency is granted so long as it can be argued there was "reasonable belief" the appeal fell under any of Holder's provisions. In order to allow the "widest allowable aperture" for targeting, the directives do not place the burden of proof upon an analyst. Even with the aid of NSA databases and access to external files and records, if an analyst cannot arrive at a conclusive answer, shadow of a doubt is not granted. The attorney general's orders explicitly instruct the analyst to assume a person is abroad and non-American when no definitive location data is available: "A person reasonably believed to be located outside the United States or whose location is not known will be presumed to be a non-United States person unless such person can be positively identified as a United States person." All international communications are granted free license for surveillance: "Information indicates that the telephone number [and in a subsequent clause, 'electronic communications account/address/identifier'] has been used to communicate directly with another telephone number [etc.] reasonably believed by the U.S. Intelligence Community to be used by an individual associated with a foreign power or foreign territory." This also allows for targeting of anyone with foreign associations via electronic "buddy lists," such as Facebook. In any situation where an American is communicating with a foreigner, the data can be intercepted.

If American Bob is on vacation in France and emails American Mary, they may be surveilled. If Bob is in San Francisco and Mary is in New York their conversation can be recorded if an analyst isn't able to determine where Bob's telephone is transmitting from or easily locate Mary's naturalization papers. Also, if Bob is believed to be associated with a foreign political group after posting on a socialist Internet forum based in Venezuela, has a foreign telephone account or utilizes a non-domestic email service, he may become a suspect. Anyone who has electronically "friended" a non-American can be made a target. It is clear that under this policy, reverse targeting can occur. If a person of potential interest does not elicit lawful targeting, all an analyst needs to do is look at the web of associations and find one foreign contact at a distance of two or fewer hops to substantiate an investigation upon the otherwise legally-protected individual. Once the American's identity is removed, collected data can be disseminated to other agencies or "friendly governments." After Bob and Mary's names are removed from their emailed love letter, the NSA can hand it over to the CIA, FBI or GCHQ with no questions asked.

Once a person is verified to be within the United States, all targeting is to cease, with the exception of bulk data collection. The NSA is permitted to retain non- and American information using this method based upon the premise that the intelligence agency is unable to filter the two types of communication. If the NSA dragnets American "backbone" hubs, this would permit almost all American communications to be collected with impunity. Contrary to Clapper's claims, if it is later revealed during "post-target analysis" that a subject was within the U.S. during transmission or interception, the accrued information is granted grandfather amnesty and retained for review. All of this directly contradicts Obama and the intelligence community's reassurances that the U.S. government cannot use purloined domestic data without individual, court-issued consent.

The most condemning passage found in the disclosures is the only one marked "Top Secret" within a document already labeled "Top Secret." It reads, "In addition, in those cases where NSA seeks to acquire communications about the target that are not to or from the target, NSA will either employ an Internet Protocol filter to ensure that the person from whom it seeks to obtain foreign intelligence information is located overseas, or it will target Internet links that terminate in a foreign country. In either event, NSA will direct surveillance at a party to the communication reasonably believed to be outside the

United States." By being allowed to "acquire communication *about* [my emphasis] the target" that is not "to or from" the suspect, an analyst is given license to follow leads that do not necessarily begin outside the United States but "terminate in a foreign country." The only way to determine if communications are "about" a target is to collect bulk data and analyze the contents.

Greenwald closes by mindfully stepping back to provide a comprehensive picture of the legal implications. Holder's orders force the PRISM-affiliated companies to surrender all data for anyone who falls under these 2009 provisions. Under these clauses, American information is freely handed over without a warrant. In many respects, "The top secret rules that allow NSA to use US data without a warrant" is the most condemning article to date because when placed alongside the NSA's "hopping" protocol, on paper the NSA has the right to surveil most every American due to happenstance association.

Almost seven hours after Gellman's PRISM rewrite appeared—complemented by *The Guardian*'s "UK gathering secret intelligence via covert NSA operation," both of which implicated GCHQ in the espionage controversy—sensing its association with the NSA and its own intelligence programs might be further comprised, the British government issued a "D-Notice" to the English press.[54] A "D-Notice" or "Defence Advisory Notice" is an official request for the media to remain silent on an issue pertaining to national security. The non-Snowden-leaked D-Notice reads, in part, "Although none of these recent articles has contravened any of the guidelines contained within the Defence Advisory Notice System, the intelligence services are concerned that further developments of this same theme may begin to jeopardize both national security and possibly UK personnel."[55] A day after the island nation learned the whistleblower's identity, British authorities sought retribution by issuing a global travel alert. It instructed airlines around the world to deny Snowden flight privileges because "the individual is highly likely to be refused entry to the U.K."[56] The warning was largely symbolic because Britain could not force non-English airports to comply (merely charge a reimbursement fee of $3,100 for detention and removal of Snowden if he stepped foot on British soil), nor did it reasonably believe Snowden would be foolish enough to enter the country. Snowden would have his just desserts 11 days later. It was now 11 days later.

As Washington was kept busy by yet another Greenwald-sponsored media blitz, *The Guardian* returned its attention to Britain. Greenwald passed the journalistic baton back to MacAskill's team, which gave Snowden a birthday present titled, "GCHQ taps fibre-optic cables for secret access to world's communications."[57] The journalists based their report on data Snowden had stolen while at Dell.[58] Predictably Washington knew restrictive legal hurdles would remain even if it used covert court orders to collect domestic information. It would be much more prudent to have another country spy on "foreign" America. The U.S. could then exchange foreign intelligence data to gain insight into its own citizenry.[59] That is exactly what it does with GCHQ's Tempora program.

Even though GCHQ had copies of PRISM, it didn't need it. Tempora debuted in 2008 before being fully inaugurated at the beginning of 2012. It is a program that vacuums everything that crosses fiber-optic cables, storing metadata for 30 days and live content for three, thereby granting ample time for the information to be categorized, analyzed and recorded. Its access points are intercept probes where transatlantic cables enter British shores. This includes cables used by American Internet servers.

After Americans had been allowed to use Tempora on a provisional basis, they were granted full access. By May 2012, 300 GCHQ and 250 NSA analysts were tasked with sifting through Tempora's incoming data. Thirteen months later, Clapper would testify on national television, "We [the intelligence community] couldn't do it [access, analyze, and record domestic data] even if we wanted to."[60] Human sifting occurs after Tempora has winnowed frivolous information. Relevant data is captured using "selectors" chosen by both agencies.

Tempora's aperture is wide. GCHQ chose 40,000 and the NSA 30,000 triggers. A "trigger" is a term or designation which, when found, culls the host document for further review. Each trigger adds another weave to the surveillance net. The denser the weave, the greater the amount of information is pulled out of the World Wide Web. Yahoo and Gmail use a similar program to scan the content of email in order to insert content-related advertising into user accounts.

The greater the number of triggers, the more data there is to analyze. Admittedly, even after filtration, the influx of information outpaces the joint effort. In 2012 GCHQ had taps on over 200 cables, cataloging the information as it went, but was only able to successfully analyze the contents of 46 lines. Each cable is able to process 21 petabytes a day. This is 192 times the amount of information found in all of the books in the British Library. The British Library houses over 150 million items. Due to bulk data analysis being labor and money intensive, Britain is increasing its storage capacity. If it cannot immediately analyze the data, it intends to keep it until it has the time and resources to do so.

GCHQ was not modest when outlining the program's agenda. Two of its key components are titled "Mastering the Internet" and "Global Telecoms Exploitation." Not to be outdone in respect to ambition, during a June 2008 visit overseas, General Alexander pondered, "Why can't we collect all the signals all the time? Sounds like a good summer project for Menwith." The quotation is included as a slogan on one of the disclosed Tempora slides.

Under the ruse of national self-defense, the countries have carte blanche license to gather anything and everything "foreign" to that particular country, including the contents of telephone calls and email messages, Facebook entries and browser history. In the event Holder's disclosure is met with an American citizen who never leaves the country and has no foreign contacts, Britain is free to investigate the "foreigner" on America's behalf. MacAskill reports that *The Guardian* was given to understand 850,000 NSA employees and contractors have access to GCHQ databases. *The Guardian* team leaves the reader to assume reciprocity applies to America's surveillance records since England is a "friendly government."

Like America, Britain also has domestic commercial "intercept partners"—BT, Verizon Business, Vodafone Cable, Global Crossing, Level 3, Viatel and Interoute—which comply under covert legal "agreements" complete with gag orders. Analogous to U.S. law, British wiretapping requires a signed warrant unless surveillance involves foreign communications, then a notarized blanket certificate suffices. A portion of domestic communications is conveniently relayed abroad before returning to Britain.

MacAskill conclusively documents America's joint espionage enterprises with Britain. He also introduces a worldwide conspiracy which answers why GCHQ was not concerned about Canada or Australia during the G20 summits. The United States and England's data sharing is not bilateral. They are only two of what is referred to as the "Five Eyes" of the world. Canada, Australia and New Zealand are included in the surveillance coop. (In intelligence terms, the United States is the first party, members of the Five Eyes are deemed second parties and all other nations are labeled third parties.)[61] In 2012 Britain reported it had the "biggest internet access" of any of the clandestine association's members. This is due to location but also because Britain, in GCHQ's attorneys' words, has "a light oversight regime compared with the U.S." As NSA analysts were being briefed on Tempora, when they asked what the legal limits of surveillance were in England, the Americans were informed it was "your call."

The Five Eyes are not a recent surveillance development. They are an extension of post-World War II alliances between the five English-speaking countries. An intelligence exchange program was designed, agreed upon and signed in 1947. It was referred to as the "Secret Treaty."[62]

Of the various reactions to Tempora, the most adamant was Germany. In a matter of days, local newspapers reported one of the main cables connecting northern Germany to the

United States was compromised at its British transition point. Federal Minister of Justice Sabine Leutheusser-Schnarrenberger referred to Tempora as a "nightmare."[63] Berlin demanded legal justification for England's actions. Jan Philipp Albrecht, German member of the European Parliament, requested infringement procedures begin because Article 16 of the Treaties of the European Union had been violated.[64] The United Nations (U.N.) had not been informed about Tempora and a vote had not been taken which permitted international surveillance.

Once it was established that GCHQ's spying was not limited to isolated political events and operated at a level which made PRISM appear juvenile, as the world waited for more information about the other "three eyes" of global espionage, Snowden nodded his consent for the *SCMP* to continue its reporting on the NSA's surveillance of China. On June 22, the day following the Tempora disclosures, *SCMP* premiered three articles.

Characteristically sparse, the Eastern periodical debuted "Snowden reveals more US cyberspying details"[65] and "US spies on Chinese mobile phone companies, steals SMS data"[66] an hour apart. The two exposés reveal the global telecommunications provider with over 46,000 kilometers of fiber-optic cable worldwide, Pacnet, had been mined by the NSA for its SMS data. SMS data is short for "small message service" and refers to the interception of millions of Chinese text messages. Pacnet's headquarters are in Singapore and Hong Kong. The cable connects to data centers in mainland China, Hong Kong, Japan, Singapore, South Korea and Taiwan.

The NSA conducted its Pacnet espionage by exploiting technology gaps in American-made-and-sold Pacnet components which granted the agency backdoor access. The nation's second-largest communications provider, China Unicom, finished replacing its American-made Cisco routers by Halloween 2012.[67] Through these deliberately flawed[68] products, the NSA had been spying on China Unicom's 258 million users. Though China Unicom found this exploitation point on its own, Snowden's disclosures undoubtedly spurred all Chinese tech-

nology firms to begin replacing and banning American communication hardware. But Snowden's files were a
double-edged sword. They also provided the Chinese government justification for implementing even stricter Internet
controls.

"NSA targeted China's Tsinghua University in extensive
hacking attacks, says Snowden"[69] arrived a little under two
hours later. The report focuses on NSA-led cyberespionage on
the computers and servers at another central Asian hub, this
time in mainland China: Tsinghua University in Beijing. As
with Chinese University, because the data collected includes
specific IP addresses, foreign possession of the data confirms
NSA hacking. The revealed documents also show the attacks
were focused efforts. Within a single day in January 2013, a
minimum of 63 computers and servers had been compromised
by the American agency. The U.S. intelligence community has
a preoccupation with the Tsinghua system because it houses
the world's largest national research portal, the China Education and Research Network.

The *Global Times*, a pro-party newspaper, issued a call to
arms as it vehemently condemned American foreign surveillance while periodically lapsing into hypocrisy. The daily
stopped short of referring to America as a corporatocracy,
wherein corporations are the governing bodies. Instead it announced that the division between American business and U.S.
government had become indistinguishable, "Along with the
expansion of American Internet barons which have extremely
close relations with Washington, the ownership the Internet is
now being used by Washington to serve its own interests.
Snowden sounded the alarm, and we cannot cover our ears."
It lambasted American capitalism for having failed as an ideology, after making its inevitable plunge into a dictatorship:
"Washington keeps a firm grip of the Internet where it abuses
its power. But other countries are not united in fighting US
hegemony in cyberspace."[70] *The Sinocism China Newsletter* outlined the possible economic implications of U.S. intelligence's
intrusive international surveillance: "If [Mark] Zuckerberg [the

CEO of Facebook] had any remaining shred of hope that Facebook could come to China, he can kiss it goodbye thanks to Snowden."[71]

By willfully hand-delivering proof of America's hypocrisy, the Chinese equivalent to Twitter, Sina Weibo, exploded with applause for Snowden. Many commentators believed the NSA leaker's Eastern approval was due to the hope that he might inspire one of their own in mainland China to tear down the Great Firewall of Internet censorship and surveillance. One Weibo user, nicknamed "Pretending to be in New York," high-lighted the irony of Snowden being in China and the two countries' paradoxical political positions: "If Snowden were a Chinese citizen, 1) Hong Kong would agree to hand him over to the Chinese government; 2) the US would hail him as hero and then try to rescue him immediately; 3) his name would become a 'sensitive word' on the social media in China and all discussions related would be banned; 4) [o]ver a thrilling struggle, he would finally board the airplane to New York; 5) people would acclaim the escape on the social media in China; 6) New York University would invite him to be a visiting scholar." Another user named Leigh Chiang sardonically noted, "It looks like Obama has been assimilated by a certain political party (Communist Party of China)."[72] People took to the streets of Hong Kong, and protests were staged at the U.S. Consulate.[73] But it was semi-autonomous Hong Kong which filled its headlines with Snowden; barring a few exceptions such as *Global Times* and *The Sinocism China Newsletter* (the latter is edited by an American living in Beijing), mainland China largely ignored him, for fear it would incite domestic upheaval.

Snowden told the *SCMP*, "My intention is to ask the courts and people of Hong Kong to decide my fate. I have had many opportunities to flee Hong Kong, but I would rather stay and fight the United States government in the courts, because I have faith in Hong Kong's rule of law." He was subtly inform-ing Hong Kong, and consequently the world, that he was prepared to use the local court system to his advantage should the need arise. Snowden could stay 90 days on his visa.[74] It was confirmed he was working with human rights attorneys Robert Tibbo, Albert Ho and Jonathan Man, the latter two of Ho, Tse, Wai & Partners. Tibbo and Man had a history of battling extradition proceedings.[75] They had attempted to sue Hong Kong for detaining then extraditing Sami al-Saadi in 2004. Their client had cited fear of unfair treatment and abuse at the hands of dictator Muammar Gaddafi if he were returned to Tripoli.[76] On June 19, a WikiLeaks consulting team arrived in Hong Kong to further aid Snowden.[77] During their discussions, as he had with Poitras and Greenwald, Snowden insisted all parties remove their cell batteries and place their phones in a refrigerator.[78]

Snowden was aware that for deportation to occur, the U.S. would have to make a convincing case. It needed to find equivalent charges in the country's extradition agreement.[79] If it could not, Hong Kong would be unable to consider him a criminal for an act it didn't consider illegal. Both countries had espionage laws, and "unlawful use of computers" was included in the treaty. The U.S. knew regardless of what ensued, Snowden would appeal his detention, which would force his case to be heard before he could be lawfully extradited. The process could take months, if not years. Washington's greatest concern was that he make a bid for asylum citing the fear of abuse by U.S. authorities. Fellow whistleblower Bradley Manning had already filed this complaint. While waiting trial, he was placed in solitary confinement in Quantico, Virginia. He reported inhumane treatment at the hands of his guards.[80]

On June 14, a day after the *SCMP* reports that the U.S. had hacked Chinese University, a federal court signs and seals charges against Snowden.[81] It is accompanied by an arrest warrant.

On June 15, the American government quietly asks for Snowden to be provisionally arrested and detained. A provisional arrest expedites the detainment proceedings and supersedes the need for a standard arrest, which can only be executed after the charges have been recognized by the host country.

On June 17, Washington anxiously inquires as to why Hong Kong had not met its demands. Hong Kong responds that the matter is still "under review."

On June 19, as disclosures continue to appear, U.S. Attorney General Eric Holder places a personal call to Hong Kong Secretary for Justice Rimsky Yuen. He pleads for Hong Kong to detain Snowden.

On June 21, as the sealed charges are made public, citing Snowden with theft, "unauthorized communication of national defense information" and "willful communication of classified communications intelligence information to an unauthorized person," Hong Kong finally responds to Washington. It asks for more details concerning Snowden's case.[82]

Washington made several mistakes while attempting to convince Hong Kong to surrender the whistleblower. The most obvious blunder was listing Snowden's middle name as "James" instead of "Joseph" on a number of officially submitted papers. The Justice Department had also failed to include his passport number.[83] The paperwork was rushed because Washington arrogantly assumed where the request was coming from was justification enough. It had failed to explain "how two of the three charges the US mentioned in its arrest request fell within the scope of a US-Hong Kong rendition of fugitive offenders agreement signed in 1996."[84] This undoubtedly refers to the latter two charges which Snowden himself had predicted would be the U.S. government's vital misstep. During his June 9 interview with Greenwald and MacAskill, he said, "But I don't think I have committed a crime outside the domain of the U.S. I think it will be clearly shown to be political in nature."[85] By including espionage charges instead of merely indicting him on theft, the U.S. permitted Hong Kong to argue Washington's motive was political as opposed to strictly criminal. This automatically placed Snowden in debatable refugee status. To cover all of its bases, Washington would have had to request that Interpol issue a Red Notice for Snowden. Interpol is the world's police agency, and a Red Notice would force 190 countries' airports to stop Snowden's departure. Though an Interpol official later commented that the agency would have been unable to act upon an alleged political crime, the symbolic gesture by the U.S. would have nonetheless reinforced how severe the charges put to Snowden were.[86] When requesting further details about the charges, which Washington vainly denied having ever received,[87] Hong Kong also asked the U.S. to address claims of hacking as reported by the *SCMP*.[88] At this juncture, the United States should have read between the lines. It wasn't getting Snowden back.

Snowden left China because the country's officials knew that when Washington didn't immediately respond to the request for more detailed information about the American exile, the Capitol was up to something. The U.S. government was unwilling to content itself with Hong Kong playing political opossum, so the Justice Department changed tactics. It was going to pin Snowden down and then bury China in paperwork until it submitted.

The U.S. was planning to revoke Snowden's passport. China anticipated this and tipped him off.

On June 22, Snowden's passport is revoked.[89]

Though Beijing refuted the claim, Ho reported Snowden had been informed by a government representative that he was a free man and should act upon it. True to the word he'd given the *SCMP*, when Snowden was asked to leave, he did. Ho could not confirm whether the diplomat was from Hong Kong or Beijing but strongly suspected the latter.[90] Chief Executive and President of the Executive Council of the Hong Kong Special Administrative Region (HKSAR) Leung Chunying interjected, stating Hong Kong's hand had not been forced, and Beijing only offered its advice. An anonymous source familiar with Snowden's case said, "One hundred percent there was communication between Hong Kong and the central government regarding how to handle Snowden."[91] Regardless of whether Beijing issued an explicit or implicit "suggestion," it was clear mainland China did not want to contend with the political implications of harboring Snowden.

Washington's gravest mistake was dragging its feet in revoking Snowden's passport atop bowing to public pressure in revealing the charges before the purported fugitive was in custody. It allowed the world to know exactly what Snowden was up against and enabled him to prepare accordingly.

China sought neutrality when it came to Snowden. By neither detaining him nor protecting him, it had essentially ignored him. China's official communist newspaper, *People's Daily*, made sure to highlight this fact: "China is generous enough not to hype this incident in consideration of the Sino-US relationship."[92] It had likewise refused to neither help nor hinder the U.S. government just as the U.S. had for China the year before. Heralded police official Wang Lijun was thought to be seeking political asylum when he entered the U.S. Consulate in Chengdu on February 6, 2012. Washington neither recognized an appeal if one was made nor did it arrest the Chinese fugitive. It merely asked him to leave. China had now returned the indifferent favor.[93] Representative King was perhaps unaware of this piece of historical trivia when he stated, "For some reason Hong Kong and China wanted to let Snowden get away and this is a direct slap at the U.S."[94]

A Shanghai official speaking on a condition of anonymity rightly observed that Snowden served no purpose to China: "It is also impractical for China to hope Snowden will cooperate with us. If he wanted to do that, he'd have flown to Beijing."[95] Not only did mainland China acknowledge the implied and later overt message by Snowden in his decision to land in Hong Kong instead of China's capital, it realized he meant what he said on June 17. He was only willing to work with the press, not governments. From a political perspective, apathy had been met with apathy.

On Sunday, June 23, to the U.S. government's dismay, it discovers Snowden has flown to Russia.

Midday Sunday, after 34 days in the Pearl of the Orient, Ho and Man accompanied Snowden to Chek Lap Kok Airport.[96] He boarded Aeroflot SU213 with WikiLeaks' Sara Harrison, a close advisor to Julian Assange.[97] At 5 p.m. local time, they landed 4,500 miles away at Moscow's Sheremetyevo International Airport.[98] WikiLeaks footed the tab for the flight as well as a portion of his lodgings while in Hong Kong and later Russia.[99]

Though the American government thought it was on the verge of cornering Snowden and forcing China to hand him over, Washington satisfied itself believing it had him on the run.

What the Capitol didn't know was that it was about to be cast in the role of the fool in one of the most beautifully orchestrated multinational political ploys in modern history. Weeks before, Snowden had received a quiet offer to make the former Soviet Union his home. In order to avoid straining already-taut relations between America and Russia, all he had to do was wait until it appeared he had no other choice but flee Hong Kong. To make his coincidental arrival in Russia appear convincing, an expertly choreographed plot involving international intrigue and denial was devised. The script was ambitious. The fact that it succeeded is nothing short of breathtaking.

Chapter 5
Polar Bear in a Snowstorm

> "Perhaps, in such times, loving one's country means being hated by its government."
>
> –Edward Snowden, letter to former congressman Gordon Humphrey, July 15, 2013[1]

SNOWDEN ORIGINALLY BELIEVED ICELAND was his ideal adopted home because of its shared ideals on Internet freedom.[2] Though it had an extradition treaty with the U.S., Iceland had never surrendered anyone to America.[3] A day after the WikiLeaks team arrived in Hong Kong, Icelandic entrepreneur and head of WikiLeaks partner conglomerate DataCell, Olafur Sigurvinsson, told Channel2 television, "We have a plane and all the logistics in place. Now we are only awaiting a response from the [Icelandic] government."[4] A Gulfstream G550 had been contracted from a Chinese firm at a cost of nearly a quarter-of-a-million dollars. Funds had come from individual donations made to Datacell.[5] The only problem is Snowden had not formally sought refuge in Iceland. WikiLeaks and Sigurvinsson had taken it upon themselves to make inquiries on Snowden's behalf starting June 12.[6] Only after he arrived in Russia did he begin submitting asylum requests. His first were to Iceland and Ecuador. Snowden was informed he needed to be on Icelandic soil to apply for asylum.[7] Then he requested Icelandic citizenship which, if granted, would supersede the extradition treaty.[8] Having previously voiced his preference for Iceland to the media, the U.S. government quietly pressured the U.N. to lobby the island nation. The U.N. sent its secretary general to meet with Icelandic parliament.[9] Four days after his citizenship paperwork arrived, only six members of Iceland's 63-seat legislative body voted in favor of putting the matter on the government's agenda.[10] Even if it had been placed on parliament's docket, Iceland's legislature was going on summer vacation and would not reconvene until September.

Assange and WikiLeaks were putting on a good show because sometime between June 12-18 WikiLeaks representative Kristinn Hrafnsson had been informed by Icelandic officials that Snowden would have to apply in person.[11]

What should have tipped off the U.S. government that something was amiss was that the entire month Snowden was in China, every waking second wasn't being spent filing asylum requests. Instead he provided more disclosures to the local press and conducted interviews despite American authorities exerting more and more pressure upon Hong Kong and Beijing to detain him. That a plot was afoot is retrospectively obvious because of all of the legal powerhouses working on Snowden's behalf, it was an apparent surprise to everyone that several countries he would later petition had clearly defined legislation requiring an asylum applicant to apply in person. If Snowden's concern for safety was genuine—especially since impending felony charges would almost invariably involve passport nullification—as soon as WikiLeaks affirmed it had a working budget of at least $240,000, Snowden would have set to globetrotting as he dropped off asylum requests along the way. Snowden already knew all of this. If he was astute enough to have researched which country would have difficulty extraditing him before coincidentally traveling to another which had no such treaty with the U.S., it is reasonable to assume he also knew which countries would accept his application without his presence. He was playing opossum. Nonetheless, by filing asylum requests Snowden would also delay extradition proceedings until a determination was made with each sanctuary plea. It was now obvious his statement during the live Q & A session that he hadn't flown directly to Iceland because "Iceland could be pushed harder, quicker, before the public could have a chance to make their feelings known, and I would not put that past the current US administration"[12] meant he did not have incriminating evidence against the U.S. government in respect to Iceland. He couldn't mount popular support as easily. However, being on Icelandic soil, Snowden could prolong extradition proceedings after submitting an asylum request in person.

Snowden didn't do any of this because he wasn't worried.

Two days after it learned of his identity, amid global outrage as most every country distanced itself from Snowden for fear of American backlash, Russia made a curious announcement. The Russian president's spokesman, Dmitry Peskov, boldly informed the local newspaper *Kommersant*, "If such an appeal [from Snowden] is given, it will be considered."[13] The next day the *SCMP* interviewed Snowden and asked if he'd been offered Russian asylum. He answered, "My only comment is that I am glad there are governments that refuse to be intimidated by great power."[14]

At the time of the interview, Snowden was still mulling over the offer. It is likely he made up his mind on June 20, the day after Harrison arrived in Hong Kong. After the two discussed the matter and came to a decision, a celebratory pre-birthday party was thrown at the apartment he'd taken after leaving the Mira, the same one he would move out of the following day under the veil of night. By this birthday, he was settled into the Russian Embassy, which was located on the 21st floor of a skyscraper.[15] Another indication Snowden and Russia had been speaking was that the G20 disclosure was released a week after Russia discovered who he was. As he had done with China, he was endearing himself to his soon-to-be adopted country as he pitted the Soviet government and citizenry against Washington. All that was left to do was to make Snowden's entry into Russia appear convincing and plausible.

The first step was to find a way to get him to Russia but not make it apparent he was there to stay. The day Hong Kong requested more information from the American government about his case, Snowden was instructed to purchase a ticket from Hong Kong to Havana, Cuba via Moscow on Aeroflot, Russia's national airline.[16] Russia and Snowden now had to wait for his passport to be revoked. Both Russia and Snowden knew China would not detain him. Because he was on a connecting flight, he would be permitted to alight in the geopolitically neutral transit zone at Sheremetyevo International Airport. As a safety precaution and for the sake of appearance, on June 22 he had been issued an Ecuadorian safe pass from the London Embassy. The refugee document allowed "the bearer to travel to the territory of Ecuador for the purpose of political asylum."[17] To make the scenario more believable, Ecuadorian Embassy cars would be sitting at the airport when he arrived.[18] Upon landing, he would be "stuck" in Russia. Signs that he never intended to arrive in Cuba were glaring and obvious. It was understood Snowden was flying through Russia to get to Cuba in order to board a flight to Venezuela to gain refuge in Ecuador.

Amid the frenzy, no one seemed to notice the incongruity of Snowden fleeing through one and to another country with American extradition treaties; his having to pass through U.N. and American airspace to reach Cuba; in 2006 Cuba had given assurances to the U.S. that it would not accept "new" American fugitives as a gesture of good faith amid a history of strife between the two nations;[19] and in order to apply for asylum in Ecuador, one had to either be standing in the country or file at an Ecuadorian Embassy[20] (not one report appeared confirming or denying whether Snowden had filed Ecuadorian asylum paperwork while in Hong Kong). Snowden had no intention of traveling to Cuba. The giveaway should have been that his first stop was in a country which did not have an extradition agreement with the United States.

Despite the suspicious conditions which brought him to Russia, on June 24 journalists piled onto Aeroflot SU150 to Cuba.[21] Snowden's seat, 17A, was vacant. *Kommersant* made sure to mention the flight and seat number a full day prior to departure. It was estimated that a quarter of economy and over half of business class was comprised of reporters. When he failed to appear by takeoff, photojournalists were left with nothing to do over the course of the 12-hour flight but take pictures of the unoccupied seat. As Maxim Shemetov of *Reuters* admitted a day later, "It looked suspicious that everyone knew when and how a top secret target was going to leave Russia."[22] By comparison, passengers on Snowden's arrival flight could not confirm whether he had been aboard. He and Harrison had been seated separately from the other passengers, were released and greeted on the tarmac by numerous Russian security agents and their baggage was loaded directly from the plane.[23]

The United States realized it had been duped on Wednesday, June 26, when Spanish-language network Univision displayed Snowden's Ecuadorian safe passage certificate. It was unsigned.[24] The capital had not approved it. It no longer mattered that Snowden had arrived in Russia illegally. He was there and because he was in a transit zone, nothing could be done about it. People demanded to know who was responsible for the invalid document.

In June 2012, Julian Assange entered the Ecuadorian Embassy in London. He would be granted asylum two months later but remained stranded at the consulate.[25] The WikiLeaks founder would have to step onto English soil in order to board a plane to his adopted country. If he were to do so, he would be immediately arrested. A European arrest warrant had been issued as part of a sexual assault investigation.[26] It was here he met local Ecuadorian consul Fidel Narvaez. The diplomat had been assigned to stay in the embassy at night to deter police harassment of Assange. Over time, a bond was forged between the refugee and a person with a known history of social and civil activism. Narvaez had issued Snowden's travel voucher at Assange's behest.[27] A few days after Snowden had settled into his suite at Sheremetyevo's V-Express Capsule Hotel, Naraez appeared in Moscow.[28]

Regardless of who was ultimately responsible for getting Snowden to Russia, everyone had to plead ignorance and innocence.

China released an official statement regarding Snowden's release: "The US Government earlier on made a request to the HKSAR Government for the issue of a provisional warrant of arrest against Mr. Snowden. Since the documents provided by the US Government did not fully comply with the legal requirements under Hong Kong law, the HKSAR Government has requested the US Government to provide additional information so that the Department of Justice could consider whether the US Government's request can meet the relevant legal conditions. As the HKSAR Government has yet to have sufficient information to process the request for provisional warrant of arrest, there is no legal basis to restrict Mr. Snowden from leaving Hong Kong."[29] It made sure to add, "Meanwhile, the HKSAR Government has formally written to the US Government requesting clarification on earlier reports about the hacking of computer systems in Hong Kong by US government agencies. The HKSAR Government will continue to follow up on the matter so as to protect the legal rights of the people of Hong Kong." Yuen confirmed, "Until the minute of Snowden's departure, the U.S. government hadn't yet replied to our requests for clarification."[30] Legal experts later confirmed China had operated within the bounds of law.[31]

What would appear to be an admission of guilt but a political formality nonetheless, Ecuador's secretary of political management threatened legal action to whoever was responsible for leaking the illicit document to the press. The statement could be construed as Ecuador not wanting to be seen in the same disorganized light as America when it came to filing official paperwork or vain whitewashing because it hadn't wanted the existence of the travel pass to be made public. Predictably, by Wednesday Narvaez was apologetic: "I am conscious of my responsibility and I assume it in its totality." During his regular weekend address to the nation, Ecuador's president, President Rafael Correa, stated, "If it is [true] that he [Narvaez] went beyond his authority, he will be disciplined accordingly." But Ecuador had no intention of investigating Narvaez. In an ironic twist, the day after Correa's announcement, metadata revealed the travel voucher had arrived in the in-box of Ecuador's secretary of judicial affairs. It was undoubtedly presented to the president's office.[32]

America had assumed Ecuador's waiving trade agreement rights with the U.S. on Thursday was an indication it was intending to grant Snowden asylum. The country's official statement was that economic privileges should not be contingent upon blackmail. The country was preempting the United States revoking the preferential tariffs granted in the 2002 Andean Trade Promotion and Drug Eradication Act (ATPDEA). Ecuador's secretary of communications pithily suggested the U.S. should take its $23 million in savings and apply it to human rights education.[33] He took the opportunity to add, "Finally, we would enjoy (sic) that the U.S. respond with the same urgency that they are asking of us to deliver Mr. Snowden when he enters Ecuadorian soil, to our requests to the U.S. Embassy in Ecuador, via communication POL 081/2013 that they deliver to us the many fugitives from Ecuadorian justice who are currently living in the United States, particularly the corrupt bankers who knowingly destroyed our economy in 1999, whose extradition has been repeatedly denied by the United States."[34] It was a wonderful show. Only U.S. and Ecuadorian officials knew the trade agreement status was on shaky ground before Snowden came into the picture. Neither party had expected it to be extended in the upcoming weeks.

Two days after Snowden's arrival, Russian president Vladimir Putin told the press, "It is true that Mr. Snowden arrived in Moscow, which was completely unexpected for us."[35] He added, "As for his possible extradition, we can extradite foreign nationals only to those countries with which we have relevant international agreements on the extradition of criminals. We have no such agreement with the United States. Mr. Snowden has committed no crimes in the Russian Federation." During a press conference five days later, Putin stated, "Russia never gives anyone up and doesn't plan to give anyone up and no one has ever given us anyone" atop "[...] [Snowden] is essentially a fighter for human rights, and for democracy."[36]

Having served 16 years in Soviet intelligence,[37] Putin knew the value of a foreign intelligence worker. He was making it expressly clear that Russia had no intention of surrendering the American whistleblower. Russia's leader was overtly declaring he was going to stand firm on international and national law. By referring to Snowden as a civil rights activist, Putin was also telling the world how his country perceived Snowden.

Whereas it could exert pressure upon nearly autonomous Hong Kong until Beijing stepped in, Washington had a stalwart political adversary in Russia. Shortly after Snowden arrived, Russian Foreign Minister Sergey Lavrov took the offensive: "We consider the attempts to accuse Russia of violation of U.S. laws and even some sort of conspiracy, which on top of all that are accompanied by threats, as absolutely ungrounded and unacceptable. There are no legal grounds for such conduct of U.S. officials, and we proceed from that." The U.S. government had to change tactics. As White House Press Secretary Jay Carney lambasted Hong Kong for allowing Snowden to fly to Russia, "This was a deliberate choice by the government to release a fugitive despite a valid arrest warrant, and that decision unquestionably has a negative impact on the U.S.-China relationship,"[38] the Capitol had decided it best to downplay Snowden's importance. Washington was fearful it would be made a fool again and anxious that if it tried to flex its rhetorical muscles, it might incur political backlash. Four days after Snowden landed in Russia, Obama told reporters, "We've got a whole lot of business that we do with China and Russia and I'm not going to have one case of a suspect who we're trying to extradite suddenly being elevated to the point where I've got to start doing wheeling and dealing and trading on a whole host of other issues, simply to get a guy extradited so that he can face the justice system here in the United States."[39] However, the U.S. government was discreetly offering Russia increased political cooperation in exchange for Snowden.

It was a wonderful drama, but what truly sold the world that Snowden's association with the former Soviet Union was mere coincidence was Putin's closing statement at a press conference following the first day of the Gas Exporting Countries Forum Summit. Russia's leader declared, "He [Snowden] must stop his work aimed at harming our American partners, as strange as that sounds coming from my lips."[40] Snowden had applied for Russian asylum the previous day, June 30.[41] The day after Putin's conditions were made public, Snowden rescinded his asylum application. It was a convincing ruse because it appeared as if Snowden's odds were good that he would find a temporary home with one of the 18 other countries which he'd applied on July 1.

It took Norway, Austria, Finland, Germany, Ireland, the Netherlands, Spain, Switzerland, Brazil, India and Poland less than a day to turn Snowden down. The first eight countries promptly absolved themselves of responsibility by deferring to their legal technicality that asylum applicants must be on native ground to be considered. Even though a nation's foreign ministry is considered to reside on the respective country's soil, they denied Snowden's application because he had been unable to present it in person. Contenting itself with already having done its share, Ecuador would use this alibi after American vice president Joe Biden called Correa.[42] Ecuador's president politely bowed out of the Snowden affair by allowing his previous declaration that Snowden's safe passage document had been a "mistake"[43] to speak for itself. India rejected his claim outright, as did Poland, but the latter reinforced its stance by citing an applicant's need to be on Polish land. Brazil responded by stating it wouldn't respond, a decision it would later regret.[44] As the world awaited answers from Iceland, China, Cuba, Bolivia, Venezuela, Nicaragua, France and Italy,[45] suspicions were immediately raised and conjectures made that the remaining countries' hesitation signaled possible acceptance and admittance of Snowden.

Few thought France or Italy would humor him due to their ties to the U.S. It was obvious if China had wanted him, it would have kept him. Because the press had yet to account for why Snowden had not proceeded to Cuba, many suspected there was unvoiced reason for him not already being there. Only a handful of people were aware Iceland was a foregone conclusion before it was ever a consideration. France would later deny having received any paperwork before saying no, and Italy would use the well-worn excuse of needing him in the country to acknowledge his request. China stated it had no information to issue pertaining to Snowden.[46] Cuba never responded. This left Venezuela, Bolivia and Nicaragua.

Four days later, WikiLeaks announced Snowden had applied for asylum in six more countries. The website refused to name them, citing potential American influence as seen with Ecuador and what was reasonably assumed to have taken place with other nations.[47] An unnamed U.S. government official later confirmed this: "There is not a country in the hemisphere whose government does not understand our position at this point."[48]

As with his theoretical flight to Cuba, many of Snowden's asylum applications were meant to lend verisimilitude to the feigned proceedings. The other tip-off that Snowden's applications were not sincere was that six days before, he had given the *SCMP* approval to run another exposé, the one which he obligated the newspaper to sit on until the U.S. had filed its charges against him. Only after Snowden had landed where he'd intended to stay did he give the news outlet permission to release incriminating information about him.

On June 24, the day after the whistleblower arrived in Russia, Los Angeles awoke to "Snowden sought Booz Allen job to gather evidence on NSA surveillance."[49] The article opens succinctly, "Edward Snowden secured a job with a US government contractor for one reason alone—to obtain evidence of Washington's cyberspying networks," before adding, somewhat sardonically, "the *South China Morning Post* can reveal." It quotes Snowden, "My position with Booz Allen Hamilton granted me access to lists of machines all over the world the NSA hacked. That is why I accepted that position about three months ago." As before, due to scarcity of material, the *SCMP* inserted its new information between previous and current press reports. Yet it made sure to send a chill down Washington's spine by quoting Snowden's long-term intention: "[…] I would like to make it [confidential American intelligence disclosures] available to journalists in each country to make their own assessment, independent of my bias, as to whether or not the knowledge of US network operations against their people should be published." It is highly doubt-ful Snowden would have made such a bold, incendiary declaration if Russia hadn't guaranteed him a safe haven two days before he sat down to speak with the *SCMP*.

Pundits immediately began to speculate whether Greenwald, Poitras and Gellman had asked Snowden to get hired on at BAH in order to extract data.[50] Greenwald and Poitras were too offended to hold their tongues. If proven true, the accusations could implicate the journalists in one or more of the charges put to Snowden. Poitras claimed[51] she was un-clear where Snowden had worked before meeting him in Hong Kong. To her credit, since the documents he had in his posses-sion related to various facilities, operations and stations worldwide, it would be difficult for an untrained eye to deter-mine where he had stolen the information. Regretting he'd hedged the details of his communication timeline with Snowden, Greenwald called the allegation "baseless innu-endo."[52] Gellman kept characteristically silent. Snowden had revealed in his interview with Poitras that he'd worked for another intelligence agency, the CIA, and the *Post* reporter knew it would be revealed he'd been employed as a NSA con-tractor for another firm. Less than two months later, the press broke the news that Snowden had an extended tenure with Dell.[53]

Snowden was not worried he would not be permitted to continue his journalistic pursuits in Russia. He had already distributed a considerable amount of information to his cho-sen journalists, and, as he would declare on July 12, he "cannot control them [the writers and their decision to act upon the material]."[54] During the week they'd spent with him in Hong Kong, Greenwald and Poitras had been briefed by Snowden over what the documents were, how to interpret them, their meaning and their implications. He was still in contact with Gellman.[55] At this stage Snowden was merely acting as an advisor, permitting the press to do its work. He even admitted his role in the proceedings wasn't vital. On June 17 he'd in-formed the world, "All I can say right now is the US Government is not going to be able to cover this up by jailing or murdering me."[56] The day after the *SCMP* released its jaw-dropping report regarding Snowden's reasons for joining BAH, *The Daily Beast* published an interview with Greenwald which explained Snowden's cryptic statement.[57] It also served to increase the severity of Washington's Snowden-induced migraine.

Greenwald relays that Snowden had made copies of all the purloined files and distributed them to several unnamed people, sealing the files' contents under heavy encryption. However, as Greenwald reports, "If anything happens at all to Edward Snowden, he told me he has arranged for them to get access to the full archives." [58] Snowden had created a timed contact release program much like the ones used by outdoor enthusiasts. An account is created which specifies when the user will be departing, the individual's destination and the latest time the person should return. If the user fails to log into the account before the slated deadline, an email is automatically sent to those placed on an emergency contact list with the relevant information. If Snowden missed resetting the account's timer, the key to the encrypted files would be released to his chosen data bankers. It is characteristic of Snowden to want to control the files and explains his demand for Internet access while in exile.[59] This also sheds light on Snowden's statement, "The truth is coming, and it cannot be stopped." When he originally made the declaration during the June 17 Q & A session, it had ostentatious overtones. With Greenwald's report, the statement is understood to be more literal than figurative.

Snowden had told the *SCMP* that he intended to release top secret disclosures to the nations to which the surveillance applied. The world didn't have to wait long to see whether Snowden would keep his promise. Even though he was unable to reach Western Europe, he had associates that could.

Poitras had remained in Hong Kong on the off chance Snowden might request a follow-up interview atop wanting to get footage of the ensuing protests and support rallies for the NSA leaker. However, the day after her Snowden interview aired, she was forced out of her hotel room. She began receiving anonymous calls, and people were repeatedly knocking on her door. After being escorted by security through a back exit, she relocated and tried to meld into the city's seven million people. She surrendered after a CNN reporter identified her on June 15. She summarily flew to Berlin. Her flight from recognition was an attempt to supersede authorities from intercepting the data Snowden had recently issued her. It was also a reprieve into the sanctuary of her German apartment, which she maintained to escape harassment by American intelligence. There she continued editing her interview footage and, in line with Snowden's wishes, prepared her own series of disclosures that related to Europe and Germany for the German press.[60]

Europe took little notice of Snowden's BAH admission because *Norddeutscher Rundfunk*, also known as North German Broadcasting (NGB),[61] and Germany's largest newspaper, the Munich-based periodical *Süddeutsche Zeitung*, broke another story an hour later.[62] "Britain Draws from German Internet" reveals that GCHQ was using Tempora to wiretap transatlantic Telephone Cable No. 14 or "TAT-14." TAT-14 is a major fiber-optic backbone connecting Germany with the United States through Britain. The hub is utilized by Denmark, France and the Netherlands and approximately 50 international companies route phone calls and Internet connections through the line. As with Greenwald's Verizon exposé, *Süddeutsche Zeitung* reports English telecoms Vodafone and British Telecommunications were willful surveillance participants.

Vodafone reported it was within the legal confines of the countries in which it was operating. British Telecommunications offered no comment. German intelligence as well as Telekom, the primary German communication provider that uses TAT-14, claimed to have no knowledge of the surveillance practice.

Steffen Seibert, spokesperson for German Chancellor Angela Merkel, demanded NATO (North Atlantic Treaty Association) allies answer "what legal basis and to which extent" the TAT-14 surveillance had been conducted. Albrecht stated, "We urge the Federal Government and the EU Commission to initiate infringement proceedings against the UK government." [63] It was the first of many revelations for Germany.

Another indication Snowden's safety was never in doubt is that after June 17, Greenwald disappeared for 10 days. He had been busily preparing to lead yet another cavalcade of disclosures. He commenced with a before-and-after pair of reports which appeared 17 minutes apart, "How the NSA is still harvesting your online data"[64] and "NSA collected US email records in bulk for more than two years under Obama."[65]

The latter, poignantly opening with a picture of Obama alongside his predecessor, tells of a now-defunct, highly controversial surveillance program which originated in 2001 called Stellar Wind or "The Program" to NSA insiders.[66] Initially the program permitted bulk collection of online metadata without the need for a court's approval. As a consequence of internal complaints being ignored by then-president Bush—followed by threatened resignations from FBI Director Robert Mueller, acting Attorney General James Comey and bedridden Attorney General John Ashcroft[67]—Stellar Wind was terminated in May 2004. The program was revived two months later by requiring an FISC judge sign-off on all operations. Judge Collen Kollar-Kotelly proceeded to rubber stamp blanket orders every 90 days. Greenwald reports after being goaded by the attorney general's office, Bush restructured the program once again. Stellar Wind 3.0 allowed for more invasive procedures. The program ran under Obama before it "was discontinued in 2011 for operational and resource reasons and has not been restarted."

An accompanying 51-page disclosure[68] discusses Stellar Wind. The report includes a signed, 16-page 2007 Department of Justice memo[69] requesting the NSA be granted the authority to surveil "communications metadata associated with United States persons and persons believed to be in the United States."[70] The memo followed then-Secretary of Defense Robert Gates' October 2007 signature verifying the accompanying "Supplemental Procedures" pertaining to Internet metadata.

The memo's justification rests upon the intelligence agency already housing a large amount of American data and believing "[...] it is over-identifying numbers and addresses that belong to United States persons and that modifying its practice to [contact] chain through all telephone numbers and addresses, including those reasonably believed to be used by a United States person, will yield valuable foreign intelligence information primarily concerning non-United States persons outside the United States." It is paradoxically admitting that there is already too much information but nonetheless wants the NSA's "hop" policy to be made legal.

Though this form of collection does not include the content of emails, Internet metadata reveals who is sending and receiving emails (the information appearing on all of an email's address lines) and discloses a user's IP address, which can reveal an individual's location. Greenwald considers the greatest privacy violation to be IP address retrieval. Yet he makes a novice IT assumption.

He defers to Julian Sanchez of the Cato Institute who, though he is not incorrect in his information relating to IP logs, was obviously confused about what Greenwald was asking. Sanchez states a user's IP log reveals what websites a person has visited, in what order and how frequently. In essence, an IP catalog provides a biography of a person's thoughts as they occur. As with Verizon, AT&T and other providers' metadata collections, this type of information permits an analyst to easily assess a person's interests, habits and proclivities.

However, a static IP address listed in the header of an email is inactive. For an analyst to retrieve the contents of an IP log and exploit its recording device—in this case what is referred to as a first-person cookie—an individual would have to either have been granted access to that particular computer or hacked it. The most common hacking method for this type of information retrieval is the insertion of spying software or "spyware." Greenwald fails to make a distinction between static and kinetic IP addresses or expound upon how an IP log can be captured.

Greenwald goes on to play attorney and lets the government attempt justification before deconstructing its reasoning. Deputy Attorney General James Cole told the House Intelligence Committee on June 18, "Toll records, phone records like this [i.e., telephone metadata], that don't include any content, are not covered by the Fourth Amendment because people don't have a reasonable expectation of privacy in who they called and when they called. That's something you show to the phone company." Greenwald is quick to point out that unlike a telephone invoice, Internet billing does not include an itemized report of whom a person emailed or what websites were visited during the preceding month. The same logic can be applied to other personal records an individual shares with another party but nonetheless has a "reasonable expectation" to assume will remain confidential, such as medical records.

Others have compared metadata to the information on the outside of a mailed envelope.[71] A letter's mailing instructions include who is writing and from what location, who is receiving the missive and at what location, and when the exchange is taking place. This is vital transmission data which allows material to be delivered. Though a postal carrier can see this information, the individual is not permitted to view the contents of the envelope. However, unlike the federal government's approach to electronic metadata, only the trusted third party— the postal service—has been granted permission by the sender to access the envelope's transport information. The only other person aside from the postal worker who is legally permitted to handle the envelope, as well as read its contents, is the addressee. Using this analogy, only a contracted carrier, be it the postal service or an electronic communication company, has the right to access delivery data. Yet the argument would prove futile. The U.S. Postal Service would admit a little over a month later it takes photographs of every piece of mail it receives and transports.[72] This is reportedly done to ease the processing burden but the files are kept on record and freely surrendered upon receipt of a government request.

Stellar Wind was grossly ineffective. Intelligence agents referred to the program's target profiles as "Pizza Hut cases" because 99 percent of red flags were triggered by fast food takeout orders.[73] Somewhat dubiously, since Stellar Wind's objective was to track potential terrorist activity, the program was responsible for unveiling former New York governor Eliot Spitzer's solicitation of prostitutes.[74]

As with his report on Obama's order to draw up a global cyberattack hit list, Greenwald's article does not reveal previously unknown information. Its novelty is that it confirms and expounds upon what is suspected by providing official documentation. In spite of this, the article remains somewhat vague. Greenwald announces more invasive surveillance measures commenced in 2007, but the disclosed memo is merely a request. No known finalized, signed law confirms that in its later stages Stellar Wind's Internet mining unapologetically included United States citizens directly, only incidentally. Snowden obviously could not locate or access such incendiary materials if they do exist. However, in Greenwald's defense, the report was merely a primer for current United States surveillance practices.

In "How the NSA is still harvesting your online data," Greenwald opens by rejecting the Obama administration's claim that domestic Internet surveillance had ceased in 2011. He states it is clear a division within the NSA called the Special Source Operations (SSO) Directorate, "collects and analyzes significant amounts of data from US communications systems in the course of monitoring foreign targets."

Though he cannot confirm it is Stellar Wind's immediate successor, "EvilOlive" is presumed to be the replacement program the SSO announced the day after Christmas in 2012. Its purported ability to get 75 percent of traffic to "pass through the filter" is the result of having "opened the aperture" so more data can be "identified, selected and forwarded to NSA repositories." Given its characteristics, EvilOlive appears to be the American response to Tempora.

EvilOlive's vague nature could be self-sustaining or a component or complement to another program periodically mentioned in the referenced documentation, "ShellTrumpet." Five days after EvilOlive was activated, an SSO official bragged that ShellTrumpet had just processed its one-trillionth metadata record. Though it was in its fifth year of operation, half of the data it had vacuumed up was collected during 2012. ShellTrumpet capabilities include "near-real-time metadata analysis" and "direct email tip alerting." Since the program operates in "near-real-time," "direct email tip alerting" may refer to triggers which call an analyst's attention to a target having just received an electronic message or, as suggested by its prefix, a filter which alerts the NSA to the mention of a person, item or activity within the content of an email.

Greenwald relays that "a substantial portion" of the data which the NSA analyzes is provided by allied governments, most likely the other Four Eyes. By at least August 2012, GCHQ began providing its American counterpart with data through a program titled "Transient Thurible." Greenwald reports U.S. intelligence was also expanding its collection capabilities at this time. A February 6, 2013, SSO disclosure mentions the addition of two more programs by September 2013: "MoonLightPath" and "Spinneret."

Greenwald's return is somewhat disappointing. Though his report on Stellar Wind is more thorough, it contains inaccurate IT data, fails to provide the final chapters of the program's history, and is inconclusive. (This is perhaps due to Snowden not being readily available after his Russian arrival;[75] he and Greenwald purportedly remained in steady contact after Hong Kong.[76]) Granted, it is a springboard for what he wants to discuss—contemporary American domestic surveillance programs—but his companion article pales by comparison. His exposé on EvilOlive and ShellTrumpet, which may or may not be the primary mechanisms for U.S. domestic spying, is emaciated and fails to provide a clear, convincing picture of the NSA's current operations. Greenwald even admits, "It is not clear how much of this collection concerns foreigners' online records and how much concerns those of Americans. Also unclear is the claimed legal authority for this collection." The referenced documentation to the various programs could conceivably be the result of delicate information which *The Guardian* was not comfortable releasing. As witnessed with previous partially redacted disclosures where, at times, a censored slide bore little more than its title, the possibility exists that nothing of interest would have remained for Greenwald's audience post-redaction. Yet, unlike all of his preceding articles, his EvilOlive report did not attempt to confirm the documentation or add comment.

While the U.S. Army spent the day attempting to justify the decision it had made 24 hours before to include filtering *The Guardian*'s website as part of its routine Internet "network hygiene,"[77] the German periodical *Der Spiegel* ran the first of many Poitras-produced editorials on June 29. *Der Spiegel* is a German-language weekly with a circulation of over one million subscribers.

The article "NSA Spied on European Union Offices"[78] opens by citing a classified September 2010 document retrieved by Snowden proving U.S. intelligence "not only conducted online surveillance of European citizens" but surveilled EU offices in Washington and the New York headquarters of the United Nations. Audio bugs were installed, computers hacked and telephone and Internet data was compromised. The EU offices are unapologetically designated as a "location target."

American intelligence also monitored the member states on their native soil. The NSA allegedly tapped the home of the Council of the European Union, the Justus Lipsius Building in Belgium's capital, Brussels. "A precise analysis showed that the attacks on the telecommunications system had originated from a building complex separated from the rest of the NATO headquarters that is used by NSA experts." The on-site European spying is presumed to have taken place no later than 2008.

In a subsequent report, Poitras would remark that almost all foreign diplomatic surveillance is recognized by the U.S. as illegal: "With few exceptions, this electronic eavesdropping not only contravenes the diplomatic code, but also international agreements. The Convention on the Privileges and Immunities of the United Nations of 1946, as well as the Vienna Convention on Diplomatic Relations of 1961, long ago established that no espionage methods are to be used. What's more, the US and the UN signed an agreement in 1947 that rules out all undercover operations."[79]

The festival of disclosures would end with an international double feature starring *The Guardian* and *Der Spiegel* on June 30. MacAskill presented "New NSA leaks show how US is bugging its European allies"[80] a few hours before Poitras issued, "NSA Snoops on 500 Million German Data Connections."[81] The bookend reports appeared a week before the U.S. was scheduled to discuss free-trade policies with the European Union in Brussels.[82]

MacAskill's work is less of a follow-up than a companion piece to Poitras' *Der Spiegel* debut. It outlines that U.S. intelligence was not only spying on the European embassies in New York and Washington but the previously cited September 2010 document lists a total of 38 missionary "targets," including France, Italy, Greece, Japan, Mexico, South Korea, India and Turkey.

Each embassy's spy program was given its own code name. The EU mission at the U.N. office in New York was designated "Perdido" and included a floor plan of the embassy. France's New York U.N. mission was "Blackfoot," its Washington operation, "Wabash." In some cases separate titles were issued to differentiate an embassy from its American surveillance. Operation "Klondyke" focused upon Greece's U.N. Embassy, "Powell." Italy's Washington office was known both as "Bruneau" and "Hemlock."

Aside from audio bugs and cable interception, the NSA spied using "Dropmire." Though granted a code name, Dropmire is not a target or assignment: given the context provided by MacAskill, it is a physical espionage device. An accompanying 2007 slide states that Dropmire is "implanted on the Cryptofax at the EU embassy, DC." Dropmire gathers information as faxes are sent between foreign affairs offices and their respective European capitals. The timing of Dropmire's incorporation suggests it was installed for the same purpose that G20 surveillance had been initiated. U.S. intelligence sought "knowledge of policy disagreements on global issues and other rifts between member states" after the 2008 banking crisis.

Following less than a week after *Süddeutsche Zeitung*/NGB's joint TAT-14 report, Poitras' article focuses upon the NSA's preoccupation with its G20 partner and U.N. ally, Germany. It relays that American intelligence readily collects German telephone calls, emails, text messages and chat transcripts in bulk. The metadata is stored overseas at Fort Meade, Maryland.

The report is alarming because of America's alliances with Germany, especially when compared to U.S. surveillance of other European nations. In France the average American data capture is two million pieces of information per day from its 65 million citizens. A normal surveillance day for Germany's 80 million residents is 15 times as much, 30 million intercepts per diem. Poitras does not attempt to offer conjecture as to why America is overly concerned with Germany. She does highlight that the report is consistent with Boundless Informant's leaked heat map. Germany is in the same color code as Saudi Arabia, China, Iraq, Lithuania, Afghanistan and Kenya. Snowden's stolen document also confirms Germany's immediate response to the Tempora release was accurate. As with TAT-14, the NSA's main German intercept points are the country's Internet hubs linking it to the outside world. Though she tries to remain objective by not providing tentative explanations for the intense spying, Poitras succumbs to the temptation to mention that the classified documents explicitly exclude the other Four Eyes—Australia, Canada, New Zealand and Britain—from U.S. intelligence's prying eyes. Should any of the Five Eyes want to surveil another espionage member, it must first obtain permission.[83]

Martin Schulz, the president of the European parliament, was reported as being "deeply worried and shocked about the allegations of U.S. authorities spying on EU offices" and made the statement, "On behalf of the European Parliament, I demand full clarification and require further information speedily from the US authorities with regard to these allegations."[84]

France even chimed in. The country's foreign minister, Laurent Fabius, responded, "These acts, if confirmed, would be completely unacceptable."[85] Germany's minister of justice became livid once more. Leutheusser-Schnarrenberger labeled America's actions as "utterly inappropriate."[86] Steffen Seibert proclaimed, "The monitoring of friends ... this is unacceptable. It can't be tolerated. We're no longer in the Cold War." During a press conference the day after Poitras' article premiered, Obama rebutted by snidely telling reporters, "If I want to know what Chancellor Merkel is thinking, I will call Chancellor Merkel. If I want to know what President Hollande is thinking on a particular issue, I'll call President Hollande. If I want to know what David Cameron is thinking, I call David Cameron. Ultimately, we work so closely together, that there's almost no information that's not shared between our various countries."[87] Yet some critics speculated that Germany knew about and was complicit in the domestic spying.[88]

Snowden's first public statement since his arrival in Russia came on July 1.* Posted on WikiLeaks,[89] Snowden outlines Washington's hypocrisy by juxtaposing Obama's declaration that he would not "wheel and deal" to get the intelligence leaker back with his subsequent "order" for Biden to pressure Ecuador to reject Snowden's asylum petition. He continues to comment on his abandoned nation's political duplicity: "Although I am convicted of nothing, it [the United States] has unilaterally revoked my passport, leaving me a stateless person. Without any judicial order, the administration now seeks to stop me exercising a basic right. A right that belongs to everybody. The right to seek asylum." It is clear Snowden does not consider the charge of theft to be legitimate, because he

---

* On July 1, *Der Spiegel* published a three-part review of NSA surveillance titled "How the NSA Targets Germany and Europe." It includes two previously unreleased slides—a map showing the world's fiber-optic network and a Boundless Informant graph comparing French and Italian phone traffic to German communications—but does not offer exclusive infomation aside from 35,321 people were employed by the NSA in 2006, which had a budget of $6.115 billion.

acknowledges and refers to The Universal Declaration of Human Rights (UDHR). Article 14 of UDHR has two clauses: "(1) Everyone has the right to seek and to enjoy in other countries asylum from persecution. (2) This right may not be invoked in the case of prosecutions genuinely arising from non-political crimes or from acts contrary to the purposes and principles of the United Nations."[90] Snowden closes by announcing he is "unbowed" in his convictions.

The courageous indictment arrived at a time when Washington was becoming very concerned about two of the three most viable future homes for Snowden. The presidents of Venezuela and Bolivia were alongside Putin during the two-day Gas Exporting Countries Summit. As it had done several times before, the U.S. government was on the verge of stacking the deck against itself when Snowden was concerned. A world divided was about to make one Latin American country's asylum decision very easy.

Venezuela's leader, Nicolás Maduro, was preparing to leave the energy conference when he told Russia's Interfax news agency, "We [the people of Venezuela] think this young person has done something very important for humanity, has done a favour to humanity, has spoken great truths to deconstruct a world that is controlled by an imperialist American elite." When asked if he intended to take Snowden back to Venezuela with him, Maduro sardonically responded, "What we're taking with us are multiple agreements that we're signing with Russia, including oil and gas."[91]

Bolivia's president, Evo Morales, informed *Actualidad*, the Spanish-language provider for the Russia Today news network, "If there were a request, of course we would be willing to debate and consider the idea."[92] Morales had also recently congratulated Correa for threatening to back out of the ATPDEA.[93] Neither world leader had been informed that their country had already received Snowden's asylum request.

Late Tuesday, Bolivian Air Force flight FAB-001 left Moscow with Morales onboard en route to Bolivia's capital, La Paz. As it passed over Austria, Portugal informed Morales' flight crew that the aircraft's reservation to refuel in Lisbon had been cancelled for "technical reasons." As the Dassault Falcon 900EX[94] changed flight paths and rerouted to the Canary Islands off the coast of Africa, French authorities reported it could not permit FAB-001 to fly over due to "technical issues."[95] Morales had no choice but to make a circle and land in Vienna. Once in Austria's capital, the aircraft was subjected to a "routine" inspection by Austrian authorities, and all of its passengers' passports were verified. Twelve hours later,[96] Morales departed. FAB-001 was now cleared to refuel in the Canary Islands on the condition its passengers consent to another inspection, this time by Spain.

Austria later claimed it had merely responded to FAB-001's request to refuel. Audio records confirm that the flight crew had cited a possible fuel indicator problem. Purportedly, they were unsure how much fuel they had. Even if this were the case, they could have easily made it to Lisbon: Assuming it had not been refueled during the two-day layover in Moscow and granting the greatest benefit of the doubt in respect to distance, the FAB-001 would have been forced to refuel in Lisbon after crossing 5,382 Atlantic miles. During the return voyage to Bolivia, it would have been scheduled to stop in Vienna and not Lisbon because the Dassault Falcon 900EX has a flight range of only 4,598 miles.[97] The aircraft wouldn't have had the fuel to make the 4,850-mile round trip to Portugal from Moscow. Vienna and Lisbon are 1,037 and 2,425 miles from Moscow respectively. It is clear the FAB-001 had been refueled in Moscow and could have easily made it to Lisbon.

The problem Morales encountered was that he had attempted to cross allied airspace. After expressing support for Correa and suggesting Bolivia might harbor Snowden, Washington wanted to intimidate Morales as well as confirm that the American exile, which had not been seen in days, was not being flown out of Russia. After Morales was forced to land, the U.S. ambassador to Austria, William Eacho, made several calls from his embassy to various officials. He "claimed with great certainty that Edward Snowden was onboard" while referencing a "diplomatic note requesting Snowden's extradition."[98] After first denying Morales had been forbidden passage, Spain's minister of foreign affairs, José Manuel García-Margallo, conceded on national television, "They told us that the information was clear, that he [Snowden] was inside [the airplane]." He did not specify who "they" were and declined to comment whether he'd been contacted by American authorities, yet he added that other European countries' similar responses were based on the same information he'd been issued.[99] When later questioned, France's president, Francois Hollande, apologetically stated there had been "conflicting information" about the airplane's flight manifest.[100] The U.S. government declined to comment, saying the matter should be redirected to the countries involved.[101]

Morales arrived in La Paz close to midnight on Wednesday, July 3.[102] He was met by cheering crowds. An emergency meeting was quickly organized, and a portion of the Union of South American Nations (Unión de Naciones Suramericanas or "UNASUR") assembled the following day. As protesters burned France's flag in front of Bolivia's French Embassy[103] and international headlines quoted Bolivian vice president Alvaro Garcia's assertion that Morales had been "kidnapped by imperialism,"[104] the presidents of Ecuador, Argentina, Uruguay, Venezuela, Suriname and Bolivia met in Cochabamba, Bolivia, to discuss the issue. Since it had already refused to acknowledge Snowden's asylum petition, Brazil felt it only needed to be represented by an advisor. Due to their strong ties to the U.S., Colombia, Peru and Chile were not in attendance. Juan Manuel Santos, Colombia's president, tried to remain politically neutral. He tweeted, "We're in solidarity with Evo Morales because what they did to him is unheard-of, but let's not let this turn into a diplomatic crisis for Latin America and the EU."[105] Maduro informed the UNASUR congregation that U.S. Secretary of State John Kerry had contacted his government officials, attempting to pressure them not to accept Snowden's asylum request.[106]

It could be argued the U.S. knew Snowden wasn't on the flight but had deliberately commandeered Morales' airplane to set an example for any nation that might want to host him.

It proved Snowden's arrival in a receptive country would be arduous, if not impossible. But this is unlikely. To merely make the point in the wake of any present asylum offers atop creating international ill will while asking favors of already hostile EU members would be politically expensive. France had recently suggested the free-trade talks between America and the European Union should be postponed.[107] The most likely explanation for Washington's actions was it merely acted before thinking. What it accomplished was inflaming already-strained relations with South America and gave various Latin American nations a reason to collectively discuss Snowden.

The impact of the Morales incident was twofold. It solidified the Latin American coalition whose members already viewed the U.S. and its allies as antagonistic to their countries' political philosophies and practices. "We are not colonies anymore," announced José Mujica, president of Uruguay. "We deserve respect," he continued, "and when one of our governments is insulted we feel the insult throughout Latin America."[108] In a speech in Buenos Aires, Argentina's President Cristina Kirchner declared, "[These actions are] vestiges of a colonialism that we thought were long over. We believe this constitutes not only the humiliation of a sister nation but of all South America."[109] Morales had told the UNASUR summit members, "My only sin is that I'm indigenous and anti-imperialist, [that I question] those economic policies planned and implemented by politicians that just starve us to death."[110]

The other consequence was that economic sanctions against the offending nations might ensue. In response to the Spanish ambassador to Austria first requesting to inspect FAB-001 when it was grounded in Vienna before telling Morales he could refuel in the Canary Islands only if he consented to another search, Maduro proclaimed, "We're going to re-evaluate our relations with Spain."[111] Morales left the impromptu conference stating, "My hand would not tremble to close the US Embassy. We have dignity, sovereignty. Without America, we are better off politically and democratically."[112] Morales was so outraged that he refused to accept an apology from France's foreign minister, who professed there was "never any intention to block the access to our air space." Bolivia's leader shot back, "What happened these days is not an accident but part of policies to continue intimidating the Bolivian people and Latin American people."[113]

Upon arriving in Cochabamba for the UNASUR meeting, Maduro said, "We're here to tell president Evo Morales that he can count on us. Whoever picks a fight with Bolivia, picks a fight with Venezuela."[114] It was little surprise that the next day, July 5, Venezuela granted Snowden asylum. Nicaragua did as well. Maduro implied his country's decision was based in part on the Morales plane incident: "I, as head of state of the Bolivarian Republic of Venezuela, offer humanitarian asylum to the young American, Edward Joseph Snowden, the ex-functionary of the CIA, so that he can come to live in the country of [Venezuela's founder Simon] Bolivar and [late President Hugo] Chavez and [escape] U.S. imperial persecution."[115] Nicaraguan president Daniel Ortega quietly justified his nation's motives: "We are an open country, respectful of the right of asylum, and it's clear that if circumstances permit, we would gladly receive Snowden and give him asylum in Nicaragua." Both countries had already received and rejected extradition requests from the U.S.[116] The Central American country's entry onto the international stage was largely symbolic. Pundits doubted the sincerity of Ortega's offer. They suspected he was using the opportunity to appeal to regional heads of state.[117] Even though it was not delivered in person, Snowden's application had been accepted at Nicaragua's foreign ministry in Moscow.[118] As expected, the next day Morales announced Bolivia was "willing to give asylum" to Snowden.[119] Unlike Maduro, Morales explicitly affirmed Bolivia's offer was due to the European debacle. He stated the offer was a "justified protest" in response to what had taken place.[120]

Until now the United States had appeared justified in its persecution and hunt for Snowden because a large number of nations had rejected him in less than a day, and a majority had done so in under a week. But when not one but three countries suddenly consented to host the American exile, it insinuated that Snowden's actions could be legitimate, especially since the offers came from smaller, less powerful nations which many believed would be made to suffer for their decision. Publicly the White House characteristically downplayed the countries' defiance. When asked for an official response to the first nation that made an asylum offer, an unnamed U.S. official stated, "You'd have to ask the Venezuelans what it means, as it is their offer."[121]

In actuality, Washington could say little to Venezuela. Even though Kerry called Venezuelan Foreign Minister Elias Jaua mere hours after Maduro made his announcement,[122] declaring that if Snowden should arrive in the South American country, the U.S. would close NATO airspace and cease oil deliveries, Venezuela's officials knew he was bluffing. The global economy could not survive without the resources provided by the world's largest oil exporter.[123] As expected, Capitol Hill let the ATPDEA expire,[124] but as a sign of protest, Bolivia had resigned from the treaty four days prior.[125] The U.S. government didn't take Nicaragua's offer seriously: For Snowden to arrive in the country, he would first have to travel through Venezuela.[126]

Washington's comparatively complacent response was odd. Perhaps the Capitol realized it had overstepped its bounds and created asylum offers which might not have otherwise been made. Maybe the U.S. government had slowly come to understand that Snowden did not intend to leave Russia. But if history is any guide, Washington was exhibiting humility because it believed that Snowden was trapped and it was only a matter of time before the U.S. could convince the former Soviet Union to hand him over.

For Snowden to arrive in any of the receptive countries, he would have to transverse American and U.N. airspace if traveling by commercial jet. When en route to Latin and South America, Russia's Aeroflot airline passes through Cuba and other nations with extradition treaties with the U.S.[127] In spite of this, Snowden now qualified for unquestioned safe passage. America is a signatory on UDHR. In principle the U.S. is obligated to recognize asylees from all countries, especially participating UDHR nations. Nicaragua, Venezuela and Ecuador are also UDHR signatories. If he had not been granted asylum, the United States would have the right to ask any U.N. member to land Snowden's plane once it entered their territory. Since he was granted asylum by another UDHR nation and not charged with a crime outside of the U.S., the other United Nations members had no right or cause to detain him. As the United Nations High Commissioner for Refugees makes clear, "As such it [principle of non-refoulement or the returning of the persecuted to the persecutor] is binding in all States, regardless of whether they have acceded to the 1951 [Refugee] Convention or 1967 Protocol [Relating to the Status of Refugees]. A refugee seeking protection must not be prevented from entering a country as this would amount to refoulement."[128] A commercial flight also has the international right to fly over and refuel as needed, whereas government and private aircraft must request permission to enter each country's airspace and land. But as the world witnessed, international politics trumps theoretical law.[129] Washington was violating international law and justifying it by stating its own legislation had been broken. The irony of the situation was not lost on the press.[130] The U.S. government desperately chased an individual whose alleged crimes were committed under the same reasoning.

It was clear Snowden's safety could not be guaranteed even if Maduro sent a government aircraft to pick him up. Snowden's only viable option would be to take a private airplane with the fuel capacity to travel directly from Moscow to its western destination while avoiding American or allied airspace along the way. The Bombardier Global 8000 can travel 7,900 miles. It is geographically possible to bypass hostile zones by flying north from Moscow to the Barents Sea, alongside Norway then between Britain and Iceland on the Norwegian Sea. Snowden could arrive safely after carefully navigating through Caribbean territory. Barring prevailing headwinds, even Bolivia resting on the western coast of South America is within Snowden's hypothetical flight range.[131]

But neither Olafur Sigurvinsson nor WikiLeaks began scrambling to get Snowden to long-term safety. No official announcement was immediately released or plans put in place to relocate the whistleblower. Snowden remained hidden from public sight. He was where he wanted to be and couldn't have planned it better. It had been sheer luck Morales and Maduro had voiced support for Snowden while they were in Moscow. He now had a legitimate reason to stay in Russia.

MacAskill had been working alongside Greenwald in his home in Rio de Janeiro when the Dropmire report premiered.[132] The synchronicity of the *Der Spiegel* EU article thematically matching MacAskill's editorial was the obvious product of Poitras and *The Guardian* team being in steady communication. But Greenwald had not left Hong Kong merely to seek refuge. Like Poitras, he was delivering classified data to the country which it applied: Brazil. After waiting for the headlines to clear, Greenwald led another succession of classified exposés.

Arriving on the coattails of Latin America's discontent with the U.S., on the Saturday afternoon that Morales told the world he would accept Snowden, Greenwald published "U.S. spied on millions of e-mails and calls of Brazilians"[133] and "U.S. expands the surveillance apparatus continuously"[134] in *O Globo*, a Portuguese-language newspaper based out of Rio de Janeiro. Greenwald speaks fluent Portuguese.[135]

Referencing confidential U.S. intelligence documents, in his first article Greenwald announces that by January 2013 the NSA had monitored 2.3 billion Brazilian calls. The number was just below those that American intelligence had domestically surveilled. The Brazilian surveillance is reported to be "constant and [of] large scale." The NSA accomplishes this using an internal labor force of 35,200 employees and "strategic partnerships" with more than 80 of the "largest global corporations." However, the relationship between America's clandestine agency and foreign communication firms is not as benign or mutual as the term "partnerships" implies.

When U.S. intelligence found international data lacking, the NSA began using its domestic "partnerships" to gain greater access to foreign information. American intelligence exploits the U.S.-foreign business alliances by "bridging" them: "The partners operate in the U.S., but do not have access to information passing [through] networks of a nation, and for corporate relationships, provide exclusive access to the other [telecommunications companies and service providers' internet]."

The agency collects the data using a program called Fairview and includes a "corporate portfolio" filled with foreign assignments' code names: "Darkthunder," "Steelflauta," "Monkeyrocket," "Shiftingshadow," "Orangecrush," "Yachtshop," "Orangeblossom," "Silverzephyr," "Bluezephyr," "Cobaltfalcon," among others. It is unclear whether the foreign communication providers are complicit in, or even aware of, the data release.

Having regained his journalistic stride, Greenwald's disclosure of Fairview provides a better understanding of how the NSA is able to obtain its monumental amount of foreign data. He also answers one of the lingering questions from the PRISM debate. It was now understood that the previously revealed Chinese and German intercepts were not the sole product of hacking but of the U.S. government forcing its domestic providers to allow American intelligence to "bridge over" into foreign communication systems. This undoubtedly breaches the U.S. communication providers' confidentiality agreements with its foreign partners and also subtly implies that other nations may also be exploiting their domestic telecom and Internet firms' U.S. relations, especially interactions involving the other Four Eyes and "friendly governments."

"U.S. expands the surveillance apparatus continuously" serves as a teaser rather than a comprehensive exposé. Greenwald begins by reviewing the director of national intelligence's contradictory claims regarding American surveillance then makes passing reference to Boundless Informant before revealing XKeyscore.

Greenwald's treatment of XKeyscore is peculiar. It is cursory and not immediately seconded by another publication's reporting. In almost all previous instances in which he issues an exclusive about a particular top secret surveillance program, he explores it at length. But Greenwald teases his audience by merely relaying that XKeyscore is software that uses over 700 servers worldwide to spy on a surplus of 150 countries. The program has the ability to log onto and track a target in real-time as the individual moves across the Internet. He does not go into greater detail about how the program functions or provide any data showing its effectiveness. However, an included XKeyscore training slide asks, "My target uses Google Maps to scope target locations—can I use this information to determine his email address? What about the web searches—do any stand out and look suspicious?" The tutorial outlines, "XKEYSCORE extracts and databases these events including all web-based searches which can be retrospectively queried." It emphasizes that the NSA retains data because "retrospectively" appears in red.[136]

Greenwald was not content to let the Brazilian populace merely read about American surveillance. He had also gone to the Brazilian television network Rede Globo with a handful of previously unseen classified slides tucked under his arm. After America's ABC network, Rede Globo has the largest annual revenue of any broadcast company in the world.[137] Hot on the heels of the twin *O Globo* articles, an eight-minute exposé aired the next day,[138] Sunday, July 7. Audiences learned that "Brazil became a strategic focus of the U.S. 'Big Brother' because the data that transits through here is less protected than the same data in other countries." The additional slides deal with the NSA programs Fairview and Boundless Informant. They show the South American country was surveilled in 2012 because of the amount of Internet traffic which was being directed to Pakistan and North Korea.[139]

There is an incongruity in reports that follow Greenwald's articles. Brazil's television program *Fantastico* announced[140] that the purported 2.3 Brazilian and three million American pieces of retrieved data were cumulative totals amassed over a 10-

year period.[141] This contradicts Greenwald's initial *Guardian* statement that the Boundless Informant slides were displaying monthly accumulations.[142] Considering the advanced technology and the fact Greenwald was consulting with Snowden in Hong Kong while drafting his June exposé, it is more likely the original statistic is correct. This is reinforced by the proportional figures found in Poitras' examination of the NSA's German surveillance.

Predictably, Greenwald's Fairview exposé automatically brought into question the nature of U.S. communication providers' relationships with their foreign associates, but it was Brazil's response that made headlines. The nation's president, Dilma Rousseff, called an emergency cabinet meeting as soon as the reports were made public. On Monday she issued a statement through her foreign affairs minister, Antonio Patriota: "The Brazilian government has asked for clarifications through the US embassy in Brasília and the Brazilian embassy in Washington." Brazil was politically astute. It refused to wait for Washington to address the grievance. Though a member, Brazil did not bother asking the U.N. to investigate. Instead it demanded regulations be put in place "to impede abuses and protect the privacy" of people worldwide. In the meantime, the South American nation instigated a full internal investigation of its own. Federal police and the national Brazilian Telecommunication Agency looked into exactly how the data was being accessed. They suspected that satellites signals were being intercepted but also examined the transatlantic cables connecting the country to the outside world. Brazil questioned domestic communication providers in their possible role in the matter.[143] The U.S. stated it would not publicly comment on the reports, and its responses to Brazil would be limited.[144]

Poitras left Berlin the day after she revealed that the NSA was spying on Germany. She met Greenwald and MacAskill in Rio de Janeiro on July 1 and continued working on her interview footage.[145] As Greenwald had a few days prior, she was about to present her own doubleheader of classified disclosures.

Shortly before Snowden left Hawaii, Poitras was still unsure about the authenticity of the person she was having anonymous discussions with over the Internet. She wanted to confirm Snowden was who he said he was. She enlisted the aid of Jacob Appelbaum. Though neither party was aware of who they were speaking to at the time, Snowden undoubtedly knew of Appelbaum's work.

Appelbaum is probably one of Snowden's few IT peers. He is a Internet security innovator and famed hacker. A proponent of online privacy, Appelbaum has traveled the world engaging audiences in talks about the latest advances in Internet safety. He is a consultant for the online anonymity venture the Tor Project and has worked for Greenpeace and the radical environmental group Rainforest Action Network. In 2005 he snuck past the National Guard and set up wireless Internet so victims of Hurricane Katrina could register for FEMA housing. Like Poitras, he has been repeatedly detained at airports and had his personal possessions confiscated. After Appelbaum spoke on behalf of Assange and WikiLeaks at the 2010 HOPE Conference,[146] the Justice Department requisitioned the contents of his Twitter accounts. Cleverly the social network petitioned the court system to unseal the request. This allowed the company to place the order's contents and demands online.[147] Because of consistent American security harassment, Appelbaum resides in Berlin, which is perhaps where he met Poitras (or through her interaction with Assange).[148] He had provided one of the questions during Snowden's June 17 online Q & A session.[149]

After Appelbaum had revealed his identity to Snowden, the whistleblower gave him and Poitras permission to publish the contents of the interview when they felt it appropriate. The media had saturated the public with basic IT and intelligence jargon since June 5, and the average reader could now follow the otherwise technical conversation. On July 8 using *Der Spiegel* as the venue, Poitras allowed Snowden to vicariously and retroactively address the current state of world affairs.[150]

Shortly into the interview and due in part to geographical self-interest, Appelbaum bluntly inquires whether the German government or authorities were privy to the NSA's domestic spying. "Yes, of course," Snowden responds. "We're in bed together with the Germans the same as with most other Western countries. For example, we tip them off when someone we want is flying through their airports (that we for example, have learned from the cell phone of a suspected hacker's girlfriend in a totally unrelated third country) and they hand them over to us. They don't ask to justify how we know something, and vice versa, to insulate their political leaders from the backlash of knowing how grievously they're violating global privacy." Snowden makes it retrospectively clear the European Union was colluding with the U.S. when Morales' airplane was forced down in Vienna. Obviously France, Spain, Portugal and Austria's actions were the product of American pressure, U.N. obligation and—as Snowden mentions—the desire to not question how Washington "knew" Snowden was onboard the Bolivian aircraft.

Appelbaum quickly follows with, "Does the NSA partner with other nations, like Israel?" Snowden replies it does but undoubtedly knew it was a leaning question. Appelbaum then asks if the NSA aided in the creation of Stuxnet. Stuxnet was a fabled state-of-the-art computer virus which infected Iran's nuclear facilities. Its origin was long believed to have been a joint effort between Israel and the United States. Stuxnet was discovered because of poor programming. It inadvertently spread beyond its intended target and extended globally, infecting Iran, Indonesia, India, Azerbaijan, America and Pakistan.[151] It was later duplicated and sold on the black market.[152] Snowden simply replies, "NSA and Israel co-wrote it."

Able to finally get answers to lingering personal questions, Appelbaum continues down the same geopolitical vein. As Snowden responds, he mentions in passing the existence of the "Five Eye Partners" before divulging the true lifespan of recorded data. Referring to Tempora he states, "Right now the buffer [information storage unit] can hold three days of traffic, but that's being improved. Three days may not sound like much, but remember that that's not metadata. 'Full-take' means it doesn't miss anything, and ingests the entirety of each circuit's capacity." His disclosure counters both America and Britain's reassurances that all retrieved data is first filtered and subsequently anonymized prior to being recorded. Reinforcing the contents of the revealed XKeyscore training slide two days prior, Snowden adds that if an analyst requests data, because it has been highlighted, it is stored "forever and ever, regardless of policy." He reports that the NSA's objective is to store all metadata permanently because live data's "content isn't as valuable as metadata because you can either re-fetch content based on the metadata or, if not, simply task all future communications of interest for permanent collection since the metadata tells you what out of their data stream you actually want." In the event someone's is targeted, Snowden states the person is "just owned." He adds, "An analyst will get a daily (or scheduled based on exfiltration summary) report on what changed on the system, PCAPS ["packets of capture" or units of collected data] of leftover data that wasn't understood by the automated dissectors, and so forth. It's up to the analyst to do whatever they want at that point—the target's machine doesn't belong to them anymore, it belongs to the US government." Given Snowden's description, this is probably akin to EvilOlive's real-time tip alerting capabilities.

Toward the end of the interview, Snowden presents what he views as the only viable solution to the privacy problem because, in his words, those who are accountable will never be made to answer. He tells Appelbaum, "Laws are meant for you, not for them." Snowden states that civil liberty groups should push the corroborating companies to include privacy clauses in their contracts. For those that refuse, they are free to be "punished by consumers in the market."

The interview's publication served several purposes. It implicated Germany in the previously reported domestic surveillance. The discussion outlined how America could have possibly pulled the European Union's puppet strings to bring down Morales' flight. As always, it exposed new confidential information. Yet this is the first time Snowden offers solutions to the problem. Seibert, the German representative who a little over a week prior proclaimed that the NSA's German spying was reminiscent of the Cold War, did not deny or even seek rhetorical neutrality regarding Snowden's claims. Instead he blatantly confessed and admitted government compliance: "The BND [Bundesnachrichtendienst or German foreign intelligence agency] has been co-operating for decades with partner agencies, including the NSA. We can only protect our citizens if we cooperate. This cooperation is following rules and laws very strictly and is subject to parliamentary control."[153] The German populace did not approve. An opinion poll conducted a few weeks before showed half of Germany considered Snowden a hero, and 35 percent of the country's population said it would be willing to hide him in their homes.[154] The latter is a telling historical metaphor revealing how a large minority of Germans viewed America's hunt for the NSA whistleblower.

The same day, Poitras released seven more minutes of interview footage.[155]

The audience is met by a black screen before "SNOWDEN" appears in the center of the frame; immediately below it, "Interview Part 2." The letters fade out as viewers are greeted by the familiar sounds of waves lapping upon the banks of Victoria Harbor. In the lower, left corner of the screen, "Excerpts of interview with Edward Snowden" fades in and is followed by "HONG KONG June 6, 2013" before a return and then "GLENN GREENWALD, interviewer" rests upon "LAURA POITRAS, filmmaker."

Snowden's face suddenly appears, and the camera aggressively closes in on it. He looks the same as before. It is obvious this is a continuation of the same interview the world flocked to see almost a month before. Poitras is a masterful filmmaker. The documentary plays a similar role as the Appelbaum interview because Poitras chose footage that reflects what the world and Snowden had experienced the preceding month.

The interview begins with Greenwald asking Snowden what he believes the U.S. government's response to his actions will be. He correctly estimates Washington would proclaim he's "violated the Espionage Act. They're going to say, I've aided our enemies [...]." Greenwald then puts to Snowden whether he entered the intelligence community with the intention of becoming a mole or to undermine the U.S. government. Snowden laughs before pausing to recollect. He reminds his audience that after the invasion of Iraq, he enlisted in the Army because he "believed in the goodness of what we [the U.S.] were doing. I believed in the nobility of our intentions to free oppressed people overseas." He relays that his perspective changed after having been exposed to "true information," information that "had not been propagandized in the media." Snowden announces, "We [the U.S. government] were actually involved in misleading the public and misleading all publics, not just the American public, in order to create a certain mindset in the global consciousness, and I was actually a victim of that. America is a fundamentally a good country. We have good people with good values who want to do the right thing, but the structures of power that exist are working to their own ends to extend their capability at the expense of the freedom of all publics."

Whereas the initial whistleblowing reports where meant to catch the American public's attention, more recent revelations panned back to include "all publics." It is clear Snowden meant what he typed during the June 17 online chat: "This country is worth dying for," but due to his experiences in U.S. intelligence, his concern became more cosmopolitan. Though some could argue that his American disclosures were aimed at harming America, he chose to also extract foreign data to show non-U.S. citizens their governments were also engaging in similar practices. At worst, he could be labeled a misanthrope, but with each theft, he made himself more vulnerable to being caught.

Though audiences were hard-pressed to believe the claim in June, Poitras lets Snowden repeat, "There are literally no ingress or egress points anywhere in the continental United States where communications can enter or exit without being monitored and collected and analyzed." He lists the most important excised files as being, "The Verizon document," because "it literally lays out they're [members of the intelligence community] using an authority that was intended to be used to seek warrants against individuals and they're applying it to the whole of society by basically subverting a corporate partnership through major telecommunications providers and they're getting everyone's calls, everyone's call records and everyone's internet traffic as well." He then lists Boundless Informant. He pauses before labeling it "a global auditing system for the NSA's intercept and collection system that lets us track how much we're collecting, where we're collecting, by which authorities and so forth. The NSA lied about the existence of this tool to Congress and to specific congressmen in response to previous inquiries about their surveillance activities." He then adds PRISM, "which is a demonstration of how the U.S. government co-opts U.S. corporate power to its own ends. Companies like Google, Facebook, Apple, Microsoft, they all get together with the NSA and provide the NSA direct access to the back ends of all of the systems you use to communicate, to store data, to put things in the cloud [online storage sites], and even to just send birthday wishes and keep a record of your life. And they give NSA direct access that they don't need to oversee so they can't be held liable for it. I think that's a dangerous capability for anybody to have but particularly an organization that's demonstrated time and time again that they'll work to shield themselves from oversight."

Poitras has Snowden reiterate his motives for action before closing the interview: "I don't want to live in a world where everything that I say, everything I do, everyone I talk to, every expression of creativity or love or friendship is recorded. And that's not something I'm willing to support, it's not something I'm willing to build, and it's not something I'm willing to live under. So I think anyone who opposes that sort of world has an obligation to act in the way they can. Now I've watched and waited and tried to do my job in the most policy-driven way I could, which is to wait and allow [...] our leadership, our figures, to sort of correct the excesses of government when we go too far. But as I've watched, I've seen that's not occurring. In fact, we're compounding the excesses of prior governments and making it worse and more invasive, and no one is really standing to stop it."

The declaration that his motive was to take a personal stand and to set an example is one which the world had yet to hear. Snowden reveals that his initial goal was to clear his conscience and avoid hypocrisy by no longer supporting what he believed was unjustifiable. Snowden ceased being complicit in the mechanisms which he deemed were responsible for exploiting personal freedoms and removed himself from the advantages which that society offered.

The same day, the *O Globo* team was left by Greenwald to report, "NSA and CIA have maintained staff in Brasilia to collect satellite data."[156] Guided by a document dated 2002 which was leaked by Snowden, the Brazilian newspaper relays that 75 "monitoring stations" are jointly controlled throughout the world by both the CIA and NSA. Sixty-five are in various world capitals, some on military outposts, and five are located in Central and Latin America: Colombia, Venezuela, Panama, Mexico and Brazil. Two are specifically cited as residing in New Delhi and Misawa, Japan. (A subsequent report would reveal two more reside in Vienna and Frankfurt.)[157] The code name for such operations is "Stateroom."[158] Like Snowden, the "Special Collection Service" agents assigned to these outposts are given diplomatic covers by their American embassies. The agents' mission is to collect foreign satellite collection information or "FORNSAT." This is to be done using established "alliances with private companies, owners, or operators."

A September 2010 document shows the Brazilian Consulate in Washington and the South American nation's U.N. offices in New York were American targets. As with the Cryptofax in the EU Embassy in Washington, Dropmire had been implanted in private digital networks, and other physical alterations were made to computer systems in Brazil. At this time, "Highlands" was the code name for digital signal collection, computer screen captures were dubbed "Vagrant" (a screen capture or "screencap" is a single-frame picture of what appears on a computer monitor), and "Lifesaver" designated the copying of disk drives. All three methods were utilized to extract Brazilian data.

Greenwald returned the next day. "U.S. spies spread through Latin America"[159] appeared July 9 in *O Globo*. It opens by declaring that the U.S. spying that takes place in Brazil is not exclusive to the South American country. Classified documents reveal that, again, the NSA is not engaging in counterintelligence to solely determine military activity, intent and capability abroad. In February 2013 American intelligence was preoccupied with "oil" in Venezuela and Mexico's "energy."

From 2008 to at least March 2013, U.S. intelligence's foremost southern concerns after Brazil were Colombia and Mexico. They were followed by Venezuela, Argentina, Ecuador, Panama, Costa Rica, Nicaragua, Honduras, Paraguay, Chile, Peru and El Salvador respectively. During February 2013, the NSA gleaned its information from these nations using Boundless Informant and PRISM, the latter of which had been actively recording data from undersea fiber-optic cables as far back as 2007. Boundless Informant was used to chart how many domestic partnerships were being exploited by Fairview. In one case, telephone calls, faxes and emails were obtained through "Steelknight," the code name for a regional private satellite operator. Colombia, Venezuela and Ecuador were monitored using XKeyscore during 2008.

Officials from various Latin American countries condemned the reports, which were epitomized by Gilberto Carvalho, aide to President Rousseff, stating a "very hard" response was in order, lest the American government "trample all over us tomorrow."[160] Argentina's leader announced, "[These reports are] [m]ore than revelations, these are confirmations of what we thought was happening." In anticipation of the Mercosur summit, when numerous Central and Latin American countries would meet at the end of the week to discuss free-trade agreements, President Kirchner expressed the hope that summit members would consent to issuing a strong, unified response and demand an explanation from the U.S. government.[161] Brazil's U.S. ambassador, Thomas Shannon, reportedly informed Brazil's communications minister, Paulo Bernardo, that America does not conduct Brazilian surveillance and was not working with the nation's communication providers.[162] Shannon's response unequivocally implicated private South American business owners. Whereas Greenwald's findings in "U.S. spied on millions of e-mails and calls of Brazilians" suggest U.S. intelligence might have been tapping into foreign communications without the companies' consent, the ambassador's pronouncement clarified *The Guardian*'s "NSA and CIA have maintained staff in Brasilia to collect satellite data" use of the term "alliances." American intelligence's relationship with "private companies, owners, or operators" was literal and not the NSA's euphemism for covert surveillance. It would later be revealed that Shannon (with the implication that all U.S. ambassadors) worked closely with the NSA.

The morning Greenwald informed the world that the NSA was watching most of Central and South America, the head of the foreign affairs committee of Russia's Lower House of Parliament, Alexei Pushkov, posted on Twitter that Snowden had accepted Venezuela's asylum offer. But controversy quickly ensued. Within minutes he removed the tweet. Another post promptly filled the void, "Information about Snowden accepting Maduro's offer of asylum comes from [Russian TV channel] Vesti 24 newscast at 18:00. Contact them for all questions." However, the press reported two different "original" notices. The most often quoted original announced, "Predictably, Snowden has agreed to Maduro's offer of political asylum. Apparently, this option appeared most reliable to Snowden."[163] An alternative version read, "According to News 24, with reference to Maduro, Snowden accepted his offer of asylum. If so, it is (sic) found that the safest option."[164] Regardless of translation differences, it cannot be denied that "News 24" is mentioned in the alternative version. Since the former was the most frequently cited atop the unlikely possibility someone edited out "News 24" to incriminate Pushkov, this edition is probably the true original. It is also more plausible that the latter rendition was inserted into the media flow to buffer the Russian official's misstep. News 24 posted on its website that Maduro had recently confirmed his offer of asylum, not that Snowden had accepted.[165] Strangely, later that afternoon WikiLeaks announced, "Tomorrow the first phase of Edward Snowden's 'Flight of Liberty' campaign will be launched. Follow for further details."[166] However, by the morning of July 11 nothing had been announced nor had Snowden made an appearance. Instead a bombshell of a disclosure debuted.

Greenwald came editorially and thematically home. Working from his house in Rio de Janeiro, he, Poitras and MacAskill presented "Microsoft handed the NSA access to encrypted messages" in *The Guardian* on July 11. They set out to do nothing short of prove Microsoft is a willing participant in the PRISM program.

They begin by reminding their audience that online companies first feigned ignorance of PRISM, proceeded to deny allowing the NSA access to their servers, then insisted data extraction took place only under individual court orders, progressed to admitting a blanket order forced compliance, before attempting defense by criticizing the federal government for not permitting them to release their unfiltered requisition data. "But," says *The Guardian*, "internal NSA newsletters, marked top secret, suggest the co-operation between the intelligence community and the companies is deep and ongoing."

Proof is provided by documentation from the NSA's SSO division. In July 2012, Microsoft began trials runs of a new encryption service for its personal information manager program Outlook.com. The NSA was worried users would be able to encode chats and email. It is revealed in a newsletter dated December 26, 2012, that the issue had been resolved two weeks prior. Microsoft had granted the intelligence community pre-encryption access to Outlook, Live and Hotmail. The Outlook.com portal was released to the public on February 18, 2013. Microsoft boasted the program possessed new, tighter security features.[167]

The intelligence community's other concern was Microsoft's online storage accounts. By April 8, 2013, PRISM had been given free access to Microsoft's cloud device, SkyDrive. The agreement was fashioned so "analysts will no longer have to make a special request to SSO for this [access to the cloud]—a process step that many analysts may not have known about."

The NSA had already acquired full, direct access to Skype video transmissions by this time: "The audio portions of these sessions have been processed correctly all along, but without the accompanying video. Now, analysts will have the complete 'picture.'" The company's privacy policy states, "Skype is committed to respecting your privacy and the confidentiality of your personal data, traffic data and communications content."[168]

Citing an August 3, 2012 classified document, Greenwald and Co. report that PRISM's collected data is freely available to the FBI and CIA. All an agent has to do to get an NSA analyst's findings is file a copy request. The document declares that file sharing makes PRISM a "team sport!"

Aside from the SSO's admission that analysts "will no longer have to make a special request," the NSA wanting pre-encryption access reveals it is conducting live surveillance without court oversight. Otherwise it would obtain and present an FISC order for a specific target's materials. The encrypted data would then be taken to cryptanalysts to decode. Though some could argue cryptanalysis is time and labor-intensive, by law this is the process which the NSA should follow. As with his Verizon exposé, Greenwald judiciously left this reader to make a fair assumption of other software providers' true relationship and roles with American intelligence.

This follows a 100-year tradition of American communication providers colluding with U.S. intelligence. The two largest telegraph companies, Western Union and Postal Telegraph, willfully violated the Radio Communication Act of 1912 and provided the first covert government intelligence agency, the Black Chamber, with daily supplies of its telegrams.[169]

Microsoft's response to the claims added another chapter to its book of defenses: "[...] when we upgrade or update products legal obligations may in some circumstances require that we maintain the ability to provide information in response to a law enforcement or national security request." The company's failure to deny or even shy away from the proceeding allegations implies the software corporation is haggardly admitting it is guilty of customer privacy violations.

After the Microsoft exposé, the steam train of disclosures inexplicably comes to an abrupt stop. Few knew the silence was an indicator that Greenwald and Poitras had been in contact with Snowden.[170] As they had done before, they were deliberately leaving the headlines open.

On Friday, July 12, it was made public that the day before, Snowden had contacted 13 Russian officials, lawyers and the human rights advocacy organizations Amnesty International and Human Rights Watch as well as the international political and corporate watchdog group Transparency International.[171] He asked them to meet in 24 hours—at 4:30 p.m.—in Sheremetyevo Airport where, at 5 p.m., he would be making a brief statement. Some invitation recipients were apprehensive because they had no way of confirming whether the summons was authentic. Tonya Lokshino of Human Rights Watch wrote on Facebook, "I'm not sure this is for real, but compelled to give it a try" and she "[w]ouldn't want to create an impression that HRW is not interested in what Snowden has to say." Others highlighted that Snowden's request anomalously used the British spelling "centre" and "behaviour." The same orthographical criticism had been leveled at his July 1 WikiLeaks announcement.[172] However suspect, like Lokshino, no one who was invited was willing to take the chance of being wrong.

In traditional Snowden fashion, the NSA leaker had instructed his guests to be on the lookout for an individual bearing a sign which read "G9." This would aid in separating the press from those which Snowden expressly wanted in attendance. When the G9 sign holder appeared, the invitees quietly followed. The press sensed a plot was afoot and summarily did the same. At 5:00, the gray doors emboldened with "Staff Only" closed within a room in Terminal E.[173] The press had been refused admittance. Reporters and cameramen crowded outside, anxiously hoping for follow-up interviews. Snowden then appeared before his chosen audience. Despite his request that the conference not be photographed or recorded for security reasons, five minutes later the world got to see Snowden for the first time since he arrived in Russia. In the now iconic picture taken by Lokshina, he appears to be wearing the same or a similar shirt as in Poitras' video and is in need of a haircut. He is flanked to the camera's right by his Russian interpreter as Sarah Harrison sits on his left. He thanks everyone for coming and begins his announcement.

Given everything which preceded the meeting, his statement merits full disclosure.

Hello. My name is Ed Snowden. A little over one month ago, I had family, a home in paradise, and I lived in great comfort. I also had the capability without any warrant to search for, seize, and read your communications. Anyone's communications at any time. That is the power to change people's fates.

It is also a serious violation of the law. The 4th and 5th Amendments to the Constitution of my country, Article 12 of the Universal Declaration of Human Rights, and numerous statutes and treaties forbid such systems of massive, pervasive surveillance. While the US Constitution marks these programs as illegal, my government argues that secret court rulings, which the world is not permitted to see, somehow legitimize an illegal affair. These rulings simply corrupt the most basic notion of justice—that it must be seen to be done. The immoral cannot be made moral through the use of secret law.

I believe in the principle declared at Nuremberg in 1945: "Individuals have international duties which transcend the national obligations of obedience. Therefore individual citizens have the duty to violate domestic laws to prevent crimes against peace and humanity from occurring."

Accordingly, I did what I believed right and began a campaign to correct this wrongdoing. I did not seek to enrich myself. I did not seek to sell US secrets. I did not partner with any foreign government to guarantee my safety. Instead, I took what I knew to the public, so what affects all of us can be discussed by all of us in the light of day, and I asked the world for justice.

That moral decision to tell the public about spying that affects all of us has been costly, but it was the right thing to do and I have no regrets.

Since that time, the government and intelligence services of the United States of America have attempted to make an example of me, a warning to all others who might speak out as I have. I have been made stateless and hounded for my act of political expression. The United States Government has placed me on no-fly lists. It demanded Hong Kong return me outside of the framework of its laws, in direct violation of the principle of non-refoulement—the Law of Nations. It has threatened with sanctions countries who would stand up for my human rights and the UN asylum system. It has even taken the unprecedented step of ordering military allies to ground a Latin American president's plane in search for a political refugee. These dangerous escalations represent a threat not just to the dignity of Latin America, but to the basic rights shared by every person, every nation, to live free from persecution, and to seek and enjoy asylum.

Yet even in the face of this historically disproportionate aggression, countries around the world have offered support and asylum. These nations, including Russia, Venezuela, Bolivia, Nicaragua, and Ecuador have my grati-

tude and respect for being the first to stand against human rights violations carried out by the powerful rather than the powerless. By refusing to compromise their principles in the face of intimidation, they have earned the respect of the world. It is my intention to travel to each of these countries to extend my personal thanks to their people and leaders.

I announce today my formal acceptance of all offers of support or asylum I have been extended and all others that may be offered in the future. With, for example, the grant of asylum provided by Venezuela's President Maduro, my asylee status is now formal, and no state has a basis by which to limit or interfere with my right to enjoy that asylum. As we have seen, however, some governments in Western European and North American states have demonstrated a willingness to act outside the law, and this behavior persists today. This unlawful threat makes it impossible for me to travel to Latin America and enjoy the asylum granted there in accordance with our shared rights.

This willingness by powerful states to act extra-legally represents a threat to all of us, and must not be allowed to succeed. Accordingly, I ask for your assistance in requesting guarantees of safe passage from the relevant nations in securing my travel to Latin America, as well as requesting asylum in Russia until such time as these states accede to law and my legal travel is permitted. I will be submitting my request to Russia today, and hope it will be accepted favorably.

If you have any questions, I will answer what I can. Thank you.[174]

By referencing international as well as American law, Snowden is clearly attempting to reach a global audience. His Thoreauvian citation of the Nuremberg War Crime Tribunal in 1945-6 cleverly aligns the U.S. government's dogged hunt for him with the infamous persecution of the Jews in Nazi Germany. It also implicitly alludes to a subsequent era of heightened government surveillance with East Germany's Staatssicherheit, or state security, better known as the Stasi. Though Snowden reiterates that he believes he has only broken unjust American law and not universal principle, his moral conviction is best displayed in his stated intent to one day visit the countries which have "refused to compromise their principles." He goes on to testify that his motives to whistleblow were irrefutably egalitarian because, in his words, "I did not seek to enrich myself. I did not seek to sell US secrets. I did not partner with any foreign government to guarantee my safety." He then imparts that the U.S. government's pressuring of other nations to refuse him asylum undermines international law and the countries' ability to make autonomous political decisions. By expressly commending the nations which have either aided him or offered their assistance, he subtly condemns those in the European Union for their involvement in the Morales plane incident. He appeals to have these nations conform to the international law of permitting a recognized asylee access and the freedom to enjoy the liberty he has been granted. Not surprisingly, he closes by stating his hand has been forced and he will be reapplying for Russian asylum until he is able to travel to his adopted land.

Fourteen minutes after beginning the meeting, Snowden started taking questions. Amid the awkward pauses during translation and Sheremetyevo Airport's perpetual travel announcements, he remained jovial, laughing periodically, but the stress of the situation was ever present in his voice. He graciously accepted question upon question long after declaring the G9 summit had come to a close. Conversations with various individuals included discussion of the legal technicalities of seeking and accepting asylum in multiple countries, his political affiliation, the U.S. government's hypocritical refusal to respect other nations' decisions to grant him refugee status since America is a signatory on UDHR and how Snowden viewed Washington's persecution as "purely political" and driven solely upon the desire to evoke fear in anyone who would doubt or challenge its policies.

Snowden informed the G9 gathering he had been recognized by the United Nations High Commissioner for Refugees, but, though a member, the United States did not accept the Commissioner's judgment. He reported that during a private meeting in Iceland, the U.N. secretary general, South Korean diplomat Ban Ki-moon, disagreed with Snowden's actions and was "biasing" the Federation's opinion of him. When questioned how he received the information, Snowden reported that Birgitta Jónsdóttir, a sympathetic member of the Icelandic party who had voted to put Snowden's citizenship application on the government's docket, made the report. [175] It is the U.N. agency's mandated mission to aid refugees' repatriation to their adopted country.[176] Even amid harsh criticism that its pursuit of Snowden was extreme, the U.S. government made sure its presence was known and felt. Eight minutes into the Q & A session, Lokshina told Snowden the U.S. Embassy had instructed her to relay to him it did not consider him a whistleblower and he should be "punished for breaking the law."[177] Snowden quickly countered by stating that the American populace's will was being better represented by various foreign governments because 55 percent of U.S. citizens agreed with him. The meeting had lasted 42 minutes.

Washington started to show signs it was catching on. The White House chastised Moscow for giving Snowden a "propaganda platform."[178] It is reasonably believed that the meeting was only possible through the Kremlin's guidance; otherwise the successful organization of a variety of Russian officials, attorneys and human rights groups would not have been possible on such short notice, especially in a sea of over 200 reporters.[179] The Kremlin is metaphorically and literally analogous to the American White House. It is both the residence and symbol of Russian politics.

Whereas the White House viewed Snowden's extending invitations to the human rights organizations was political innuendo that implied his innocence, its true purpose was to blur the Kremlin's role in the American exile's plight. Snowden needn't have called a conference to make the announcement he was applying for Russian asylum. He could have merely filed his paperwork as he had before. Furthermore, as one attorney pointed out during the Q & A, Snowden could not accept asylum status in multiple countries.[180] He had coincidentally found himself obligated to void all other refugee offers in order to reapply in Russia. He made sure to add, "I am only in a position to accept Russia's offer because of my inability to travel."[181]

Though it was reported he never left,[182] Snowden somehow managed to always evade the press, which perpetually swarmed Sheremetyevo Airport.[183] It was possible for him to stalk around the Mira undetected until June 9 but now the world knew what he looked like and was conducting its own surveillance. He was so much of a ghost that during the G9 meeting he was asked for an official photograph to confirm his existence in the terminal.[184] Bearing in mind the only first-hand reports that surfaced about Snowden after the conference came from Anatoly Kucherena, a Russian lawyer with Kremlin ties to whom Snowden had coincidentally extended a personal G9 invitation, unofficial sources claim he was staying in a safe house under the protection of the Federal Security Service, the successor to the KBG.[185] Kucherena is a Federal Security Service board member, agreed to process Snowden's Russian asylum paperwork *pro bono* and during this time held an office in the Kremlin.[186]

But it was unlikely the Kremlin would chance Snowden being seen outside the airport. It would give away Russia's position and violate him being permitted on Russian soil without a passport. In all likelihood, either WikiLeaks or the Kremlin was paying for him to stay in Sheremetyevo's V-Express Capsule Hotel located in the transit zone. Yet if Kucherena can be believed, he did so at great personal risk. Throughout his stay, he was supposedly without protection or additional security.[187]

The U.S. government became infuriated when it could no longer ignore the obvious. The night of the G9 meeting, Obama called Putin. The conversation ended in a stalemate with respect to the American exile.[188] Four days later, Snowden submitted his asylum application. When his paperwork was officially acknowledged by the Russian Federal Migration Service on July 24, thereby giving him license to leave the airport while his case was being decided, it was accompanied by his attorney's statement that Snowden no longer sought refuge in South America.[189] Kerry was back on the telephone with his Soviet equivalent, Sergey Lavrov,[190] and members of the Senate Appropriations Committee started preparing speeches which would result in a unanimous vote to move toward imposing sanctions on any country aiding Snowden.[191] The U.S. government and the world waited for Snowden to emerge from Sheremetyevo.

At 6 p.m. a man much larger than Snowden emerged from the transit area. It was Kucherena. He told reporters Snowden would not be leaving the airport.[192] *Der Spiegel* had run a follow-up to XKeyscore three days after Putin reiterated "any actions by [Snowden] connected with harming Russian-American relations are unacceptable."[193] Snowden had reapplied for Russian asylum the day before.

Chapter 6
From Russia, With Love

"'Where is it?' thought Raskolnikov. 'Where is it I've read that someone condemned to death says or thinks, an hour before his death, that if he had to live on some high rock, on such a narrow ledge that he'd only room to stand, and the ocean, everlasting darkness, everlasting solitude, everlasting tempest around him, if he had to remain standing on a square yard of space all his life, a thousand years, eternity, it were better to live so than to die at once!'"

–Fyodor Dostoevsky, *Crime and Punishment,* given to Snowden by his Russian attorney, Anatoly Kucherena[1]

❈ ❈ ❈

IN A POORLY TIMED, UNCREDITED ARTICLE titled, "'Prolific Partner': German Intelligence Used NSA Spy Program,"[2] *Der Spiegel* reports that the BND and Germany's domestic intelligence agency, *Bundesamt für Verfassungsschutz* or the Federal Office for the Protection of the Constitution (BfV), had been given XKeyscore by the U.S. intelligence. Its source is a 2008 classified presentation released to the German press by Poitras.

Though hardly surprising since it was revealed a month before that the NSA had provided GCHQ with PRISM, the exposé provides greater insight into the mysterious program. Using metadata, XKeyscore can "retroactively reveal any terms the target person has typed into a search engine." This includes "full-take" data which the recording of metadata is said to exclude. *Der Spiegel* relays this is of particular interest to Germans because XKeyscore was one of the primary tools used to collect the previously reported 500 million pieces of domestic information. In December 2012 alone, 180 million data captures were made. The program was first issued to the BND, which then trained the BfV to use the program. A subsequent *Der Spiegel* report would relay that the vice president of Germany's domestic intelligence agency "formally requested" the program after watching it successfully wiretap a DSL connection.[3]

Prior to discovering there was a breach of faith between the two nations' intelligence divisions as America narrowed its focus upon its U.N. colleague, in January 2013 Germany was working toward "relax[ing] [the] interpretation of the [nation's] privacy laws to provide greater opportunities of intelligence sharing" with the NSA. At the end of April, BND officials were invited to meet with NSA specialists to discuss "data acquisition" and "behavior detection."[4] The BND was already considered a "most prolific partner" to the NSA as a result of joint information gathering in Afghanistan.

The BfV, BND and NSA offered no comment.

Aside from the obvious implications of Germany's domestic intelligence agency using XKeyscore, the article verifies Snowden's previous *Der Spiegel* interview claims. Even though metadata is used to determine the need for further investigation, XKeyscore's ability to retroactively cull supposedly uncollected full-take data refutes any claims that only anonymous metadata is being gathered. The report also establishes, as with GCHQ, that the NSA sought a mutual data exchange with its German counterparts.

To make matters worse, a Brazilian periodical new to the classified disclosure field debuted a rather incriminating article three days after Russia had recognized Snowden's paperwork.

Well-meaning but under present circumstances contrary to its masthead, *Epoca* premiered "Spies of the digital age"[5] on July 27. It bears no byline by Greenwald. The exposé follows in the footsteps of *The Guardian*'s G20 report and tells the riveting tale of a 2010 U.S.-initiated U.N. sanction meeting. The topic was Iran's plan to enrich uranium on native soil. Brazil's then-president Luiz Inácio Lula da Silva courageously stepped into the crossfire and accepted the role of mediator. Because the Middle Eastern country had already broken its verbal agreement not to pursue nuclear activities, Brazil and Turkey wanted an alternative to sanctions, which would only enrage Iran. Turkey bravely offered to permit Iran to continue its nuclear research within its neighbor's borders. The logic was simple. A U.N. member could then keep an eye on Iran.

The United States was worried. The Security Council needed nine of 15 votes to pass a resolution. Russia and China threatened to veto the vote. Other nations weren't showing their cards. With a plan in place and carrying along Washington's blessing, Brazil's president traveled to Tehran to try to get then-Iranian president Mahmoud Ahmadinejad's signature promising he'd play nice.

If he refused, the argument would automatically become that there was no other choice but to instate sanctions. But the U.S. had no intention of humoring Ahmadinejad's autograph even if Brazil somehow managed to acquire it. The South American nation had been given the green light by Washington because it wanted to prolong the proceedings. While Brazil's leader was burning through political capital, America was leveraging the other nations. It was able to do so because the NSA had conducted espionage on eight U.N. members. U.S. diplomats therefore knew where their counterparts stood on the issue and had modified the debate accordingly.

Exhausted, Brazil and Turkey miraculously presented Ahmadinejad's agreement to the U.N. council. To the countries' dismay, the U.S. suddenly announced that France, Britain, Russia and China were ready to vote. The Iranian sanction resolution passed by an overwhelming margin. Only Brazil and Turkey had dissented.

Epoca had framed the NSA. Though primarily concerned with German surveillance, the July 20 *Der Spiegel* article implicated the American intelligence agency. Snowden remained ominously hidden after the reports' publication. *The Guardian* relayed that his only physical contact with the outside world was through Kucherena.[6] WikiLeaks claimed Harrison had remained by his side since his departure from Hong Kong.[7]

When entering the transit zone to meet with Snowden on July 24, Kucherena was brandishing a brown paper bag. As he left to announce that Snowden would not be leaving the airport, the bag was nowhere to be seen. When questioned, Kucherena stated he'd brought Snowden clothes, a pair of shoes and books to pass the time and gain a better understanding of the history and culture in which he had found himself. Snowden had been given Fyodor Dostoevsky's *Crime and Punishment*, the works of Anton Chekhov and Russia's history by Nikolai Karamzin.[8]

The media quickly wondered whether Kucherena was attempting to impart something to the American exile by handing him Dostoevsky's 1866 classic. It is the tale of Rodion Raskolnikov, a lowly dropout living in squalor in St. Petersburg. He kills a pawn broker who financially and emotionally preyed upon those around her. He justifies his decision using Utilitarian reasoning: The malevolence of the murder is counterbalanced by the world no longer having to suffer the pawn broker's existence and her money going to charity. The largest portion of the novel deals with Raskolnikov mentally contending with the consequences of his actions. Snowden's attorney obviously saw real-life parallels in his client.

In Kucherena's words, he had given Snowden a copy of the Russian attorney's favorite writer, Chekhov, for "dessert."[9] Chekhov is known for his short stories and plays. Though sometimes comical, they are by no means light reading. His characters are often morally ambiguous and frustratingly human. Chekhov's work could only be considered dessert because the portions are smaller than Dostoevsky's 200,000-word main course.By comparison, this text is a little over 110,000 words.

Conservative in its interpretation and novelistic in its presentation, Karamzin's history of Russia was the true literary compensation for Dostoevsky. Kucherena had only provided Snowden with an abridgment of the 12-volume collection. Within a few days, Snowden had devoured Dostoevsky and, after surveying Karamzin, asked for the historian's complete oeuvre.[10] Apparently Snowden expected to remain at Sheremetyevo for a long time.

As the world awaited Snowden's fate, former NSA director Michael Hayden presented an op-ed piece to CNN on July 24.[11] In lieu of the preceding, documented reports, he audaciously claims the location of communicants is not tracked and recorded. Hayden states, "No data mining engines or complex logarithmic tools are launched to scour the data for abstract patterns." Even though *Der Spiegel* had granted the world greater insight into the inner workings of XKeyscore only four days before, Snowden had indirectly spoken of the program's ability to do just that. He had told Appelbaum, "An analyst will get a daily (or scheduled, based on exfiltration summary) report on what changed on the system, PCAPS of leftover data that wasn't understood by the automated dissectors, and so forth." The former NSA director then contradicts himself by announcing the data which the NSA hasn't collected "lies fallow until the NSA can put a question to it based on a predicate related to terrorism and only terrorism." Interestingly, though the media attempted to discredit Snowden's credentials by labeling him a "low-level contract consultant,"[12] Hayden reports that the ability to draw up this concise data is only granted to "a little more than 20 people in the NSA." There are over 1,000 NSA employees and contractors that hold the same position Snowden did.[13] Hayden tells his readers NSA surveillance is "not about targeting Americans" but "[...] who in America deserve[s] to be targeted."

Following the tradition started by his congressional counterparts, Hayden attempts to legitimize the various American surveillance programs by reminding his audience the programs were court approved. He flippantly observes, "After all, the Supreme Court had determined decades earlier (Smith v. Maryland, 1979) that metadata carried no expectations of privacy." He goes on to quote Steve Bradbury, former head of the Justice Department's Office of Legal Counsel, "At least 14 federal judges have approved the NSA's acquisition of this data every

90 days since 2006 under the business records provision of the Foreign Intelligence Surveillance Act (FISA)." Hayden, like many of his political peers since June 5, assumed his audience hadn't grown tired of the fallacy that an action's justifiability is determined by its ability to win a majority vote, the best historic example being American slave laws.

On July 31, the U.S. government set out to rectify some of the damage its reputation had incurred. In Washington, Clapper—20 years ahead of schedule—declassified the first half of the previously leaked FISC order demanding telecommunication providers turn over metadata records. He also disclosed two letters, dated 2009 and 2011, addressed to various intelligence committee members concerning the use of bulk surveillance.[14] Clapper was trying to absolve himself of responsibility by releasing the letters and incriminating members of Congress. They ask congressional heads of intelligence to inform their peers that information pertaining to government surveillance was available for review for a limited time. There is no evidence the messages were forwarded, as witnessed on June 11 at the close of an emergency congressional briefing after the first disclosures had premiered. Leaving the meeting, Representative Bill Pascrell stated, "There was a letter that we were supposed to have received in 2011 but I can't find it and most of my friends in Congress did not receive this either."[15] Clapper had declassified the documents amid a Senate Judiciary Committee hearing which established that only one terror plot, not 54 as had been previously reported, were foiled using current surveillance methods. During the proceedings, Senator Charles Grassley reprimanded General Clapper for having lied to Congress in the March 2013 hearing when he unequivocally answered "No sir" to the question "Does the NSA collect any type of data at all on millions or hundreds of millions of Americans?" Grassley declared, "Nothing can excuse this kind of behavior from a senior administration official of any administration, especially on matters of such grave importance."[16]

While Clapper sat before Congress, the person who famously queried, "Why can't we collect all the signals all the time?" tried appeasing a younger crowd. NSA Director Keith Alexander was the keynote speaker at Black Hat USA 2013 in Las Vegas. Black Hat is a yearly IT security convention. Alexander assumed his techie audience wouldn't be familiar with Freud and attempted to convince the attendees that NSA analysts play the same role as civilian IT technicians. He was met by jeers and demands for him to read the United States Constitution.[17]

Somewhat surprisingly since Snowden's fate could hang in the balance, the same day Greenwald presented "XKeyscore: NSA tool collects 'nearly everything a user does on the internet.'"[18] Greenwald does nothing short of put the first nail in the surveillance debate's coffin.

It begins, "A top secret National Security Agency program allows analysts to search with no prior authorization through vast databases containing emails, online chats and the browsing histories of millions of individuals." Greenwald dubiously adds, "according to documents provided by whistleblower Edward Snowden." The documentation includes 32 PowerPoint training slides. The NSA accomplishes this by using, in the agency's terms, its "widest reaching" tool for surveillance, XKeyscore. Greenwald reports that the program's capabilities are much more expansive than had been previously revealed. They include the ability to search by "name, telephone number, IP address, keywords, [...]" and even the type of browser used. The results of the query are staggering. XKeyscore can produce "every email address seen in a session by both username and domain," "every phone number seen in a session (e.g., address book entries or signature block [automatic signatures placed at the bottom of a email])" and "webmail and chat activity, [...] username, buddylist, machine specific cookies [which house IP logs] etc." XKeyscore's reach is near absolute.

The program "searches [the] bodies of emails, webpages and documents," including the "To, From, CC, BCC lines" as well as 'Contact Us' pages on websites." By utilizing a tool called "Presenter," an analyst can freely read Facebook chats or private messages. This is as simple as entering a user's Facebook name and listing a date range for the desired online conversations. An analyst can even investigate what terms have been entered into a search engine and the locations a person has explored using Google Maps. In the NSA's assessment, XKeyscore allows access to "nearly everything a typical user does on the internet." The slides boast of "provid[ing] real-time target activity" which alerts analysts to new online activity conducted by a target. Analysts are told to be on the lookout for people "searching the web for suspicious stuff." After "suspicious stuff" is detected, XKeyscore is used to reveal who has visited a particular website by accessing the website's IP cookie address catalog. One training prompt dauntingly asks for XKeyscore to "Show me all the exploitable machines in country X."

As an example of the program's prowess, when an analyst queries a person's email, XKeyscore brings up everything that has been collected, and the analyst can then pick which emails to read. The available information includes "communications that transit the United States and communications that terminate in the United States." In other words, the surveillance tool gathers any communications that travel through American networks. Accompanying documentation shows XKeyscore is positioned in Washington State, Texas and the upper northeast, presumably New York.

In order to retroactively access this data, the NSA must record and index the World Wide Web's "raw unselected bulk traffic" flow. Poitras would later add that it does this using "DeepDive" buffer technology. This slows down Internet connections so data captures can be made more easily.[19] The classified slides relay that up to two billion records are added daily. During one month in 2008, XKeyscore had vacuumed up nearly 42 billion live, full-take records. By 2012, an average of 150 bits of data for every Internet user in America was stored in the NSA's 30-day buffer. Confirming Snowden's previous *Der Spiegel* statement, XKeyscore has "customizable storage times."

Targeting takes places using templated forms that permit an analyst to select justification from a simple dropdown menu. Analysts are allowed to pick from several choices, including "Phone number country code indicates person is located outside the U.S.," "Phone number is registered in a country other than the U.S." and the easiest alibi for an inquiry, "In direct contact w/tgt [target] overseas, no info to show proposed tgt in U.S." As Greenwald makes clear, after an analyst hits "send," the NSA employee does not have to wait for an FISC order or even in-house clearance before proceeding with the investigation. The only time a request is reviewed is after the fact should an audit take place. But, as Snowden informed his journalistic team in Hong Kong, "It's very rare to be questioned on our searches and even when we are, it's usually along the lines of 'Let's bulk up the justification.'" Using typical linguistic ambiguity, the NSA's official statement regarding Greenwald's report was, "Every search by an NSA analyst *is* [my emphasis] fully auditable," not that searches were regularly audited in much the same manner a person *can* take a walk every day not necessitating the individual actually does.

The documentation substantiates Greenwald's June 20 warrantless data acquisition exposé as well as *The Guardian's* July 11 Microsoft encryption report. Just as American citizen Bob's foreign telephone is cause for an investigation, XKeyscore analysts are told to be mindful of "someone who is using encryption." An example prompt also tells the program, "Show me all the VPN [virtual private network] startups in country X, and give me the data so I can decrypt and discover the users." A VPN is often used for security purposes and grants the user the theoretical safety of a private network while permitting data to travel freely over the Internet. VPN's are frequently utilized by corporate personnel to keep confidential business information out of a competitor's grasp.

XKeyscore also validates one of the whistleblower's most controversial statements. On June 9, Snowden told the world, "Not all analysts have the ability to target everything, but I, sitting at my desk, certainly had the authorities to wiretap anyone from you or your accountant, to a federal judge, to even the President if I had a personal e-mail." A week before Greenwald's XKeyscore article premiered, Hayden stated in his op-ed, "To be sure, Snowden was reaching for dramatic effect, but if his words were true, he would have been violating not only the laws of the United States, he would also have been violating the laws of physics. He had neither the authority nor the ability to do what he has claimed he could do." Nine days after Snowden had made his dubious announcement, Alexander met with members of Congress to discuss the NSA's surveillance programs. When asked the leaning question by Chairman of the House Intelligence Committee Mike Rogers, "So the technology does not exist for any individual or group of individuals at the NSA to flip a switch, to listen to American's phone calls or read their emails?" Alexander replied, "That is correct."[20] This is the same senator who, on October 3 during the 2013 Cybersecurity Summit, joked with Hayden about placing Snowden on an assassination list.[21]

Pundits had focused upon what they considered the highly dubious claim by Snowden. Now they had proof. However, in the last line of his live June 17 chat, Snowden substantiated why he would need a letter to spy on the president, "The US Person / foreigner distinction is not a reasonable substitute for individualized suspicion, and is only applied to improve support for the program. This is the precise reason that NSA provides Congress with a special immunity to its surveillance."[22] Obviously, a warrant is required to spy upon anyone in the White House or Capitol Hill because the intelligence community considers such data "in-house." Everyone else is fair game.

Though it was known Germany had been given XKeyscore, the classified certification listed at the bottom of each slide grants the other Four Eyes permission to view the contents of the PowerPoint presentation. It is less obvious but nonetheless apparent that XKeyscore's point-and-click dropdown menu was created for convenience and expediency but serves a greater internal purpose. Its design subtly imparts to analysts that nothing is legally amiss in what they are doing. The ease and speed to proceed with an investigation in lieu of a court order implies an analyst's activities are being automatically processed and therefore are lawful and freely permitted. (Staff morale is perhaps the reason the PowerPoint pauses to announce "300 terrorists captured using intelligence generated from XKEYSCORE.") Yet the choices an analyst is given to validate an inquiry are so broad, when placed alongside the grossly nondescript justification "suspicious stuff" being cause for alarm, almost any reason that can be articulated complies with NSA policy. For example, because terrorists want knowledge of the inner workings of the NSA, after criminal justice major Bob clicks on nsa.gov while researching a class project, he is a legitimate target once the analyst chooses XKeyscore's option of "no info to show proposed tgt in U.S." Under NSA policy, since Bob is now a target, all of Bob's Facebook friends and email contacts (first hop) and subsequently his friend's friends (second hop) are under surveillance.

After waking up the world by exposing PRISM, Greenwald dispensed piecemeal disclosures to counter each progressive refutation by Washington that it was not committing invasive privacy violations. With each report, he further restricted the U.S. government's argumentative wiggle room. Aided by a global editorial team, he gradually built up his case while taking the time to show that the surveillance abuses were not exclusive to the United States. But Greenwald had saved the best for last. After proving Washington had cleverly given itself the legal authority to domestically spy under the ruse of foreign targeting protocols, he established that it also had the technological capability to do so. It was his most condemning exposé to date. The only thing left to prove was that the technological capability was being abused.

During Washington's July 31 public relations effort, Hayden appeared on CNN. When Erin Burnett asked about Greenwald's XKeyscore report, "So you're [Hayden] saying they [NSA analysts] can search through any given civilian ...

the text, the databases, the email searches, the internet searches, all those things [to] find that needle in the haystack," a notably flustered Hayden reluctantly grumbled, "Yes."[23]

As with the meticulous timing of most every report, Greenwald knew Washington was sending out its best to help curb the world's discontent with U.S. intelligence programs. *The Guardian* released Greenwald's story on Wednesday morning. Even if the various government representatives compensated for XKeyscore by quickly editing what they were planning to say, their mere presence put a bad taste in the audiences' mouths, especially after the same audiences had just finished reading Greenwald's headline piece. Still, those familiar with Snowden's plight could not help but wonder about the journalist's poor timing. He had even made a point to specifically name Snowden as the responsible party.

The appearance of Greenwald's report could be read in two ways. Snowden had either told the journalist the two of them had nothing to fear because he was about to be granted Russian asylum, or all hope was lost because he'd been informed that his application was going to be denied and he was about to be deported. Though Greenwald had been delicate with what information he released and was conscientious about when he released it, Snowden not taking advantage of his newfound freedom after the Russian Federal Migration Service recognized his paperwork signaled something was wrong. Another ominous sign was Lon Snowden had given up hope of visiting his son in Russia.

Snowden's father had been reticent to speak to the press after he and the world learned that his son was the one responsible for the NSA disclosures. By June 17, Eric Bolling of Fox News had convinced Lon to conduct an exclusive interview.[24] This was "after days of talking, emailing, and texting," once Snowden's father had "[...] reached out to someone in [Washington] D.C. whom he trusted." That person, in Bolling's words, "happen[ed] to trust me."

From the commencement of the dialogue, it is clear Edward inherited his linguistic dexterity. Lon speaks of "political discourse" and reports that the last time he saw his son was "in the shadow of the National Security Agency" on April 4. He exhibits a familiarity with law, incorporating the frequently heard legalese defense "I can't speak to that" when asked if Edward had broken the law. Like his son, Lon is a thinker.

Even though he is Edward's father, Lon refuses to produce a blanket defense for his son's actions. Lon announces he "served [the] nation for over 30 years honorably" and admits "that's [stealing classified data] not something I could have done" but adds, "I'm not in Ed's shoes." He judiciously states because he is not aware of what Edward saw or experienced, he cannot rightly pass judgment.

Lon acknowledges that a distinct line between right and wrong does not exist as he nonetheless stands on principle. The audience comes to understand where Edward derived his ethical sensibilities. Lon eloquently reports that his son had been confronted by what he viewed to be a "moral hazard," the conflict between Edward's oath to guard national security while simultaneously respecting the tenants of the Fourth Amendment.

Lon states he personally does not "want the government listening to my phone calls, I don't want the government archiving the places that my other children visit on the internet [...]. I don't want them reading my email. I don't want them reading my texts," even under the guise of "we need to keep you safe." He offers the analogy of the NSA's snooping being akin to the government walking up to a person's mailbox, nonchalantly opening an individual's mail, looking and copying the contents "in case you do something wrong sometime in the future" and resealing the envelopes before putting them back as if nothing happened.

Despite his intellectual acumen, it is painfully clear he is outside his element. Lon plays directly into the hands of the media. He instantly becomes a clichéd caricature of the bereaved parent. Less a minute into the interview, he is brandishing a childhood photo of Edward. It is obvious he does not possess his son's sociopolitical understanding of the media. Lon placates Bolling and makes an appeal directly into the camera. He asks his son not to release any more classified information for fear of being accused of treason, a concern a former military employee has been trained to dread. He declares, "I would rather my son be a prisoner in the U.S. than a free man in a country that did not have the freedoms that are protected, that we have." Lon would have many more opportunities to get a handle on the media and the political maelstrom that had engulfed his boy.

Lon proceeded to search for a legal defense team in case Edward was apprehended. He also wanted to contact and possibly travel to meet his son. Famed Washington attorney and former assistant deputy attorney general under Ronald Reagan, Bruce Fein, offered his services for free. Fein's interest in the Snowden affair was a supposed matter of principle. As part of the Reagan administration, he followed the "fundamental premise of who we are as a people—the right to be left alone."[25]

Less than two weeks later, on Lon's behalf, Fein presented a letter to Attorney General Holder.[26] It outlines terms Lon purportedly believed would goad Edward to return to the U.S. on his own volition and stand trial. Three extremely idealistic provisions are cited.

1. He [Edward Snowden] would not be detained or imprisoned prior to trial.

2. He would not be subject to a gag order.

3. He would be tried in a venue of his choosing.

The request asks that these guarantees be made and should any of them not be honored, Snowden's case would be "dismissed without prejudice." Fein failed to punctuate the last sentence.

The next day, June 28, Lon appeared on the *TODAY*[27] program on NBC. During the interview with Michael Isikoff, Lon inadvertently creates a divide between his son's supporters. He doubts the sincerity of WikiLeaks' interest in his son, stating the anti-secrecy group's agenda was not to uphold the Constitution but to "release as much information as possible."

It is obvious Lon had not yet been in contact with Edward, otherwise he might have been more reluctant to pass judgment on the organization that had recently pulled strings to get his son to safety.

It is possible the former warrant officer had spent a long 11 days meditating upon Edward's predicament and come to a handful of conclusions, but later evidence suggests Fein was already directing Lon's media approach. Whereas he had been reserved and indisposed to pass judgment on June 17, Lon now declared his son, "[...] has in fact broken U.S. law, in the sense that he has released classified information. And if folks want to classify him as a traitor, in fact he has betrayed his government. But I don't believe that he's betrayed the people of the United States."

That weekend, Assange personally contacted Fein. WikiLeaks' founder relayed a message from Edward, asking that Fein and Lon refrain from commenting on matters pertaining to him.[28] A month and a half later, Snowden would provide a definitive 170-word statement to *The Huffington Post*, declaring that neither Fein, his wife (a politician and business partner to Fein) or his father spoke for or represented him.[29]

Undeterred by the whistleblower's polite demand, Fein published an open letter[30] to Edward on July 2. Fein's verbose address is less a note of support than a platform the Washington attorney uses to project his political philosophy. He alludes to American revolutionary Thomas Paine, makes a pained reference to 18th-century German philosophy, and speaks of the "vicissitudes" of life and Clapper's "stupendous mendacity" before addressing Edward's "reduction to *de facto* statelessness." It is unclear who he believes his audience to be. He tells Snowden, "You have forced onto the national agenda the question of whether the American people prefer the right to be left alone from government snooping absent probable cause to believe crime is afoot to vassalage in hopes of a risk-free existence." He closes by modestly announcing, "[...] [W]e will be unflagging in efforts to educate the American people about the impending ruination of the Constitution [...]."

175

Fein informed the website *Politico* that he'd posted the letter online because Lon was unable to contact his son directly.[31] The statement brings into question Fein's interest in Lon. If the letter was solely meant to be a personal address to Edward, Fein had a channel to Assange. Centered at the top of both letters, the address and telephone number of Fein's legal firm rests above his personal email address.

On July 26 two things became clear. Lon's abruptly aggressive approach to the media had been at Fein's instruction, and Edward's father realized he'd lost control of the situation. This is apparent in the third chapter of Fein's letter-writing campaign[32]—to none other than the president—and Lon's trio of complementary interviews.

Fein's presidential missive is propaganda thinly disguised as a "concerned citizen" letter. He does nothing short of accuse Obama of committing evil acts before arriving at his second paragraph: "You are acutely aware that the history of liberty is a history of civil disobedience to unjust laws or practices. As [18th-century philosopher and politician] Edmund Burke sermonized, 'All that is necessary for the triumph of evil is that good men do nothing.'" Fein proceeds to dig the hole deeper. While providing an account of civil disobedience, he quotes Thoreau's titular essay and cites the Nuremberg Trials before making the—if not politically incorrect, at least embarrassing—mistake of including slavery as another example. Granted, it is a fine illustration of corrupt, unjust law, but presenting it to an African-American as well as highlighting it by devoting a single-line paragraph to the subject is nothing short of exploiting the reader's ethnicity in hopes of evoking empathy. Fein would go on to quote Martin Luther King, Jr., while plagiarizing portions of his letter to Holder.

Referring to himself in the third person even though he is credited as the author, Fein proceeds to condemn Obama's congressional members who have deemed Edward a "traitor" before he has been placed on trial, cites the Morales plane incident, observes that Snowden had effected the change Obama promised but failed to deliver, and proclaims the president "belatedly and cynically embraced" a national debate only after Edward left him no other choice. He closes by "urg[ing]" the president "to order the Attorney General to move to dismiss the outstanding criminal complaint against Edward."

In the process, Fein makes an eyebrow-raising note: "Since 2005, Mr. Snowden had been employed by the intelligence community." Fein could have misheard his client's timeline of Edward's life, or Lon could be vague on matters which took place almost a decade before, but the disclosure accounts for Snowden's first "dark year" and suggests his entry into American intelligence started at least five months before it was initially reported.

Lon returned to speak on *TODAY*.[33] He had figured out that Fein scheduled the talks to correspond with letter releases. (In a July 1 telephone interview[34] with Ralph Hallow of *The Washington Times*, Lon said he was shocked to discover the media had copies of his attorney's letter to Holder. The State Department did not want to give any unnecessary air time to the issue, which left the Washington attorney as the likely culprit, especially once Fein's letter to the president was placed online.) Though Fein appears alongside him, Lon shifts gears. Asked by Matt Lauer if he believes WikiLeaks was exploiting Edward, Lon replies, "I'm thankful for anybody who is providing him with assistance." He had also taken the time to educate himself in matters pertaining to national security. While Fein, in his own words, attempted to repeatedly "interject," Lon mentions Rogers, Wyden, King, Feinstein and Clapper. He makes the astute observation that defense contractors lobby and donate to politicians, thereby influencing and buying support for surveillance programs where it might not otherwise exist. In the process, he quotes his son: "I've watched closely the balance of the 36 members on the two intelligence committees within Congress, particularly the House. And the American people don't know the full truth, but the truth is coming."

By the end of the month, Lon had grown wise to the stringent sociopolitical atmosphere, media and Fein. Though slightly

177

evident in telephone interviews he conducted with the *Associated Press*[35] the day of his second *TODAY* chat and earlier with Ralph Hallow—and to a lesser extent during a brief discussion[36] with Anderson Cooper on July 29—Lon admitted he'd undergone "intellectual evolution" and had an "epiphany" since June. On July 30 Lon took center stage.

In the interview[37] where he would incorrectly recall that Edward started working in American intelligence in 2003, *The Washington Post's* affable reporter Jerry Markon asks questions while the infamously talkative Fein sits idly by.[38] Lon announces he'd rejected the FBI's offer to send him to Russia to see his son, because the agency could not guarantee the two would meet. Edward's father shrewdly responded, telling the intelligence bureau, "Wait a minute, folks, I'm not going to sit on the tarmac to be an emotional tool for you." When asked how Edward's patriotic upbringing had ultimately manifested itself, Lon makes an about-face from his admission on NBC a month before. He was now "[…] absolutely thankful for what he [Edward] did." He states that his son's devotion to his country is evident by the actions he'd taken. The greatest revelation for the 30-year military officer was that he'd recognized the political reality Edward was facing. Lon no longer wanted his son to return to America: "If he comes back to the United States he is going to be treated horribly. He is going to be thrown into a hole. He is not going to be allowed to speak." He goes on to say the jury pool had been "poisoned" because the charges arose from the hub of national intelligence, Alexandria, Virginia, where a person could not "throw a rock without hitting a defense contractor." Edward's father ends by declaring, "He [Edward] knows he has done the right thing." The duo sat down with Jake Tapper on CNN's *The Lead* the same day. Lon expressed many of the same opinions.

Then something strange happened. On the day Greenwald's masterpiece debuted, July 31, Lon appeared on Russia's Rossiya 24 news channel via the network's station in Washington. He thanked Putin, the Kremlin and the people of Russia for keeping his son safe.[39] The reason the FBI wanted

Lon to be waiting on the tarmac for Edward instead of merely walking into Sheremetyevo where his son would be sitting is the same reason Greenwald had taken the liberty of publishing his coup de grâce XKeyscore exposé. The FBI couldn't guarantee the two would meet because Edward would be leaving the airport. Lon knew this because Kucherena had contacted him earlier that morning.[40]

Snowden was granted Russian asylum the next day.

All the indications had been there. Greenwald's suddenly publishing after an unprecedented furlough of silence despite Putin's warning and Lon's slip of the tongue on national television made it obvious the FBI knew—probably through surveillance Russia deliberately made readily available—that Snowden was about to be a free man, as did Snowden, who had given Greenwald the green light. The press even found it suspicious the U.S. government did not have advance notice of Snowden's impending freedom as it later pushed the White House on the issue.[41] It had been no coincidence that one of the pieces of reading material Kucherena left with Snowden on July 24 was an alphabet book: The American needed to begin learning Russian. The same day, Snowden's attorney told Rossiya 24 his client intended to settle in Russia.[42] Less than a week after Snowden had submitted his second Russian asylum request, Andrey Pilipchuk, representative for Russia's Interior Ministry, made a point to tell the press, "[Russian] [l]aw agencies asked the US on many occasions to extradite wanted criminals through Interpol channels, but those requests were neither met nor even responded to."[43] As with China and Ecuador, America expected a favor despite a history of being unwilling to do what was being asked by other nations.

The plan had worked perfectly despite the *Der Spiegel* and *Epoca* staffs' publication faux pas. Kucherena announced Russia had consented to the fact Snowden could not control what journalists did with material previously handed to them.[44] Snowden had told his editorial entourage to keep quiet to make the show convincing. Through it all, Russian officials reassured the world that Snowden's appearance had been happenstance.

Long before August 1 arrived, Putin's denial of interest in Snowden had become redundant to the point of parody. He'd informed a group of geology students on July 15, "He [Snowden] arrived on our territory without an invitation, we did not invite him. And indeed, he wasn't coming here; he was in transit to other nations. But as soon as he was in the air, it became known, and our American partners essentially blocked him from traveling further. They scared all the other countries and essentially blocked him into our territory themselves. A Christmas gift, you could say."[45] Putin let it be known that the U.S. had inadvertently positioned and kept its exile in a country without an American extradition treaty by first revoking his passport then prohibiting other nations from letting him leave Russia. Whereas passport nullification was to be expected, America penning him in Russia was the true Christmas present for both the former Soviet Union and Snowden. For good measure, Putin told the geology collective, "[...] as soon as there is some kind of opportunity to move on, I hope he will do so."[46] Furthermore, the Russian Federation had not issued him a passport along with his asylum certificate, so while he was free to roam Russia, he could not leave the country.[47] When it was made public at the end of the month that Snowden had been in contact with Russia while in Hong Kong, Kucherena automatically refuted the claim.[48] Less than a week later, Putin came clean and admitted Russian diplomats had been speaking with the whistleblower long before he boarded Aeroflot SU213.[49]

The masterstroke of Snowden's eventual entry into Russia was the revocation of his first asylum petition in feigned protest to Putin's refusal to tolerate further U.S. harm at the whistleblower's hands. The dirty little secret is he couldn't have released any information even if he wanted: He had given all his files to Poitras and Greenwald back in Hong Kong.[50] The pause before granting him asylum had given other nations the opportunity to first declare that Snowden's actions were justifiable, therefore lending credence to Russia's decision to do the same. Washington had done the former Soviet Union a favor by making a show over the whole of Europe a little over a week later. Through exquisite planning, reasonable expectation and helpful coincidence, Snowden and Russia could have hardly made it more convincing that neither party had a choice but to let him stay where he was. But the U.S. government had made one other mistake which all but absolved Russia of responsibility.

In his asylum request to Ecuador, Snowden stated, "Also, prominent members of Congress and others in the media have accused me of being a traitor and have called for me to be jailed or executed as a result of having communicated this information to the public." He adds, "My case is also very similar to that of the American soldier Bradley Manning, who made public government information through WikiLeaks revealing war crimes, was arrested by the United States government and has been treated inhumanely during his time in prison. He was put in solitary confinement before his trial and the U.N. anti-torture representative judged that Mr. Manning was submitted to cruel and inhumane acts by the United States government." In his conclusion, he reiterates and emphasizes, "I believe that, given these circumstances, it is unlikely that I would receive a fair trial or proper treatment prior to that trial, and face the possibility of life in prison or even death."[51] His Nicaraguan asylum bid is almost verbatim.[52]

Snowden and his legal advisors knew most countries were sympathetic to refugees who voiced concern that they might be confronted with death if returned to their abandoned nation. The United Nations High Commissioner for Refugees mandates, "Where a threat to the life and/or personal safety or other fundamental human rights guarantees of a refugee exists, resettlement may be the only solution."[53]

Though he had not been accused of committing a capital offense and was facing only 30 years based on the three charges brought against him, the United States retained the right to indict him on additional charges.[54] The possibility remained that Snowden might be cited for treason. Under United States law, the maximum penalty for treason is death.[55] The U.S. government's mistake was it did not declare that the charges had been finalized. It did not help that Snowden's specified fear of abuse and mistreatment was well founded on very recent events in a case not unlike his own. Countries were also having difficulty issuing benefit of the doubt to the United States government. They had recently witnessed the extent to which Washington was willing to go in hopes of capturing Snowden. The media had also been quick in pointing out that the Obama administration appeared to have an unprecedented vendetta against whistleblowers who leaked classified data to the press. Snowden's lawsuit was the seventh in the five years Obama had been in office. Before him, only three people had been arraigned in the whole of American history.[56]

Thirty-nine days after filing charges against Snowden, 23 days after he'd applied for asylum in over 20 countries and 17 days after his first refugee requests were honored, the U.S. still left open the option of the death penalty. The irony was that Washington could see the specific terms of Snowden's appeals. Ecuador had released his asylum request to the press on June 24.[57] Only a week after he'd reapplied for Russian asylum did the U.S. inform Russia it would not pursue capital punishment if Snowden was turned over.[58] Stunningly, Washington's letter[59] to Russia all but admits the U.S. government intended to charge Snowden with treason. It states that the U.S. court system "would not seek the death penalty even if Mr. Snowden were charged with additional, death penalty-eligible crimes." Included in the appeal is a somewhat sardonic but nonetheless desperate attempt to discredit Snowden: "We understand from press reports and prior conversations between our governments that Mr. Snowden believes that he is unable to travel out of Russia and must therefore take steps to legalize his status. That is not accurate; he is able to travel. […] He is eligible for a limited validity passport good for direct return to the United States." The letter subtly acknowledges that the Justice Department had finally caught onto Russia's game: "We believe that these assurances eliminate these asserted grounds for Mr. Snowden's claim that he should be treated as a refugee or granted asylum, temporary or otherwise." Snowden was not seeking political but temporary asylum. Doing so expedited his claim and made Putin exempt from blame. Temporary asylum requests only require the approval of the Russian Federal Migration Service, not the signature of the Russian president.[60] As a temporary refugee he would be permitted to remain in Russia for a year, but his status could be extended indefinitely.[61]

But Washington's assurances came too late. Maduro had already set the precedent. He implied he was saving the American exile's life by granting him "humanitarian asylum" instead of political refuge.[62] The speaker of Russian Parliament, Sergei Naryshkin, explicitly stated that Snowden needed a safe haven to avoid the death penalty.[63]

It remains unclear why Snowden remained in Sheremetyevo International Airport after July 24. When he did not exit the airport with Kucherena on the evening of July 24, the Russian attorney told reporters Snowden's paperwork "was not a standard process" and was still being considered.[64] But law enforcement and airport officials stated he had received his Russian Federal Migration Service asylum recognition certificate that permitted him to pass through border control. Interfax had even reported that Snowden presented the document to border control.[65] Vladimir Volokh, former head of Russian Immigration Services, announced on July 23 that even if a certificate were to be issued, though Snowden had the right to move freely throughout the country, there would be safety concerns.[66] Russia had instructed Snowden to remain in the airport for three reasons. One, it did not want to be held accountable if something were to happen to Snowden, especially on Russian soil, before he'd been granted asylum. Two, the airport had proven safe for the last 31 days. Three, the former Soviet Union did not want to appear as if it was handing Snowden his freedom immediately after acknowledging his asylum application.

On Thursday afternoon,[67] August 1 at 3:30 p.m., after 38 days in Russian limbo, Snowden left the airport. He got into a taxi[68] and was escorted to a secure location inside Russia where he would live with other American expatriates.[69] Though the gesture would have been largely symbolic due to obvious travel difficulties, because he did not go directly to the Venezuelan Embassy, renounce his Russian asylum status and—similar to Assange—remain at the consulate until he had been acknowledged as a South American refugee, it was clear he intended to remain in Russia. In much the same manner that Fein would continue to question the integrity of Snowden's editorial connections,[70] Kucherena persistently refuted WikiLeaks' claims of the organization's physical proximity to Snowden. WikiLeaks implied Harrison had stayed in Sheremetyevo with Snowden after the G9 meeting.[71] (In Kucherena's defense, unlike his flight to and arrival in Russia, there were no status updates regarding Snowden's welfare during this time period on WikiLeaks' characteristically loquacious Twitter account.)[72] WikiLeaks also reported that Harrison entered the cab with him.[73] Kucherena said Snowden left by himself.[74] The bickering remained between the various parties. Snowden later announced he had no conflicts with any of the journalists or legal personnel who had and were continuing to help him.[75]

What is irrefutable is that little is known about his time in Russia. Aside from WikiLeaks posting his statement about receiving Russian asylum 30 minutes after he left the airport, "Over the past eight weeks we have seen the Obama administration show no respect for international or domestic law, but in the end the law is winning. I thank the Russian Federation for granting me asylum in accordance with its laws and international obligations."[76]—amid brief communications with the press and various foreign nations—Snowden summarily disappeared into the deep recesses of the former Soviet Union.

He had gotten his wish. He had finally removed himself from the media spotlight and left the intelligence disclosures in his wake. In less than six weeks, a multitude of sources, both new and old, would file over two dozen original reports revealing classified data Snowden had liberated. Donning disguises, he purportedly walks undetected amongst the people whose daily lives had been consumed by stories of their adopted American brother.[77]

Chapter 7
Black Rain

"The immoral cannot be made moral through the use of secret law."

–Edward Snowden, public statement made during the G9 meeting, July 12, 2013[1]

The fallout was catastrophic, but it could have all been avoided if it hadn't been for seven people.

After declaring on July 19, "We [the White House] call on the Russian government to cease its campaign of pressure against individuals and groups seeking to expose corruption, and to ensure that the universal human rights and fundamental freedoms of all of its citizens, including the freedoms of speech and assembly, are protected and respected,"[2] Press Secretary Jay Carney produced the U.S. government's first official response to Snowden's asylum shortly after Russia granted the whistleblower his freedom. Washington's fatigue and exasperation was obvious. Carney issued the subdued statement, "[...] we are extremely disappointed by this decision by Russian authorities" before glibly inserting, "This move by the Russian government undermines a longstanding record of law enforcement cooperation."[3]

Various U.S. senators went on record. Charles Schumer announced, "Russia has stabbed us in the back." Former presidential candidate John McCain proclaimed, "We cannot allow today's action by Putin to stand without serious repercussions." Lindsey Graham stood by his previous call to boycott the 2014 Winter Olympics in Sochi, Russia, if Snowden wasn't returned to the United States.[4] The latter two congressmen also suggested ignoring America's nuclear disarmament agreement with Russia.[5] They called for the completion of the last phase of America's European missile-defense program. In anticipation of Russia providing Snowden safe harbor,[6] several politicians had already begun to pressure the president[7] to cancel his meeting with Putin, which was scheduled to take place before the commencement of the G20 Summit in Moscow on September 5 in Saint Petersburg. Carney reported that the White House was now "evaluating the utility" of a pre-summit conversation.

The U.S. government immediately set out to engage in damage control as it had attempted but failed to do the day before.

Hours after news agencies across the globe started reporting Snowden had been granted asylum, CNN announced[8] the U.S. would be—in an "unprecedented" move—closing 22 embassies and consulates on August 4. Two days later, the motive for the security precaution was unveiled. U.S. intelligence had intercepted a message by senior-level al-Qaeda operatives which suggested a planned attack.[9] CNN obliged the Obama administration's request not to broadcast any further details concerning the matter due to "the sensitivity of the information."[10]

National Security Analyst Peter Bergen and Bailey Cahall, a research associate at the New America Foundation (where Bergen is a director), offered a reason for the heightened security alert in their op-ed CNN piece, "What's behind the timing of the terror threat."[11] They state that it is the date, August 4, which—in the authors' determination—is "seen by al Qaeda's would-be martyrs as a particularly auspicious day to die." This is because August 4 is when the holiest of holy days, Laylat al-Qadr or the "Night of Destiny" during Islam's hallowed month, Ramadan, would take place in 2013. A photographic history of attacks by Islamic extremists accompanies the report. It includes attacks which took place on February 1, 2013; September 11, 2012; September 13, 2011; April 5, 2010; September 17, 2008; July 9, 2008; January 12, 2007; September 12, 2006; March 2, 2006; December 7, 2004; February 28, 2003; October 13, 2002; June 14, 2002; March 20, 2002; January 22, 2002;

and August 6, 1998. Within the article, Bergen and Cahall add that in 2000, during that year's Night of Destiny, al-Qaeda factions tried to bomb the *USS The Sullivans* on January 3 and failed. However, on October 12 of the same year, al-Qaeda succeeded in destroying the *USS Cole*. The co-authors list the Riyadh U.S Embassy attack on May 12, 2003, as well as the violence that erupted at the Jeddah Consulate on December 6, 2004, which ended in what the CNN reporters catalog as five (actually nine)[12] deaths. Their editorial also includes the first attempt to destroy the embassy in Yemen on March 18, 2008.

But there is a problem with the headline. Just one of Bergen and Cahall's 21 cited examples took place within the corresponding dates of Ramadan for the representative year: the September 17, 2008 attack upon the U.S. Embassy in Yemen. September 11, 2001 didn't even occur within the confines of the Islamic holy month.

The answer as to why two noted experts on the Middle East, specifically al Qaeda, representing one of the world's leading news sources produced such a highly suggestive and misleading report is found in CNN's agreement not to provide further details about the alert. The U.S. government was wagging the dog. Instead of a media blackout, which prohibits specific topics from being broadcast or discussed in the news, the White House instigated a whiteout. Like the blinding weather conditions for which it is named, the Obama administration hoped to suffocate Snowden-related headlines to distract from its failure to capture and try the American exile. Not only had three countries implied the whistleblower's actions were justified by granting him asylum, but Russia had taken a definitive stand by issuing Snowden asylum and providing him a home.

Washington's primary concern wasn't that a Quinnipiac poll conducted in the last three days and released when Snowden was granted Russian asylum showed 55 percent of American voters labeled Snowden a "whistleblower" as opposed to 34 percent which considered him a "traitor."[13] The U.S. government's fear was that the number might grow. *The*

Huffington Post had published a study in June that found that the more educated a person is in relation to Snowden's case, the greater the likelihood the former statistic will rise, "[Those] paying the most attention to the leak story were more likely to say they thought Snowden had done the right thing" and "Among those who said they had 'heard a lot' about the story, 50 percent said that they thought Snowden had done the right thing, and 34 percent said he had done the wrong thing."[14]

The Capitol was simultaneously distracting the public and undermining the NSA leaker's character and impact. Without once mentioning his name, Bergen and Cahall's story relates— but by no means gives free air time—to Snowden's role as a national security agent who had released confidential intelligence information. A 21st-century rendition of Jonathan Edwards' hellfire sermon "Sinners in the Hands of an Angry God," the exposé reminds readers that national security is still a very relevant concern and its secrets should remain hidden because America is always on the brink of war. In this literary context, the co-authors equate God with national intelligence because it is only due to the good graces of both agencies that America does not wake to find itself engulfed in flames.

Perhaps under pressure from those who found the article's timing and contents suspicious, four days after the first ambiguous security announcement was made a news leak occurred.[15] The information had been released by a group of newspapers owned by one of the largest publishing companies in America, the McClatchy Company. The editorials revealed that al-Qaeda leader Ayman al-Zawahiri had spoken to Nasser al-Wuhayshi, the head of the Yemen-based al-Qaeda faction in the Arabian Peninsula. Al-Zawahiri had told al-Wuhayshi to "do something."[16] Late that afternoon, CNN did a follow-up highlighting that McClatchy had already divulged the delicate information.[17]

By midday on August 4, the one-day closures of several of the diplomatic posts were extended to an entire week.[18] Additionally and somewhat predictably, in the early hours of August 6 security sources told CNN "[a] pair of suspected U.S. drone strikes killed four al-Qaeda militants in Yemen […]." The report made sure to include that the strikes were initiated three days before Snowden had been granted asylum. Strangely, the military was just getting around to releasing this information, information that can readily be assumed to be about top secret operations which remained in effect before Ramadan had ended. CNN's intelligence source "didn't offer additional details" after reluctantly admitting, "None of those killed on Tuesday were among the 25 names on the country's most-wanted list."[19] The timing and content of the report bears striking resemblance to the ironic synchronicity of the 1998 Al-Shifa pharmaceutical factory bombing amid then-president Bill Clinton's impending impeachment hearings.

As a capstone, hours before the close of Ramadan and in the wake of an embassy attack by al Qaeda, President Obama appeared on *The Tonight Show*.[20] The phrasing and order of the pre-screened questions makes an easy case for the White House having scripted the entire interview. After opening banalities, host Jay Leno began the interview with the diplomatic post closings, moved directly into the leaned question of how the president intends to answer those claiming the White House's response to the Middle East security threats was "overreact[ion]," before segueing into Snowden. Leno introduced the latter by asking, "Is it safe to say that we learned about these threats through the NSA intelligence program?" Of the 19 questions put to him, the president took the longest amount of time, 1:58, to address this concern. Three questions directly pertained to the NSA or Snowden yet the president only mentioned Snowden's name once. In the process, he alarmingly announced, "There have been times where they [Russia] slip back into Cold War thinking and Cold War mentality."

After Ramadan had ended the next day and no embassy had been attacked, the White House announced Obama would not meet with Russia's president before the G20 Summit.[21] Though a list of justifications for the canceled discussion were offered, Putin's aide, Yuri Ushakov, unhesitatingly proclaimed,

"It's clear that the decision is linked to the situation around former CIA contractor Edward Snowden."[22] The cost of Washington's unwillingness to accept that it had lost the Snowden battle was a reported 31 lives, two of which were confirmed civilians,[23] by the close of Ramadan. No "high-value targets" had been destroyed after a minimum of seven drone attacks. It was later reported that U.S. intelligence had not been in possession of "specifics of any al-Qaeda plot."[24]

After a week of diverting the public's attention away from Snowden and amid more disclosures, the White House realized the issue of privacy violations and the American surveillance system was not going away. Obama consented to give his first press conference in four months[25] on Friday, August 9, in the East Room of the White House. He opened the meeting by announcing he had called for a four-step review and reconstruction of American surveillance programs.[26]

The first is "reforms to Section 215 of the PATRIOT Act" even though "[I]t does not allow the government to listen to any phone calls without a warrant. But given the scale of this program, I understand the concerns of those who would worry that it could be subject to abuse." Obama stated adjustments will be made to these two laws to ensure "greater oversight, greater transparency, and constraints on the use of this authority."

He then proposed FISC oversight in the form of a legal representative being present to review request orders, because the court currently "only hears one side of the story, may tilt it too far in favor of security, may not pay enough attention to liberty." Obama, a Harvard lawyer, acknowledged a kangaroo court was in effect because no defense attorney was present to represent those whom the U.S. government was attempting to target.

The president went on to announce, under his directive, that declassification of intelligence data pertaining to how the NSA functions will begin. He proclaimed this act will be a testament to the administration's pledge of greater transparency. Declassification will be accompanied by a new NSA website which will "serve as a hub for further transparency." In addition, "The NSA is taking steps to put in place a full-time civil liberties and privacy officer and release information that details its mission, authorities, and oversight."

Lastly, he stated a "high-level group of outside experts" will be assigned to "review our entire intelligence and communications technologies" because, he admitted, "governments, including our own, [have the] unprecedented capability to monitor communications." Three days later Obama announced he had appointed the Director of National Intelligence, James Clapper, to establish the external oversight review committee. The motley crew had been given the title, "Director of National Intelligence Review Group on Intelligence and Communications Technologies."[27]

The impact of the international disclosures—especially those pertaining to China, Germany and the EU—was obvious during the conference. The president very gingerly acknowledged, "[...] how these [surveillance] issues are viewed overseas [is important] because American leadership around the world depends upon the example of American democracy and American openness, because what makes us different from other countries is not simply our ability to secure our nation; it's the way we do it, with open debate and democratic process." He went on to state, "[...] to others around the world, I want to make clear once again that America is not interested in spying on ordinary people. Our intelligence is focused above all on finding the information that's necessary to protect our people and, in many cases, protect our allies."

Without mentioning Snowden once, Obama closed by taking a jab at the American exile, "And I believe that those who have lawfully raised their voices on behalf of privacy and civil liberties are also patriots who love our country and want it to live up to our highest ideals."

During follow-up questions from the press, Obama was asked to account for his shift from being a senator critical of surveillance practices to a president who avidly supports them, especially after the Snowden affair. After subtly testifying he was an advocate of oversight before the first disclosure by referring to his speech on the afternoon of May 23 at the National Defense University (which was arguably instigated after the *The Washington Post* alerted the U.S. government it had a leak), he accepted responsibility for the programs and laws, "When I looked through specifically what was being done, my determination was that the two programs in particular that had been an issue—215 and 702—offered valuable intelligence that helps us protect the American people, and they're worth preserving." Even though a large portion of the American surveillance data released to the press contains information from the start of 2013 until April, he reported, "What we also saw was that some bolts needed to be tightened up on some of the programs. So we initiated some additional oversight reforms, compliance officers, audits and so forth." Despite acknowledging, "[Disclosures have been released] one a week to kind of maximize attention and see if they can catch us at some imprecision on something," he made the mistake of offering the defense, "[W]hat you're not reading about is the government actually abusing these programs and listening in on people's phone calls or inappropriately reading people's emails." Blatantly ignoring *The Guardian*'s Microsoft exposé, he lent the reassurance, "[I]f people don't have confidence that the law, the checks and balances of the court and Congress, are sufficient to give us confidence that government's not snooping, maybe we can embed technologies in there that prevent the snooping regardless of what government wants to do. There may be some technological fixes that provide another layer of assurance." Though he continually reiterates he is confident current surveillance mechanisms are not being abused, he failed to address the issue of the NSA hiding specific programs such as Boundless Informant from Congress in order to evade government oversight.

As a testament of his commitment to transparency, Obama's press conference was accompanied by the release of two documents, the "Administration White Paper: Bulk Collection of Telephony Metadata under Section 215 of the USA

PATRIOT Act" and an NSA memorandum.[28] They are both dated June 9. By issuing a white paper instead of a green one, Washington was making its position clear before uttering a word. A "white paper" is a government report which takes a firm, resolute stance upon an issue. It is in contrast to a "green paper," which opens and invites discussion. Much like Bergen and Cahall's CNN exposé which simultaneously defends national intelligence while implicitly incriminating Snowden, the presentation of the two documents is a calculated double-edged sword. The White Paper (WP) and memo respectively declare they are intended to provide "as much information as possible to the public concerning the legal authority for this [215] program" and "a succinct description of NSA's mission, authorities, oversight and partnerships." Rather than apologetic confessions, they are angry, finger-pointing acknowledgements disguised as legal defenses. By their conclusions and through the use of phrases such as "catastrophic terrorist attacks" and "the only practical means," it is clear that the government's stance is stricter, more invasive surveillance measures could have stopped 9/11 and are the only way to provide effective, continued national security.

The memo unrepentantly opens with "[w]e now know that 9/11 hijacker Khalid al-Midhar, who was on board American Airlines flight 77 that crashed into the Pentagon, resided in California for the first six months of 2000. While NSA had intercepted some of Midhar's conversations with persons in an al-Qaeda safe house in Yemen during that period, NSA did not have the U.S. phone number or any indication that the phone Midhar was using was located in San Diego. NSA did not have the tools or the database to search to identify these connections and share them with the FBI." Though other programs, such as Fairview, are mentioned, the document conveniently overlooks ThinThread, which was available but unused due to political reasons at the time of the American attacks.

Obama even admitted during the Q & A segment of the press conference, "There's no doubt Mr. Snowden's leaks triggered a much more rapid and passionate response than if I had simply appointed this review board." The whistleblower's influence is evident throughout the two documents as is the pressure that had been perpetually exerted upon the U.S. government by service providers after Washington refused to permit them to release data proving their hand had been federally forced. The memo states, "[...] the government compels one or more providers to assist NSA with the collection of information responsive to the foreign intelligence need." The WP validates intelligence had open-door access to provider's servers: "Providers would also be forced to review daily requests of differing docket numbers, rather than merely complying with one ongoing request, which would be more onerous on the providers and raise potential and unnecessary compliance issues." The U.S. government admits individual court orders were never issued.

The WP owns up to Greenwald's June 20 report on warrantless surveillance: "[...] the FBI must rely on publicly available information, other available intelligence, or other legal processes in order to identify the subscribers of any of the numbers that are retrieved." Determining a person's identity via cell number is as easy as querying Facebook. In order to receive a vanity URL, a person must have an authorization code which is sent by Facebook once an individual provides a working cell number. Many email providers ask for a phone number for "security purposes." The WP goes on to state that "other available intelligence," which is designated under the phrase "tangible things," includes "books, records, papers, documents, and other items," such as electronically stored documents one might put into an online cloud service. Using legal precedent, "tangible things" are collected if it is "reasonable to believe" the information relates to terrorism. The requisition can include "entire repositories of records" and, under "Prospective Orders," it is not necessary to submit individual orders after an initial request on a target has been recognized and approved, because the requirement would "impose entirely unnecessary burdens on both the Court and the Government."

The impact of the Tempora and Fairview articles is also felt. The memo confesses that the United States is partnered with "over 30 nations" but does not ask any foreign relation "to do what NSA is itself prohibited by law from doing." The WP even blatantly states, "[...] a large amount of metadata is consolidated and preserved by the Government [...]" and relays that the NSA has a five-year raw data retaining buffer.

The NSA survey makes sure to deny only metadata is collected: "This process will *often* [my emphasis] involve the collection of communications metadata [...]." The WP seconds this: "Section 215 permits the FBI to seek a court order directing a business or other entity to produce records or documents when there are reasonable grounds to believe that the information sought is *relevant* [my emphasis] to an authorized investigation of international terrorism." Under relevancy, contact chaining is acknowledged, but nothing else is said about the protocol. The document's failure to provide further comment on the policy implies the answer to the question left open in Greenwald's Stellar Wind report: The surveillance practice was made freely and impenitently permissible through a later law. It confirms Greenwald's June 20 warrantless surveillance exposé by adding, as with "tangible things," "[...] [metadata] can be reliably identified only through analysis of a large volume of data [...]" because "It would be impossible to conduct these queries effectively without a large pool of telephony metadata to search, as there is no way to know in advance which numbers will be responsive to the authorized queries." In the middle of all its assurances, the WP confesses that a dragnet is cast and analysts *then* go through the data captures. It is clear the intelligence community's policy is information is not surveilled until it has been viewed by an analyst in the same manner that Clapper's books do not officially become books until he begins reading them.

But even collectively the documents are far from being an admission of guilt to all of the preceding editorial charges. The WP dauntingly admits, "Intrusion on privacy interests is limited" and "If any Fourth Amendment privacy interest were implicated by collection of telephony metadata, which does not include the content of any conversations, it would be minimal." Though the government's perspective is clear when the WP references a 1989 Supreme Court case, "[...] it is necessary to balance the individual's privacy expectations against the Government's interests to determine whether it is impractical to require a warrant [...]," the memo continually reassures the reader that only international communications or those by "foreign persons" who are "reasonably believed" to be "wholly outside the United States" are targeted and domestic surveillance is incidental. The surveillance survey decrees U.S. citizens' rights are adamantly protected. Despite a PRISM slide which states it is "nothing to worry about," the WP imparts, "[...] compliance incidents are also reported to the Intelligence and Judiciary Committees of both houses of Congress [...]." It does not state whether the reports include incidental data captures nor does it claim that domestic information is immediately destroyed.

The document refutes that interagency data exchange is a pre-review "team sport": "[...] [B]efore the NSA disseminates any information about a U.S. person outside the agency, a high-ranking NSA official must determine that the information identifying the U.S. person is in fact related to counterterrorism [...]." Amazingly, the NSA overview opens a new door for criticism by announcing that identifiers have been put in place to highlight people who "[...] are *likely* [my emphasis] to receive foreign intelligence information authorized for collection under an approved certification." (The WP states that only 300 identifiers are used instead of 30,000 as cited in *The Guardian*'s Tempora report.) Though both articles contain subjective, broadly defined terms which legally permit overreach, the WP reveals that an FISC order is not needed for "an investigative activity that does not require any particular factual predication," otherwise known as a "threat assessment." A suspicion which is not based upon a "factual predication" is often referred to as a "hunch." This clemency is granted because a "federal prosecutor need only sign and issue a grand jury subpoena to obtain similar documents in criminal investigations, yet national security investigations have no similar investigative tool." This is analogous to New York outlawing child pornography by passing legislation making it illegal while San Francisco freely permits it simply because the city never got around to banning it.

Amid the two documents' backpedaling and whitewashing, the U.S. government finds itself facing a chicken-or-the-egg conundrum. If one agency cannot release data to another without first verifying that targeting is legitimate, but to establish legitimacy interagency cross-referencing is required, it is logistically impossible for any substantiation to occur. Because the WP discusses American law, it does not attempt to address claims of international data swapping used to evade domestic surveillance legislation.

It was clever. Over the course of a single day, the president of the United States assumed the role of "good cop" by doling out assurances that measures were being taken to quell any concerns about domestic surveillance. Meanwhile two government issued documents played the part of "bad cop." They informed the populace that its grievances were unfounded, and, in truth, Washington was being legally frugal because it reserved the right to be much more intrusive. With the same hubris used to pressure various European nations after Morales took flight, the WP stays true to its political and literary tradition by adamantly proclaiming unconstitutional privacy invasions have and do occur, though they are "limited" and "minimal." Without so much as a hint of green, it shrugs at the law having been gerrymandered to permit blanket warrants. Despite the implied, admitted guilt involved in releasing a statement upon programs and laws which the public had been repeatedly informed needed no justification or explanation, the WP and accompanying memo marks a turning point for the Obama administration. They contain much of the same defensive postures Washington had committed to memory since June 5. However, a fair degree of offense is contained within their pages. Though presented under the ruse of transparency, the Capitol seized the opportunity to exploit the American public's demand for answers and gave it fervently spun propaganda and a firm reprimand for doubting its authority.

The media whiteout, bombings, Obama's appearance on *The Tonight Show*, his long overdue White House press conference and the publication of the NSA memo and White Paper might not have happened if it hadn't been for seven individuals. The time when the American people and corporations could be satisfied with answers had long past. They now demanded change. A week before Snowden was granted asylum, Congress voted on legislation which would have proved something was being done about the current state of American surveillance. The legislation lost by six votes. The rest was a domino effect. In the end, the president had no choice but to personally reassure everyone change was coming, even if it had to be at his own hands.

Various members of Congress had set to work addressing American espionage practices soon after Greenwald reported on Verizon. Some were unrealistically radical and merely put forth as a testament to one's party platform or constituency. Representative Rush Holt's "Surveillance State Repeal Act"[29] demanded that the PATRIOT Act be eradicated. House Resolution No. 205 by Tom McMillin insisted Clapper be prosecuted. Senator Patrick Leahy would revise his prophetic March proposal, Electronic Communications Privacy Act Amendments Act of 2013,[30] and reissue it in June as FISA Accountability and Privacy Protection Act of 2013.[31] Several politicians wanted variations on the first piece of sponsored legislation to arise out of the Snowden debacle, Senator Jeff Merkley's June 11 public transparency plan. The Ending Secret Law Act[32] asked for FISC opinions to be made available to Congress and the court's decisions released to the American people. Other tentative laws narrowly focused on one aspect of the surveillance debate. Representatives John Conyers and Justin Amash's LIBERT-E Act[33] argued blanket monitoring was illegal and stipulated only individual cases involving probable cause be allowed. Many called for the expiration date on the FISA Amendments Act be moved forward so its legislation could be reviewed and revised before 2017. A handful thought the problem was with the appointment of FISC judges. A multitude of bills offered resolutions. A few lawmakers had pity on the telephone and Internet providers. They made the appeal that the companies be allowed to publicly release their FISC request figures. Obama had entered the press conference having absorbed a number of Capitol Hill's suggestions, such as placing a defense attorney in America's secret court. Despite Congress members' efforts, U.S. intelligence and the White House did everything they could to make sure nothing would change.

The LIBERT-E Act had over 50 sponsors. It was the product of two Michigan politicians. Amash, a Republican with Libertarian leanings and the sixth-youngest representative, had been joined by Conyers, a Democrat born in 1929 who was the second-longest serving incumbent on Capitol Hill now in his 48th year in Congress. But the two politicians knew the controversial law would not pass on its own. They judiciously took another approach. The decision wound up testing the moral fabric of democracy.

Unlike the Senate, where all members can force a vote, the House Speaker reigns supreme. If the speaker doesn't deem a topic worthy of consideration, it isn't put on the docket. Amash walked gingerly around Speaker Boehner, who had already decreed Snowden a traitor. He made his bill into an amendment to the Department of Defense Appropriations Act, 2014.[34] Any lawmaker can propose an amendment to a bill so long as it can be proven to relate to the legislation it is trying to piggyback. The amendment's relevance was obvious and irrefutable. It dealt with defense spending. Amash was calling to cancel the NSA's authority to conduct blanket surveillance.[35] There were two sides to the legislative coin. In theory, Amash's proposal should have been agreeable to the fiscally conservative Republican-led House because it would cut costs. In reality, House Republicans strongly supported national defense, which the bill sought to limit. It was nonetheless Amash's best bet for getting the law passed.

It was also a prime example of why politicians hate amendment riders. Piggybacked legislation frequently puts them in a difficult position with their party, campaign donors and constituency. In the case of Amash's proposal, a lose-lose scenario ensued. If the amendment was attached, a House member would be simultaneously voting for and against national defense, and the press and public rarely issued benefit of the doubt after final votes were cast. Because of this, leaders of the House started humoring the unthinkable. The amendment process was a liberty which assured all voices were heard. Talk about limiting the number of amendments to a bill began to circulate. Democracy remained intact for one reason. If an actual move toward blocking a vote on the amendment ensued, Amash's legislation had enough support for the entire Defense bill to be held up.[36] Republicans reluctantly consented. The amendment was ruled to be in order on Monday, July 22.[37] It was then scheduled to be debated on Wednesday evening, July 24, before going up for a tentative vote the next day.

The White House was so nervous, it broke character. Carney publicly denounced the pending legislation during a press conference on Tuesday, "[…] we [the White House] oppose the current effort in the House to hastily dismantle one of our intelligence community's counterterrorism tools. This blunt approach is not the product of an informed, open or deliberative process. We urge the House to reject the Amash Amendment, and instead move forward with an approach that appropriately takes into account the need for a reasoned review of what tools can best secure the nation."[38] The White House chose to ignore the irony of the statement being made moments after another closed-door briefing had come to an end.[39]

The White House and intelligence community knew that little could be done about Monday's ruling. It was a mere technicality. The day after the amendment was declared legal and could therefore proceed, amid promises of greater transparency, invitations to a top secret meeting with General Alexander were extended to select members of the House.[40]

The Republicans had a right to be worried. After 15 minutes of debate the day before,[41] Amash's amendment was narrowly defeated 205-217 on Thursday.[42] Ninety-four Republicans and 111 Democrats voted in favor, 134 Republicans and 83 Democrats had been against the legislation. Surprisingly, the author of the PATRIOT Act, James Sensenbrenner, voted for Amash's law.[43] He said he had done so because, "The time has come to stop it."[44] Since a majority of Democrats supported the amendment, it would have likely passed in the Democrat-led Senate. Aside from what might have been said by Alexander, a look behind the campaign contribution curtain suggests Lon Snowden was right. The 217 "nay" voices received 122 percent more money from the intelligence and defense industries than the 205 "yea" voters.[45]

The $594 billion Defense bill was passed with over 60 amendments[46] by a vote of 315 to 109.[47] The tab was five billion dollars below current spending and the White House threatened to veto it in order to continue to fund the Pentagon. Its emotional appeal was that the reduced budget would force compensatory cuts to other programs such as health research and education.[48]

However, one of the amendments that did pass relates to U.S. government surveillance. It was put forth by Mike Pompeo of Kansas and declares that the NSA cannot use its budget to "acquire, monitor, or store the contents [...] of any electronic communication" of a U.S. citizen.[49] It passed by a vote of 409-12.[50] The reason Pompeo's law was met with little fanfare and passed by an overwhelming margin is because it is essentially flaccid. It prohibits what the NSA stated it was not doing and currently steering around. Pompeo's legislation does not ban the bulk collection of metadata.

As Congress, the White House and the intelligence community continued to fight against and amongst themselves, the press sallied forth. It seized every opportunity to pounce upon a corporation's whitewashed statement or an exaggeration by Washington, all the while further displaying the depth and range of American and international surveillance.

Chapter 8
The Band Played On

"These programs were never about terrorism: they're about economic spying, social control, and diplomatic manipulation. They're about power."

–Edward Snowden, open letter to the people of Brazil, December 16, 2013[1]

✼ ✼ ✼

AFTER GIVING SNOWDEN HIS ASYLUM PRESENT of XKeyscore, Greenwald's exposés became sporadic. He had signed a book deal in the middle of July to produce an entire volume of new surveillance revelations. However, in a matter of weeks he—and not his writing—would make headlines. Poitras dutifully fed and explained classified data to the German press as she worked on the final chapter of her post-9/11 trilogy. Her last installment focuses on how the War on Terror was brought home to American soil. One of its themes is United States surveillance. Gellman even resurfaced to contribute one of the better, more penetrating, vital and timely post-asylum disclosures.

The day Snowden was granted asylum, *The Guardian* celebrated with another exclusive: "NSA pays £100m in secret funding for GCHQ."[2] It proudly proclaims "Secret payments revealed in leaks by Edward Snowden." The article answers the question left from the June 21 Tempora report of which intelligence agency calls the shots.

Largely because Britain's comparatively lax surveillance laws are a "selling point," the U.S. government started financially supporting many of GCHQ's intelligence stations and programs after GCHQ suffered substantial domestic budget cuts. One such British spy project hopes to ultimately "exploit any phone, anywhere, any time." Having poured over 100 million pounds into contracted British intelligence services from 2010-2013, the NSA is allowed to prioritize surveillance affairs at some of Britain's spy stations. Half the cost of GCHQ's Cyprus station is paid by U.S. taxpayers. But Washington is not always happy with what it gets for its citizens' money. Internal, classified documents comment, "GCHQ must pull its weight and be seen to pull its weight" because the U.S. government had "raised a number of issues with regards to meeting NSA's minimum expectations." This is perhaps because 60 percent of Britain's filtered data still comes from American intelligence. It is obvious a portion of the nine-figure paycheck, revealed in GCHQ's "investment portfolios," was for foreign surveillance of U.S. citizens and subsequent data-swapping services. One classified review brags of how GCHQ made "unique contributions" to the NSA investigation of the American citizen behind the failed 2010 Times Square car bomb attack. The plot by Faizal Shahzad was foiled by a T-shirt vendor who noticed that a suspiciously parked car happened to be smoking.[3]

A companion article titled, "GCHQ: inside the top secret world of Britain's biggest spy agency"[4] appeared the same day. Its focus is largely on the daily life within GCHQ, its history, but also its plans. The report admits, "Of all the highly classified documents about GCHQ revealed by the whistleblower Edward Snowden, this has to be one of the least sensitive." The exposé discusses the nuances of working inside the world's largest surveillance facility whose annual budget is one billion pounds. (The NSA's yearly allotment is 17 times greater.)[5] Employees have bake sales, annual in-house sporting events, team vacations and chat using an internal networking site sardonically named "SpySpace," a titular mockup of Facebook's predecessor, MySpace.

But the article moves to more substantial matters by grabbing the loose thread of cellular phone surveillance that its bookend report left dangling. The British intelligence agency seeks to "[collect] voice and SMS and geo-locating phone" data and "intelligence from all the extra functionality that iPhones and BlackBerrys offer." A classified document recognizes the technological climate and sets the agenda: "Google Apps already has over 30 million users. This is good news. It allows us to exploit the mobile advantage." As with telecommunications providers' government compliance, on February 8, 2011, it was noted that "Legal assurances [by cell phone manufacturers were] now believed to be good."

In its conclusion—a review of GCHQ's contribution to American intelligence—the report states that the British intelligence agency "[…] had given the NSA 36% of all the raw information the British had intercepted from computers the agency was monitoring. A confidential document declares new technological advances permit the British to "[…] interchange 100% of GCHQ End Point Projects with NSA."

Also on August 1, NGB[6] expanded on British communication providers' roles in government surveillance. It was another joint feature with *Süddeutsche Zeitung*, which would release "Snowden revealed names of spying telecom companies"[7] the next day.

Together the news sources report that not two but seven major domestic telecoms, alongside their respective code names, provided GCHQ with access to their fiber-optic cables in 2010: Verizon Business ("Dacron"), British Telecommunications ("Remedy"), Vodafone Cable ("Gerontic"), Global Crossing ("Pinnage"), Level 3 ("Little"), Viatel ("Vitreous") and Interoute ("Streetcar"). The British spy agency used Tempora to hack the various data backbones across Europe. GCHQ has 102 "points of presence" over Europe, 15 of which are in Germany.

The British communication companies' involvement with GCHQ is of particular interest to Germany, because Level 3 owns data centers in Berlin, Hamburg, Dusseldorf, Frankfurt and Munich. Global Crossing and Interoute are also major German communication distributors. For readers familiar with the American surveillance story, Viatel's response was pre-

dictable as well as somewhat laughable: "We do not cooperate with the GCHQ or grant access to our infrastructure or
customer data." The company representative continues, "Like
all telecommunications providers in Europe, we are obliged to
comply with European and national laws including those regarding privacy and data retention. From time to time, we
receive inquiries from authorities, [which are] checked by our
legal and security departments, and if they are legal, [they]
will be processed accordingly." The reports also reveal that
the Five Eyes, whose acronym is revealed as "FVEY," operate
a "ring of satellite monitoring systems around the globe." The
group project is code-named "Echelon."

Epoca's sophomore disclosure effort appeared on August
2. Greenwald is the first credited writer of "Letter from the
American Ambassador in Brazil thanks the NSA for its Support."[8] He presents a classified missive dated May 19, 2009,
addressed to General Alexander thanking him and the NSA
for their work with SIGINT. The top secret document was
written by Thomas Shannon, who at the time was assistant
secretary to the Bureau of Western Hemisphere Affairs. Shannon states he was impressed by the quality of information
provided by the spy agency during the Fifth Summit of the
Americas. The Summit of the Americas, originated by Bill
Clinton, occurs every few years and brings together the leaders of the Western Hemisphere to discuss chosen themes. Topics
for 2009 included the economic crisis, environmental issues
and alternative energy. Shannon proudly announces, "We
succeeded and our rivals failed, and our success owes in good
measure to the abundant, timely, and detailed reporting that
you [Alexander and the NSA] provided." Over 100 reports
had been received which revealed the "plans and intentions
of the other Summit participants." Seven months after he
penned the thank you note, Shannon was appointed ambassador to Brazil.

Poitras' return to the printed page after Snowden stepped
freely onto Russian soil, "Mass Data: Transfers from Germany
Aid US Surveillance,"[9] conveniently, implicitly and themati-

cally follows *The Guardian*'s discussion of GCHQ and the NSA's relationship. Though her report substantiates an assumption any regular reader of the Snowden affair would have about the BND's kinship with American intelligence, it also provides a vital piece of the surveillance puzzle.

Working in adjoining buildings, the NSA receives intercepted data from the BND on a daily basis. But the German foreign intelligence agency paradoxically assures its citizenry the information it gives to U.S. intelligence is not only wiped clean of any identifying features, it does not include any domestic data. In turn the NSA claims it complies with the rules and regulations of the country in which it is operating. Under Germany's G-10 Law, domestic surveillance is illegal. However, an accompanying Boundless Informant graph shows daily reports of telephone and Internet traffic in Germany from December 10, 2012 and January 8, 2013. Though the information could have been retrieved and transferred as foreign intelligence by the NSA from U.S. soil or by another surveillance organization such as GCHQ, the revealed code or SIGINT Activity Designator (SIGAD) for one interception site is "US-987LA." This is strongly believed to be one of two domestic outposts. The numeric suffix is also indicative of a third-party contractor, implying the BND was spying on its own people for the NSA. The report suggests either German foreign intelligence is lying to its government, or Germany's representatives are feigning ignorance.

There is a third possibility. The programs used and their respective monthly figures are as follows: XKeyscore, 182 million; Lopers (used for monitoring traditional "hard-line" telephone connections), 131 million; Juggernaut (used for spying on mobile network transfers such as vocal communication, fax and text messaging), 93.5 million; Cerf Call Moses, 39 million; and Matrix, almost eight million records. (By comparison, Spain, Italy, France and the Netherlands had almost no Internet data surveilled in the same 30-day period.) Due to the bloated figures, solely blaming the BND is logistically difficult. Though not definitive due to the lapse of time, a travel report relays that only 100 BND employees were stationed in a single German surveillance facility in 2006. It is possible the outpost is smaller than US-987LA, but by ratio, Menwith is staffed with 1,600 employees for a country of 63 million. As previously noted, Germany has a population of 80 million. If the BND was gathering domestic data, unless there was a massive growth in Germany's intelligence budget over the last seven years, it is unlikely the immense amount of data could be collected, analyzed and filtered by such a small workforce. The *Der Spiegel* report states, "Officially, the German government is still waiting for an answer from Washington as to where in Germany the metadata documented in the NSA files was obtained." Regardless of which party is responsible, Germany and America's reliance on XKeyscore to gather data is also a concern since the program has full-take capabilities.

The article also cites two of Germany's spying tools, Mira4 and VERAS, which were given to the NSA in exchange for nondescript intelligence assistance. Poitras' report closes on the frightening note of the classified documents mentioning a discussion between the two agencies. They spoke of analysis programs able to detect behavior patterns. This technology is used by civilian data mining companies to predict consumer behavior. By gauging and comparing an individual's past and current purchasing patterns and Internet browsing habits with previous, established models, analysis programs guess what a person intends to buy next. In 2012 the American corporation Target began sending maternity-related coupons to a Minneapolis teenager based on purchasing patterns. The consumer wasn't aware she was pregnant. She was.[10]

Poitras' article on August 5 serves another purpose. By placing her explanation of SIGADs alongside Greenwald's *O Globo* Fairview exposé, readers could step back and see a blurred outline of the bigger surveillance picture. It becomes even clearer once two previous citations are considered. On June 8, *The Guardian* released an additional, edited PRISM slide but admitted it had difficulty interpreting its meaning due to lack of context.[11] The slide mentions the Fairview and "Blarney" programs. On July 10, Gellman released a similar slide without redactions.[12] Readers could see that the program names "Oakstar" and "Stormbrew" had been censored by *The Guardian*.[13]

Gathering bulk data from corporate, government and private telecom and Internet providers, each spy program has a different function and purpose, as indicated by its related SIGAD. For example, an unseen slide briefly mentioned in Gellman's original PRISM report states Blarney is "an ongoing collection program that leverages IC [intelligence community] and commercial partnerships to gain access and exploit foreign intelligence obtained from global networks." Blarney can be assumed to utilize PRISM for its data analysis because PRISM's assigned SIGAD is US-984XN. The two known SIGAD's associated with Blarney are US-984 and US-984X. Blarney is believed to be installed in Room 641A in San Francisco and somewhere in New Jersey.

SIGADs classify hosts as well as location. Oakstar's SIGADs were revealed in the *O Globo* report. US-3206 is the code for the collections gleaned from Monkeyrocket; US-3217 for Shiftingshadow; US-3230 for Orangecrush; US-3247 for Yachtshop, which is the access point for the private contractor Blueanchor; US-3251 for Orangeblossom; US-3273 for Silverzephyr, which is the access point for the private contractor Steelknight; US-3277 for Bluezephyr and US-3354 for Cobalfalcon.[14]

Like Blarney, Stormbrew's data collection is largely focused on domestic communications. Its corporate and private affiliates are located in Washington, California, Texas, Florida, New York, Virginia and Pennsylvania. Stormbrew's SIGAD is US-983. Examining the location of known SIGADs, it appears suffixes beginning with the number 3 designate foreign surveillance and 9 denote domestic spying activity. One of Stormbrew's assigned SIGAD's is US-3140 for an entity codenamed "Madcapocelot." Its name and numeric indicator imply it is an eastern lookout point for European communications.

In Greenwald's July 31 XKeyscore report, a classified slide shows that XKeyscore contains "[u]nique data beyond user activity from front end full-take feeds." The belated PRISM slide tells analysts to use both "upstream" data alongside PRISM. Upstream is the common term for "front end." It is "active" information sent *from* a computer. For example, when a person sends an email, it goes "upstream." It is "down-stream" or "passive" after the email message has been received and downloaded. The revealed documents come together to imply data is deposited into the storage reservoirs "Marina," "Pinwale" and "Trafficthief" only after it has been received, reviewed and filtered.[15] An example data flow would be a user's email originating in Brazil. As it is transferred to a South American Internet firm's fiber-optic cables contracted by Orangecrush, it is picked up by Fairview, and PRISM processes it before it is deposited and stored in Pinwale for later refer-ence. XKeyscore can then retrieve files from this catalogued system. Astute readers were able to begin getting a handle on how American surveillance functioned two months after the debate began.

Even though Snowden was safe in the confines of Russia, the U.S. government was still trying to make life difficult for him. The encrypted email service Lavabit, based out of Texas, announced it was shutting down on August 8.[16] The company's owner, Ladar Levison, stated on the website's index page that he had decided to close the firm's doors after 10 years because he didn't want to "become complicit in crimes against the American people."[17] This was after the federal government filed a lawsuit in early July once he refused to grant access to one particular user's email account.[18] Snowden had held a Lavabit account since January 2010.[19] He used the email ad-dress edsnowden@lavabit.com to extend his G9 meeting invitations and communicate with human rights groups and his Russian attorneys afterward.[20] Even though Levison could say little about the content of Snowden's emails because Lavabit files are asymmetrically encrypted on the company's server and only the account holder possesses the key, Levison was put under a gag order. Though initially shut out of their accounts, the 400,000 Lavabit users were later given a 72-hour window to retrieve, record or transfer the contents of their files.[21] Levison told *The Guardian*, "We are entering a time of state-sponsored intrusion into our privacy that we haven't seen since the McCarthy era. And it's on a much broader scale."[22] He has since started a legal defense fund, and has raised over $100,000.[23]

After Obama's speech, *The Guardian* set to refute any claims that U.S. intelligence was not legally entitled to conduct surveillance on a U.S. citizen. On August 9, "NSA loophole allows warrantless search for US citizens' emails and phone calls"[24] appeared.

It reveals an FAA 702 "Update," which is believed to have been in effect since 2011 but metadata establishes was instituted no later than June 2012. The clause gives the NSA authority to investigate "non-US citizens […] outside the US at the point of collection" without a warrant. A slippery slope then ensues through contact chaining of "incidental" domestic data. Until this time, even though the U.S. intelligence admitted "it is not reasonably possible to identify the number of people located in the United States whose communications may have been reviewed under Section 702 authority,"[25] intelligence had hidden behind the assertion it had no lawful right to conduct domestic surveillance. Essentially the FAA addendum eradicates the minimization procedures set to protect Americans from being surveilled. The disclosure of the FAA update permitted Senator Wyden to discuss the previously classified surveillance policy, "Once Americans' communications are collected, a gap in the law that I call the 'back-door searches loophole' allows the government to potentially go through these communications and conduct warrantless searches for the phone calls or emails of law-abiding Americans." The NSA silently pled guilty after Wyden and Udall informed[26] General Alexander that an NSA FAA fact sheet[27] posted on the agency's website misled readers into believing "the law does not allow the NSA to deliberately search for the records of particular Americans." The fact sheet was later removed.[28]

Whereas Greenwald's sister report in June left arguable room for doubt, the existence and implied need for 702's amendment speaks for itself. It also explains the semantic delicacy incorporated in Washington's guarantee that Americans were not being watched. Much like data is not considered to be surveilled until it is seen by human eyes, the insinuation was that no *direct* targeting was taking place. The FAA update proves, at worst, Americans are indirectly targeted; at the very least their data is being retroactively searched.[29] XKeyscore's querying of entire databases of full-take records is now understood to be the administration's definition of "indirect surveillance." In an accompanying report titled, "NSA surveillance: the long fight to close backdoor into US communications,"[30] it is clear who is at fault. Intelligence agencies and the Department of Justice "reaffirmed" to the chair of the Senate Intelligence Committee, Dianne Feinstein, that database searches "do not provide a means to circumvent the general requirement to obtain a court order before targeting a U.S. person under FISA." As intelligence hid the existence of law-violating surveillance programs from Congress, it was also misinforming and misdirecting oversight committees.

On Monday, August 12, *Der Spiegel* produced what begins as a less volatile article, "Ally and Target: US Intelligence Watches Germany Closely."[31] Using classified documents, it reports how the United States views various nations from a surveillance perspective. By its conclusion, the exposé answers a long-standing question about American spying.

By at least April 2013, the NSA prioritized its surveillance of foreign nations. It does so using a sliding scale that gauges a multitude of espionage categories. With 1 being the greatest concern and 5 being the least, foreign policy, economic stability and financial systems, arms exports, new technologies, "advanced conventional" weapons, international trade, counter-espionage and the risk of cyberattacks, energy security and food are all rated. (A subsequent report would include human rights, war crimes, environmental issues and raw materials.)[32] Overall, China, Russia, Iran, Pakistan and Afghanistan are "intelligence priorities." France, Germany and Japan are mid-level concerns while Italy and Spain reside below them. Cambodia, Laos, Nepal, Finland, Denmark, Croatia and the Czech Republic are "more or less irrelevant from a US intelligence perspective."

U.S. intelligence is mindful but not preoccupied with the foreign policy, economic stability and financial systems of Germany, having issued a grade of 3 to each. The country's arms exports, new technologies, advanced conventional weapons and international trade earned a rank of 4. The risk of cyberattacks or counter-espionage by its U.N. partner is the least of America's worries, having merited a score of 5.

The article goes on to discuss an NSA report painfully dubbed, "Tales from the Land of Brothers Grimm." In it, one German analyst expresses legal and moral apprehensions about using XKeyscore, stating in *Der Spiegel*'s terms, "[H]e always felt that he had one foot in prison when he was using the program." The agent's anxiety suggests that the individual was aware Xkeyscore violated or skirted G-10 laws. However, German spies are also reported to have reveled in their newfound snooping capabilities using the surveillance program. A unit manager relayed that he had finally been able to acquire materials from the Tunisian Interior Ministry which had doggedly eluded his grasp. This was after XKeyscore's training was broken down into the program's respective components and presented in 20-minute briefings. Analysts stated the frantic instruction felt like "speed dating."

The article shifts gears once more and reveals why American intelligence has an infatuation with Germany. After 9/11, the NSA wanted to establish a core surveillance hub in the center of Europe so the agency could readily track terrorists, "most" of which move through Germany during their travels. It also needed a place to watch the international gray hat organization, Anonymous. (It would later be reported that the federal government's preoccupation with the vigilante organization was not rooted in undermining rebel cyber collectives. The U.S. government sought to arrest and extort Anonymous members by getting them to consent to international NSA hacking missions as part of a plea bargain.)[33] It succeeded. The NSA's European Cryptologic Center in Griesheim is reported to have the "largest analysis and productivity in Europe."

The Washington Post's return to the disclosure field is somewhat of a surprise. The day Snowden applied for bulk asylum status and made his first public announcement after reaching Russia, Gellman's home office presented, "Plugging the leaks in the Edward Snowden case."[34] It is nothing short of a pro-Washington renunciation of Snowden which conveniently overlooks that the periodical was side-by-side in breaking the first whistleblowing reports.

The *Post* admits, "Documents published so far by news organizations have shed useful light on some NSA programs and raised questions that deserve debate." But the newspaper has apprehensions that future disclosures will sacrifice national security. It provides a rap sheet of current geopolitical casualties resulting from the Snowden affair, including damage to Obama's European reputation and U.N. free-trade talk complications as—referring to the ATPDEA contingency—Ecuadorian workers' livelihoods hung in the balance. Wiping retrospective egg off its face, the *Post* announces the day the American exile applied for mass asylum, Latin American countries were already "holding Mr. Snowden at arm's length" due to his "toxicity." Even though the periodical acknowledges Snowden has only acted upon political and not military data, it nonetheless proceeds to evoke fear: "[...] Mr. Snowden is reported to have stolen many more documents, encrypted copies of which may have been given to allies such as the WikiLeaks organization." Despite the NSA leaker's great efforts to only dole out carefully chosen materials to select parties with a proven track record of journalistic integrity, the citation does nothing short of insist that an unfiltered, Manning-like data dump will occur. The article conveniently ignores that the *Post*'s own rendition of the PRISM scandal was published after Gellman took an editorial stand not to publish all 41 classified slides, which consequently kept the exposé from being an exclusive feature. The newspaper proceeds to highlight that it cannot substantiate whether China or Russia had obtained Snowden's trove of classified materials, though his handing them over in exchange for asylum appears to be a growing possibility. It calls for the whistleblower to surrender himself, but admits it is unlikely because "the supposed friends of this naive hacker are likely advising him otherwise."

Greenwald was quick to respond. He posted on Twitter, "Shouldn't media outlets need—y'know—facts or evidence before asserting that Snowden 'may' have given secrets to Russia and/or China govts?"[35] Greenwald's former employer, *Salon*, stated the editorial was "journalists against journalism."[36] It does not blame Gellman for the article. The online news source conjectures that the "higher-ups" in the boardroom had "issu[ed] a jeremiad" to the *Post* newsroom. *Salon* believes the newspaper's retraction of its previous groundbreaking report is akin to the same news outlet which broke the 1972 Watergate Scandal announcing President Nixon should "prevent Deep Throat [the whistleblower who was reporting to the *Post*] from leaking information." It laments the brief renunciation's underlying theme, that cultivating sources will be frowned upon for future *Post* writers and perhaps all journalists. *Salon* considers the missive indicative of all major news outlets eventually kowtowing to political pressure.

On August 15, Gellman reemerged to put a rather large nail in the surveillance coffin. Since June 5, it had become clear that American intelligence did indeed have the technological capability to spy on its citizens. The question remained whether it broke privacy laws. In "NSA broke privacy rules thousands of times per year, audit finds,"[37] Gellman answers the inherent question in every preceding disclosure.

Gellman refuses to dance around the issue and opens with the "National Security Agency has broken privacy rules or overstepped its legal authority thousands of times each year since Congress granted the agency broad new powers in 2008, according to an internal audit and other top-secret documents." It includes two classified and one unclassified file as well as a page from a newsletter.

Confirming Snowden's statement that, during audits, analysts were not held accountable for targeting violations but instead are told to "bulk up the justification," a top secret document titled, "Targeting Rationale"[38] informs the NSA employee, "While we do want to provide our FAA overseers with the information they need, we DO NOT [the NSA's emphasis] want to give them any extraneous information." It goes on to state, "Your rationale MUST NOT [the NSA's emphasis] contain any additional information including: probable cause-like information (i.e. *proof* [the NSA's emphasis] of your analytic judgment), how you came to your analytic conclusions, any RAGTIME information, classification marking, or selector information." "Ragtime" is bulk data collected on and, per 702's update, "around" targets. One example of target justification is a social media hop: "Selector was found on buddy list of Al-Qaeda East Africa associate." The NSA intended to keep these instructions in-house for a long time. "Dated: 20070108" is found on the bottom, right corner of the first page. Immediately below the timestamp is "Declassify On: 39480914." The NSA's targeting procedure was scheduled to be made public on September 14, 3948.

Another top secret document is a compliance memo dated May 3, 2012.[39] No oversight committee, including the FISC, read it because it was addressed to the SIGINT director from the head of Oversight & Compliance within Security and Intelligence. The chief of Oversight uses the occasion to file procedural grievances and appeal for more surveillance latitude. It is a comparative quarterly report of "incidences of non-compliance" from January 1 through March 31. Violations had increased by 11 percent since the last quarterly filing, and 89 percent of incidences involved raw, or full-take, intelligence. Of the 865 violations which had taken place so far in

2012, 63 percent were due to "operator error." In specifying the nature of operator infractions, the NSA report makes the crotchety insinuation that the errors might not have occurred if the agency was permitted greater legal girth by which to conduct its spying, "Analysis identified that these incidents could be reduced if analysts had more complete and consistent information available about selectors and/or targets at the time of tasking [...]."

Thirty-seven percent of violations are attributed to system error. Without the slightest hint of irony, the NSA states that regulations are the cause of the greatest volume of laws being broken under this category: "[S]ystem lacks the capability to 'push' real-time travel data out to analysts, system/device unable to detect changes in user." The memo obtusely reinforces this point by supplying a pie chart. It breaks human error into respective classifications to visually imply the largest single cause of violations is system limitations.

Ten percent of the FISA breaches were due to "delayed detasking" or failure to quickly stop an investigation once the agency discovered a target was domestic. Dauntingly, when four drop-down menu selectors were discovered to have targeted 913 people with U.S. green cards, the directorate did not order to have the program updated or, in Gellman's terms, create "built-in safeguards to prevent unlawful surveillance." Instead analysts were instructed to first research if a suspected target had American rights and privileges before proceeding with the investigation. Within the report, the various intelligence databases are listed: "Cloud/ABR," "Dishfire," "Fastscope," "Marina," "Octave," "Pinwale," "Sigint Navigator," "Tracfin" (used for tracking bank transfers),[40] "Transx," "Tuningfork," "UTT," "XKeyscore," "Nucleon," "Anchory" and, rather disturbingly, "unknown."

Analysts took the Targeting Rationale's advice to heart. During the first three months of 2012, 74 percent of database query violations were due to "broad syntax." Admittedly a few analysts were cited as not having been "familiar enough to use the tool [program] used for query." Though "lack of due diligence" and "training and guidance" are listed as culprits, "workload issues" is also included. Of the 865 privacy violations committed during the first quarter of 2012, auditors found 83. "Automated alerts" discovered 553. Undoubtedly the wider the regulatory aperture is programmed, the fewer number of queries will be flagged as violations. In laymen's terms, a computerized auditing program can be set up to consider "X" but not "Y" as a violation. This means the person programming the alert system determines what is and is not a violation. The violation triggers have an inverse relationship to selectors. The NSA wants as many selectors as possible in order to net data. The agency wants as few violation triggers as possible keeping it from reeling in information. "VLR," "Spyder," "Chalkfun" and "TransX" are part of the alert systems.

On February 16, 2012, it was discovered that the five-year legal limitation on 3,032 files had long since expired. This was due to Stellar Wind being copied over to another database. The files' origination times had been overridden, or reset, during the transferal process. The end of the report admits that a group of cryptanalysts had been given unauthorized access to "NSA Establishment FISA data." On average, a violation occurred every three hours from April 1, 2012, to May 31, 2013, for a yearly total of 2,776. The memo is a report for NSA outposts in and around Washington. The statistics do not include the quarterly or yearly data for the NSA stations in Denver; San Antonio; Honolulu; Oak Ridge, Tennessee; or Augusta, Georgia.

A third disclosure is an October 12, 2011, article from the NSA's internal electronic newsletter, "SSO News." It provides evidence that the FISC did find the NSA in violation of the Constitution, "However, in the 80-page [FISC] opinion, the judge ordered certain 'upstream' or 'passive' FAA DNI collection to cease after 30 days, unless NSA implements solutions to correct all deficiencies identified in the opinion document." "DNI" is "digital network intelligence" and the technical term for Internet communications. The ruling was based on "[deficiencies] on statutory and constitutional grounds." Little else is known about the secret ruling or the conditions surrounding the decision.[41] Gellman reports, much like Boundless Informant being hidden from Congress, that the invasive program being used had been put into operation without the court's knowledge. The FISC had found PRISM and its corporate relationships to be legal. (Six days later, after the Obama administration diligently fought a Freedom of Information Act lawsuit by the Electronic Frontier Foundation, the U.S. government redacted and declassified the court's 85-page opinion of the ruling. "Wholly domestic" communications had been retrieved in the attempt to capture, store and then filter upstream data. Because the NSA purged its upstream data repositories in April 2012, it is assumed the upstream collection took place from 2008 to 2011. Contrary to the SSO article, a footnote within the opinion states the court's approval of phone record collection was "premised on a flawed depiction of how the NSA" would use the data.)[42]

Whereas the violation report is alarming in retrospect, the last disclosure is startling in its potentiality. Revised 20 days after the FISC determination, an unclassified training slide[43] guides analysts through the procedure if an American is targeted. In the comments sections under the headings "Intentional," "Inadvertent" and "Reverse" (where an analyst targets a foreign individual to gather data on an American through contact chaining), an analyst is told, "If collect (sic) on U.S. Person is needed, seek additional authority if eligible and a valid foreign intelligence requirement." In the comments sections under the heading "Incidental," unlike all other action headings, an analyst is not told to "Stop collection immediately!" Confirming what Greenwald had claimed in his PRISM exposé, the intelligence worker is advised, "Focus your report on the foreign end of the communication." The slide explicitly states that the violation need not be reported because it does not violate any specified law. Likewise, the only type of information that houses legal constraints is metadata; therefore full-take data captures are not considered illicit and not likely to be destroyed.

Gellman also discusses undisclosed classified information. His report quietly establishes that Snowden was not exaggerating when he stated he had "the authorities to wiretap anyone." One in 10 violations involved an analyst typing the wrong number into a database and inadvertently retrieving an American's phone calls or emails. The public had been reluctantly reassured only "incidentally collected" data could be extracted for analysis, which, as Gellman notes, implies a firewall prohibiting domestic surveillance had been put in place. Still, the *Post* journalist reports, "A notable example in 2008 was the interception of a 'large number' of calls placed from Washington when a programming error confused the U.S. area code 202 for 20, the international dialing code for Egypt." The surveillance breach did not involve metadata and therefore did not need to be reported. Nor was it included in the quarterly memo that a team of Hawaiian analysts abused their power and queried the Swedish telecommunication provider Ericsson along with the keywords "radio" and "radar."

Gellman reminded the White House why it had grown to dislike the *The Washington Post* 40 years before. The journalist had provided irrefutable proof that thousands of privacy violations had occurred. He had also shown there is no way of definitively knowing what goes unreported due to gaping holes in surveillance law and spy programs the NSA keeps hidden from oversight committees. He even exposed a handful of privacy abuses. Washington's window for excuses was getting progressively smaller with each report.

The Washington Post reporter would not hold the limelight long. In what could be viewed as unintentional journalistic rivalry, Greenwald took center stage three days later. However, he undoubtedly would have preferred to have done so under vastly different circumstances.

On Sunday, August 18, at a little past 8 a.m., Greenwald's partner, David Miranda, was detained at Heathrow Airport in London. Having arrived from Berlin with Greenwald (after spending a week with Poitras)[44] en route to Rio de Janeiro, Miranda was held under Schedule 7 of the Terrorism Act (of)

2000.[45] He underwent an eight hour, 55 minute[46] interrogation by London authorities.

A controversial law, Schedule 7 applies only to airports, border areas and ports of call. A terror suspect has no right to legal representation and can be held without being charged for up to nine hours.[47] Official figures relay that under the law, 97 percent of detainees are held for less than an hour. Only one in 2,000 people are kept for more than six hours.[48]

The authorities had become wise to the safety precaution Poitras had long since adopted of having a friend, acquaintance or business partner check in and carry delicate information. Miranda's camera, laptop, DVDs, mobile phone, memory sticks, video game consoles and two watches[49] were confiscated. Greenwald had previously stated he held between 15-20,000 classified documents.[50] It was later reported Miranda had been in possession of over 58,000 files.[51]

This followed a series of attempts by the U.S. government to intimidate journalists through challenging and undermining the First Amendment right to source confidentiality. On May 13, 2013, the *Associated Press* (*AP*) announced five of its reporters and an editor's telephone records for April and May 2012 had been subpoenaed by the Department of Justice. The requests had been quietly presented to the journalists' telecommunications providers, not the account holders. Two reporters were Verizon customers. Verizon failed to inform its clients of the subpoenas and did not challenge the orders.[52] No other information was provided, but it was noted that the U.S. attorney's office was investigating a May 7 *AP* report[53] detailing the CIA's role in foiling Yemeni terrorist Fahd al-Quso's plot to blow up a commercial flight.[54] Gary Pruitt, President of *AP*, announced there was no security risk because the story had been held until the U.S. government granted permission to print the information.[55]

The next week and just three days before Snowden would board a flight to Hong Kong, *The Washington Post* broke the story[56] of Fox News reporter James Rosen having been tracked and his telephone and email monitored by the Justice Department. The 2010 investigation followed a June 11, 2009, exposé by Rosen which explores how North Korea intended to react to the threat of U.N. sanctions if the communist country were to conduct another nuclear test after completing a successful detonation on May 25.[57] It was believed Rosen had gathered his information from Stephen Jin-Woo Kim, a senior analyst at the Office of National Security at Lawrence Livermore National Laboratory.

Two days after the *AP* report premiered and two days before the *Post* story debuted, Attorney General Holder testified before Congress that he was not in charge of the inquiry into the *AP* reporters' telephone records. He added, "With regard to the potential prosecution of the press for the disclosure of material, that is not something that I've ever been involved in, heard of or would think would be a wise policy."[58] His testimony was brought into question six days later when NBC verified Holder had given the Justice Department the green light to investigate Rosen.[59] The warrant listed Rosen as a "possible co-conspirator" in violation of the Espionage Act.

Scotland Yard knew the risks involved in detaining the partner of a well-known journalist and attorney. It anticipated *The Guardian*, civil rights groups and the Brazilian government would get involved. It accepted a lawsuit would ensue.[60] But intimidation or even knowledge of what Greenwald and Co. had in their possession was not the British government's primary goal. It was trying to close another security gap.

Few knew that aside from the D-Notice, British authorities had already gone to great lengths to silence the Snowden press. *The Guardian* was content to sit on the information until Scotland Yard attacked one of their own. Two days after Greenwald's partner was released, the newspaper revealed[61] that a month before, on July 20, GCHQ officials accompanied the newspaper's deputy editor, Paul Johnson; news and media executive director, Sheila Fitzsimons; and computer expert David Blishen to the basement of *The Guardian*'s King's Cross offices. The officials watched as the three newspaper employees took angle grinders and drills to the hard drives and memory chips containing Snowden's purloined data.

Five days after the news source reported on GCHQ's G20 spying, two government officials—Jeremy Heywood, the Cabinet secretary to Prime Minister David Cameron, and Craig Oliver, Cameron's director of communications[62]—darkened the doorway of *The Guardian*'s editor, Alan Rusbridger, shortly after he arrived at work. After a cordial but direct chat, the two officials were satisfied, believing they'd intimidated the staff enough to keep it from releasing more classified information. Hours after the government officials left, the world learned of Tempora's existence. Cameron's office held its tongue. More reports appeared. Heywood returned to *The Guardian*'s headquarters the day after the newspaper revealed Microsoft had granted pre-encryption access to the government. A call from Oliver followed three days later. The officials' argument was that the sensitive information could be hacked. Rusbridger explained the material had been air gapped (a technique used by Poitras).[63] Air gapping involves downloading information to and from a computer which has no Internet connection and is therefore physically isolated from the world. As *The New Yorker* reported, "[…] on five white Formica tables sat five new laptops, unconnected to the Internet or to any other network. The trove of documents from Snowden was kept on these computers, in encrypted file containers. Accessing each container required three passwords, and no individual knew more than one."[64] The only possible way for the information to be compromised was for it to be physically stolen. Rusbridger had hired security to guard the Snowden files around the clock.

Rusbridger refused to give in, but then between July 16 and 19, "government pressure intensified, and in a series of phone calls and meetings, the threat of legal action or even a police raid became more explicit." Oliver Robbins, Britain's deputy national security adviser, told Rusbridger on July 18 the government would be sending agents to *The Guardian* offices. After he made it clear that copies of the files existed in America and Brazil, Rusbridger submitted, "I preferred to destroy our copy rather than hand it back to them." He did not want the confiscated material to be used in court if Snowden was apprehended.[65] He also feared the authorities would make good on their threats. Rusbridger was not worried for two reasons.

He knew *The Guardian* could continue reporting from its New York base, and long before the computers and recording devices were destroyed, Rusbridger had sent a thumb drive of selected Snowden documents to the United States. The materials eventually reached their destination: the former editor of the *Wall Street Journal* (*WSJ*) and founding editor of *ProPublica*, Paul Steiger.[66] *The New York Times* had also been given copies. Snowden consented to the arrangement.[67] Representatives from the British Embassy in Washington would later attempt to coerce *The Times* into relinquishing its copies of the Snowden files.[68]

When the American justice system's questionable pursuit of its own citizen journalists is placed alongside U.S. intelligence's predominant role with GCHQ, it is not unreasonable to humor whether the NSA had a silent role in Miranda's detention and the destruction of *The Guardian*'s hardware, especially considering the agency's propensity to capitalize upon Britain's looser national security and press laws. Britain does not offer its press analogous First Amendment rights. What is clear was two of the Five Eyes refused to admit wrongdoing and were willing to go to great and very questionable lengths to keep the press from informing the world about their surveillance methods, policies and practices. The unspoken consequences were clear. Journalism was suddenly viewed as criminal, and under British law, Miranda's detention meant the press's efforts were being equated with acts of terrorism.

Perhaps coincidental, the day *The Guardian* revealed its Snowden cache had been destroyed, the *WSJ* published, "New Details Show Broader NSA Surveillance Reach."[69#] Eleven days before, readers were reassured by the NSA memo the agency only "touches about 1.6 percent" of the information

#All material from *The Wall Street Journal* is based on secondary sources. The publication refused to provide primary documentation.

carried by the Internet on a daily basis. It was understood that a very large number of the 1.6 percent is foreign correspondence after carefully monitored minimization procedures, reverence for the Fourth Amendment, and advanced, exacting technology carefully filtered out almost all American communications. Yet the report's subtitle implies otherwise, "Programs Cover 75% of Nation's Traffic, Can Snare Emails."

The *WSJ* relays that the NSA has recourse to surveil the American populace through Blarney, Fairview, Oakstar, Stormbrew and a newly revealed and little known program titled "Lithium." When met by the assertion U.S. intelligence spies on citizens' email as well as metadata, NSA spokesperson Vanee Vines replied, "[M]inimization procedures [are used] that are approved by the U.S. attorney general and designed to protect the privacy of United States persons." The newspaper's response is surprising.

Whereas *The Guardian* and *The Washington Post* are known for their liberal perspectives and reporting, the *WSJ* is one of the most conservative newspapers in America. It quickly counters Vines' claim, "For the 2002 Winter Olympics in Salt Lake City, officials say, the Federal Bureau of Investigation and NSA arranged with Qwest Communications International Inc. to use intercept equipment for a period of less than six months around the time of the event. It monitored the *content* [my emphasis] of all email and text communications in the Salt Lake City area."

The *WSJ* proved the ability for the NSA to spy on Americans' data as well as metadata had been deliberately used, albeit, in the terms of the White Paper, the "intrusion on privacy interests [was] limited." Nonetheless, premeditated—and not incidental—violations had taken place.

On August 22, MacAskill returned to present, "NSA paid millions to cover Prism compliance costs for tech companies."[70] It is a historical marker to the recently revealed FISC ruling supposedly barring the NSA from continuing surveillance until it could remedy privacy invasions.

As the court was coming to a decision on whether American intelligence was breaking the law, the NSA's data providers' annual "certifications," which allowed the agency to continue its collaborative surveillance work, were withheld. The Internet providers were nonetheless granted temporary extensions. This forced PRISM participants to incur the costs of maintaining program compliance. A December 2012 newsletter tells the tale but adds that their expenses were ultimately reimbursed by SSO and, by extension, the taxpayer. MacAskill's report incriminates all participating companies' claims of ignorance of the program with the possible exception of Apple, which had been inducted into the program the month the court decision was passed. It also brings into question why PRISM providers were expected to meet new certification standards if the court previously ruled that the data relay program was constitutional.

Yahoo acknowledged the disclosure by stating, "We have requested reimbursement consistent with this law" (two years after it took place), and Facebook claimed it had never been reimbursed. MacAskill reports that in lieu of the published evidence, Google still "den[ied] [having] joined Prism or any other surveillance program." Both Microsoft and Google added in their comments that the firms were still waiting for permission to release their individual FISC orders to the public. Much like Hong Kong's official statement regarding its decision not to detain Snowden, the companies' incriminatory, blunt statements complemented by their pithy footnotes reveal they were tired of playing along with the federal government.

However, this is not the most telling portion of the newsletter. It reads, "It is important that these Certifications were renewed [by FISC], because they authorize FAA702 operations until 23 September 2013, even if Congress fails to pass, or delays passage of, a replacement bill for the 2008 FAA legislation which enable all FAA collection." The announcement adds, "[...] the law permits operations to continue as long as the Certifications are in effect." An ethically dubious practice analogous to Bush's stopgap which circumvented the FISC's edict that open wiretapping was illegal, the license to grand-father in legislation grants powers not given by Congress. This means the FISC has the ability to interpret as well as retroactively create law by overriding future legislation. The newsletter ends with the note that the Office of General Counsel intended to appeal the court's decision if it believed the NSA's new collection methods failed to meet compliance standards.

Eight days after Gellman exposed the NSA's deliberate abuses to the world, numerous news sources flocked to the *WSJ*'s "NSA Officers Spy on Love Interests" on August 23.[71] The short but brutally condemning exposé put yet another nail in the debate coffin. It does so not by what it states but what it implies.

While discussing with journalists Gellman's report, NSA Chief Compliance Officer John DeLong let slip during a conference call that willful domestic compliance violations have occurred. The incidences, which are mockingly referred to as "LOVEINT," involve NSA employees spying on former and current boyfriends, girlfriends and spouses. Most misdirected targeting was self-reported because analysts are contractually obligated to undergo regular polygraph examinations. Some violations were found during audits. Yet there is an incongruity in the story.

When Feinstein informed her intelligence committee of the LOVEINT violations, she paradoxically assured everyone that "in most instances" the violations didn't involve American data. Gellman had previously announced, "Some [classified NSA] reports make clear that an unauthorized search produced no records."[72] Placed alongside one another, the contradictory statements suggest XKeyscore and PRISM's filters do not guard American information from spying eyes. If they did, Feinstein would have had nothing to say to her peers because proper programming would not have allowed American surveillance. Furthermore, there shouldn't have been a report, because it is permissible to surveil any non-U.S. person, therefore the "instances" which didn't involve domestic spying would not have been in an issue.

A month later,[73] still under pressure by the media over the *WSJ*'s LOVEINT report, a September 11, 2013 letter from Inspector General George Ellard to the ranking member of the Senate Judiciary Committee, Charles Grassley, was released to the press.[74] It is a response to Grassley's request for answers four days after the *WSJ* broke the story.

Ellard opens by stating his office is currently conducting two instigations involving violations of misdirected domestic surveillance on past and present love interests and spouses. He was also in the process of reviewing another allegation. He goes on to outline several previous cases. For five years an NSA employee engaged in illicit contact chaining and collected American intelligence on two separate occasions. Another analyst spied on her husband, whom she suspected was having an affair. On the first day on the job, an individual queried the six email addresses of a former girlfriend. His violations went undetected for four days. One analyst, who was employed by the military, surveilled his wife, who was also a soldier. One privacy offender had made it a practice to research phone numbers of individuals whom she'd met at social settings.

Most resigned before investigations were completed. An agent who was found guilty was issued a letter of reprimand. Another received the same along with a 10-day suspension. Ellard admits in one case, "The Agency has been unable to locate records as to whether a referral was made to DoJ [the Department of Justice]." The Inspector General does not report a single instance where criminal charges were filed. The letter states some surveillance attempts found no results because the target was American. In others, domestic data was retrieved and removed. This would support the claim that once domestic information had been inadvertently collected, it is openly available whereas a general public search is protected by automated safeguards.

The day the original LOVEINT report filled headlines, another publication made its editorial debut with Snowden material. The British tabloid *The Independent* presented "UK's secret Mid-East internet surveillance base is revealed in Edward Snowden leaks"[75] on August 23. The article states that the news source had been informed "Britain runs a secret internet-monitoring station in the Middle East to intercept and process vast quantities of emails, telephone calls and web traffic." It does so by tapping underwater fiber-optic cables within the region. The data goes to GCHQ, which is then shared with the NSA. The report explicitly declares the "information on its [the station's] activities was contained in the leaked documents obtained from the NSA by Edward Snowden." It repeats this claim several times throughout the exposé.

There are several oddities within and about the editorial. It was the first of its kind to solely focus upon classified Middle Eastern surveillance activities. Also, after relaying an overview of the purloined data, the article devotes approximately half of its time to *The Guardian* having destroyed its files and "agree[ing] to the Government's request not to publish any material contained in the Snowden documents that could damage national security." *The Independent* argues *Süddeutsche Zeitung* having published "Snowden revealed names of spying telecom companies" on August 2, even though "[*The Guardian*] had details of the highly controversial and secret programme for over a month," was further evidence Snowden's chosen source had been silenced. The censored news outlet was therefore forced to find another venue for the remaining disclosures. The tabloid incorrectly reports that Greenwald's partner, David Miranda, had been *arrested* on August 18.

The day the story appeared on *The Independent*'s front page, Snowden issued a 150-word statement to *The Guardian*: "I have never spoken with, worked with, or provided any journalistic materials to [T]he Independent. The journalists I have worked with have, at my request, been judicious and careful in ensuring that the only things disclosed are what the public should know but that does not place any person in danger." He estimates, "[…] the UK government is now seeking to create an appearance that [T]he Guardian and Washington Post's disclosures are harmful, and they are doing so by intentionally leaking harmful information to *The Independent* and attributing it to others."

Snowden's announcement is accompanied by a response from Greenwald. The journalist adds, "[*The Independent*'s report is] the type of disclosure which journalists working directly with NSA whistleblower Edward Snowden have thus far avoided" and "Speaking for myself, let me make one thing clear: I'm not aware of, nor subject to, any agreement that imposes any limitations of any kind on the reporting that I am doing on these documents."[76] Another pundit acutely observed, "*The Independent* is owned by Alexander Lebedev and his son Evgeny. Lebedev Senior, a Russian oligarch, is a noted critic of Vladimir Putin. Putin has granted Snowden temporary asylum."[77]

Snowden was aware the British government had taken advantage of a new periodical, *The Wall Street Journal*, having recently released classified data. It would appear plausible to the public, especially after *The Guardian* made known that it had destroyed its files, for the muted newspaper to have passed the classified baton to another British news source. Snowden assumes and all indications suggest GCHQ leaked delicate military information to frame *The Guardian* and the NSA leaker. Also, if military personnel were harmed as a result of the disclosure, the British government could better justify its detention of Miranda. The article explicitly states, "One of the areas of concern in Whitehall is that details of the Middle East spying base which could identify its location could enter the public domain. The data-gathering operation is part of a £1bn internet project *still being assembled* [my emphasis] by GCHQ." Like "the White House," "Washington" and "the Kremlin," "Whitehall" is a metonym for British government. The report makes sure to add that satellite dishes reside on the premises.

Britain's version of the U.S. government's faux terror threat was a less subtle but much more ingenious media whiteout. *The Guardian* had evoked sympathy by reporting it had been forced to destroy the Snowden files. This also implied the government had something to hide. GCHQ had *The Independent* lay the groundwork to point the finger if GCHQ's station was attacked. To Britain's credit, though an English surveillance base in the Middle East wasn't targeted, it didn't wag the dog further by evoking or feigning an attack. However, the damage had been done. The implication had been made that Snowden and Co. put Britain at risk.

The Independent and GCHQ would be caught red-handed in a week. Included in its report is "Information about the project [British intelligence's station in the Middle East] was contained in 50,000 GCHQ documents that Mr. Snowden downloaded during 2012." The fact Miranda had been in possession of 58,000 documents would not be released to the press for seven more days.[78] The note could have been a complete fabrication which just happened to nearly hit the mark a week later. Until August 30, it was understood there was at most 20,000 files.[79] Only the British government knew any different. Not surprisingly, *The Independent* issued its own rendition of the *Post*'s anti-disclosure editorial on October 13.[80]

On August 26, Poitras premiered, "Codename 'Apalachee': How America Spies on Europe and the UN."[81] It is equal parts follow-up to MacAskill's June 30 report, "New NSA leaks show how US is bugging its European allies" and Greenwald's July 8 article, "NSA and CIA have maintained staff in Brasilia to collect satellite data," atop a general mishmash of miscellaneous data much like her July 1 review of NSA surveillance, "How the NSA Targets Germany and Europe." The editorial's exacting detail and description of particular surveillance practices is fascinating.

"Apalachee" is the code name for the U.N. offices in New York. "Magothy" is the American surveillance label for the EU Embassy in Washington. Two months before, MacAskill only mentioned that the NSA had blueprints for the U.N.'s 31st floor offices. Poitras includes them in her report. Interestingly, the two consulates are not monitored domestically. They are surveilled by NSA analysts and technicians in Brussels. The spying is made easier by both embassies being linked through a VPN, which affords the NSA certain technological advantages. One NSA employee reported, "If we lose access to one site, we can immediately regain it by riding the VPN to the other side and punching a whole (sic) out. We have done this several times when we got locked out of Magothy." NSA technicians have also decrypted the U.N.'s internal video teleconferencing system using Blarney. In a three-week period, the number of decrypted messages went from 12 to 458. The documents cited in the report correspond with signed orders for diplomatic espionage by then-U.S. secretary of state Hillary Clinton. Frighteningly, the 2009 directive included the surveillance of biometrics. Biometric spying uses highly advanced technology to catalog a person's physiological characteristics. This includes facial, voice and retinal recognition.

Poitras goes on to mention that the International Atomic Energy Agency in Vienna is surveilled by American intelligence, Blarney produces 11,000 pieces of data a year, before citing two previously unknown program names: "Dancingoasis" and "Rampart-T." The latter has been in operation since 1991 and its objective is "penetration of hard targets at or near the leadership level" or, in laymen's terms, it is being used to spy on 20 different world leaders. Like Lithium, little is known about Dancingoasis.

As with her August 5 exposé, "Mass Data: Transfers from Germany Aid US Surveillance," Poitras provides enough new information for a reader to connect the dots. In "Apalachee" she notes that the NSA monitors U.S. offices from abroad. In "Mass Data," she relays that the NSA abides by the surveillance laws of the nation in which it is stationed. She makes a point to reiterate it is legal for intelligence agencies to eavesdrop on foreign communications in "How the NSA Targets Germany and Europe" on July 1. Echoing the purported American practice of extraordinary rendition, wherein authorities transport a suspected criminal to a foreign country whose criminal justice laws are more lenient so harsher interrogation techniques can be used, Poitras' note forces the question of whether the NSA is surveilling its own country from abroad so that it may legally spy on its citizens.

Two days later *Süddeutsche Zeitung* and NGB added to the international conspiracy with "British Officials Have Far-Reaching Access to Internet and Telephone Communications."[82] Like Poitras' article, the German new sources continue where they had previously left off, "Britain Draws from German Internet." Having revealed that the international fiber-optic line TAT-14 was tapped by GCHQ, the German media goes on to report that other primary distribution cables are under British surveillance: Atlantic Crossing 1, Circe North, Circe South, Flag Atlantic-1, Flag Europa-Asia, Sea-Me-We 3 and Sea-Me-We4, Solas, UK France 3, UK Netherlands-14, Ulysses, Yellow and the Pan European Crossing. For German readers, the new concern was Sea-Me-We 3 and AC-1, which rest on native soil. More alarmingly, the German portion of Sea-Me-We 3 is owned by Telekom which, predictably, denied any knowledge of its communications being watched. Interestingly, one of the communications providers previously implicated in the English spying conspiracy, British Telecommunications, is reported to have designed some of GCHQ's surveillance hardware and software.

Though GCHQ had probably issued a report by this time to the NSA about what had been found in Miranda's possession, there was no proof there was not more. The intelligence community continued to investigate. By August 29 it felt confident enough to announce it was getting closer to answers of how Snowden managed to acquire the monumental amount of data that even he didn't have the authority to access. An anonymous former U.S. official who was familiar with the investigation relayed to NBS News, "Every day, they [intelligence officials] are learning how brilliant he [Snowden] was. This is why you don't hire brilliant people for jobs like this. You hire smart people. Brilliant people get you in trouble."[83] Senator Feinstein had told reporters in late June she'd been informed Snowden had stolen approximately 200 documents.[84] Two months later, after the number had risen to 20,000, then skyrocketed to 58,000, the NSA admitted it was still unable to determine exactly what the whistleblower had pilfered. But the agency had discovered one method he'd used. Snowden had learned his lesson from his first futile attempts to access highly classified files when he was with the CIA and Dell. Instead of trying to steal them himself, he stole them as someone else: Snowden had gained access by borrowing other NSA employees' identities. As a system administrator, he had the ability to create and modify user accounts. The whistleblower cherry-picked who he wanted to be and with what level clearance. The ongoing forensic investigation revealed he had used other personnel's accounts when they were on vacation or called in sick so as not to arouse suspicion. It also saved him the trouble of having to remove his electronic footprint afterward. The anonymous source stated, "The damage, on a scale of 1 to 10, is a 12."[85] By December, the NSA would admit to *60 Minutes* that the actual number of stolen items was closer to 1.7 million.[86]

The discovery provided enough pieces of the puzzle to gain a glimpse of Snowden's methodology. He would tell former CIA analyst Ray McGovern on October 9 the laptops he had been seen with in Hong Kong were "diversions"[87] or decoys. The computers were not empty, but they did not contain all the stolen documentation. Snowden could not risk having all the data confiscated. He knew if he were apprehended, he would be searched. The laptops had to house something incriminating, otherwise security would continue looking. He was aware it would take time for forensics to discover his identity theft, and by providing the authorities with something substantial, he could be tried and sentenced before they found the full contents of his lifted catalog. Therefore he had created and initiated the timed contact release program for his encrypted passwords before he left America in case he was apprehended before he met Greenwald and Poitras. He undoubtedly told them—should he be caught—to withhold reporting until after his trial. There was no worry of China draining the contents of his laptops because they contained little or nothing of consequence. As noted, by the time he landed in Russia, he didn't have a single classified file in his possession.

August 29 was also a day for disclosures. The Australian news source *The Age* and *The Washington Post* published a total of four reports in less than 24 hours.

It was inevitable more information would come to light about the other Three Eyes—Australia, New Zealand and Canada—and their respective roles in collaboratively monitoring the world. *Süddeutsche Zeitung* passed along regionally applicable disclosures to an Australian journalist named Philip Dorling. A trained historian, Dorling became a political staffer in 1996 after working in the Australian Department of Foreign Affairs and Trade. He remained in politics and government until 2008. As with Poitras and Greenwald, Dorling had already earned his whistleblowing badge. Police raided his home in 2000 upon suspicion he had leaked information to the press about East Timor, a country occupying half an island in Southeast Asia.[88] Dorling became a journalist and got raided again in 2008 after he published an article which contained excerpts from a classified brief intended for the Australian minister of defense.[89] He was the sole Australian journalist to get direct access to the WikiLeaks "Cablegate" release in late 2010. Cablegate was the leak of 251,287 cables between the White House and numerous diplomatic missions around the world. He writes for *The Age* and *The Sydney Morning Herald*,[90] subsidiary publications of Fairfax Media.

"Australian spies in global deal to tap undersea cables"[91] expounds upon *Süddeutsche Zeitung*'s report on GCHQ's commandeering multiple fiber-optic lines. Dorling states the Australian Signals Directorate is working alongside British government, the NSA, as well as Singapore intelligence in order to surveil undersea cables connecting Australia, Asia and the Middle East. One of the tapped communication lines is one of world's largest, the previously mentioned Sea-Me-We 3.

An accompanying slide shows Sea-Me-We 3 runs across the entire eastern hemisphere and connects to Germany, Belgium, Britain, France, Portugal, Morocco, Italy, Greece, Turkey, Cyprus, Egypt, Saudi Arabia, Djibouti, Oman, the United Arab

Emirates, Pakistan, India, Sri Lanka, Myanmar, Thailand, Malaysia, Indonesia, Singapore, Australia, Brunei, Vietnam, the Philippines, Macau, Hong Kong, China, Taiwan and Japan. The data following through a portion of the cable is freely surrendered to federal intelligence—not by a private provider—but by its administrator, SingTel, a company owned by the Singaporean government and the country's Defense Ministry. Singapore authorities "cooperate" with the Australian Signals Directorate which, in turn, hands over the information to GCHQ. Because Australia's only connection to the cable runs through Singapore, GCHQ is able to monitor "much of Australia's telecommunications and internet traffic with Europe" through Sea-Me-We 3.

"NSA paying U.S. companies for access to communications networks"[92] arrived on August 29. It is the first in a series of seven nearly consecutive reports by Gellman, complete with an interactive slideshow. The article explores how the intelligence community intended to account for its $52.6 billion "Black Budget" from the latter half of 2012 through the beginning of 2013. The information was derived from Clapper's leaked FY 2013 Congressional Budget Justification report.[93] Though the numbers are overwhelming, they do not include the funding for military intelligence gathering.

Clapper spends the first two pages of the 178-page report bemoaning prior budget cuts. The first action item under "Signals Intelligence" is "[...] bolstering our support for clandestine SIGINT capabilities to collect against high priority targets, including foreign leadership targets." The director of national intelligence proceeds to ignore that millions of what he had already been given in previous years went to non-terrorist-related industrial, political and economic espionage as he acridly announces "[...] we will continue to house some of the IC [intelligence community] workforce in older and less capable facilities that may not meet current antiterrorism/force protection requirements [...]." It is unclear whether Clapper is stating these personnel will be in physical danger or obligated to use outdated surveillance equipment that does not abide by current law. The first item of concern under "Investments" is not the protection of American citizens but "[p]rioritizing our requirements [...] to produce a budget that meets customer needs [...]." As revealed in previous disclosures, the "customer" is corporate partnerships and other nations who have contracted NSA's services. Under "Mission Focused Science & Technology," Clapper wants biometrics to continue to be funded and further developed.

The report proceeds to list anticipated operational expenses. The individual budgets for the data-mining programs alone are massive. Blarney cost $65.96 million, Fairview $94.74 million, Stormbrew $46.04 million and Oakstar's tab was $9.41 million. The remaining $61.85 million goes unaccounted.

The report reveals that "Corporate Partner Access" data is expected to cost $278 million. Yet this fund is clearly for clandestine domestic partnerships. A separate line is allotted for "Foreign Partner Access," which is a comparative bargain at $56.6 million. The 500 percent difference shows where the NSA's surveillance priorities lie. Partnership money pays for data as well as the corporations' "network and circuit leases, equipment hardware and software maintenance, secure network connectivity, and covert site leases." At over 80 companies worldwide, the average payout is almost $4.1 million per contracted business.[94]

Paul Kouroupas, a former Global Crossing security officer, is paraphrased by Gellman. Kouroupas stated that some companies receive the payment with open arms and willfully sign government contracts. Doing so is not only convenient but lucrative. These businesses realize they would draw less revenue if they were to merely charge for individual court orders. Gellman summarizes attorney Albert Gidari, who reported that firms also enter into agreements with Washington to defer the legal cost of having each FISC order reviewed. As witnessed by Yahoo and Facebook's grievances, he added that the U.S. government uses the Machiavellian tactic of dragging its feet when it comes to reimbursing those who insist on receiving individual orders. This gives companies even more incentive to sign on the dotted line.

The next article, "U.S. spy network's successes, failures and objectives detailed in 'black budget' summary"[95] reveals that the U.S. intelligence community consists of 107,035 employees and its largest department is the CIA. Its budget was $14.7 billion. The NSA's spending allotment was $10.8 billion.[96] Gellman relays, "The surge in resources for the [CIA is] funded secret prisons [i.e., rendition camps or "black sites"], a controversial interrogation program, the deployment of lethal drones and a huge expansion of its counterterrorism center." One-fifth of intelligence workers—21,575—are CIA. Of its total budget, $68.6 million went to "creating and maintaining 'cover'" for overseas operatives to present themselves as peaceful diplomats. Though Clapper wanted more money for biometrics, monumental advances in this state-of-the-art technology had taken place since Clinton's 2009 directive. The CIA was using drones to conduct physiological espionage in the Middle East. U.S. intelligence could now identify a person from thousands of feet in the air.

Depending on a reader's perspective, Gellman's next topic can be viewed as either an objective or a failure. Ironically, the people who are paid to be suspicious were growing paranoid of one another. The NSA had started to worry about "potential insider compromise of sensitive information." The agency intended to reinvestigate 4,000 of its civilian employees. It wanted to review "high-risk, high-gain applicants and contractors" or the anti-establishment, anti-authoritarian computer geniuses the agency couldn't function without. It knew that a cultural and philosophical divide dwells within the current generation of analysts. As former NSA inspector general Joel F. Brenner remarked, "There were lots of discussions at NSA and in the intelligence community in general about the acculturation process. They were aware that they were bringing in young people who had to adjust to the culture—and who would change the culture."[97] This generational antagonism was evident in the crowd's response to Alexander during the Black Hat conference in Las Vegas. But the reception could have been a lot worse. The General had been advised not to represent the intelligence community at the DefCon conference which took place the same week. As a security conference, the Black Hat convention attracted professional technicians and would be more accepting of government authority figures. DefCon was a hacker meeting.[98] The NSA knew it needed to recruit from both groups but had difficulty trusting Generation X's IT wizards. The disproportionate rate of pay to education, even for analysts holding college degrees, is offered in an attempt to quell the inherent discontent. Most lawyers and psychologists fail to earn what Snowden did at BAH. Many doctors and surgeons are below the whistleblower's pay grade when he worked for Dell.[99] The NSA also worried about double agents infiltrating the agency. Gellman goes into greater detail about this facet of the Black Budget in a later exposé.

Shifting gears once more, Gellman relays, like Germany, Washington views Israel as both a surveillance partner and target because the country "has a history of espionage attempts against the United States." Iran, China and Russia's systems are admitted to have strong spy defenses, but the greatest surveillance stronghold is North Korea. There are "critical gaps" in intelligence on North Korea. The NSA knows "virtually nothing" about its leader, Kim Jong-un. Other intelligence omissions include concise knowledge of Lebanon's Hezbollah movement and China's aircraft capabilities.

The third installment in the Black Budget series is "To hunt Osama bin Laden, satellites watched over Abbottabad, Pakistan, and Navy SEALs."[100] The article tells how the al-Qaeda leader was found. With the aid of 387 high-resolution and infrared images gathered during the previous month, the commando raid that discovered and killed bin Laden had been directed by satellites. Using metadata then cell phone GPS, the Navy SEALs were led to where bin Laden was hiding in Abbottabad. Eight hours later, DNA confirmed his identity. The determination was made after having covertly obtained blood samples from those around the terrorist. The lab results verified his immediate circle consisted of relatives. The CIA had recruited a Pakistani doctor, Shakil Afridi, whose cover was that of a public health worker distributing vaccinations. Afridi was later convicted and sentenced to 33 years for crimes against the State. The sentence has since been overturned but is set for retrial.

Gellman returned on August 30 to present, "U.S. spy agencies mounted 231 offensive cyber-operations in 2011, documents show."[101] It is a companion article to Greenwald's June 7 cyberattack directive report. It reveals Obama's order was not an exercise in hypothetical espionage. It followed a year in which Operation "GENIE" produced over 200 U.S.-led cyberattacks.

It costs American taxpayers $652 million for intelligence workers to infiltrate foreign networks and computers. Once in, they insert malicious software or "malware," so analysts can remotely control "thousands of machines." An anonymous official is quoted as saying the NSA's agenda is to "[...] pry open the window somewhere and leave it so when you come back the owner doesn't know it's unlocked, but you can get back in when you want to." Gellman reports the ultimate goal is to infect millions of systems. GENIE includes a program code-named "Turbine" which monitors all of its spyware bugs. It has the capability to run "potentially millions of implants." As Snowden did, the implants are designed to ensure no electronic footprint is left behind. System logs are automatically modified or deleted after a hack has taken place.

Recalling the *SCMP* reports, the NSA's targets extend well beyond terrorist networks and include foreign banks, universities and civilian computers and networks. As outlined in the President's directive, other objectives are "to manipulate, disrupt, deny, degrade, or destroy information resident in computers or computer networks, or the computers and networks themselves."

The first stage of American cyberespionage is assigned to the NSA division with an oxymoronic acronym, Tailored Access Operations (TAO). TAO is comprised of engineers who construct tailor-made software and hardware for the secret agency to deploy. They have a range of ready-made templates engineered to fit a variety of standard "routers, switches and firewalls from multiple product vendor lines." TAO's spying products are designed to copy stored files, survive program updates and retrieve communications. The department's current project is to create biometric software that can detect and record an individual's conversation out of a sea of chatter. Once realized, it will be analogous to being able to distinctly and clearly understand what a single person is saying in a stadium full of roaring fans.

Gellman then decided to take a day off. *Der Spiegel* took the disclosure helm with the uncredited exposé, "NSA Spied on Al Jazeera Communications."[102] It is a brief overview of the NSA's surveillance of the Arab broadcaster Al Jazeera. The news outlet has broadcast al-Qaeda video messages for more than 10 years. A March 23, 2006 classified document shows American intelligence hacked into Al Jazeera's internal network. The espionage effort was considered a "notable success." The agency accessed and read communications by many "interesting targets." In the process it had gained access to Russia's Aeroflot flight reservation service database. It is possible the U.S. government knew Snowden was en route to Cuba via Russia before his flight made headlines.

Gellman returned the next day to publish the fifth editorial in the Black Budget series, "U.S. intelligence agencies spend millions to hunt for insider threats, document shows."[103] Following his report on the NSA's success and failures, Gellman devotes more time to the threat of internal spies within the intelligence community. The sudden alarm was the result of Manning having given thousands of documents to WikiLeaks in 2010. Congress demanded Clapper conduct an investigation of current employees. Interestingly, Capitol Hill had given the director of national intelligence an October 2012 deadline to install an automated detection system. If he had met the project's cut-off date, the world might not have heard of Edward Snowden.

The previously cited investigation of 4,000 current intelligence employees was the result of keystroke monitoring raising eyebrows. The NSA discovered agents were irregularly accessing databases and downloading multiple documents. Though Snowden had done the latter, he failed to arouse suspicion because of his job title and by masking his identity under other employee's accounts. Gellman suggests the administration's anxiety applies to a previous budget year because it took place "long before" Snowden leaked his information. Even if the proposed reevaluations were for the present year under discussion, 2012, Snowden's USIS background check had occurred in 2011. Strangely, if the timeframes were aligned, the whistleblower wouldn't have needed to worry. An anonymous NSA representative stated "contractors like Snowden" weren't being put under the magnifying glass. No further explanation was given why he would have been automatically exempt from suspicion.

However, the intelligence community's primary concern was not whistleblowers. It was infiltration. It is reported that one in five CIA applicants within a particular employment "subset" are turned down because something in their background suggests a potential terrorist element or, in the agency's terms, the candidates possess "significant terrorist and/or hostile intelligence connections."

The report reveals Washington freely and unapologetically views all leaks as a treasonous or terrorist act. Obama instituted an insider threat policy through an Executive Order issued in November 2012.[104] It designates the unauthorized release of classified material as "espionage" and equates it with terrorism. Gellman quotes Steven Aftergood, a government secrecy expert, "It's disturbing, because they [whistleblowing and terrorism] are not the same. There are such things as a good leak. Some classified things should be public. The official policy does not admit that distinction."

Sixth in the collection of exposés is "U.S. documents detail al-Qaeda's efforts to fight back against drones."[105] It premiered on September 2. An accompanying document[106] maintained by the *Post* reports 358 drone attacks have occurred in Pakistan since 2004, averaging a bombing every nine days. There have been a total of 70 in Yemen and Somalia since 2002, averaging one attack every two months. The Snowden disclosures report Al-Queda is attempting to develop and implement antidrone tactics because of the persistent threat. These include satellite interference "with GPS signals and infrared tags that drone operators rely on to pinpoint missile targets." Gellman makes sure to add he is not revealing delicate classified information. As researchers at the University of Texas proved in 2012, radar confusion is as simple as replicating a drone's GPS signal and redirecting the aircraft. However, to date al-Qaeda has been unsuccessful in disrupting a single attack. The satellite transmissions are encrypted.

Unfortunately, the U.S. military has failed to encrypt drones' video relays. In 2009 Iraqi insurgents on the ground could see where a drone was traveling the same as the Americans who were flying the aircraft. Video feed encryption for drones will not be completed until 2014. Gellman also relays that a drone's inherent weak point is identical to the Achilles Heel of a remote controlled car. Once it moves out of range, a drone cannot be manually navigated. American intelligence must wait for the autopilot program to return the aircraft to a receiving area. On rare occasions drones have crashed before intelligence regained control.

Classified documents show the intelligence community is also concerned with public opinion. In the same manner that the phrase "The War on Iraq" was consciously changed to eliminate the human element and replaced with the more abstract "The War on Terror," military intelligence was aware the term "drone" possesses a cold, apathetic sensibility. Amongst the lexicon substitutions offered was "robot warfare" despite the opposition having no aerial weaponry. Gellman refrains from noting similarities in intelligence labeling an individual under surveillance a "target"—an inanimate object which is designed to be fired upon—as opposed to a "suspect" who has yet to be convicted of a crime.

Gellman closed the Black Budget series on September 3 with "Top-secret U.S. intelligence files show new levels of distrust of Pakistan."[107] In lieu of the United States bombing the nation almost weekly, Washington considers Pakistan an ally but keeps it at arm's length much like Germany and Israel. Paradoxically, and perhaps due to a guilty conscience, the U.S. has given the country an average of two billion dollars in aid per year over the course of the last decade. Still, America's actions reveal its attitude. As Pakistan's former ambassador to the United States, Husain Haqqani, observed, "The mistrust now exceeds the trust."

Though it would serve American intelligence well to remain on good terms with the Middle Eastern country due to its proximity to centralized Islamic concentrations, the United States is apprehensive about Pakistan because of its estimated 120 nuclear arms, human rights abuses and biological and chemical weapons stores. The root of the intelligence community's trepidation is the security of the foreign land. Washington worries that if Islamic militants were to take over, Pakistan's weapons would be turned toward America. One of the most critical intelligence gaps regarding Pakistan is how the country transports and builds its nuclear weaponry. Because of this, the U.S. intelligence is making full use of its surveillance abilities in Afghanistan in order to keep an eye on the country's eastern neighbor.

At best, the Pakistani-U.S. alliance is an uncomfortable one. Washington has been caught more than once turning a blind eye to Pakistan's human rights abuses. A September 2009 cable from the U.S. Embassy in Islamabad to Washington reported extrajudicial militant killings by the Pakistan army. The Obama administration sought to silence the incident for fear of bad press because of America's political affiliation. When the message was leaked and later disclosed on WikiLeaks the following year, the White House informed the public it had remained quiet in order to keep the foreign nation's military from suffering retaliation. In November 2010, a video appeared online showing six bound and blindfolded men being executed by the Pakistani militia. Only "low-level Pakistani army units" the White House believed to have been responsible were refused their regular financial support. U.S. intelligence discovered in May 2012 that Pakistani officers aimed to "eliminate" human rights activist Asma Jahangir "to quiet public criticism of the military." Neither the U.S. military nor U.N. intervened. Once Jahangir was told of the plot, she quickly conducted a series of interviews to raise public awareness. She is still alive.

As Gellman was informing the world of the NSA's internal trust issues, *Der Spiegel* presented a very brief disclosure, "NSA Targeted French Foreign Ministry."[108] With the exception of the Morales plane incident and U.N. spying allegations, France had avoided the disclosure spotlight. The article states that a June 2010 classified document shows the NSA was monitoring French diplomats' computer networks and, like the U.N. offices in New York and Washington, did so by exploiting the VPN. The hack granted access to diplomatie.gouv.fr and resulted in a "collection of computer screens." It is unclear if this is intelligence jargon for multiple screenshots or continued, open access to a number of computers. Though a medium intelligence priority at best, the NSA was data mining America's ally in hopes of stealing information relating to France's weapons trade and economics. The nation's president, Francois Hollande, had already threatened to suspend free-trade talks with the U.S. after the initial U.N. spying reports were released.

Rounding out September 1 was an 11-minute *Fantastico* news report.[109] Using an internal NSA document dated June 2012, the news program displayed intercepted text messages by then-Mexican president Enrique Pena Nieto. The purloined intelligence included the then-candidate's considerations for cabinet members. The nine other presidential candidates were also placed under surveillance over a course of two weeks. A program called "Mainway" collected bulk data, and "Dishfire" filtered the communications. The NSA had also surveilled Brazil's leader, Dilma Rousseff, and her chief advisors. During the production of the news broadcast, Greenwald set up an encrypted chat with Snowden and the *Fantastico* staff. (Knowing he would be quoted, Snowden made sure to state he was unable to comment directly on the contents of the classified documents lest he hurt Russia's ally.)

The NSA viewed the espionage assignment as proof it could "find a needle in a haystack." Another series of confidential slides show that after a "hop," the intelligence community attempts to establish connections and associations between secondary targets. This is referred to as "Hop 1.5." Another slide asks, "Friends, Enemies, or Problems?" and lists Brazil, Egypt, India, Iran, Mexico, Saudi Arabia, Somalia, Sudan, Turkey, Yemen and "others" for the project years 2014 to 2019. An internal newsletter dated May 2005 states, "ISI (the International Security Issues division of the NSA) is responsible for [the surveillance of] 13 individual nation states in three continents. One significant tie that binds all these countries together is their importance to U.S. economic, trade, and defense concerns. The Western Europe and Strategic Partnerships division [of the NSA] primarily focuses on foreign policy and trade activities of Belgium, France, Germany, Italy, and Spain, as well as Brazil, Japan and Mexico." It goes on to add, "The Aegean and Ukraine division works all aspects of the Turkish target" including diplomatic relations. ISI is also tasked with gathering "financial intelligence." The newsletter announces the NSA intends to establish ISI divisions outside of its Washington bases. The expansion includes ISI technicians in Georgia, Hawaii, Texas and the European Security Command. ISI workers were scheduled to begin arriving in Texas in June.

As had been the case with previous exclusives, the news station's timing was deliberate. *Fanastico*'s latest exposé premiered shortly after Mexico's minister of justice, Jose Eduardo Cardozo, had returned home following talks with vice president Biden about the *O Globo* disclosure reports. Biden was slated to travel south shortly after the newscast to discuss Mexico's economic policy. Rousseff was scheduled to arrive in Washington in October. It was a highly anticipated visit signifying Brazil's growing stature on the world's stage. The day after *Fanastico* aired its report, Rousseff summoned Brazil's U.S. ambassador.[110] She demanded answers.

In 2010, *The Guardian, Times* and *Der Spiegel* blanketed the globe with headline-grabbing news. They simultaneously reported on the U.S. government's "War Logs," a data dump consisting of 91,731 files pertaining to the Afghanistan War which WikiLeaks posted online on July 25.[111] Three news sources came together again, this time with *ProPublica* filling in for *Der Spiegel*, to issue one of the biggest exposés within the Snowden files. The reports took two months to produce.[112]

Greenwald reemerged on September 5 to present, "Revealed: how US and UK spy agencies defeat internet privacy and security."[113] Not content with having access to only Microsoft's operating systems, Greenwald reports that GCHQ and the NSA developed and are using technology that cracks encryption codes across the Internet. A classified 2010 GCHQ documents states, "For the past decade, NSA has lead (sic) an aggressive, multi-pronged effort to break widely used internet encryption technologies. Vast amounts of encrypted internet data which have up till now been discarded are now exploitable." Despite Internet companies' assurances that their transmissions were secure, the intelligence agencies have access to the contents of protected email, web searches, online chats, banking transactions and even medical records.

Both spy agencies view encryption as a domestic war, as evidenced by the chosen code names for their collection and decoding programs. The NSA's is "Bullrun," the namesake of one of the primary battles fought during the American Civil War. GCHQ's is "Edgehill," the first major conflict of the English Civil War.

The intelligence communities use many decryption methods. One is the standard brute force attack. As previously noted, a supercomputer runs all of the possible permutations of numbers, letters and symbols until it finds the correct password or phrase. But this time-consuming technique is not their primary weapon against encoding. Gellman hinted at it six days before when presenting the various cyberattack techniques deployed by the NSA.

The NSA had snuggled closer to private Internet companies and become bedfellows with online security firms. With the latter, a portion of SIGINT's $254.9 million Black Budget bought American intelligence knowledge of antivirus programs' vulnerabilities as well as ensured backdoors would be—and would remain—available. In short, the spy agency's Commercial Solutions Center division contracted Internet defense businesses to ignore or create and install exploitable weakness in their programs which would only be known by the intelligence community. In the NSA's terms, the funds allowed the agency to "[...] covertly influence and/or overtly leverage their [U.S. and foreign IT industries'] commercial products' design." This includes the heightened security 4G cell phones are said to provide. When questioned if computer protection programs had built-in backdoors, many major antivirus distributors refused to comment or claimed ignorance of possible government involvement.[114]

GCHQ and the NSA were also forced to confront private Internet companies that had responded to consumer demands for greater security. In online encryption surveillance, two types of secure data transfers are carefully monitored, Transport Layer Security (TLS) and Secure Sockets Layer (SSL). The technology was first made widely available to the public by financial institutions and then online merchandisers before becoming standard practice for most major websites worldwide. This programming assures a web surfer that only the person browsing the Internet is communicating with a specific website. A secure connection is made by a browser simultaneously sending an asymmetric or public key alongside its website request. If the browser recognizes that the website has a SSL certificate, it uses the key to establish a secure, symmetric connection between the user and website. Any website with the URL prefix "HTTPS" (as opposed to the highly vulnerable "HTTP") is using TLS/SSL technology. The universal sign for a secure connection is a green padlock in a computer screen's address bar.

A security certificate is an electronic document which verifies that the owner of the website has the rights to the website domain or, in laymen's terms, it ensures a user that when a web address is entered, the individual or company claiming to own the website actually does. However, a classified document reveals in 2006, the NSA convinced the agency that oversees certificate licensing, the U.S. National Institute of Standards and Technology, to issue the NSA's version of the draft standard. The next year two cryptographers discovered the agency had included exploitable flaws in its proposal. The result, as American intelligence itself admits, was "[...] NSA became the sole editor." U.S. intelligence sought to further weaken the authority's power in 2013. A slated agenda within the Black Budget application is to "influence policies, standards and specifications for commercial public key technologies."

Without the encryption key, successful SSL infiltration that avoids detection is difficult and requires a large budget but is nonetheless possible. The safety feature can be compromised by instigating a "Man in the Middle" (MITM) attack.[115] Essentially, this type of hack does not break the SSL code but captures user data by impersonating a secure website. It reroutes a website request to a faux Internet location (which must look and operate like the desired, authentic, certified website). While the user browses the fake webpage, data is gathered without the web surfer noticing. But this is unnecessary if a spy has the encryption key for the website's SSL certificate. The analyst merely unlocks and records the data flow.

GCHQ already had three major companies under its thumb and could access 30 types of VPNs by 2010. It hopes to have the codes of 15 Internet firms and 300 VPNs by 2015. A 2012 quarterly update suggests British intelligence has compromised Google's security after "new access opportunities" presented themselves. GCHQ was still working on Hotmail, Yahoo and Facebook's encryption programs. Where the information couldn't be bought, GCHQ put personnel on the ground. British intelligence recruited and deployed undercover agents to get hired by Internet firms in order to gain access to encryption keys.

Information regarding the agencies' decryption programs is one of their most closely kept and guarded secrets. A classified instruction slide insists, "Do not ask about or speculate on sources or methods underpinning Bullrun." Analysts are told there is no "need-to-know" basis for relaying information about the spy tool. Even decoded data cannot be stamped as a Bullrun product: "Reports derived from BULLRUN materials shall not reveal (or imply) that the source data was decrypted. The network communication technology that carried the communication should not be revealed." Loss of surveillance capabilities as a result of "damage to industry relationships" is the greatest fear. (Washington had asked the *Post* to censor the names of the nine Internet companies which appear on the PRISM slides.)[116] By comparison, public backlash is listed as a "moderate" concern.

Whereas *The Guardian* presented its own account of the encryption scandal, *ProPublica* and the *Times* joined forces. *ProPublica* christened its article, "Revealed: The NSA's Secret Campaign to Crack, Undermine Internet Security"[117] while the *Times* opted for "N.S.A. Able to Foil Basic Safeguards of Privacy on Web."[118] Aside from their titles, only a few editorial amendments and two excised lines from the *ProPublica* version divide the work. As with any case of multiple reports on the same issue, the joint exposé covers much the same ground as *The Guardian* but places emphases in particular areas of interest while only mentioning aspects of the discussion Greenwald deemed more relevant. Mindful of its audience, the *Times/ProPublica* report is less concerned than *The Guardian* about GCHQ's role in undermining encryption technology. It devotes a large portion of its time to the NSA's pursuit of coded data.

As revealed in Greenwald's June 20 warrantless surveillance exposé, the editorial reminds readers it is NSA policy to (capture and) store encrypted communications regardless of its (revealed) place of origin or the nationality of its sender. It adds that Bullrun had a predecessor, "Manassas." Manassas is the Confederate title for the Battle at Bull Run but is also the name of an iron-clad ship used by the South during the Civil War. Ironically, the CSS Manassas was decommissioned shortly after being put into battle.

One of the article's primary concerns is the manner in which encrypted data is acquired. The report notes, "In some cases, companies say they were coerced by the government into handing over their master encryption keys or building in a backdoor." (This line was excised from the *ProPublica* rendition, as was the redundant, "Some companies have been asked to hand the government the encryption keys to all customer communications, according to people familiar with the government's requests.") Just as it had paid Cisco to install exploitable defects in its routers,[119] when a foreign intelligence target ordered new American computer hardware, the U.S. government had the manufacturer install a backdoor into the product.

The NSA's collection of encryption keys is large enough have its own named database, the Key Provisioning Service. If the storehouse doesn't have a key the NSA needs, the politely titled "Key Recovery Service" (GCHQ's equivalent division is code-named "Cheesy Name") is sent out to procure it. Following Greenwald's claim that ground agents are given cover and engage in social engineering to get passwords companies diligently refuse to hand over, the news sources report the NSA also hacks into businesses' databases in order to get encryption codes. Because of this, the Five Eyes only share decrypted messages if they were gathered using legally obtained keys. As an incriminatory GCHQ document states, "Approval to release to non-Sigint agencies will depend on there being a proven non-Sigint method of acquiring keys." Yet this clause may only exist for staff morale. Snowden told Appelbaum, "They [foreign nations] don't ask to justify how we know something, and vice versa, to insulate their political leaders from the backlash of knowing how grievously they're violating global privacy."[120] Regardless, this leaves open the possibility the quintet of spy agencies—much like U.S. intelligence's relationship with Pakistan, Israel and Germany—could be less than forthright in their joint surveillance activities since all have an alibi for withholding information. An internal NSA document even acknowledges that GCHQ has "unspecified capabilities against network technologies."

Though the NSA expects to have "full unencrypted access" to an unnamed Internet company, a Middle Eastern Internet service, as well as the data from three foreign governments by the close of 2013, its goal is not comprehensive retrieval of encrypted data. To save time, energy and resources, it hopes to obtain the power to do to all communications what it does with Microsoft: gain direct and live pre-encryption access.

Between the two reports, the British and American spy agencies' encryption agenda is clear. In the event they don't already own a website's public key, they first attempt to financially coerce the Internet company into surrendering its key. If the business refuses, it is threatened with a court order. If it obstinately stands on principle, a hacking directive is issued. Should the company's defenses prove to be impenetrable, moles are placed within the business to commandeer the code.

Fantastico returned on September 8 with a 13-minute feature[121] over the NSA's monitoring of the Brazilian oil giant Petrobras, specifically the company's internal computer network. The Rede Globo production also includes insight into the NSA and GCHQ's surveillance techniques. Petrobras was not only surveilled, it was deemed a prime example of a target in a series of NSA training slides outlining how to conduct corporate, government and financial espionage. It includes the SWIFT network, "the cooperative that unites over ten thousand banks in 212 countries." All international banking transfers use SWIFT. The slides cite Google and the private network of France's Ministry of Foreign Affairs as other exemplary targets.

As with diplomatic surveillance operations, access to financial and business records provides what is essentially insider trading information to the United States. Petrobras is one of the 30 largest companies in the world.[122] When questioned, GCHQ failed to respond, but the NSA reassured Brazil its economic surveillance was conducted only to aid in determining if an impending financial crisis was looming. It stated the intelligence was in no way used "to steal the trade secrets of foreign companies on behalf of—or give intelligence we collect to—U.S. companies to enhance their international competitiveness or increase their bottom line." Clapper stated, "It is not a secret that the intelligence community collects information about economic and financial matters, and terrorist financing."[123] It seems unlikely the NSA suspected the oil entrepreneur of having links to terrorism. Despite the American grievance that Chinese cyberspies hacked into the Pentagon and stole millions of dollars in military defense planning, the NSA had gained access to the latest technological advances in oil detection and extraction through Petrobras. Ethically, China's espionage dealt with a foreign nation's defense capabilities; America's spying focused on the private sector.

Accompanying documents also reveal two GCHQ operations code-named "Flying Pig" and "Hush Puppy." They are used to spy on TSL and SSL data transfers. The existence of the programs implies the agency does not have access to all encryption codes because MITM attacks were being used to intercept these coded communications.[124] The training slides tell analysts, "foreign government networks, airlines, energy and financial organizations" are susceptible to MITM intrusions.

On the first day of the G20 Summit, Brazil's president confronted Obama about the allegations that she had been the victim of American espionage. She'd told the president, "I want to know everything that they [American intelligence agencies] have. Everything."[125] It was confirmed she still intended to go to the White House in October.[126] A little over a week after the Petrobras report, Rousseff canceled the meeting.[127]

When *O Globo* first revealed American intelligence had been spying on her country, Rousseff initiated internal and external investigations into the claims. The country summarily started planning to reroute mainline undersea fiber-optic cables to bypass American connections and link directly with Europe and Africa. By August Brazil had signed a joint satellite venture with France and Italy to further secure the nation's communications. Because of the disclosures, Brazil will have its own national encrypted email system by 2014 so citizens can abandon American communication services such as Hotmail and Google.[128] After returning from the summit, Rousseff started pushing her legislators to pass a bill which would force foreign communication companies to store her country's domestic data on Brazilian servers.[129] Only the U.S. and India have more Facebook account holders.[130]

The next day *Der Spiegel* issued "iSpy: How the NSA Accesses Smartphone Data."[131] From a public relations perspective it was a deadly blow to the surveillance debate. It confirms that GCHQ's dream of "exploit[ing] any phone, anywhere, any time" had become a reality. The Poitras editorial begins with the tale of then-NSA chief Michael Hayden being solicited by an Apple salesperson. The employee bragged that the new iPhone had over 400,000 apps ("apps" are additional applications or programs a cell phone user can elect to download). Hayden turned to his wife and announced, "This kid doesn't know who I am, does he? Four-hundred-thousand apps means 400,000 possibilities for attacks."

The ability for intelligence agencies to use cell phones to spy on their owners is the result of the evolution of cellular technology. Cellular communication had gone from the basic cell phone which was only able to make and receive calls, to the "feature phone" that had the capability to receive texts and emails (and, later in its development, take pictures), to the smartphone which is a handheld computer. Poitras reports that half of mobile subscribers in Germany, over two-thirds of the British and 50 percent of Americans who own a cell phone—130 million—have smartphones. The three main types of smartphones are Apple's iPhone, Google's Android and the independently owned Canadian BlackBerry.

In early 2013 smartphones surpassed feature phone sales.[132] Because of smartphones' popularity, prevalence and capability, the NSA had found its long-awaited surveillance Mecca. An NSA presentation asks the analyst, "Does your target have a smartphone?" and lists spying techniques which can be used to exploit iPhones. The NSA has the ability to monitor 38 features and four operating systems of the Apple product. This includes a phone's texting, voicemail, photos, Facebook and Yahoo messenger features. The agency can tell where a smartphone owner has been, is, and plans to be through a user's Google Earth searches, GPS and mapping programs. The NSA acknowledges the process is made even easier because most users don't know these features have been activated. In most cases, the factory default for these programs is set to initiate when the phone is turned on for the first time.

This is not a new discovery. In late 2011 a systems administrator named Trevor Eckhart found that software designed by Carrier IQ was programmed to record dialed numbers (even if they are not transmitted), texts, Internet searches and keystrokes. The information was then relayed to the phone's provider which, by law, would be available to the NSA. Contrary to telecoms' denials, statistics suggest Carrier IQ's product was installed on virtually every smartphone. Andrew Coward, a Carrier IQ marketing manager, confirmed the report.[133] Nine days later, the company adamantly refuted Coward's statement. Echkart was presented a cease-and-desist letter. When the Electronic Frontier Foundation offered the computer technician legal assistance, Carrier IQ suddenly backed down.[134]

Poitras reports that additional classified data shows family photos, images of war zones and group pictures of friends that the NSA had stolen from smartphones. One picture is a self-portrait by a former foreign government official. Poitras suggests it is pornographic. U.S. intelligence can even tell where pictures were taken. A photo's GPS is inserted into the code of every picture captured by a smartphone as an Exif tag.

However, as witnessed in Snowden's precaution of having Greenwald, Poitras, Harrison and Russian attorneys remove the batteries and place their phones in the refrigerator, merely disabling these features is futile. Cell phones are designed to run at a low frequency even when they are turned off. This is perhaps one of the reasons why many models of smartphones have imbedded, or built-in, power sources. American intelligence calls the covert espionage capability "The Find." It was first utilized in 2004 and uses a type of spyware which is installed when a person innocently agrees to download a product update.[135] It was discovered in 2009 when a design flaw in the spyware crashed servers.[136] But Snowden wasn't merely attempting to keep his location a secret. He didn't want U.S. intelligence hearing what he had to say. The ability for authorities to remotely listen to conversations even when a phone is turned off was revealed in a 2006 court ruling.[137]

Even the smartphone which is marketed on its reputation for security has been compromised by the NSA. Poitras includes a screenshot of an instructional slide titled, "Your target is using a BlackBerry? Now what?" It contains a BlackBerry's decrypted email from a Mexican government agency. Because of its security features, BlackBerry was once the preferred cell phone for government employees. Now less than half of federal workers use the product.

Poitras states that users make it even simpler for the NSA to spy. Because most smartphone owners have their phones programmed to "synch" or relay all of the phone's data to their personal computer, the NSA has two outlets to retrieve information. But the particulars are not important because a three-frame overview[138] labeled "Top Secret" and titled, "iPhone Location Services" reveals the NSA's attitude, approach and capabilities.

The first slide, which bears the caption, "Who knew in 1984 … ," contains two pictures from Ridley Scott's iconographic Apple commercial which aired during that year's Super Bowl. The advertisement is an adaptation of a scene from George Orwell's classic 1949 dystopian tale, *Nineteen Eighty-*

Four. It is thematically relevant because Orwell presents a totalitarian state which is under constant and absolute government surveillance. The next slide shows former Apple co-founder and CEO Steven Jobs presenting the latest iPhone to audiences. The caption continues from the first slide, " ... that this would be big brother ... ." This is referring to the cell phone and not Jobs. Big Brother is the metaphor for the omnipresent eye in Orwell's novel. The last slide houses two pictures: an enthralled, dancing customer who has just purchased an iPhone and a person with "iPhone 4" painted on his cheek. The caption finishes the sentence, " ... and the zombies would be paying customers?"

"Who knew in 1984 that this would be big brother, and the zombies would be paying customers?" The individuals in the final slide do not appear to be terrorists.

The NSA had turned the people's phones against them. The intelligence agency even mocks the fact that the watched are, through their own taxes, paying the watchers to spy on them. The "zombies" don't even own the legal rights to the phones which are tracking their every move and thought. When a cell phone's contract is paid off, the phone's owner receives an "unlock code" which is essentially the digital deed to the device. Only after the code is entered, thereby "rooting" the phone, can a person have complete control over the machine's programming. (In January 2013, Congress made it illegal to unlock a cell phone without the provider's consent.)[139] Until then, because the phone is property of the manufacturer, the company decides which programs are mandatory. Obama's reassurance on August 9 that skeptics of federal oversight can rely on private industry to develop and provide privacy measures was insulting to all but the most uninitiated. The businesses offering the technology were issued court orders and paid millions of dollars to obtain and surrender user data to the government. The communications providers and U.S. government have little worry that the masses will one day control their phones. Long before most smartphone owners pay off their contact, they are hungry for the latest technology and freely enter into another agreement. Until then, the phone as well as the data within it is property of the provider.

As the last slide states, the irony is that the government didn't have to convince or coerce its citizens that surveillance was necessary. Nor did it have to spend money to do so. The watched have shown they are willing and eager to hand over their rights and hundreds of thousands of dollars for what is essentially government surveillance tools disguised as an all-in-one phone, computer and personal manager. There are even biometric apps that users can download free of charge. They monitor sleep patterns, recognize fingerprints and track walking and running rates. Most smartphones come equipped with voice recognition software. Moreover, smartphone clients are not only allowing themselves to be freely surveilled, they are working for American intelligence. With Exif tags, the NSA is able to create a layout of the inside of a building, business or home without having to place bugs or implants within the facility because smartphone users are unconsciously acting as undercover spy agents each time they take a picture.

The U.S. government had been watching its citizens since the advent of the telegram, but only recently has it been able to do so with near-absolute precision, accuracy and mind-numbing ease. Though it was inevitable, it had been predictable. Since the time of the wired cable, each step of technology afforded the U.S. government greater and greater surveillance opportunities. From the widespread use of the telephone to the advent of the Internet, federal spies clipped the heels of technology as it moved toward the panopticon. The NSA is correct, 1984 is now.

Afterword

"They who can give up essential liberty to obtain a little temporary safety, deserve neither liberty nor safety."

–Benjamin Franklin, *Memoirs*[1]

❈ ❈ ❈

DOES THE U.S. GOVERNMENT INTENTIONALLY, exclusively spy on innocent Americans?

Former intelligence workers, the press and foreign governments claim it does; the White House, NSA and American corporations swear it does not. Everyone has an opinion but one thing is obvious. The intelligence community has the necessary ingredients. It possesses both capability and initiative. The next stage of surveillance, biometrics, is no longer science fiction. The newest wave of technology isn't sauntering up the porch steps and preparing to ring the doorbell. People are holding it in their hands. The newest incarnation of iPhones offer fingerprint identification. Most every smartphone comes equipped with voice recognition. (The iPhone's program title even sounds like an intelligence code name: "Siri.") People can freely download sleep analysis software. The newest gaming consoles house environmental scanners which detect motion, tracks players' heart rates and conduct motion-pattern analysis, which reads and creates a physiological fingerprint of an individual's unique body movements and mannerisms. As novelist John Lanchester noted, "Members of the security establishment always want more abilities, more tools, more powers for themselves and fewer rights for us. They never say 'thanks a lot, we're good from here, we have everything we need.'"[2] Governments across the globe continue to put immense amounts of time, labor and taxpayer money into creating a comprehensive Big Brother program and they intend to make the electronic panopticon a reality by any means necessary. As the joint encryption exposés make clear, private industry's compliance with government surveillance will be achieved through willful participation, court order, social engineering or outright theft. Those in power have also proven they are willing to go to great lengths to keep people from seeing what lies behind the lead-lined surveillance curtain.

Some argue America is on the brink of an all-seeing electronic eye, that the surveillance state has already arrived, and Tony Scott's 1998 action thriller *Enemy of the State* is now a domestic drama. Lanchester observed a surveillance state— like a police state—is not one where there are watchmen on every corner. It is a world in which the spies are free to do whatever they want.[3] Surveillance laws are drawn so broadly almost anything is permitted. In Snowden's terms, the aperture is very, very wide. Through the gerrymandering of language and the aid of a hidden court's covert rulings, incidental collection is not viewed as illicit since it is not "direct" spying on Americans; investigations are green lit without "factual predication" because the U.S. government never bothered installing the same system of checks and balances found in local courts; any communication involving a foreigner is considered fair game, as is collected data since only metadata is protected by law; no "reasonable expectations" exist for the privacy of communication records; surveillance is permitted if it can be argued an American is *likely* to receive, not terrorist, but foreign intelligence; any data an analyst can categorize as "suspicious stuff" is pursued; the permissible contact chaining limit leaves less than a 15 percent chance a random U.S. citizen has not been monitored; all while U.S. intelligence has designated the terms "exercise," "prevention," "response," "metro," "forest fire," "recall," "power," "smart," "ice," "help," "pork," "cancelled," "recovery" and "watch" as dangerous and cause for immediate review.[4] U.S. intelligence has abandoned using a spy dragnet on its citizens; on paper, it now has the legal license to cloak the entire country in a surveillance blanket.

Many hope the worst has past. The world stared into the surveillance abyss when it learned Boundless Informant's existence had been hidden from Congress, the FISC ruled against another program which had been in operation for months before the court was aware it even existed and millions of dollars of the Black Budget are unaccounted in the congressional record. It is natural to wonder what else is going on that only the watchers know about. The nation shook when White House Press Secretary Jay Carney tried legitimizing illicit international espionage by declaring, "As a matter of policy, we have made clear that we do what other nations do, which is gather foreign intelligence."[5] The "everyone is jumping off a bridge" approach to political decision-making left the American populace crossing its fingers, praying Washington doesn't adopt the same line of reasoning when debating the topic of Syrian genocide.

The true fear lies not in what is occurring that will never be known, but what has yet to be revealed. History has shown intelligence agencies are aware what they are doing is wrong, because they have tried hiding it from those who would shut them down. The surveillance debate is punctuated with reluctant confessions. The NSA has grudgingly confessed it does accidentally and has, on occasion, deliberately watched its people. The head of National Intelligence admitted he was lying when he said domestic information wasn't collected. The admission "only metadata" gradually transformed into "live, raw, full-take data." The American people discovered if a U.S. citizen is talking to a foreign friend, analysts have permission to "focus [...] on the foreign end of the communication." Listening to only half of a conversation is a technique most find difficult to conceive but one which Washington has clearly mastered. On September 28 *The New York Times* announced the NSA has created profiles of Americans since 2010. "Irrespective of nationality or location," the spy agency "augment[s] the communications data with material from public, commercial and other sources, including bank codes, insurance information, Facebook profiles, passenger manifests, voter registration rolls and GPS location information, as well as property records and unspecified tax data" as long as the surveillance somehow relates to foreign intelligence.[6] Four days later, the public would be informed the agency had in fact tracked citizens' locations through their cell phones.[7] Eleven days after that an NSA slide would irrefutably display 250 million address books had been collected in the course of a single year. Officials estimate the statistic includes "tens of millions" of Americans' names, email and street addresses, telephone numbers and business and family relations.[8] Offshore surveillance is no longer a conspiracy theory. Because the FISC prohibits the collection of contact data, address book information had been gathered on foreign soil. In December, the world learned American intelligence has been placing agents in the virtual field of online gaming.[9] The public expressed concern that surveillance was taking place within a communication medium in which a large minority of users are minors,[10] atop the futility of spying on individuals who readily assume pseudonyms. The more the media pushes, the more U.S. intelligence grudgingly squeals.

For those who had faith, most has been lost. It is one thing to assume those sworn to protect a nation's interests are up to no good. The citizenry are allowed to live under the happy delusion everything is in order. A government that tells its populace it is undermining the trust of its people is unfortunate, but nonetheless permits everyone to deal with reality as it stands. It is an entirely different affair to contend with the psychological burden of being lied to. Much like Watergate forced Baby Boomers to abandon their post-war vision of utopia, the Snowden affair shattered Generation X's idyllic notion of a shinier, happier postmodern tomorrow. And the two eras are connected by a thematic bridge. In the 1950s, young Boomers were told technology would eventually solve humanity's problems. The advent of the Internet all but assured Gen X's teenagers the pledge had almost been met. As Boomers eased into retirement and their children slid into middle age, the promise was finally fulfilled. However, only the problems of the few had been remedied. For everyone else, technology had made life worse.

As Snowden had observed, part of the collateral damage are those who believed in President Obama's campaign promises of dismantling the surveillance state that was erected by his predecessor, George W. Bush. Obama's supporters felt betrayed when he defended the various spy programs. They were all but crushed after the press revealed he had made a point to strengthen them. Ron Paul's constituencies were left shaking their heads. American voters' apprehension is palpable. Washington was offering xeroxed reassurances to its people in the same condescending tone it was ladling verbal pats on the back to its purported espionage allies, nation states which the Capitol had duplicitously put under a covert surveillance lens. The U.S. populace wanted answers. The Administration gave it platitudes. Washington expected its citizens to innately trust what they were being told and adhere to rules it refused to follow. The White House continues to ignore a petition which had garnered the requisite number of signatures in half the required time, yet the Capitol seemed surprised that people were willing to stop and listen to a 29-year-old who had given up a long-term relationship, six-figure salary and a home in paradise in order to tell his fellows Americans something was wrong. Very, very wrong.

Ecuadorian foreign minister Ricardo Patiño acutely observed, "It's a paradox of life that now the whistleblower is being chased by the one being accused."[11] It is little wonder Snowden did not choose to follow in the footsteps of fellow whistleblower Daniel Ellsberg, who had leaked the Pentagon Papers 40 years before. Ellsberg opted to remain in America and stand trial. Snowden elected to leave. As Washington fanatically chased him around the globe, upsetting foreign relations as it went, U.S. representatives cited Snowden's flight as evidence of his guilt. But the damage had already been done. The Capitol's dogged pursuit was rightly viewed as a vengeance campaign. American intelligence and the White House had been undermined by a single video game-playing computer genius. Snowden had recruited his information conduits before he began his final round of document liberation. Once completed and after initiating a trio of journalists in the political and technological intricacies of what lay before them, he summarily walked away, leaving his whistleblowing apostles to spread the surveillance word and Washington no other option but to sidestep then whitewash the issue.

Snowden had set out to start a debate. But he served another purpose. He was a litmus to how the U.S. government, corporations, foreign nations and the media interact with one another. Shortly after he'd landed in Russia, an unnamed White House official quipped, "Mr. Snowden's claim that he is focused on supporting transparency, freedom of the press, and protection of individual rights and democracy is belied by the protectors he has potentially chosen: China, Russia, Cuba, Venezuela, and Ecuador. His failure to criticize these regimes suggests that his true motive throughout has been to injure the national security of the U.S., not to advance Internet freedom and free speech."[12] It was not that these foreign countries hypocritically agreed with Snowden's philosophy. China's willingness to stall for Russia as Ecuador, Venezuela, Nicaragua and Bolivia lent a hand in his escape was merely a reflection of these nations' opinions of the United States. Snowden's acceptance by these countries is also a subtle indicator of the level of degradation American civil liberties had fallen. The mandated privacy invasions in Russia and China were being eclipsed, if not already bypassed, by U.S. law and policy. Six years before the Snowden affair, Privacy International had downgraded the United States from an "extensive surveillance society" to an "endemic surveillance society." The country founded upon freedom now resided at the bottom of the liberty class alongside Russia, Britain and China.[13] Moreover, the Chinese and Russian people had been told they were being watched. By comparison, American government had installed a secret court whose rulings were hidden from the public and U.S. intelligence was running programs only it knew about.

Regardless of which side of the Snowden affair a person takes, there is little argument the Weibo user's looking-glass hypothetical reflects political reality. If a North Korean dissident arrived in New York with documents proving the communist country was spying on America, Washington would not happily acknowledge an arrest warrant and gladly consent to extradition proceedings that didn't exist. It is unlikely the press would be publishing pictures of Obama shrugging off the political lunacy after his airplane had been forced down over Iraq upon unfounded suspicions he was taking a "patriot of democracy" to safety. If the shoe were on the other foot, America would not be canceling dinner dates with foreign leaders. It would be at war.

And for anyone familiar with history or politics, it came as no surprise both the American and British governments used war as a ruse to whitewash their tarnished reputations. It had been done many times before and the tactic is unlikely to end with Snowden. The reason Obama was disgruntled over the press's "drip and drab" reporting was because he was working blind. The NSA could not tell him what he was up against. Washington had no other option but to dig in its heels and hope the world had a short memory. Greenwald and Poitras hadn't invented a new technique by countering each fallacious claim with hard-copy evidence, giving the White House less and less argumentative wiggle room with every utterance. The novelty of the Snowden affair resides in its prolonged timeframe. In most cases where the media dances with the government, the conversational waltz is relatively brief. With the NSA disclosures numbering in the thousands and possibly hundreds of thousands, the idea of a marathon debate that could extend well into the next presidency is a very likely possibility. Washington is enraged because the mere thought is exhausting.

The masterstroke of the media's presentation of the Snowden files is not its timing but its delicacy. It was a Herculean effort to assess what the NSA leaker had provided and decide on how to present the information. The press made sure to only refute the government's latest exaggeration, fabrication or outright lie while never showing the other classified cards in its hand. At best, it would only hint at what was coming next so as to keep Washington sweating. The genius of the media's presentation format was complemented by its decision to humanize the issue. Though Snowden made it clear he wanted the argument to be about the message and not the messenger, he realized the necessity of being the face behind the disclosures. Without him, the government could claim the documents were fabricated. Without him, no one could rightly confirm what was taking place within the confines of the world's most secretive agency. Without him, the world wouldn't care as much. He could have easily fled directly to Russia or any other country without an American extradition treaty but the whistleblower opted to put himself in the crosshairs, repeatedly.

No one is contesting Snowden has nerves of steel. Poitras had fled from the computer screen once she realized what her anonymous emailer had sent her. The whistleblower had stolen the top secret data over a course of several *years*. It is illegal to have classified documents outside a secure area. The consequences of his actions were compounded every time the NSA leaker stuck around to nab more, because his treasure trove of criminality grew with each theft. But he continued snatching one confidential file after another in order to make his argument more cohesive, more comprehensive, more condemning. Greenwald learned the severity of the situation in August. As Snowden acknowledged, he will live with fear and anxiety for the rest of his life. But the question of motive lingers.

Though the "Snowden Question" is largely irrelevant, people still wonder if he can be trusted; despite the catalyst being secondary to the result, it is human nature to nonetheless attempt to complete the puzzle. History has already proved one thing. He abided by the first law of whistleblowing: Don't lie, fabricate or hedge on the details, because the world will put both the claims and the claimant under a microscope. Poitras made sure Snowden was telling the truth so the surveillance debate wouldn't be buried under a character assassination once he was greeted by the public. The journalists had done their homework. After meeting the man behind the Rubik's Cube and learning his agenda and motives, they knew each time someone tried to say he was lying, the Snowden collective could prove otherwise.

While the NSA leaker said he was only an American who wanted to initiate a much needed discussion, others sus-pected—and have conjectured—he was a double agent whose mission was to undermine the United States.[14] It may never be revealed what Snowden did during his two "dark years" be-tween the summer of 2005 until the spring of 2006 and April or May 2012 until March 2013. It is remarkable that in less than half a year of working *around* intelligence, he had been recruited as an undercover CIA agent. It is equally daunting Snowden accomplished this without a degree. For academes, it is nothing short of a miracle to be accepted into a graduate program without a college diploma. He hadn't been given a cover to enroll into the University of Liverpool, because the college recognized his name. It does not help his case that he once worked for the notorious Defense Intelligence Agency. Without hints, it is tempting to let one's inner Ian Fleming run wild.

History might prove Snowden simply spent his first dark period unemployed and playing Tekken. His trip to Ireland could have been a gift from a rich relative. Perhaps he earned his bachelor's degree while working overseas and had grown accustomed and opted to promote the image of the unedu-cated savant spy. His second dark year is less promising for those looking to cast him in the role of a 21st-century Cold War espionage antihero. Snowden had already stolen a number of documents by this time. Alexander even suggested the NSA leaker worked for an intelligence contractor between Dell and Booz Allen Hamilton. Moreover, if he was conducting coun-terintelligence for another country, as the whistleblower himself stated, it makes sense he would have flown directly to his employer, delivered the information and disappeared into obscurity. But he didn't. It would be wise to let the ambiguities of life lie but Snowden's case is different. Too many questions remain unanswered.

For some it is implausible Snowden would risk being caught in Hong Kong if he didn't already have protection. For others the convenience of his selected reporters residing in countries where he needed distribution is too coincidental. Then there is the matter how he expertly pilfered from two of the world's most clandestine agencies. But his being a foreign spy seems unlikely. A career double agent who has completed his last assignment knows the risks of stepping into the light outweigh the temptation to thumb one's nose at those who have been duped. He took risks, very serious personal risks, in order to tell his fellow Americans what was being done in their name with their taxes as well as inform the world that much the same was taking place across the globe. His falling into the lap of Russia suggests he had come to an early agreement with the country shortly after the former Soviet Union learned who he was on June 9. His willingness to answer instead of simply refusing to respond to the *South China Morning Post*'s question of whether Russia had offered him asylum is the knowing tap on the side of the nose. The proof is Russia's harboring him in its Hong Kong embassy. The rest of the story is epilogue. My assessment of how he arrived in Russia may prove to be wide of the mark. Snowden could get a passport and travel to Venezuela tomorrow. But this is improbable. He seems content in Russia. He has done his duty. He has left the work for the next shift.

Regardless of who or what Snowden is and was, his impact is irrefutable.

In America, bill upon bill is being proposed on Capitol Hill. The White House's premature declassification of data and release of The White Paper is a simultaneous confession and defense of its surveillance activities. Numerous privacy and Fourth Amendment lawsuits have been filed against the federal government.[15] Restore the Fourth, a grassroots movement supporting the Fourth Amendment, held rallies nationwide on the Independence Day following the first disclosures.[16] A protest march on Washington took place on October 26. Attendees included Thomas Drake and former presidential candidate Gary Johnson.[17] In late October after it was revealed that the German chancellor's phone had been tapped,[18] the White House continued to deny wrongdoing by deliberately ignoring the past. Carney announced, "And I noted the other day a readout from a phone call the President had with Chancellor Merkel made clear that we do not and will not monitor the Chancellor's communications."[19] Under immense political pressure, Senate hearings ensued. During the proceedings Rogers echoed Chambliss's circular defense of American surveillance, "You can't have your privacy violated if you don't know your privacy is violated."[20] Using the congressman's logic, it is morally permissible to rob someone so long as the crime goes undetected. The chair of the House Intelligence Committee obviously sees the only misstep the NSA has made is having been caught. As for the NSA, Keith Alexander and Deputy Director John Inglis will leave their respective positions in the spring of 2014. Though new faces will be emerging, the spy agency shows no signs of slowing down.

Somewhat predictably given Clapper's adamant defense, the NSA hasn't changed its policies; it has merely tightened its security. Instead of conducting surveillance in a manner that won't plague an employee's conscience and spur another Snowden to action, the agency instituted an information lockdown. Shortly after the disclosures stared appearing, a two-person data extraction rule was instituted.[21] Whenever a file needs to be moved, another agent or analyst must be present. The same in-house legislation had been implemented in 2010 after Manning was suspected of having stolen thousands of files.[22] It is anyone's guess why the regulation was not being reinforced or did not apply to contractors handling top secret documents. Regular audits now take place.[23] Snowden was also found to have used the intelligence community's cloud service to steal files. The surveillance cloud was the product of pre-9/11 interagency information dispersal issues. Ironically and out of stubbornness and hubris, instead of cataloguing the data contained within the various departments' databases, the post-Snowden NSA decided to keep the massive security liability open and available as well as expand its capabilities. The super storage unit is code-named "Wildsage."[24]

Many critics of Snowden pondered whether the surveillance state is as omnipotent as the whistleblower has made it out to be. Their argument is Snowden himself. They cite his ability to evade detection as proof that not everything is being watched and recorded.[25] Ignoring that Snowden knew the intelligence community's blind spots, he also exploited the NSA's Achilles' Heel: volume (that is, if one doesn't count its atrocious grammar, poor spelling and juvenile PowerPoint construction and design). But U.S. intelligence had already begun to remedy this problem pre-Snowden. The NSA has since finished building the $1.5 billion Intelligence Community Comprehensive National Cybersecurity Initiative Data Center at Camp Williams, near Bluffdale, Utah. It is five times the size of the U.S. Capitol. The facility's capacities are modest. It houses the capability to store emails, cell calls, Internet searches and parking and banking receipts. Its mission is to be able to record and catalog a person's entire life. The Utah Data Center is estimated to be able to retain between three to 12 exabytes of data, or up to 12,000,000,000,000,000,000 bits of information.[26] The intelligence community no longer has to dump its full-take buffer after three days and metadata is now immortal.

Snowden had been wrong about one thing. He understated the NSA's ability to break encryption codes. He told Poitras, "Assume that your adversary is capable of a trillion guesses per second." Currently the intelligence agency has "Jaguar," a supercomputer capable of executing 2.33 quadrillion operations per second. In laymen's terms, Snowden's trillion is the next series of zeroes after a million. A quadrillion is the round after that: 1,000,000,000,000,000. Jaguar was slated to be upgraded and metamorphose into "Titan" by the end of 2013, which should enable the NSA to make 20,000,000,000,000,000 password guesses per second.[27]

Abroad, an entire continent has been alienated. Snowden had inadvertently unified all of Latin America. Brazil may never speak to Washington ever again and U.S. administration has dashed any hopes of forming an alliance with Venezuela after Hugo Chavez's death. It is not fairing much better with its southern neighbor. *Der Spiegel* followed *Fantastico's* September 1 report with a more in-depth look at American intelligence's Mexican surveillance.[28] Across the Atlantic, divisions have formed. Merkel's reelection bid was challenged on the issue of NSA surveillance[29] but she ultimately won. Due to the spying allegations, she now insists all U.S.-German joint spying activities be contractually bound.[30] In late September, India learned its diplomatic offices in New York and Washington were surveilled.[31] Instead of responding with technological counterintelligence, India instituted a security technique that makes espionage much more challenging: All sensitive documents are now composed on typewriters and Indian officials have top secret meetings outside embassy buildings.[32] France finally found itself center stage in mid-October when the long-standing daily *Le Monde* reported the NSA had intercepted 70 million French calls and texts in a 30-day period.[33] The European Union has proposed legislation which would force Internet companies to disclose when user data is being retained and to whom it is being reported.[34] The EU also moved to instate punitive measures against the United States. Various members of European Parliament have called to suspend the SWIFT Agreement with America.[35] The first step was taken two days after *Le Monde's* exposé premiered: a European council passed a non-binding resolution by a vote of 280-254 to boot the United States from the Terrorist Finance Tracking Program.[36] Clear lines of demarcation with America have been drawn by China and Russia. Obama did not meet with Putin at the G20 Summit though he talked with Hollande, Jinping and Japan's Prime Minister Shinzo Abe.[37]

Snowden's cultural influence threatens to rival his political impact.

German lingerie ads have used his name to promote their products, "Dear Edward Snowden, there's still a lot to uncover" and "Dear NSA, intimates—don't spy them, buy them."[38] An engineering firm in China registered to trademark

Snowden's name.[39] The term "Snowball Effect" has been adapted to include sociological results. "The Snowden Effect" is loosely defined as the consequence of an initial report manifesting in direct and indirect gains in public knowledge.[40] The European Union holds no grudges. Its foreign affairs department recommended the NSA leaker for the Sakharov Prize, which is annually awarded to freedom of thought and civil rights activists. Snowden received the Sam Adams Associates for Integrity in Intelligence award on October 9. The whistleblower has been called the John Brown of the 21st century.[41] He has been nominated for the Nobel Peace Prize.[42]

His influence has also permeated the entertainment industry. The animated television satire *South Park* devoted an entire episode to NSA surveillance.[43] *Verax*, a five-minute independent film about Snowden's arrival in Hong Kong, went viral in early July.[44] Hollywood has already started initial planning on a feature film about the American whistleblower.[45] An independent, small-budget movie titled *Classified: The Edward Snowden Story* is slated for release in September 2014.[46] A three-minute PSA about suspicionless surveillance narrated by John Cusak, Maggie Gyllenhaal and Oliver Stone among others premiered in October.[47] Perhaps the greatest cultural signifier of Snowden's impact is seen in George Orwell's *Nineteen Eighty-Four*. Shortly after the world saw Snowden's face for the first time, sales of the 64-year-old classic skyrocketed. It witnessed a 5,800% overnight increase in sales. The novel went from 7,397 to 125 on Amazon's bestseller list.[48]

Though the NSA whistleblower has changed the lives of millions of anonymous individuals worldwide, he permanently shifted the life trajectory of those closest to him. After Lon fought to see his son, only to be told time and again doing so was a security risk,[49] he arrived in Russia and met with Edward a little over four months since the NSA leaker became the most wanted man in the world. To date, his mother has never spoken to the press or offered comment. She did not accompany her ex-husband to the former Soviet Union.[50] At the time Snowden was issued the Sam Adams award, Jesselyn

Radack, Director for the Government Accountability Project, reported, "Laura Poitras is living in Germany and does not feel she can return to the U.S. without being detained. I believe Glenn Greenwald harbors similar concerns because his partner was detained. [...] Also, WikiLeaks journalist Sarah Harrison is stranded in Russia with Mr. Snowden because of the prospect of being detained on terrorism charges in the UK."[51] A small legion of journalists noticed that over one weekend in October, Snowden's former girlfriend, Mills, had downloaded pictures to her blog which bore cryptic titles that included symbols. It was theorized that though she might not have forgiven Snowden for abruptly fleeing under false pretenses, she was nonetheless covertly communicating with the American exile.[52] As for Snowden, Kucherena relayed to the press that the whistleblower has a new girlfriend[53] and started working as a security technician for a Russian website on November 1.[54] To date, he has offered to personally assist both Germany[55] and Brazil[56] in their inquiries and investigations into NSA surveillance.

While Snowden, the disclosures and government and corporate reactions have been discussed, analyzed and debated, few have addressed the elephant in the surveillance room. U.S. intelligence was revealed to have additional resources by which to cross-reference data. The White Paper states, "The FBI must rely on publicly available information, other available intelligence, or other legal processes in order to identify the subscribers of any of the numbers that are retrieved." "Other available intelligence" and "other legal processes" is intelligence jargon for the sister of government spying: corporate espionage. Ironically, the industry term for this is "business intelligence." In many respects this is a graver concern than government surveillance. Though federal spying is more invasive and has the law on its side, corporate espionage is more pervasive and largely unregulated. It is often more revealing than what the government has collected. The Snowden affair makes clear Big Business and U.S. government are doting bedfellows. It is also obvious Big Business is making a pretty penny from being forced to play along. But the public has only heard of the questionable means Washington goes to acquire data directly from communication sources. What is not being talked about is the intelligence it obtains from civilian data mining enterprises. These businesses come in two flavors: Private data collection companies and corporate retailers.

The latter consists of commercial retail and fast food establishments. Considering Microsoft, Yahoo, AT&T, Google, Sprint and Verizon's relationship with the federal government, it is not unreasonable to assume the data these two types of businesses collect is also sequestered by Washington.[57] Target's ability to determine a young woman was pregnant before she knew is the tip of the spying iceberg. For example, many cell phone owners forget wifi usage is a revolving door. Most give little thought to accessing and using a store's wifi, not realizing the company's systems may be programmed to exploit the Internet connection. Once a connection is made, customer data—including gender, address, telephone number and a consumer's personal interests (via Internet searches and an individual's social network pages, which are frequently left open for convenience)—are recorded. In retail outlets, a corporation's programming may also be set to track a person's movements throughout the building and catalog the individual's browsing habits. For the customer, the result is customized advertisements and coupons; for the company, consumer analysis is completed at a fraction of the traditional cost. Sadly, advances in technology permit businesses to supersede any attempts at protecting one's privacy. Much like the U.S. intelligence's ability to stalk a phone that is turned off, corporations are now able to access phones even if they aren't deliberately connected to a store's wifi.[58]

The other and much darker side of corporate surveillance is data mining companies. These include firms such as Acxiom, Datalogix, Euclid, Federated Media, Epsilon, Digital Advertising Alliance, BlueKai and Network Advertising Initiative. Acxiom, the leader in the industry, has over 190 million profiles on American adults.[59] These entities make it their business to collect every conceivable type of knowledge about U.S. citizens. They first scour the Internet for any information a person is willing to make known before proceeding to public records. Yet these techniques are time and labor-intensive. Both data mining companies and corporations have a surveillance tool which is much more thorough, revealing and, most importantly, automated. They hire software engineers to design and implement third-party cookies.

Unlike a first-party cookie, which initiates a discussion between a user's computer and a specific website, a third-party cookie is equivalent to someone eavesdropping on a person's power lunch conversation and selling the transcript to a competitor. One method software designers use to hide third-party cookies is by embedding them in advertisements. When an individual enters a website with an ad, a third-person cookie is set. If the user moseys over to another website with an ad by the same company, a notice of the individual's continued interest—including the time, date and computer's IP address—is sent to the business. By this time, the third-party cookie is controlling a person's computer. When someone looks at shoes on a retailer's website and then checks the local news, only to eerily find an ad of the footwear in a sidebar, a third-party cookie is at work. Third-party cookies essentially track and stalk Internet users.

Aside from the invasive privacy violations, there are drastic, long-term psychological effects which result from the repetition of third-party cookies' advertising. Many were confused by Snowden's objection to surveillance on grounds that it stifled creativity and free thought. When an ad is designed to reappear time and again, it is reinforcing an idea or brand image in a potential consumer's mind. The Familiarity Principle states a person becomes more comfortable and accepting of an image the more frequently it is encountered. This is basic biology. Familiarity instills trust, often at a subconscious level. Though customers believe they are expressing freedom of choice by picking Brand X over Brand Y, they may be unaware they saw Brand X in a sidebar while browsing online recipes the week before. They purchase Brand X without realizing the subconscious motivations for doing so. They have literally been brainwashed.

Data brokers take their information, organize it into concise little profiles, and offer it to anyone with an open checkbook. This includes the obvious customers, U.S. government and corporations, but they have other steadfast clients. Many "people locator" websites purchase data mining profiles and resell them to the general public. For a nominal fee, anyone can access a person's birthday, place of birth, current and past residences, family relations, social security and phone number, educational background, email address, place of current and former employment, and medical, property and court records. Medical insurance firms are curious whether a potential client prints Internet coupons for over-the-counter headache medicine and pays in cash to avoid a rate-hiking paper trail.[60] Employment agencies want to know an applicant's hobbies and proclivities without having to ask. Loan companies are interested in a candidate's choice of recreational locales, be it a casino, truck rally or library. Once this data is combined with receipts from many of the major corporations, buying habits are then merged with wants and desires. The result is a very concise, detailed picture of an individual's possessions, activities and goals. This is then compared to established buying patterns. The end result is daunting. The owner of an analyzed profile knows who a person was, is, and is going to be. Corporations refer to this as market research. Privacy advocates consider the process an infringement upon the Fourth Amendment and argue third-party cookie usage violates the last sanctuary of privacy, one's thoughts. Orwell's prophecy is modestly conservative by 21st-century standards. The main character in *Nineteen Eighty-Four* believes, "Nothing was your own except the few cubic centimetres inside your skull."

The surveillance debate has intensified since June 5 and lent new perspectives upon the concept of the safety technology can provide. The underlying political issue is who has the right to particular varieties of information.

The public believes there are two types of conversations, public and private. The intelligence community doesn't agree.

In the Internet Age, a person can "Like" the activity of fishing enough to let the world know by making it public knowledge on one's Facebook profile. The individual can also choose to obtain a vanity Facebook URL by confidentially submitting one's telephone number to the social networking site. The phone number is used for authorization purposes to verify the request is coming from the Facebook account holder. Though it is not placed online, the number is nonetheless (questionably) stored on the company's servers. David Omand, former head of GCHQ, has no problem with collecting the publicly-known fact Bob likes fishing along with his cell number via Facebook's FISC order permitting the U.S. government access to the information.[61] For the watchers, there is no line dividing what an individual puts on the Internet and what people have privately entrusted to another party, be it a website, bank, doctor or telephone company.

Government spies also scoff at the notion of intellectual property rights. Bought-and-sold politicians agree. If something is publicly or privately posted online, it automatically becomes the property of the website's owner. (This is also why most businesses permit and encourage employees to use their company-issued phones and email accounts for personal communications—the firms have legal license to review an employee's private network and communications, because they own the devices and programs and therefore the data on them.) It is an absurd proposition analogous to stating an individual surrenders rightful ownership of a vehicle to a bank when it is parked on property whose tenant has yet to pay the mortgage in full. This policy refuses to acknowledge the resources and labor provided by the Facebook account holder, i.e., the computer used to access the social networking site, time it took to create a profile and mental ingenuity in deciding how and what to say about oneself. It is understood that the website has issued the venue which, in turn, makes the information available worldwide but the skewed exchange undermines the statement that profiles are "free." No profit sharing is offered the user. Without account holders, social networking sites would be empty voids on lonely servers and not multinational corporate affairs.

In the surveillance communities' opinion, everything is public domain and no one has the right to ask "Do you mind?" to someone eavesdropping on a conversation. Their argument is that if a person doesn't want what is being said to be known (by whomever), the individual best not speak at all. In the cloak-and-dagger world of data mining, the person having a discussion cannot reasonably expect privacy, because the individual is voicing one's thoughts, period. It does not matter whether they are spoken in confidence and directed to a particular person, much like an email is addressed "To: Bob" and not "To: Bob; Bcc: The NSA." If the speaker is naïve enough to say something at a volume where a microphone can detect it, it is *de facto* public knowledge. Whereas government surveillance only exchanges the recorded conversation with its own kind, corporate surveillance broadcasts the discussion to anyone who is willing to pay to hear it. In the surveillance world, the only guarantee of privacy is dead silence.

The U.S. government knows the difference but deliberately ignores it. It does not want a distinction to be made, because it would restrict its power and the power of those who fund political campaigns: defense contractors, telecoms, Internet companies, corporate retailers, fast food enterprises and multimillion-dollar data mining firms. The last thing the U.S. government or private business wants is account holders to have control over their own information.

Snowden's skepticism of political solutions is understandable. The people who were hired to watch the watchmen did a poor job. American citizens were told their rights were being protected as a secret oversight court rubberstamped itself into extraneousness while never bothering to see what the NSA might be hiding. Regardless whether a new law is created or a task force is assigned, it can be expected that parties in possession of private information will continue to swear a consumer's data is sacrosanct and they would never dream of violating a client's privacy; all the while information is being steadily placed on the open market, swapped and surveilled. Every data mining opt-out form absolves itself by including the clause that the representative business cannot guarantee a person's information will not conveniently fall into the company's lap at a later date. If a causal web search produces an individual's home address alongside the resident's place of employment, a robber can look up the employer's hours of operation and know when the house will likely be vacant. When situations like these are presented to those in power, the ball of accountability is bounced back and forth as witnessed when the U.S. government and telecoms pointed the finger of blame at one another after Greenwald exposed Verizon. No one is held accountable, violations continue and people are put at risk. Snowden was correct once again. Current surveillance practices make us less safe.

Regardless of how futile a circumstance may appear, it is instinct to try to defend oneself from perceived harm. Both businesses and private citizens reacted to the disclosures, some rather violently.

The NSA leaker's influence upon world economics has already been felt. Two months after the first disclosure reports showed cloud services' security had been compromised, 10 percent of network-based services and storage units provided by U.S. companies had been lost.[63] It is estimated American businesses will lose $35 million over three years to foreign cloud enterprises.[64] Simon Wardley, an executive at the Leading Edge Forum think tank, loved the surveillance revelations, because he knew the end result, "Do I like Prism? Yes, and God bless America and the NSA for handing this golden opportunity to us. Do I think we should be prepared to go the whole hog, ban U.S. services and create a 100 billon euro investment fund for small tech startups in Europe to boost the market? Oh yes, without hesitation."[65] One American business that ironically failed to suffer as a result of the Snowden affair was Booz Allen Hamilton. It renewed its contract with the U.S. government two months after Snowden went public. Along with 16 other companies, the intelligence contractor signed a six billion-dollar deal good for five years.[66] Each company will average $75 million per year.

Of all of the responses to the Snowden affair by the American public, the most interesting and distinctive was its approach to technology. People quickly set to slaying the 21st-century Argus, the all-seeing Greek god with 100 eyes for which the panopticon was named. Many fled from the U.S. government's "architecture of oppression," starting with the companies and products named in the disclosures. Google was replaced by search engines which allow users to surf the Internet anonymously.[67] Likewise, Google Chrome and Microsoft Internet Explorer were traded for proxy browsers. The proceeding weeks would reveal this was one of the NSA's greatest fears. Even though XKeyscore was shown to be able to reveal and decrypt information traveling through these pathways, the intelligence agency was reported to have difficulty tracking randomly rerouted, encrypted communications.[68] Others understood Snowden's logic as it was relayed to Appelbaum, "As a general rule, U.S.-based multinationals should not be trusted until they prove otherwise." Aside from the 11 cited Internet companies, at least 69 international corporations have yet to be named. After quoting American novelist William S. Burroughs, "A paranoid man is a man who knows a little about what's going on,"[69] IT professionals suggested swapping Windows operating system with programs run by independent distributors. Security experts pointed out free, open-source software lets people see for themselves that a backdoor hasn't been installed. Some found smartphone camera apps which do not log a picture's GPS. Many reluctantly gave up Facebook, Twitter, LinkedIn, Instagram and Pinterest.[70]

The truly worried encrypted their home computers. They found similar technology for texting and calls. But they were aware this was a speed bump at best. Though one of the godfathers of encryption technology, Phil Zimmermann, observed, "The fact that they [intelligence agencies] use PGP [Pretty Good Privacy] for government users indicates that they haven't broken it, otherwise they'd have stopped using it,"[71] Snowden had made one thing abundantly clear. When asked by MacAskill, "Is it possible to put security in place to protect against state surveillance?" the whistleblower responded, "You are not even aware of what is possible. The extent of their capabilities is horrifying. [...] Once you go on the network, I can identify your machine. You will never be safe whatever protections you put in place."[72] Even though he reported "encryption works" and suggested financially rewarding software and hardware designers which prove their privacy reliability, Snowden was aware the NSA's budget is outpacing the whole of civilian technology. It is only a matter of time before Jaguarcum-Titan peels back encryption as if it was a candy wrapper.

But one of the lessons learned from the disclosures is email is a damned-if-you-do, damned-if-you-don't privacy conundrum. It had been shown that, left open, the NSA can easily read an email's metadata and contents. If encrypted, it is NSA policy to capture, decrypt, read and store the communication. There was also the problem of location. Though Levison urged Internet businesses to operate offshore to evade unmerited NSL orders, it left no quarter for people wanting a secure email provider. An email service residing outside the Five Eyes' domain generates a foreign communication signature and the NSA and GCHQ make of hobby of snatching up third-party and "foreign" data. Levinson opted to go without email.[73] Most reluctantly admitted they couldn't afford this luxury. They chose encrypted email accounts whose files were regularly dumped to dissuade potential court orders. Their argument is if American intelligence is going to surveil any and all electronic correspondence, the users could at least make it worth the spies' time. Some even accentuated the point by mocking the NSA. Various pundits urged users to copy the intelligence agency into every email to save it the effort of having to track the communication.[74] The outcome is referred to as a denial-of-service attack, which slows or shuts down a server. These protestors are aware this wouldn't stop the surveillance state, but content themselves knowing that it will at least consume NSA agents' time and energy.[75]

The "Information Lockdown" response to privacy invasion was countered by Snowden's nightmare. After reviewing
the NSA's capabilities, others willfully surrendered to Clapper and his coalition, claiming it was impossible to function in
modern society without technology and any preventative measures were not only time-consuming, but ultimately futile. But
a third group emerged, the antipode to those who dove deeper
into the complexities of the IT world. It admired Information
Lockdown's integrity and agreed with the latter half of the
Clapper's Children philosophy. However, it criticized Clapper's
Children for giving up so easily and said those who were willing to wave the white flag before so much as stepping foot on
the electronic battlefield, had sold their privacy for a handful
of customized coupons. The third group's ideology was simple.
The NSA can't surveil what isn't there. They turned in their
phones, cancelled their social networking accounts and only
use email for business purposes. The Levinsons chose to leave
nothing but an envelope's metadata for the authorities to scan
and record. The neo-Luddites argue there is little use in own-
ing a cell phone if it has to be kept in the refrigerator and,
unlike email, it is much harder to hide the fact a letter's contents have been read. And perhaps this will be a prevailing
model: the technological haves and have-nots. This is one of
the inadvertent gains from the surveillance debacle. U.S. intelligence has offered society the opportunity to step away from
the cold, automated, quasi-human interaction of electronic
communication and return to a conversational dynamic which
is more rewarding and genuine. If this becomes the diametri-
cally opposed standard, though American intelligence used
the technology found in Aldous Huxley's *Brave New World* to
achieve its Orwellian objective, privacy's salvation might ironically lie in Huxley's character of John Savage.

The underlying philosophical issue is whether liberty and
security are mutually exclusive ideas. Some critics of Snowden
state the surveillance debate is overreaction and only those
who have something to hide need worry. Snowden's supporters are quick to inquire whether these critics use account
passwords other than "1234" and, if not, why they are con-

cerned if a random person reads their email. Bill O'Reilly made a fine point by highlighting a history of surveilled information that had been used to undermine political or economic opposition. Other privacy advocates, such as the anonymous collective behind the encrypted email provider Riseup.net, argue surveillance is used as a weapon to induce conformity:

What surveillance really is, at its root, is a highly effective form of social control. The knowledge of always being watched changes our behavior and stifles dissent. The inability to associate secretly means there is no longer any possibility for free association. The inability to whisper means there is no longer any speech that is truly free of coercion, real or implied. Most profoundly, pervasive surveillance threatens to eliminate the most vital element of both democracy and social movements: the mental space for people to form dissenting and unpopular views.[76]

Many journalists utilize anonymous web browsers to evade detection when exposing human rights violations.[77] The same programming is used by drug traffickers.[78] So the question ultimately becomes whether an individual is willing to surrender the sale of knives because there is the potential the cutlery could be used as a murder weapon.[79] But the analogy is a metaphorical Dutch door. It could symbolize the argument for surveillance or free speech; its value lies in representing the current political atmosphere. There is no gray area in which to reach a compromise, because those entrusted to protect the people have abused their power. The American populace is being forced to choose between liberty and safety. Freedom of speech and expression carries the inherent risk of personal danger at the expense of absolute security. Perfect safety eliminates freedom and privacy.

Appendix:
Chronology of disclosures supplied by Snowden

The Guardian – G | *The Washington Post* – WP | *South China Morning Post* – SCMP | *Der Spiegel* – DS | *O Globo* – OG | *Rede Globo* – RG | *Epoca* – E | *Fantastico* – F | *Norddeutscher Rundfunk/North German Broadcasting* – NGB | *Süddeutsche Zeitung* – SZ | *The Wall Street Journal* – WSJ | *The Age* – A | *ProPublica* – PP | * – accompanying documentation

Date	Publication	Article Title
While in Hong Kong		
Wednesday, June 5	G	"NSA collecting phone records of millions of Verizon customers daily"*
Thursday, June 6	G	"NSA Prism program taps in to user data of Apple, Google and others"*
Thursday, June 6	WP	"U.S. Intelligence Mining Data From Nine U.S. Internet Companies In Broad Secret Program"*
Friday, June 7	G	"Obama orders US to draw up overseas target list for cyber-attacks"*

DATE	PUBLICATION	ARTICLE TITLE
While in Hong Kong		
Friday, June 7	WP	"U.S., British intelligence mining data from nine U.S. Internet companies in broad secret program" (rewrite of previous article)*
Friday, June 7	G	"UK gathering secret intelligence via covert NSA operation"
Saturday, June 8	G	"Boundless Informant: the NSA's secret tool to track global surveillance data"*
Sunday, June 9	G	Poitras Interview, Pt. I (12 minutes)
Friday, June 13	SCMP	"Edward Snowden: US government has been hacking Hong Kong and China for years"
Saturday, June 14	SCMP	"Edward Snowden: Classified US data shows Hong Kong hacking targets"
Sunday, June 16	G	"GCHQ intercepted foreign politicians' communications at G20 summits"*
Monday, June 17	G	Online chat
Thursday, June 20	G	"The top secret rules that allow NSA to use US data without a warrant"*
Friday, June 21	G	"GCHQ taps fibre-optic cables for secret access to world's communications"*

Date	Publication	Article Title
While in Hong Kong		
Saturday, June 22	SCMP	"Snowden reveals more US cyberspying details"
Saturday, June 22	SCMP	"US spies on Chinese mobile phone companies, steals SMS data: Edward Snowden"
Saturday, June 22	SCMP	"NSA targeted China's Tsinghua University in extensive hacking attacks, says Snowden"
While in Pre-Asylum Russia		
Thursday, June 27	G	"How the NSA is still harvesting your online data"
Thursday, June 27	G	"NSA collected US email records in bulk for more than two years under Obama"*
Saturday, June 29	DS	"NSA Spied on European Union Offices"
Sunday, June 30	G	"New NSA leaks show how US is bugging its European allies"*
Sunday, June 30	DS	"NSA Snoops on 500 Million German Data Connections"
Monday, July 1	DS	"How the NSA Targets Germany and Europe"*
Saturday, July 6	OG	"U.S. spied on millions of e-mails and calls of Brazilians"*
Saturday, July 6	OG	"U.S. expands the surveillance apparatus continuously"*

Date	Publication	Article Title
While in Pre-Asylum Russia		
Sunday, July 7	RG	8-minute television report with previously unpublished classified documentation concerning the NSA's surveillance of Brazil*
Monday, July 8	DS	Appelbaum interview
Monday, July 8	OG	"NSA and CIA have maintained staff in Brasilia to collect satellite data"
Tuesday, July 9	OG	"U.S. spies spread through Latin America"*
Thursday, July 11	G	"Microsoft handed the NSA access to encrypted messages"
Friday, July 12	—	G9 meeting
Saturday, July 20	DS	"'Prolific Partner': German Intelligence Used NSA Spy Program"
Saturday, July 27	E	"Spies of the digital age"*
Wednesday, July 31	G	"XKeyscore: NSA tool collects ' nearly everything a user does on the internet'"*
While in Post-Asylum Russia		
Thursday, August 1	G	"NSA pays £100m in secret funding for GCHQ"
Thursday, August 1	G	"GCHQ: inside the top secret world of Britain's biggest spy agency"

Date	Publication	Article Title
While in Post-Asylum Russia		
Thursday, August 1	NGB	"Intelligence services use company" broadcast
Friday, August 2	SZ	"Snowden revealed names of spying telecom companies"
Friday, August 2	E	"Letter from the American Ambassador in Brazil thanks the NSA for its Support"*
Monday, August 5	DS	"Mass Data: Transfers from Germany Aid US Surveillance"*
Friday, August 9	G	"NSA loophole allows warrantless search for US citizens' emails and phone calls"*
Monday, August 12	DS	"Ally and Target: US Intelligence Watches Germany Closely"
Thursday, August 15	WP	"NSA broke privacy rules thousands of times per year, audit finds"*
Tuesday, August 20	WSJ	"New Details Show Broader NSA Surveillance Reach"
Thursday, August 22	G	"NSA paid millions to cover Prism compliance costs for tech companies"*
Monday, August 26	DS	"Codename 'Apalachee': How America Spies on Europe and the UN"*
Wednesday, August 28	SZ/NGB	"British Officials Have Far-Reaching Access to Internet and Telephone Communications"

Date	Publication	Article Title
While in Post-Asylum Russia		
Thursday, August 29	A	"Australian spies in global deal to tap undersea cables"*
Thursday, August 29	WP	"NSA paying U.S. companies for access to communications networks"*
Thursday, August 29	WP	"U.S. spy network's successes, failures and objectives detailed in 'black budget' summary"
Thursday, August 29	WP	"To hunt Osama bin Laden, satellites watched over Abbottabad, Pakistan, and Navy SEALs"
Friday, August 30	WP	"U.S. spy agencies mounted 231 offensive cyber-operations in 2011, documents show"
Saturday, August 31	DS	"NSA Spied on Al Jazeera Communications"
Sunday, September 1	WP	"U.S. intelligence agencies spend millions to hunt for insider threats, document shows"
Sunday, September 1	DS	"NSA Targeted French Foreign Ministry"
Sunday, September 1	F	11-minute television report with previously unpublished classified documentation concerning the NSA's spying on Brazil and Mexico's presidents*
Monday, September 2	WP	"Top-secret U.S. intelligence files show new levels of distrust of Pakistan"

Date	Publication	Article Title
While in Post-Asylum Russia		
Tuesday, September 3	WP	"U.S. documents detail al-Qaeda's efforts to fight back against drones"
Thursday, September 5	G	"Revealed: how US and UK spy agencies defeat internet privacy and security"*
Thursday, September 5	NYT/PP	"N.S.A. Able to Foil Basic Safeguards of Privacy on Web/ Revealed: The NSA's Secret Campaign to Crack, Undermine Internet Security"*
Sunday, September 8	F	13-minute television report with previously unpublished classified documentation concerning the NSA's surveillance of Petrobras*
Monday, September 9	DS	"iSpy: How the NSA Accesses Smartphone Data"

Sources

CHAPTER 1

1   Greenwald, Glenn. "Edward Snowden: NSA whistleblower answers reader questions." *The Guardian*. June 17, 2013. http://www.theguardian.com/world/2013/jun/17/edward-snowden-nsa-files-whistleblower.

2   Lewis, Paul and Karen McVeigh. "Edward Snowden: what we know about the source behind the NSA files leak." *The Guardian*. June 10, 2013. http://www.theguardian.com/world/2013/jun/11/edward-snowden-what-we-know-nsa.

3   Bykowicz, Julie and Greg Giroux. "NSA Leaker Was Shy, Computer-Bound Teenager in Maryland." *Bloomberg*. June 11, 2013. http://www.bloomberg.com/news/2013-06-11/nsa-leaker-was-shy-computer-bound-teenager-in-maryland.html.

4   Hallow, Ralph. "Edward Snowden's father suggests son's leaks may be protected by Constitution." *The Washington Times*. July 1, 2013. http://www.washingtontimes.com/news/2013/jul/1/father-fugitive/?page=all.

5   Toppo, Greg. "Former neighbor remembers Snowden as 'nice kid.'" *USA Today*. June 10, 2013. http://www.usatoday.com/story/news/nation/2013/06/10/snowden-neighbors-surveillance-security/2408573/.

6   BBC News – US & Canada. "Profile: Edward Snowden." *BBC News*. Aug. 7, 2013. http://www.bbc.co.uk/news/world-us-canada-22837100.

7   Markon, Jerry. "Effort to get NSA leaker Edward Snowden's father to Moscow collapses." *The Washington Post*. July 30, 2013. http://articles.washingtonpost.com/2013-07-30/politics/40895930_1_elder-snowden-washington-post-lon-snowden.

8   Shiffman, John and Daniel Trotta. "Patriot or traitor, Snowden driven by fear of government intrusion." *Reuters*. June 11, 2013. http://www.reuters.com/article/2013/06/11/usa-security-snowden-idUSL2N0EN03V20130611.

9   Fox News Insider. "Snowden's Dad Speaks Out! Preview Eric Bolling's Exclusive Interview." *Fox News Insider*. June 17, 2013. http://foxnewsinsider.com/2013/06/17/lonnie-snowden-father-edward-snowden-gives-interview-fox-news-eric-bolling-about-medias.

10 Ars Technica Forum. "State School vs. Expensive College." *Ars Technica*. Apr. 30, 2006. http://arstechnica.com/civis/viewtopic.php?f=25&t=310452&p=6791072&hilit=I+don%E2%80%99

t+have+a+degree+of+ANY+type.+I+don%E2%80%99t+even
+have+a+high+school+diploma#p6791072.

11 Geller, Adam and Brian Witte. "Edward Snowden's Background
    Surrounded By Spycraft." *The Huffington Post*. June 15, 2013. http://
    www.huffingtonpost.com/2013/06/15/edward-snowden-
    background_n_3446904.html.

12 Leonnig, Carol, Jenna Johnson and Marc Fisher. "Tracking Edward
    Snowden, from a Maryland classroom to a Hong Kong hotel." *The
    Washington Post*. June 15, 2013. http://articles.washingtonpost.com/
    2013-06-15/world/39988583_1_anime-hong-kong-world.

13 Cass, Connie, and Kimberly Dozier. "NSA leaker mysterious despite
    hours of interviews." *Salon*. June 13, 2013. http://www.salon.com/
    2013/06/13/nsa_leaker_mysterious_despite_hours_of_interviews_2/.

14 Cf. 1.5

15 Cf. 1.5

16 Ars Technica Forum. "Seducing one's girlfriend." *Ars Technica*. Nov. 7,
    2006. http://arstechnica.com/civis/
    viewtopic.php?f=27&t=247159&p=5856884&hilit=girl#p5856884.

17 Cf. 1.5

18 Itkowitz, Colby and Daniel Patrick Sheehan. "FBI visits family of NSA
    leaker in Upper Macungie." *The Morning Call*. June 10, 2013. http://
    articles.mcall.com/2013-06-10/news/mc-pa-ed-snowden-nsa-leak-
    20130610_1_fbi-agents-upper-macungie-township-public-records.

19 Broder, John and Scott Shane. "For Snowden, a Life of Ambition, Despite
    the Drifting." *The New York Times*. June 15, 2013. http://
    www.nytimes.com/2013/06/16/us/for-snowden-a-life-of-ambition-
    despite-the-drifting.html?hp&pagewanted=all.

20 Cf. 1.7

21 Mosk, Matthew, et al. "Edward Snowden's Life As We Know It." *ABC
    News*. June 13, 2013. http://abcnews.go.com/Blotter/timeline-edward-
    snowdens-life/story?id=19394487.

22 Meek, James, et al. "U.S. Fears Edward Snowden May Defect to China:
    Sources." *Yahoo*. June 13, 2013. http://news.yahoo.com/u-fears-
    edward-snowden-may-173428026.html.

23 Muller, Sarah. "Snowden 'thinks long and hard before coming to a
    decision,' friend says." *MSNBC*. Oct. 2, 2013. http://tv.msnbc.com/
    2013/06/12/edward-snowden-is-an-it-genius-says-a-friend/.

24 Shiffman, John, et al. "While working for spies, Snowden was secretly
    prolific online." *The Chicago Tribune*. June 13, 2013. http://
    articles.chicagotribune.com/2013-06-13/news/sns-rt-us-usa-security-
    snowden-onlinebre95d023-20130613_1_nsa-corporate-greed-postings.

[25] Internet archive. Snowden's Ryuhana Profile. *Archive.* Dec. 16, 2013. http://archive.is/Gv7sT.

[26] Bump, Philip. "Ed Snowden's 'Sexxxxy' 18-Year-Old Self Has Surfaced & He Wasn't a Serious Spy." *The Wire.* June 12, 2013. http://www.theatlanticwire.com/national/2013/06/snowden-teenage-photos/66180/.

[27] Cooke, Kristina and John Shiffman. "Snowden as a teen online: anime and cheeky humor." *The Chicago Tribune.* June 12, 2013. http://articles.chicagotribune.com/2013-06-12/news/sns-rt-us-usa-security-snowden-animebre95b14b-20130612_1_anime-teen-online-cia.

[28] Cooke, Kristina and John Shiffman. "Edward Snowden As A Teen Online." *The Huffington Post.* June 12, 2013. http://www.huffingtonpost.com/2013/06/12/exclusive-snowden-as-a-te_n_3430166.html.

[29] Cf. 1.27

[30] Cf. 1.28

[31] Cf. 1.10

[32] Mullin, Joe. "NSA leaker Ed Snowden's life on Ars Technica." *Ars Technica.* June 12, 2013. http://arstechnica.com/tech-policy/2013/06/nsa-leaker-ed-snowdens-life-on-ars-technica/.

[33] Ars Technica Forum. "Clicking power supply on my xbox 360." *Ars Technica.* May 19, 2006. http://arstechnica.com/civis/viewtopic.php?f=22&t=306199&p=6726096&hilit=the+sound+of+freedom#p6726096.

[34] Ars Technica Forum. "In-depth theory (sic) questions: How proxies WORK. (Difficulty: Guru)." *Ars Technica.* Oct. 14, 2003. http://arstechnica.com/civis/viewtopic.php?f=10&t=618700&p=11737503&hilit=traffic+such+as+SMTP+as+opposed+to+the+standard#p11737503.

[35] Greenwald, Glenn, et al. "Edward Snowden: the whistleblower behind the NSA surveillance revelations." *The Guardian.* June 9, 2013. http://www.theguardian.com/world/2013/jun/09/edward-snowden-nsa-whistleblower-surveillance.

[36] Poitras, Laura and Glenn Greenwald. "Edward Snowden: 'The US government will say I aided our enemies' – video interview." *The Guardian.* July 8, 2013. http://www.theguardian.com/world/video/2013/jul/08/edward-snowden-video-interview.

[37] Ars Technica Forum. "Bush Regime Playing Cards... Awesome." *Ars Technica.* Sept. 25, 2013. http://arstechnica.com/civis/viewtopic.php?f=22&t=626955&p=11886089&hilit=They+can%E2%80%99t+even+come+up+with+decent#p11886089.

[38] Ars Technica Forum. "How much time do you spend gaming per day?" *Ars Technica*. Oct. 26, 2013. http://arstechnica.com/civis/viewtopic.php?f=22&t=615139&p=11679190&hilit=eight+hours+a+day+surfing#p11679190.

[39] Ackerman, Spencer. "Edward Snowden did enlist for special forces, US army confirms." *The Guardian*. June 10, 2013. http://www.theguardian.com/world/2013/jun/10/edward-snowden-army-special-forces.

[40] Cf. 1.22

[41] Cf. 1.19

[42] Ars Technica Forum. "Does Religion Limit Humanity?" *Ars Technica*. Dec. 8, 2003. http://arstechnica.com/civis/viewtopic.php?f=24&t=636292&p=12040667&hilit=agnostic#p12040667.

[43] Marbella, Jean, et al. "Details about Edward Snowden's life in Maryland emerge." *The Baltimore Sun*. June 10, 2013. http://articles.baltimoresun.com/2013-06-10/news/bs-md-snowden-profile-20130610_1_anne-arundel-county-arundel-high-the-guardian/2.

[44] Cf. 1.39

[45] Cf. 1.21

[46] Cf. 1.21

[47] The Washington Post. "A timeline of Edward Snowden's life." *The Washington Post*. June 16, 2013. http://apps.washingtonpost.com/g/page/politics/a-timeline-of-edward-snowdens-life/235/.

[48] Finn, Peter, et al. "Probe aims to find how NSA leaker got access." *Pittsburgh Post-Gazette*. June 11, 2013. http://www.post-gazette.com/stories/news/us/probe-aims-to-find-how-nsa-leaker-got-access-691177/.

[49] Ars Technica Forum. "are you living the life you wish?" *Ars Technica*. Apr. 14, 2006. http://arstechnica.com/civis/viewtopic.php?f=23&t=315325&p=6876937&hilit=making+twice+the+average+income#p6876937.

[50] Cf. 1.10

[51] Ars Technica Forum. "Tell me about...A career in the military (or overseas)!" *Ars Technica*. Aug. 14, 2006. http://arstechnica.com/civis/viewtopic.php?f=23&t=280566&p=6352598&hilit=I+was+unemployed+for+a+full+year+%26+then#p6352598.

[52] Fein, Bruce. "Letter To Obama: Civil Disobedience, Edward J. Snowden, and the Constitution." *Popular Resistance*. July 26, 2013. http://www.popularresistance.org/letter-to-obama-civil-disobedience-edward-j-snowden-and-the-constitution/.

53 Post TV. "Snowden's father: Edward 'the brilliant one.'" *The Washington Post*. July 30, 2013. http://www.washingtonpost.com/posttv/video/thefold/snowdens-father-edward-the-brilliant-one/2013/07/30/091e3642-f964-11e2-8e84-c56731a202fb_video.html.

54 Cf. 1.23

55 Ars Technica Forum. "Living in towns - how is it possible?" *Ars Technica*. Dec. 14, 2006. http://arstechnica.com/civis/viewtopic.php?f=23&t=292779&p=6536986&hilit=some+time+in+Ireland+in+February#p6536986.

56 Shane, Scott. "Under Snowden Screen Name, 2009 Post Berated Leaks." *The New York Times*. June 26, 2013. http://www.nytimes.com/2013/06/27/world/under-snowdens-screen-name-a-declaration-in-09-that-leakers-should-be-shot.html?pagewanted=all.

57 Poitras, Laura and Glenn Greenwald. "NSA whistleblower Edward Snowden: 'I don't want to live in a society that does these sort of things.'" *The Guardian*. June 9, 2013. http://www.theguardian.com/world/video/2013/jun/09/nsa-whistleblower-edward-snowden-interview-video.

58 Cf. 1.11

59 Ferran, Lee. "Snowden's CIA Drunk Driving Claim Questioned." *ABC News*. June 12, 2013. http://abcnews.go.com/blogs/headlines/2013/06/switzerland-questions-u-s-over-cia-drunk-driving-gambit/.

60 Drew, Christopher and Scott Shane. "Résumé Shows Snowden Honed Hacking Skills." *The New York Times*. July 4, 2013. http://www.nytimes.com/2013/07/05/us/resume-shows-snowden-honed-hacking-skills.html?pagewanted=all.

61 Anderson, Mavanee. "Who is Ed Snowden? Friend shares memories, offers support for NSA leaker." *Times Free Press*. June 12, 2013. http://www.timesfreepress.com/news/2013/jun/12/who-is-ed-snowden/?print.

62 Cf. 1.35

63 Allen, Matthew. "US security snooping scandal unnerves Swiss." *Swiss Info*. June 10, 2013. http://www.swissinfo.ch/eng/business/US_security_snooping_scandal_unnerves_Swiss.html?cid=36112760.

64 Treaties.un.org. "Vienna Convention on Diplomatic Relations." *Treaties.un.org*. Dec. 16, 2013. http://treaties.un.org/doc/Treaties/1964/06/19640624%2002-10%20AM/Ch_III_3p.pdf.

65 Reuters. "Swiss president would back criminal probe against NSA leaker." *Reuters*. June 16, 2013. http://uk.reuters.com/article/2013/06/16/usa-security-switzerland-snowden-idUKL5N0ES0DX20130616.

66 Reuters. "Switzerland's oldest bank Wegelin to close after pleading guilty to aiding US tax evasion." *Reuters.* Jan. 4, 2013. http://www.telegraph.co.uk/finance/financial-crime/9779615/Switzerlands-oldest-bank-Wegelin-to-close-after-pleading-guilty-to-aiding-US-tax-evasion.html.

67 Cf. 1.4

68 Ars Technica. Ars Technica Member Profile. *Ars Technica.* Dec. 29, 2001. http://arstechnica.com/civis/memberlist.php?mode=viewprofile&u=60591.

69 Ars Technica Forum. "Perpetual market watch and securities trading thread." *Ars Technica.* Oct. 27, 2008. http://arstechnica.com/civis/viewtopic.php?f=25&t=36965&p=1091085&hilit=Holy+jesus%2C+have+you+guys+started+using+the+new+triple+levered#p1091085.

70 Cf. 1.69

71 Ars Technica Forum. "NEW PREDICTION. Dow 4000-4500." *Ars Technica.* June 30, 2008. http://arstechnica.com/civis/viewtopic.php?f=25&t=92725&p=2624123#p2624123.

72 Cf. 1.60

73 Greenwald, Glenn. "Email exchange between Edward Snowden and former GOP Senator Gordon Humphrey." *The Guardian.* July 16, 2013. http://www.theguardian.com/commentisfree/2013/jul/16/gordon-humphrey-email-edward-snowden.

74 Ambinder, Marc. "Inside the Secret Interrogation Facility at Bagram." *The Atlantic.* May 14, 2010. http://www.theatlantic.com/politics/archive/2010/05/inside-the-secret-interrogation-facility-at-bagram/56678/.

75 Cf. 1.35

76 Cf. 1.61

77 Ars Technica Forum. "Secure Systems: Launching a virtual machine from a LiveCD (or, 'Help Educate Me')." *Ars Technica.* Feb. 14, 2009. http://arstechnica.com/civis/viewtopic.php?f=15&t=64259&p=1862943&hilit=The+goal+here+is+to+be+able+to+bring+a#p1862943.

78 Schmitt, Eric. "C.I.A. Warning on Snowden in '09 Said to Slip Through the Cracks." *The New York Times.* Oct. 10, 2013. http://www.nytimes.com/2013/10/11/us/cia-warning-on-snowden-in-09-said-to-slip-through-the-cracks.html?pagewanted=1&_r=1&.

79 Schmitt, Eric. "C.I.A. Disputes Early Suspicions on Snowden." *The New York Times.* Oct. 11, 2013. http://www.nytimes.com/2013/10/12/us/cia-disputes-early-suspicions-on-snowden.html?ref=todayspaper.

80 Cf. 1.79

[81] Hosenball, Mark. "Snowden downloaded NSA secrets while working for Dell, sources say." *Reuters*. Aug. 15, 2013. http://www.reuters.com/article/2013/08/15/usa-security-snowden-dell-idUSL2N0GF11220130815.

[82] Ars Technica Forum. "Has anybody considered working as IT security in Japan?" *Ars Technica*. Feb. 18, 2002. http://arstechnica.com/civis/viewtopic.php?f=10&t=868906&p=16121410&hilit=japanese#p16121410.

[83] Cf. 1.22

[84] Witte, Brian. "Dad of Snowden's girlfriend 'shocked' by news." *The Big Story*. June 12, 2013. http://bigstory.ap.org/article/dad-snowdens-girlfriend-shocked-news.

[85] Mills, Lindsay. Personal website. *L's Journey*. Dec. 16, 2013. http://www.lsjourney.com/.

[86] Little, John. "Lindsay Mills: Reportedly the Blogging, Instagraming, Pinteresting, Flickering, YouTubing and Tweeting Girlfriend of Edward Snowden." *Blogs of War*. June 11, 2013. http://blogsofwar.com/2013/06/11/lindsay-mills-the-blogging-instagraming-pintresting-flickering-youtubing-and-tweeting-girlfriend-of-edward-snowden/.

[87] Weiss, Sasha. "We Are All Pole Dancing on the Internet." *The New Yorker*. June 13, 2013. http://www.newyorker.com/online/blogs/culture/2013/06/snowden-girlfriend-lindsay-mills-blog.html.

[88] CNN. "NSA leaker's girlfriend says she's 'lost at sea.'" *CNN*. June 12, 2013. http://www.cnn.com/2013/06/11/us/nsa-snowden-girlfriend/.

[89] La Ganga, Maria. "Lindsay Mills and other pole dancers missing in action." *Los Angeles Times*. June 13, 2013. http://articles.latimes.com/2013/jun/13/news/la-pn-lindsay-mills-missing-in-action-20130613.

[90] Ngak, Chenda. "NSA leaker's girlfriend struggles with privacy in digital age." *CBS News*. June 13, 2013. http://www.cbsnews.com/8301-205_162-57589265/nsa-leakers-girlfriend-struggles-with-privacy-in-digital-age/.

[91] Cf. 1.60

[92] Sniderman, Zachary. "'Anonymous' Now Fighting Child Pornography." *Mashable*. Oct. 24, 2011. http://mashable.com/2011/10/24/anonymous-child-pornography/.

[93] Yin, Sara. "'Anonymous' Attacks Sony in Support of PS3 Hackers." *PC Mag*. Apr. 4, 2011. http://www.pcmag.com/article2/0,2817,2383018,00.asp.

[94] EC-Council. "Dept. of Defense Directive (DoD) 8570." *EC-Council*. Dec. 16, 2013. http://www.eccouncil.org/Support/dod-8570.

[95] Knowles, William. "Former National Security Agency / Booz Allen Contractor Edward Snowden is an (ISC)^2 member." *InfoSec News*. June 11, 2013. http://www.infosecnews.org/tag/ceh/.

[96] Times Higher Education. "World University Rankings 2012-2013." *Times Higher Education*. Dec. 16, 2013. http://www.timeshighereducation.co.uk/world-university-rankings/2012-13/world-ranking.

[97] Hosenball, Mark. "NSA contractor hired Snowden despite concerns about resume discrepancies." *Reuters*. June 20, 2013. http://www.reuters.com/article/2013/06/21/us-usa-security-snowden-idUSBRE95K01J20130621.

[98] Cf. 1.60

[99] Gellman, Barton and Greg Miller. "U.S. spy network's successes, failures and objectives detailed in 'black budget' summary." *The Washington Post*. Aug. 29, 2013. http://www.washingtonpost.com/world/national-security/black-budget-summary-details-us-spy-networks-successes-failures-and-objectives/2013/08/29/7e57bb78-10ab-11e3-8cdd-bcdc09410972_story.html.

[100] USIS. "USIS Fact Sheet." *USIS*. Dec. 16, 2013. http://www.usis.com/Fact-Sheet.aspx.

[101] Lardner, Richard and Kimberly Kozier. "Watchdog faults background check of NSA leaker." *Yahoo*. June 20, 2013. http://news.yahoo.com/watchdog-faults-background-check-nsa-leaker-235639806.html.

[102] Cf. 1.35

[103] Cf. 1.1

[104] Zara, Christopher. "NSA Whistleblower Revealed: Edward Snowden Donated $500 To Ron Paul's 2012 Presidential Campaign: Does NSA Whistleblower Have Libertarian Leanings?" *International Business Times*. June 9, 2013. http://www.ibtimes.com/nsa-whistleblower-revealed-edward-snowden-donated-500-ron-pauls-2012-presidential-campaign-does-nsa.

[105] Walsh, Justin. "Edward Snowden Complete Press Conference - Moscow Airport - July 12th 2013." *YouTube*. July 12, 2013. https://www.youtube.com/watch?v=dukqMkTGEzU.

[106] Cf. 1.81

[107] Risen, James. "Snowden Says He Took No Secret Files to Russia." *The New York Times*. Oct. 17, 2013. http://www.nytimes.com/2013/10/18/world/snowden-says-he-took-no-secret-files-to-russia.html?_r=1&hp=&adxnnl=1&pagewanted=2&adxnnlx=1382135062-pbppFb/eYK3xlR8GQUumBg.

[108] Booz Allen Hamilton. "Careers/Hawaii." *Booz Allen Hamilton*. Dec. 16, 2013. http://www.boozallen.com/careers/location-careers/careers-hawaii.

109 Booz Allen Hamilton. "Improving Public Safety with Analytics." *Booz Allen Hamilton*. Dec. 16, 2013. http://www.boozallen.com/consulting/view-our-work/48383297/improving-public-safety-with-analytics.

110 Esposito, Richard and Matthew Cole. "How Snowden did it." *NBC News*. Aug. 26, 2013. http://investigations.nbcnews.com/_news/2013/08/26/20197183-how-snowden-did-it?lite.

111 Cf. 1.97

112 Wong, Alia and Eric Pape. "Paradise Lost: The Cost of Freedom for NSA Leaker Edward Snowden." *Civil Beat*. June 9, 2013. http://www.civilbeat.com/articles/2013/06/09/19246-paradise-lost-the-cost-of-freedom-for-nsa-leaker-edward-snowden/.

113 Cf. 1.104

114 Linton, Caroline. "Lindsay Mills, Edward Snowden's Girlfriend, Writes 'All I Feel Is Alone.'" *The Daily Beast*. June 11, 2013. http://www.thedailybeast.com/articles/2013/06/11/lindsay-mills-edward-snowden-s-girlfriend-writes-all-i-feel-is-alone.html.

115 Greenberg, Andy. "NSA Implementing 'Two-Person' Rule To Stop The Next Edward Snowden." *Forbes*. June 18, 2013. http://www.forbes.com/sites/andygreenberg/2013/06/18/nsa-director-says-agency-implementing-two-person-rule-to-stop-the-next-edward-snowden/.

116 Hosenball, Mark. "Feds hunted for Snowden in days before NSA programs went public." *Reuters*. June 12, 2013. http://www.reuters.com/article/2013/06/12/us-usa-security-snowden-hunt-idUSBRE95B1A220130612.

117 Cf. 1.7

118 Fox News Test. "NSA leaker's father urges son to 'come home and face this.'" *YouTube*. June 17, 2013. http://www.youtube.com/watch?v=qzVVZOVK3jA.

119 Lam, Lana. "Snowden sought Booz Allen job to gather evidence on NSA surveillance." *South Morning China Post*. June 24, 2013. http://www.scmp.com/news/hong-kong/article/1268209/snowden-sought-booz-allen-job-gather-evidence-nsa-surveillance?page=all.

120 MacAskill, Ewen. "Edward Snowden: how the spy story of the age leaked out." *The Guardian*. June 11, 2013. http://www.theguardian.com/world/2013/jun/11/edward-snowden-nsa-whistleblower-profile.

121 Waterman, Shaun. "NSA leaker Ed Snowden used banned thumb-drive, exceeded access." *The Washington Times*. June 14, 2013. http://www.washingtontimes.com/news/2013/jun/14/nsa-leaker-ed-snowden-used-banned-thumb-drive-exce/?page=all.

[122] Hofschneider, Anita. "Hawaii real estate agent: Snowden left on May 1." *Yahoo*. June 10, 2013. http://news.yahoo.com/hawaii-real-estate-agent-snowden-left-may-1-005951480.html.

[123] Vultaggio, Maria. "Ed Snowden's Girlfriend Lindsay Mills Devastated By His Disappearance Following NSA Leaks." *International Business Times*. June 11, 2013. http://www.ibtimes.com/ed-snowdens-girlfriend-lindsay-mills-devastated-his-disappearance-following-nsa-leaks-1300331.

[124] Cf. 1.116

[125] Cf. 1.1

[126] Cf. 1.120

[127] Ars Technica Forum. "So your work tells you you're going to be assigned overseas... ." *Ars Technica*. July 28, 2006. http://arstechnica.com/civis/viewtopic.php?f=23&t=286968&p=6468078&hilit=Mandarin#p6468078.

[128] Savage, Charlie. "Cryptic Overtures and a Clandestine Meeting Gave Birth to a Blockbuster Story." *The New York Times*. June 10, 2013. http://www.nytimes.com/2013/06/11/us/how-edward-j-snowden-orchestrated-a-blockbuster-story.html?pagewanted=all.

CHAPTER 2

[1] MacAskill, Ewen. "Edward Snowden: how the spy story of the age leaked out." *The Guardian*. June 11, 2013. http://www.theguardian.com/world/2013/jun/11/edward-snowden-nsa-whistleblower-profile.

[2] Snowden Edward. "Statement from Edward Snowden in Moscow." *WikiLeaks*. July 1, 2013. http://wikileaks.org/Statement-from-Edward-Snowden-in.html?snow.

[3] Bishop, Tricia. "NSA employee accused of leaking information sentenced to probation." *The Baltimore Sun*. July 15, 2013. http://articles.baltimoresun.com/2011-07-15/news/bs-md-thomas-drake-sentencing-20110715_1_jesselyn-radack-thomas-andrews-drake-nsa-employee.

[4] Cf. 2. 3

[5] Poitras, Laura, et al. "Ally and Target: US Intelligence Watches Germany Closely." *Der Spiegel*. Aug. 12, 2013. http://www.spiegel.de/international/world/germany-is-a-both-a-partner-to-and-a-target-of-nsa-surveillance-a-916029.html.

[6] Scott Pelley. "U.S. v. Whistleblower Tom Drake." *60 Minutes*. May 22, 2013. http://www.cbsnews.com/video/watch/?id=7366912n.

[7] Nakashima, Ellen. "Former NSA executive Thomas A. Drake may pay high price for media leak." *The Washington Post*. July 14, 2010. http://

www.washingtonpost.com/wp-dyn/content/article/2010/07/13/
AR2010071305992.html.

8 Cf. 2.6

9 Government Accountability Project. "WHISTLEBLOWER WITCH
HUNTS: The Smokescreen Syndrome." *Whistleblower.org*. Nov. 2010.
http://www.whistleblower.org/storage/documents/WWHfinal.pdf.

10 Shorrock, Tim. "Obama's Crackdown on Whistleblowers." *The Nation*.
Mar. 26, 2013. http://www.thenation.com/article/173521/obamas-
crackdown-whistleblowers?page=full.

11 Government Accountability Project. "NSA Whistleblowers William (Bill)
Binney and J. Kirk Wiebe." *Whistleblower.org*. Dec. 16, 2013. http://
www.whistleblower.org/program-areas/homeland-security-a-human-
rights/surveillance/nsa-whistleblowers-bill-binney-a-j-kirk-wiebe.

12 Zetter, Kim. "NSA Whistleblower to Plead Guilty to Misdemeanor."
Wired. June 9, 2011. http://www.wired.com/threatlevel/2011/06/
drake-pleads-guilty/.

13 Cf. 2.12

14 AP, "Bush program extended beyond wiretapping." *USA Today*. July 10,
2009. http://usatoday30.usatoday.com/news/washington/2009-07-10-
report-surveillance_N.htm.

15 Maass, Peter. "How Laura Poitras Helped Snowden Spill His Secrets."
The New York Times. Aug. 13, 2013. http://www.nytimes.com/2013/08/
18/magazine/laura-poitras-snowden.html?pagewanted=all.

16 Poitras, Laura. "The Program." *The New York Times*. Aug. 22, 2012.
http://www.nytimes.com/2012/08/23/opinion/the-national-security-
agencys-domestic-spying-program.html.

17 Hermann, Peter. "NSA whistle-blowers want seized computers
returned." *The Baltimore Sun*. Nov. 16, 2011. http://
articles.baltimoresun.com/2011-11-16/news/bs-md-drake-sues-fbi-
20111116-130_1_nsa-employee-thomas-andrews-drake-drake-case.

18 Radack, Jesselyn. "Judge Has Choice Words for Justice Department's
Prosecution of Drake." *Whistleblower.org*. July 18, 2011. http://
www.whistleblower.org/blog/31/1273.

19 Federation of American Scientists. "United States of America v. Thomas
Andrews Drake" indictment. *Federation of American Scientists*. Dec. 16,
2013. http://www.fas.org/sgp/news/2010/04/drake-indict.pdf.

20 Cf. 2.6

21 Hosenball, Mark. "Laptops Snowden took to Hong Kong, Russia were a
'diversion.'" *Reuters*. Oct. 11, 2013. http://www.reuters.com/article/
2013/10/11/us-usa-security-snowden-idUSBRE99A0LK20131011.

22 Risen, James and Eric Lichtblau. "Bush Lets U.S. Spy on Callers Without Court." *The New York Times*. Dec. 16, 2005. https://www.nytimes.com/2005/12/16/politics/16program.html?pagewanted=all.

23 Lichtblau, Eric. "The Education of a 9/11 Reporter." *Slate*. Mar. 26, 2008. http://www.slate.com/articles/news_and_politics/politics/2008/03/the_education_of_a_911_reporter.html.

24 Maass, Peter. "Q. & A.: Edward Snowden Speaks to Peter Maass." *The New York Times*. Aug. 13, 2013. https://www.nytimes.com/2013/08/18/magazine/snowden-maass-transcript.html.

25 Cf. 2.16

26 National Film Registry. "Registry Titles." *National Film Registry*. Dec. 16, 2013. http://www.loc.gov/film/registry_titles.php.

27 Cf. 2.15

28 The Whitney Museum. Program Guide. *The Whitney Museum*. Dec. 16, 2013. http://whitney.org/file_columns/0003/0173/2012whitneybiennial_programguide.pdf.

29 Viewfinder (Duke University's MFA Program blog). "Visiting Artist Laura Poitras Named MacArthur Fellow." *Viewfinder*. Oct. 2, 2012. http://mfaeda.org/archives/1071.

30 Poitras, Laura. "Miranda Detention: 'Blatant Attack on Press Freedom.'" *Der Spiegel*. Aug. 26, 2013. http://www.spiegel.de/international/world/laura-poitras-on-british-attacks-on-press-freedom-and-the-nsa-affair-a-918592.html.

31 Cf. 2.15

32 Cf. 2.15

33 Cf. 2.30

34 Lennard, Natasha. "Laura Poitras, the NSA, Snowden and a Rubik's Cube." *Salon*. Aug. 13, 2013. http://www.salon.com/2013/08/13/laura_poitras_the_nsa_snowden_and_a_rubiks_cube/.

35 Cf. 2.15

36 Cf. 2.15

37 Cf. 2.34

38 Cf. 2.15

39 Gellman, Barton. "Code name 'Verax': Snowden, in exchanges with Post reporter, made clear he knew risks." *The Washington Post*. June 9, 2013. http://articles.washingtonpost.com/2013-06-09/world/39856622_1_intelligence-powers-single-point.

[40] Carmon, Irin. "How we broke the NSA story." *Salon*. June 10, 2013. http://www.salon.com/2013/06/10/ qa_with_laura_poitras_the_woman_behind_the_nsa_scoops/.

[41] Auletta, Ken. "Freedom of Information." *The New Yorker*. Oct. 7, 2013. http://www.newyorker.com/reporting/2013/10/07/ 131007fa_fact_auletta?currentPage=all.

[42] Cf. 2.40

[43] Gorman, Siobhan. "Brennan Is Out of Running for CIA Post." *The Wall Street Journal*. Nov. 26, 2008. http://online.wsj.com/news/articles/ SB122764804462557485.

[44] Cf. 2.41

[45] Cf. 2.15

[46] Mierjeski, Alex. "Snoop Snoop Song: A Conversation with Glenn Greenwald." *Harpers*. July 17, 2013. http://harpers.org/blog/2013/07/ snoop-snoop-song/.

[47] Philanthropy New York. "Transitions, April 2013." *Philanthropy New York*. Dec. 16, 2013. http://www.philanthropynewyork.org/s_nyrag/ doc.asp?CID=6886&DID=61778.

[48] Time. Contributor Profile – Bart Gellman. *Time*. Dec. 16, 2013. http:// techland.time.com/author/gellmanb/?iid=redirect-counterspy/.

[49] Greenwald, Glenn, et al. "Edward Snowden: the whistleblower behind the NSA surveillance revelations." *The Guardian*. June 9, 2013. http:// www.theguardian.com/world/2013/jun/09/edward-snowden-nsa-whistleblower-surveillance.

[50] Cf. 2.39

[51] Cf. 2.39

[52] Cf. 2.39

[53] Cf. 2.39

[54] Cf. 2.39

[55] Cf. 2.49

[56] Cf. 2.39

[57] Greenwald, Glenn. "Edward Snowden: NSA whistleblower answers reader questions." *The Guardian*. June 17, 2013. http:// www.theguardian.com/world/2013/jun/17/edward-snowden-nsa-files-whistleblower.

[58] Freedom of the Press. "Board of Directors." *Press Freedom Foundation*. Dec. 16, 2013. https://pressfreedomfoundation.org/about/staff.

[59] Greenwald, Glenn. Personal Twitter account. *Twitter*. June 10, 2013. https://twitter.com/ggreenwald/status/344040301972815872.

[60] Cf. 2.15

[61] Cf. 2.15

[62] Cf. 2.40

[63] Sargent, Greg. "Glenn Greenwald pushes back hard on latest Edward Snowden 'revelations.'" *The Washington Post*. June 24, 2013. http://www.washingtonpost.com/blogs/plum-line/wp/2013/06/24/glenn-greenwald-pushes-back-hard-on-latest-edward-snowden-revelations/.

[64] Cf. 2.15

[65] Calderone, Michael. "How Glenn Greenwald Began Communicating With NSA Whistleblower Edward Snowden." *The Huffington Post*. June 10, 2013. http://www.huffingtonpost.com/2013/06/10/edward-snowden-glenn-greenwald_n_3416978.html.

[66] Cf. 2.63

[67] Cf. 2.65

[68] Der Spiegel. "Edward Snowden Interview: The NSA and Its Willing Helpers." *Der Spiegel*. July 8, 2013. http://www.spiegel.de/international/world/interview-with-whistleblower-edward-snowden-on-global-spying-a-910006.html.

[69] Cf. 2.15

[70] Cf. 2.40

[71] Cf. 2.15

[72] Cf. 2.24

[73] Cf. 2.15

[74] Davidson, Amy. "Edward Snowden, The N.S.A. Leaker, Comes Forward." *The New Yorker*. June 9, 2013. http://www.newyorker.com/online/blogs/closeread/2013/06/edward-snowden-the-nsa-leaker-comes-forward.html.

[75] Cf. 2.24

[76] Lake, Eli. "Inside the 'Q Group,' the Directorate Hunting Down Edward Snowden." *The Daily Beast*. June 10, 2013. http://www.thedailybeast.com/articles/2013/06/10/inside-the-q-group-the-directorate-hunting-down-andrew-snowden.html.

[77] Hosenball, Mark. "Feds hunted for Snowden in days before NSA programs went public." *Reuters*. June 12, 2013. http://mobile.reuters.com/article/idUSBRE95B1A220130612?irpc=932.

[78] Cf. 2.24

[79] Cf. 2.15

CHAPTER 3

[1] Greenwald, Glenn. "Edward Snowden: NSA whistleblower answers reader questions." *The Guardian.* June 17, 2013. http://www.theguardian.com/world/2013/jun/17/edward-snowden-nsa-files-whistleblower.

[2] Halperin, Carrie. "The Note's Must-Reads for Wednesday June 5, 2013." *ABC News.* June 5, 2013. http://abcnews.go.com/blogs/politics/2013/06/the-notes-must-reads-for-wednesday-june-5-2013/.

[3] Schmidt, Michael, et al. "U.S. Preparing Charges Against Leaker of Data." *The New York Times.* June 10, 2013. https://www.nytimes.com/2013/06/11/us/snowden-facing-charges-leaves-hong-kong-hotel.html?pagewanted=all.

[4] Calderone, Michael. "Washington Post Began PRISM Story Three Weeks Ago, Heard Guardian's 'Footsteps.'" *The Huffington Post.* June 7, 2013. http://www.huffingtonpost.com/2013/06/07/washington-post-prism-guardian_n_3402883.html.

[5] Greenwald, Glenn. "NSA collecting phone records of millions of Verizon customers daily." *The Guardian.* June 5, 2013. http://www.theguardian.com/world/2013/jun/06/nsa-phone-records-verizon-court-order.

[6] Cf. 3.5

[7] Gorman, Siobhan. "U.S. Collects Vast Data Trove." *The Wall Street Journal.* June 7, 2013. http://online.wsj.com/article/SB10001424127887324299104578529112289298922.html.

[8] Cf. 3.5

[9] Cauley, Leslie. "NSA has massive database of Americans' phone call." *USA Today.* May 11, 2006. http://usatoday30.usatoday.com/news/washington/2006-05-10-nsa_x.htm.

[10] Snider, L. "Recollections from the Church Committee's Investigation of NSA." *CIA.gov.* Apr. 14, 2007. https://www.cia.gov/library/center-for-the-study-of-intelligence/csi-publications/csi-studies/studies/winter99-00/art4.html.

[11] Epsley-Jones, Katelyn and Christina Frenzel. "The Church Committee Hearings & the FISA Court." *PBS.* May 15, 2007. http://www.pbs.org/wgbh/pages/frontline/homefront/preemption/churchfisa.html.

[12] Roberts, Dan, et al. "NSA surveillance: anger mounts in Congress at 'spying on Americans.'" *The Guardian.* June 11, 2013. http://www.theguardian.com/world/2013/jun/12/anger-mounts-congress-telephone-surveillance-programmes.

13 O'Keefe, Ed. "Dianne Feinstein, Saxby Chambliss explain, defend NSA phone records program." *The Washington Post*. June 6, 2013. http://www.washingtonpost.com/blogs/post-politics/wp/2013/06/06/transcript-dianne-feinstein-saxby-chambliss-explain-defend-nsa-phone-records-program/.

14 Electronic Frontier Foundation. "Hepting v. AT&T." *Electronic Frontier Foundation*. Dec. 16, 2013. https://www.eff.org/cases/hepting.

15 Criminalgovernment.com. "Communications Act of 1934." *Criminalgovernment.com*. Dec. 16, 2013. http://www.criminalgovernment.com/docs/61StatL101/ComAct34.html.

16 U.S. Government Printing Office. "Telecommunications Act of 1996." *U.S. Government Printing Office*. Dec. 16, 2013. http://www.gpo.gov/fdsys/pkg/PLAW-104publ104/pdf/PLAW-104publ104.pdf.

17 Greenfield, Rebecca. "Verizon Wants You to Blame the Government — and It's Working." *The Wire*. June 6, 2013. http://www.theatlanticwire.com/technology/2013/06/verizon-nsa-response/65978/.

18 Flaherty, Anne. "U.S. Government Pays Hundreds Of Dollars To AT&T And Verizon For Every Wiretap." *The Huffington Post*. July 10, 2013. http://www.huffingtonpost.com/2013/07/10/government-wiretap_n_3571422.html.

19 Risen, James and Laura Poitras. "N.S.A. Gathers Data on Social Connections of U.S. Citizens." *The New York Times*. Sept. 28, 2013. http://www.nytimes.com/2013/09/29/us/nsa-examines-social-networks-of-us-citizens.html?_r=1&pagewanted=all&.

20 Lake, Eli. "FBI Looks for Leaks at Foreign Intelligence Surveillance Court." *The Daily Beast*. June 18, 2013. http://www.thedailybeast.com/articles/2013/06/18/fbi-looks-for-leaks-at-foreign-intelligence-surveillance-court.html.

21 Lake, Eli. "Greenwald: Snowden's Files Are Out There if 'Anything Happens' to Him." *The Daily Beast*. June 25, 2013. http://www.thedailybeast.com/articles/2013/06/25/greenwald-snowden-s-files-are-out-there-if-anything-happens-to-him.html.

22 Bott, Ed. "The real story in the NSA scandal is the collapse of journalism." *ZDNet*. June 8, 2013. http://www.zdnet.com/the-real-story-in-the-nsa-scandal-is-the-collapse-of-journalism-7000016570/.

23 Greenwald, Glenn and Ewen MacAskill. "NSA Prism program taps in to user data of Apple, Google and others." *The Guardian*. June 6, 2013. http://www.theguardian.com/world/2013/jun/06/us-tech-giants-nsa-data.

24 RT. "NSA admits to spying on more people than previously thought." *RT*. July 18, 2013. http://rt.com/usa/nsa-inglis-three-hops-272/.

[25] Sutter, John. "On Facebook, it's now 4.74 degrees of separation." *CNN*. Nov. 22, 2011. http://edition.cnn.com/2011/11/22/tech/social-media/facebook-six-degrees/index.html?iref=allsearch.

[26] Bakhshandeh, Reza, et al. "Degrees of Separation in Social Networks." The Fourth International Symposium on Combinatorial Search. *The Association for the Advancement of Artificial Intelligence*. 2011. http://www.aaai.org/ocs/index.php/SOCS/SOCS11/paper/viewFile/4031/4352.

[27] Greenwald, Glenn and Spencer Ackerman. "NSA collected US email records in bulk for more than two years under Obama." *The Guardian*. June 27, 2013. http://www.theguardian.com/world/2013/jun/27/nsa-data-mining-authorised-obama.

[28] Davidson, Amy. "The N.S.A. and Its Targets: Lavabit Shuts Down." *The New Yorker*. Aug. 8, 2013. http://www.newyorker.com/online/blogs/closeread/2013/08/the-nsa-and-its-targets-lavabit-shuts-down.html.

[29] The Washington Post. "NSA slides explain the PRISM data-collection program." *The Washington Post*. June 6, 2013. http://www.washingtonpost.com/wp-srv/special/politics/prism-collection-documents/.

[30] Gellman, Barton and Laura Poitras. "U.S., British intelligence mining data from nine U.S. Internet companies in broad secret program." *The Washington Post*. June 6, 2013. http://articles.washingtonpost.com/2013-06-06/news/39784046_1_prism-nsa-u-s-servers.

[31] Hopkins, Nick. "UK gathering secret intelligence via covert NSA operation." *The Guardian*. June 7, 2013. http://www.theguardian.com/technology/2013/jun/07/uk-gathering-secret-intelligence-nsa-prism.

[32] Reuters. "Apple: 'We Have Never Heard Of PRISM.'" *The Huffington Post*. June 6, 2013. http://www.huffingtonpost.com/2013/06/06/apple-prism-nsa_n_3399739.html.

[33] Gupta, Poornima and Gerry Shih. "Internet giants deny granting government 'direct access' to servers." *Reuters*. June 6, 2013. http://mobile.reuters.com/article/idUSBRE9551EU20130607?irpc=932.

[34] McCullough, Charles. Letter from Charles McCullough to Senators Ron Wyden and Mark Udall. *Wired*. June 15, 2012. http://www.wired.com/images_blogs/dangerroom/2012/06/IC-IG-Letter.pdf.

[35] Meacham, T. "PRISM: The 8 Tech Companies Who Gave Your Data to the Government Have This to Say About the Scandal." *PolicyMic*. June 8, 2013. http://www.policymic.com/articles/47231/prism-the-8-tech-companies-who-gave-your-data-to-the-government-have-this-to-say-about-the-scandal.

[36] Wired. "Whistle-Blower's Evidence, Uncut." *Wired*. May 22, 2006. http://www.wired.com/science/discoveries/news/2006/05/70944.

[37] Miller, Claire. "Tech Companies Concede to Surveillance Program." *The New York Times*. June 7, 2013. http://www.nytimes.com/2013/06/08/technology/tech-companies-bristling-concede-to-government-surveillance-efforts.html?pagewanted=all&_r=0.

[38] The White House. "Statement by the President." *The White House of the United States*. June 7, 2013. http://www.whitehouse.gov/the-press-office/2013/06/07/statement-president.

[39] Zetter, Kim. "Google sends Prism data to NSA by secure FTP or 'by hand.'" *Wired*. June 12, 2013. http://www.wired.co.uk/news/archive/2013-06/12/google-prism-ftp.

[40] MacAskill, Ewen. "NSA paid millions to cover Prism compliance costs for tech companies." *The Guardian*. Aug. 22, 2013. http://www.theguardian.com/world/2013/aug/23/nsa-prism-costs-tech-companies-paid.

[41] Microsoft Corporation. "Law Enforcement Requests Report." *Microsoft Corporation*. June 14, 2013. https://www.microsoft.com/about/corporatecitizenship/en-us/reporting/transparency/.

[42] Facebook. "Global Government Requests Report." *Facebook*. June 14, 2013. https://www.facebook.com/about/government_requests.

[43] Yahoo. "Government Data Requests." *Yahoo*. June 17, 2013. http://info.yahoo.com/transparency-report/us/.

[44] Apple. "Apple's Commitment to Customer Privacy" (Government Request Report). *Apple*. June 17, 2013. https://www.apple.com/apples-commitment-to-customer-privacy/.

[45] Electronic Privacy Information Center. "Foreign Intelligence Surveillance Act Court Orders 1979-2012." *Electronic Privacy Information Center*. Dec. 16, 2013. http://epic.org/privacy/wiretap/stats/fisa_stats.html.

[46] Kadzik, Peter. Letter from Peter Kadzik to Senator Harry Reid. *Federation of American Scientists*. Apr. 30, 2013. https://www.fas.org/irp/agency/doj/fisa/2012rept.pdf.

[47] Cf. 3.39

[48] The Washington Post. PRISM slide. *The Washington Post*. Dec. 16, 2013. http://www.washingtonpost.com/wp-srv/special/politics/prism-collection-documents/images/prism-slide-2.jpg.

[49] Pingdom. Map of all Google data center locations. *Pingdom*. Dec. 16, 2013. http://royal.pingdom.com/2008/04/11/map-of-all-google-data-center-locations/.

[50] Greenwald, Glenn and Ewen MacAskill. "Obama orders US to draw up overseas target list for cyber-attacks." *The Guardian*. June 7, 2013. http://www.theguardian.com/world/2013/jun/07/obama-china-targets-cyber-overseas.

[51] The Guardian. Obama tells intelligence chiefs to draw up cyber target list – full document text. *The Guardian*. June 7, 2013. http://www.theguardian.com/world/interactive/2013/jun/07/obama-cyber-directive-full-text.

[52] Jones, Terril. "China has 'mountains of data' about U.S. cyber attacks: official." *Reuters*. June 5, 2013. http://www.reuters.com/article/2013/06/05/us-china-usa-hacking-idUSBRE95404L20130605.

[53] Cf. 3.52

[54] The White House. "Remarks by President Obama and President Xi Jinping of the People's Republic of China After Bilateral Meeting." *The White House of the United States*. June 8, 2013. http://www.whitehouse.gov/the-press-office/2013/06/08/remarks-president-obama-and-president-xi-jinping-peoples-republic-china-.

[55] Greenwald, Glenn and Ewen MacAskill. "Boundless Informant: the NSA's secret tool to track global surveillance data." *The Guardian*. June (8) 11, 2013. http://www.theguardian.com/world/2013/jun/08/nsa-boundless-informant-global-datamining.

[56] Office of the Director of National Intelligence. Transcript of Director James Clapper's interview with Andrea Mitchell. *Office of the Director of National Intelligence*. June 10, 2013. http://www.dni.gov/index.php/newsroom/speeches-and-interviews/195-speeches-interviews-2013/874-director-james-r-clapper-interview-with-andrea-mitchell.

[57] Poitras, Laura and Glenn Greenwald. "NSA whistleblower Edward Snowden: 'I don't want to live in a society that does these sort of things.'" *The Guardian*. June 9, 2013. http://www.theguardian.com/world/video/2013/jun/09/nsa-whistleblower-edward-snowden-interview-video.

[58] Greenwald, Glenn, et al. "Edward Snowden: the whistleblower behind the NSA surveillance revelations." *The Guardian*. June 9, 2013. http://www.theguardian.com/world/2013/jun/09/edward-snowden-nsa-whistleblower-surveillance.

[59] Clemons, Steve. Personal Twitter account. *Twitter*. June 8, 2013. https://twitter.com/SCClemons/status/343392529913356289.

[60] MacAskill, Ewen. "Edward Snowden, NSA files source: 'If they want to get you, in time they will.'" *The Guardian*. June 9, 2013. http://www.theguardian.com/world/2013/jun/09/nsa-whistleblower-edward-snowden-why.

[61] NBS Nightly News. "DNI's Clapper: Leaker chose to 'violate a sacred trust.'" *NBS News*. June 10, 2013. http://www.nbcnews.com/video/nightly-news/52158136#52158136.

CHAPTER 4

1   Greenwald, Glenn. "Edward Snowden: NSA whistleblower answers reader questions." *The Guardian*. June 17, 2013. http://www.theguardian.com/world/2013/jun/17/edward-snowden-nsa-files-whistleblower.

2   Moore, Michael. Personal Twitter account. *Twitter*. June 9, 2013. http://mmflint.me/11P4jva.

3   Beck, Glenn. Personal Twitter account. *Twitter*. June 9, 2013. https://twitter.com/glennbeck/status/343816286234632192.

4   Stiles, Megan. "Ron Paul: We need to know more about what the government is doing." *Campaign for Liberty*. June 10, 2013. http://www.campaignforliberty.org/national-blog/ron-paul-we-need-to-know-more-about-what-the-government-is-doing/.

5   Limbaugh, Rush. "Edward Snowden: Hero or Traitor?" *RushLimbaugh.com*. June 10, 2013. http://www.rushlimbaugh.com/daily/2013/06/10/edward_snowden_hero_or_traitor.

6   Perez, Evan. "FBI Scrutinized on Petraeus." *The Wall Street Journal*. Nov. 12, 2012. http://online.wsj.com/article/SB10001424127887324073504578113460852395852.html.

7   O'Reilly, Bill. "Data Mining and You." *BillOReilly.com*. June 10, 2013. http://www.billoreilly.com/show?action=viewTVShow&showID=3410.

8   Wing, Nick. "Jimmy Carter Defends Edward Snowden, Says NSA Spying Has Compromised Nation's Democracy." *The Huffington Post*. July 18, 2013. http://www.huffingtonpost.com/2013/07/18/jimmy-carter-edward-snowden_n_3616930.html.

9   Gore, Al. Personal Twitter account. *Twitter*. June 5, 2013. https://twitter.com/algore/status/342455655057211393.

10 Goldenberg, Suzanne. "Al Gore: NSA's secret surveillance program 'not really the American way.'" *The Guardian*. June 14, 2013. http://www.theguardian.com/world/2013/jun/14/al-gore-nsa-surveillance-unamerican.

11 Chumley, Cheryl. "GOP's Peter King: NSA leaker Edward Snowden must be extradited, prosecuted." *The Washington Times*. June 10, 2013. http://www.washingtontimes.com/news/2013/jun/10/gops-peter-king-nsa-leaker-edward-snowden-must-be-/.

12 ABC News. "Boehner on NSA Whistleblower: 'He's a Traitor.'" *ABC News*. June 11, 2013. http://abcnews.go.com/GMA/video/edward-snowden-nsa-leaker-boehner-hes-traitor-19371699.

13 Fox News. "Cheney defends NSA programs, says Snowden a 'traitor,' Obama 'lacks credibility.'" *Fox News*. June 16, 2013. http://

www.foxnews.com/politics/2013/06/16/cheney-defends-us-surveillance-programs-says-snowden-traitor-obama-lacks/.

14 Welsh, Teresa. "The NSA Leaker: Traitor or Hero?" *U.S. News.* June 11, 2013. http://www.usnews.com/opinion/articles/2013/06/11/is-nsa-leaker-edward-snowden-a-traitor-or-a-hero-whistleblower.

15 Stein, Sam. "Rand Paul Warns Edward Snowden: Don't Cozy Up To The Russians." *The Huffington Post.* June 23, 2013. http://www.huffingtonpost.com/2013/06/23/rand-paul-snowden_n_3486455.html.

16 Newport, Frank. "Americans Disapprove of Government Surveillance Programs." *Gallup.* June 12, 2013. http://www.gallup.com/poll/163043/americans-disapprove-government-surveillance-programs.aspx.

17 The White House. "Pardon Edward Snowden" petition. *The White House of the United States.* June 9, 2013. https://petitions.whitehouse.gov/petition/pardon-edward-snowden/Dp03vGYD.

18 Nelson, Steve. "White House Remains Silent on 'Pardon Edward Snowden' Petition." *U.S. News.* Aug. 23, 2013. http://www.usnews.com/news/blogs/washington-whispers/2013/08/23/white-house-remains-silent-on-pardon-edward-snowden-petition.

19 Greenwald, Glenn, et al. "Edward Snowden: the whistleblower behind the NSA surveillance revelations." *The Guardian.* June 9, 2013. http://www.theguardian.com/world/2013/jun/09/edward-snowden-nsa-whistleblower-surveillance.

20 Crow, Dwight. "Reward Edward Snowden for courageously leaking NSA docs" fundraising page. *Crowdtilt.* June 11, 2013. https://www.crowdtilt.com/campaigns/reward-edward-snowden-for-courageously-leaking-nsa-docs.

21 Itkowitz, Colby and Daniel Patrick Sheehan. "FBI visits family of NSA leaker in Upper Macungie." *The Morning Call.* June 10, 2013. http://articles.mcall.com/2013-06-10/news/mc-pa-ed-snowden-nsa-leak-20130610_1_fbi-agents-upper-macungie-township-public-records.

22 Booz Allen Hamilton. "Booz Allen Statement on Reports of Leaked Information." *Booz Allen Hamilton.* June 11, 2013. http://www.boozallen.com/media-center/press-releases/48399320/statement-reports-leaked-information-060913.

23 Wemple, Erik. "Did Snowden really earn a $200,000 salary?" *The Washington Post.* June 11, 2013. http://www.washingtonpost.com/blogs/erik-wemple/wp/2013/06/11/did-snowden-really-earn-a-200000-salary/.

24 Cf. 4.1

[25] Philips, Tom. "Edward Snowden: Hong Kong hotel hideaway of the NSA whistleblower." *The Telegraph*. June 10, 2013. http://www.telegraph.co.uk/news/worldnews/asia/hongkong/10110927/Edward-Snowden-Hong-Kong-hotel-hideaway-of-the-NSA-whistleblower.html.

[26] Mullany, Gerry and Scott Shane. "U.S. Petitions for Extradition in N.S.A. Case." *The New York Times*. June 22, 2013. http://www.nytimes.com/2013/06/23/world/asia/arrest-of-nsa-leaker-seen-as-easier-than-transfer-to-us.html?pagewanted=all&_r=0.

[27] Cf. 4.1

[28] Lam, Lana. "Whistle-blower Edward Snowden tells SCMP: 'Let Hong Kong people decide my fate.'" *South China Morning Post*. June 12, 2013. http://www.scmp.com/news/hong-kong/article/1259422/edward-snowden-let-hong-kong-people-decide-my-fate?page=all.

[29] Poitras, Laura and Glenn Greenwald. "Edward Snowden: 'The US government will say I aided our enemies' – video interview." *The Guardian*. July 8, 2013. http://www.theguardian.com/world/video/2013/jul/08/edward-snowden-video-interview.

[30] Pomfret, James and Yimou Lee. "China's 'mini-Hong Kong' eyes Internet access, shrugs off Shanghai threat." *Reuters*. Sept. 26, 2013. http://in.reuters.com/article/2013/09/26/china-qianhai-idINDEE98P08O20130926.

[31] Lai, Alexis. "Hong Kong rallies in the rain for Edward Snowden." *CNN*. June 16, 2013. http://www.cnn.com/2013/06/15/world/asia/hong-kong-snowden-protest/.

[32] Duke East Asian Nexus. "Hong Kong's Economic and Political Development in the Post-1997 Period." *Duke.edu*. Dec. 16, 2013. http://sites.duke.edu/dean/2010/11/23/hong-kongs-economic-and-political-development-in-the-post-1997-period/.

[33] Cf. 4.31

[34] Lam, Lana. "Whistle-blower Edward Snowden talks to South China Morning Post." *South China Morning Post*. June 12, 2013. http://www.scmp.com/news/hong-kong/article/1259335/exclusive-whistle-blower-edward-snowden-talks-south-china-morning?page=all.

[35] Lam, Lana. "Edward Snowden: US government has been hacking Hong Kong and China for years." *South China Morning Post*. June 13, 2013. http://www.scmp.com/news/hong-kong/article/1259508/edward-snowden-us-government-has-been-hacking-hong-kong-and-china?page=all.

[36] Lam, Lana. "Edward Snowden: Classified US data shows Hong Kong hacking targets." *South China Morning Post*. June 14, 2013. http://

www.scmp.com/news/hong-kong/article/1260306/edward-snowden-classified-us-data-shows-hong-kong-hacking-targets.

37 West, Angus. "14 disturbing things Snowden has taught us (so far)." *Global Post*. July 9, 2013. http://www.globalpost.com/dispatch/news/politics/130703/edward-snowden-leaks.

38 Morning News (Hong Kong). "Hong Kong Media: Two More Weeks of Exposure to U.S. Government's 'Secrets.'" *Morning News (Hong Kong)*. June 20, 2013. http://war.163.com/13/0620/08/91Q337HN00014OMD.html.

39 MacAskill, Ewen. "GCHQ intercepted foreign politicians' communications at G20 summits." *The Guardian*. June 16, 2013. http://www.theguardian.com/uk/2013/jun/16/gchq-intercepted-communications-g20-summits.

40 The Guardian. "How GCHQ stepped up spying on South African foreign ministry." *The Guardian*. June 16, 2013. http://www.theguardian.com/world/2013/jun/16/gchq-south-african-foreign-ministry.

41 Legislation.gov.uk. "Intelligence Services Act 1994." *Legislation.gov.uk*. Dec. 16, 2013. http://www.legislation.gov.uk/ukpga/1994/13/section/3#text%3D%22in%20the%20interests%20of%20the%20economic%20well-being%20of%20the%20United%20Kingdom%20in%20relation%20to%20the%20actions%20or%20intentions%20of%20persons%20outside%20the%20British%20Island%22.

42 Pike, John. "Menwith Hill Station, UK." *Federation of American Scientists*. Nov. 17, 2003. http://www.fas.org/irp/facility/menwith.htm.

43 Norton-Taylor, Richard. "Menwith Hill eavesdropping base undergoes massive expansion." *The Guardian*. Mar. 1, 2012. http://www.theguardian.com/world/2012/mar/01/menwith-hill-eavesdropping-base-expansion.

44 Cf. 4.42

45 Borger, Julian. "G20 summits: Russia and Turkey react with fury to spying revelations." *The Guardian*. June 17, 2013. http://www.theguardian.com/world/2013/jun/17/turkey-russia-g20-spying-gchq.

46 BBC News UK. "Spying claims: Countries demand explanation from UK." *BBC*. June 17, 2013. http://www.bbc.co.uk/news/uk-22938073.

47 Fraser, Suzan. "Turkey probes social network 'insults.'" *The Big Story*. June 27, 2013. http://bigstory.ap.org/article/turkey-probes-social-network-postings.

48 Dominiczak, Peter. "Cameron refuses to comment on G20 spying claims." *The Telegraph*. June 17, 2013. http://www.telegraph.co.uk/

news/worldnews/g8/10124795/Cameron-refuses-to-comment-on-G20-spying-claims.html.

49 The White House. "Remarks by the President at the new Economic School Graduation." *The White House of the United States.* July 7, 2009. http://www.whitehouse.gov/the-press-office/remarks-president-new-economic-school-graduation.

50 Cf. 4.1

51 Office of the Director of National Intelligence. Transcript of Director James Clapper's interview with Andrea Mitchell. *Office of the Director of National Intelligence.* June 10, 2013. http://www.dni.gov/index.php/newsroom/speeches-and-interviews/195-speeches-interviews-2013/874-director-james-r-clapper-interview-with-andrea-mitchell.

52 Royal Air Force. "RAF Menwith Hill - Personnel and Administration." *Royal Air Force.* Dec. 16, 2013. http://www.raf.mod.uk/organisation/rafmenwithhilladministration.cfm.

53 Greenwald, Glenn and James Ball. "The top secret rules that allow NSA to use US data without a warrant." *The Guardian.* June 20, 2013. http://www.theguardian.com/world/2013/jun/20/fisa-court-nsa-without-warrant.

54 Halliday, Josh. "MoD serves news outlets with D notice over surveillance leaks." *The Guardian.* June 17, 2013. http://www.theguardian.com/world/2013/jun/17/defence-d-bbc-media-censor-surveillance-security.

55 Staines, Paul and Harry Cole. "D-Notice, June 7, 2013." *Guido Fawke's Blog.* June 8, 2013. http://order-order.com/2013/06/08/d-notice-june-7-2013/.

56 AP. "NSA leaker Snowden not welcome in U.K." *USA Today.* June 14, 2013. http://www.usatoday.com/story/news/world/2013/06/14/apnewsbreak-nsa-leaker-snowden-not-welcome-in-uk/2422385/.

57 MacAskill, Ewen. "GCHQ taps fibre-optic cables for secret access to world's communications." *The Guardian.* June 21, 2013. http://www.theguardian.com/uk/2013/jun/21/gchq-cables-secret-world-communications-nsa.

58 Hosenball, Mark. "Snowden downloaded NSA secrets while working for Dell, sources say." *Reuters.* Aug. 15, 2013. http://www.reuters.com/article/2013/08/15/usa-security-snowden-dell-idUSL2N0GF11220130815.

59 Poitras, Laura. "How the NSA Targets Germany and Europe." *Der Spiegel.* July 1, 2013. http://www.spiegel.de/international/world/secret-documents-nsa-targeted-germany-and-eu-buildings-a-908609.html.

60 Cf. 4.51

[61] The Washington Post. "NSA report on privacy violations in the first quarter of 2012." *The Washington Post*. Aug. 15, 2013. http://apps.washingtonpost.com/g/page/national/nsa-report-on-privacy-violations-in-the-first-quarter-of-2012/395/#document/p8/a115763.

[62] Hopkins, Nick, et al. "GCHQ: inside the top secret world of Britain's biggest spy agency." *The Guardian*. Aug. 1, 2013. http://www.theguardian.com/world/2013/aug/02/gchq-spy-agency-nsa-snowden.

[63] Der Spiegel. "Leutheusser-Schnarrenberger: Justizministerin entsetzt über britisches Abhörprogramm." *Der Spiegel*. June 22, 2013. http://www.spiegel.de/politik/deutschland/leutheusser-schnarrenberger-entsetzt-ueber-tempora-a-907314.html.

[64] Cáceres, Javier and Christian Zaschke. "Amerikanischer als die Amerikaner." *Sueddeutsche*. June 23, 2013. http://jetzt.sueddeutsche.de/texte/anzeigen/573472/Amerikanischer-als-die-Amerikaner.

[65] Lam, Lana and Stephen Chen. "Snowden reveals more US cyberspying details." *South China Morning Post*. June 22, 2013. http://www.scmp.com/news/hong-kong/article/1266777/exclusive-snowden-safe-hong-kong-more-us-cyberspying-details-revealed?page=all.

[66] Lam, Lana and Stephen Chen. "US spies on Chinese mobile phone companies, steals SMS data: Edward Snowden." *South China Morning Post*. June 22, 2013. http://www.scmp.com/news/china/article/1266821/us-hacks-chinese-mobile-phone-companies-steals-sms-data-edward-snowden?page=all.

[67] Slashdot. "China Telco Replaces Cisco Devices Over Security Concerns." *Slashdot*. Oct. 26, 2012. http://hardware.slashdot.org/story/12/10/26/2336246/china-telco-replaces-cisco-devices-over-security-concerns.

[68] Zetter, Kim. "Router Flaw Is a Ticking Bomb." *Wired*. Aug. 1, 2005. http://www.wired.com/politics/security/news/2005/08/68365?currentPage=all.

[69] Lam, Lana. "NSA targeted China's Tsinghua University in extensive hacking attacks, says Snowden." *South China Morning Post*. June 22, 2013. http://www.scmp.com/news/china/article/1266892/exclusive-nsa-targeted-chinas-tsinghua-university-extensive-hacking?page=all.

[70] Global Times. "How big is World Washington Web?" *Global Times*. June 25, 2013. http://www.globaltimes.cn/content/791338.shtml.

[71] Bishop, Bill. The Sinocism China Newsletter 06.25.13. *Sinocism*. June 25, 2013. https://sinocism.com/?p=9635.

[72] Internet Monitor. "China's Reactions to the Snowden Story." *Harvard.edu*. Aug. 5, 2013. https://blogs.law.harvard.edu/internetmonitor/2013/08/05/chinas-reactions-to-the-snowden-story/.

[73] Cf. 4.31

[74] Whiteman, Hilary. "Scenarios for Snowden: Escape, arrest, asylum." *CNN*. June 21, 2013. http://www.cnn.com/2013/06/20/world/asia/snowden-scenarios-hong-kong/.

[75] Bradsher, Keith. "Hasty Exit Started With Pizza Inside a Hong Kong Hideout." *The New York Times*. June 24, 2013. http://www.nytimes.com/2013/06/25/world/asia/snowden-departure-from-hong-kong.html?pagewanted=all&_r=0.

[76] Lam, Lana. "Hong Kong lawyer Albert Ho says 'middleman' urged Snowden to leave." *South China Morning Post*. June 23, 2013. http://www.scmp.com/news/hong-kong/article/1267373/exclusive-human-rights-lawyers-hong-kong-reveal-they-worked-closely.

[77] Johnson, Kevin. "WikiLeaks lawyers helping Snowden in brokering asylum." *USA Today*. June 19, 2013. http://www.usatoday.com/story/news/nation/2013/06/19/wikileaks-assange-snowden-nsa-leak-asylum/2438923/.

[78] Cf. 4.75

[79] International Criminal Defense Lawyers. "China (Hong Kong) International Extradition Treaty with the United States." *McNabb Associates*. Dec. 16, 2013. http://www.mcnabbassociates.com/China%20Hong%20Kong%20International%20Extradition%20Treaty%20with%20the%20United%20States.pdf.

[80] Zetter, Kim. "UN Torture Chief: Bradley Manning Treatment Was Cruel, Inhuman." *Wired*. Mar. 3, 2012. http://www.wired.com/threatlevel/2012/03/manning-treatment-inhuman/.

[81] The Guardian. US request for extradition of Edward Snowden - full text. *The Guardian*. July 6, 2013. http://www.theguardian.com/world/interactive/2013/jul/06/us-request-extradition-edward-snowden?CMP=twt_fd&CMP=SOCxx2I2.

[82] Department of Justice. Justice Department Statement on the Request to Hong Kong for Edward Snowden's Provisional Arrest. *The United States Department of Justice*. June 26, 2013. http://www.justice.gov/opa/pr/2013/June/13-opa-761.html.

[83] The Guardian. "US got NSA leaker Edward Snowden's middle name wrong, says Hong Kong." *The Guardian*. June 26, 2013. http://www.theguardian.com/world/2013/jun/26/edward-snowden-name-wrong-hong-kong.

[84] Ying-kit, Lai. "Hong Kong minister rejects US accusations of deliberately delaying Snowden's arrest." *South China Morning Post*. June 25, 2013. http://www.scmp.com/news/hong-kong/article/1268819/hong-kong-minister-rejects-us-accusations-deliberately-delaying?page=all.

85 MacAskill, Ewen. "Edward Snowden, NSA files source: 'If they want to get you, in time they will.'" *The Guardian*. June 9, 2013. http://www.theguardian.com/world/2013/jun/09/nsa-whistleblower-edward-snowden-why.

86 Schwartz, Matthew. "NSA Leaker Snowden On The Run." *InformationWeek*. June 24, 2013. http://www.informationweek.com/security/privacy/nsa-leaker-snowden-on-the-run/240157172.

87 Bruce, Mary. "Hong Kong's 'Deliberate Choice' to Release Snowden Damages US-China Relationship, White House Says." *ABC News*. June 24, 2013. http://abcnews.go.com/blogs/politics/2013/06/hong-kongs-deliberate-choice-to-release-snowden-damages-us-china-relationship-white-house-says/.

88 Info.gov.hk. "HKSAR Government issues statement on Edward Snowden." *Info.gov.hk*. June 23, 2013. http://www.info.gov.hk/gia/general/201306/23/P201306230476.htm.

89 Cf. 4.81

90 Cf. 4.75

91 Global Post. "Edward Snowden skips flight to Havana." *Global Post*. June 24, 2013. http://www.globalpost.com/dispatch/news/regions/americas/united-states/130624/edward-snowden-expected-leave-moscow-fly-havana.

92 Global Times. "Extraditing Snowden an unwise decision." *Global Times*. June 17, 2013. http://www.globaltimes.cn/content/789238.shtml.

93 Richburg, Keith. "China confirms its official stayed one day at U.S. consulate." *The Washington Post*. Feb. 9, 2012. http://articles.washingtonpost.com/2012-02-09/world/35445973_1_bo-xilai-wang-lijun-political-asylum.

94 Osnos, Evan. "Why China Let Snowden Go." *The New Yorker*. June 24, 2013. http://www.newyorker.com/online/blogs/evanosnos/2013/06/why-china-let-snowden-go.html.

95 Cf. 4.66

96 Lam, Lana. "Snowden's last few days in Hong Kong: dramatic events prompted flight." *South China Morning Post*. June 24, 2013. http://www.scmp.com/news/hong-kong/article/1268168/snowdens-last-72-hours-hong-kong-dramatic-events-prompted?page=all.

97 Faiola, Anthony. "WikiLeaks aids Snowden on the run." *The Washington Post*. June 23, 2013. http://articles.washingtonpost.com/2013-06-23/news/40152230_1_julian-assange-wikileaks-spokesman-kristinn-hrafnsson.

98 Interfax. "Snowden's flight from Hong Kong lands at Sheremetyevo Airport." *Russia Beyond the Headlines*. June 23, 2013. http://rbth.ru/

international/2013/06/23/
snowdens_flight_from_hong_kong_lands_at_sheremetyevo_airport_
27393.html.

99 Lake, Eli and Miranda Green. "WikiLeaks Foots the Bill For Snowden's
    Global Escapades." *The Daily Beast*. June 24, 2013. http://
    www.thedailybeast.com/articles/2013/06/24/wikileaks-foots-the-bill-
    for-snowden-s-global-escapades.html.

CHAPTER 5

1   Esposito, Richard, et al. "Snowden impersonated NSA officials, sources
    say." *NBC News*. Aug. 29, 2013. http://investigations.nbcnews.com/
    _news/2013/08/29/20234171-snowden-impersonated-nsa-officials-
    sources-say.

2   Gellman, Barton. "Code name 'Verax': Snowden, in exchanges with Post
    reporter, made clear he knew risks." *The Washington Post*. June 9, 2013.
    http://articles.washingtonpost.com/2013-06-09/world/
    39856622_1_intelligence-powers-single-point.

3   Bump, Philip. "The Six Tricky Steps to Edward Snowden's Extradition,
    Explained." *The Wire*. June 20, 2013. http://www.theatlanticwire.com/
    global/2013/06/edward-snowden-extradition-explained/66433/.

4   Nelson, Steve. "Iceland-Bound Jet for Edward Snowden 'Could Take Off
    Tomorrow.'" *U.S. News*. June 21, 2013. http://www.usnews.com/
    news/newsgram/articles/2013/06/21/iceland-bound-jet-for-edward-
    snowden-could-take-off-tomorrow.

5   RT. "NSA leaker Snowden may leave Hong Kong for Iceland on private
    jet." *RT*. June 21, 2013. http://rt.com/news/snowden-iceland-private-
    jet-071/.

6   Shane, Scott. "Ex-Contractor Is Charged in Leaks on N.S.A.
    Surveillance." *The New York Times*. June 21, 2013. http://
    www.nytimes.com/2013/06/22/us/snowden-espionage-
    act.html?pagewanted=all.

7   Bloomfield, Aubrey. "Edward Snowden Iceland Asylum: Applying For
    Icelandic Citizenship May Be His Best Option." *PolicyMic*. June 21, 2013.
    http://www.policymic.com/articles/50275/edward-snowden-iceland-
    asylum-applying-for-icelandic-citizenship-may-be-his-best-option.

8   Robertsson, Robert. "Iceland parliament declines Snowden's citizenship
    bid." *Reuters*. July 5, 2013. http://www.reuters.com/article/2013/07/
    05/us-usa-security-snowden-iceland-idUSBRE9640PS20130705.

9   Pilkington, Ed. "Edward Snowden's digital 'misuse' has created
    problems, says Ban Ki-moon." *The Guardian*. July 3, 2013. http://
    www.theguardian.com/world/2013/jul/03/edward-snowden-digital-
    misuse-ban-ki-moon.

[10] McCann, Jaymi. "Running out of places to hide: Iceland Rejects Edward Snowden's bid for citizenship." *Mail Online.* July 5, 2013. http://www.dailymail.co.uk/news/article-2356995/Iceland-REJECTS-Edward-Snowdens-bid-citizenship.html.

[11] Reuters. "Iceland received informal approach over Snowden seeking asylum." *Reuters.* June 18, 2013. http://www.reuters.com/article/2013/06/18/us-usa-security-iceland-snowden-idUSBRE95H0OQ20130618.

[12] Greenwald, Glenn. "Edward Snowden: NSA whistleblower answers reader questions." *The Guardian.* June 17, 2013. http://www.theguardian.com/world/2013/jun/17/edward-snowden-nsa-files-whistleblower.

[13] Elder, Miriam. "Edward Snowden: Russia offers to consider asylum request." *The Guardian.* June 11, 2013. http://www.theguardian.com/world/2013/jun/11/edward-snowden-russia-asylum-request.

[14] Lam, Lana. "Edward Snowden: US government has been hacking Hong Kong and China for years." *South China Morning Post.* June 13, 2013. http://www.scmp.com/news/hong-kong/article/1259508/edward-snowden-us-government-has-been-hacking-hong-kong-and-china?page=all.

[15] Englund, Will. "Snowden stayed at Russian consulate while in Hong Kong." *The Washington Post.* Aug. 26, 2013. http://articles.washingtonpost.com/2013-08-26/world/41446952_1_edward-snowden-snowden-s-russian-consulate.

[16] Bradsher, Keith. "Hasty Exit Started With Pizza Inside a Hong Kong Hideout." *The New York Times.* June 24, 2013. http://www.nytimes.com/2013/06/25/world/asia/snowden-departure-from-hong-kong.html?pagewanted=all.

[17] Farivar, Cyrus. "Ecuador: Snowden travel doc issued from London embassy 'has no validity.'" *Ars Technica.* June 28, 2013. http://arstechnica.com/tech-policy/2013/06/ecuador-snowden-travel-doc-issued-from-london-embassy-has-no-validity/.

[18] Ruck, Joanna. Personal Twitter account. *Twitter.* June 23, 2013. https://twitter.com/joannaruck/status/348819065202151424/photo/1.

[19] French, Anya. "Why Edward Snowden Didn't Go To Havana, Cuba." *The Havana Note.* June 24, 2013. http://thehavananote.com/2013/06/why_edward_snowden_didnt_go_havana_cuba.

[20] Pearson, Michael, et al. "Snowden's asylum options dwindle." *CNN.* July 2, 2013. http://www.cnn.com/2013/07/02/politics/nsa-leak/.

[21] Dewey, Caitlin. "As many as 24 journalists trailed Snowden on Havana flight, but he's not on it." *The Washington Post.* June 24, 2013. http://www.washingtonpost.com/blogs/worldviews/wp/2013/06/24/as-

many-as-24-journalists-trailed-snowden-on-havana-flight-but-hes-not-on-it/.

22 Shemetov, Maxim. "Destination Cuba: Alongside empty seat 17A." *Reuters*. June 25, 2013. http://blogs.reuters.com/photographers-blog/2013/06/25/destination-cuba-alongside-empty-seat-17a/.

23 Davidson, Amy. "Edward Snowden's Flight to Moscow." *The New Yorker*. June 23, 2013. http://www.newyorker.com/online/blogs/closeread/2013/06/edward-snowdens-flight-to-moscow.html.

24 Cf. 5.17

25 Biography. Julian Assange biography. *Biography*. Dec. 16, 2013. http://www.biography.com/people/julian-assange-20688499.

26 AP. "WikiLeaks' Assange faces arrest if he leaves Ecuador Embassy." *USA Today*. June 20, 2012. http://usatoday30.usatoday.com/news/world/story/2012-06-20/wikileaks-assange-embassy/55714222/1.

27 Caselli, Irene. "Ecuador and UK impasse over Julian Assange's asylum." *BBC*. June 17, 2013. http://www.bbc.co.uk/news/uk-22928276.

28 Carroll, Rory and Amanda Holpuch. "Ecuador cools on Edward Snowden asylum as Assange frustration grows." *The Guardian*. June 28, 2013. http://www.theguardian.com/world/2013/jun/28/edward-snowden-ecuador-julian-assange.

29 Info.gov.hk. "HKSAR Government issues statement on Edward Snowden." *Info.gov.hk*. June 23, 2013. http://www.info.gov.hk/gia/general/201306/23/P201306230476.htm.

30 Kaufman, Alexander. "Whistleblower Edward Snowden's Extradition Papers From Hong Kong Denied Over Middle Name Error." *International Business Times*. June 26, 2013. http://www.ibtimes.com/whistleblower-edward-snowdens-extradition-papers-hong-kong-denied-over-middle-name-error-1323733.

31 Noble, Josh and Katherin Hille. "Legal experts back Hong Kong role in Snowden case." *Financial Times*. June 24, 2013. http://www.ft.com/intl/cms/s/cfbe6a36-dca6-11e2-9700-00144feab7de,Authorised=false.html?_i_location=http%3A%2F%2Fwww.ft.com%2Fcms%2Fs%2F0%2Fcfbe6a36-dca6-11e2-9700-00144feab7de.html%3Fsiteedition%3Dintl&siteedition=intl&_i_referer=.

32 Weinstein, Adam. "Ecuador Spinning Over Snowden 'Safe Pass.'" *ABC News*. Oct. 25, 2013. http://abcnews.go.com/ABC_Univision/ecuador-issues-denials-snowdens-safe-pass-linked-nations/story?id=19526121.

33 Valencia, Alexandra and Brian Ellsworth. "Ecuador offers U.S. rights aid, waives trade benefits." *Reuters*. June 27, 2013. http://www.reuters.com/article/2013/06/27/us-usa-security-ecuador-idUSBRE95Q0L820130627.

³⁴ Pro-Ecuador. "Correa Thumbs Nose at U.S.–Offers $23 Million Foreign Aid For Human Rights Training." *ProEcuador*. June 27, 2013. http://blog.pro-ecuador.com/correa-thumbs-nose-at-u-s-offers-23-million-foreign-aid-for-human-rights-training/.

³⁵ The Kremlin. "News conference with President of Finland Sauli Niinistö." *President of Russia*. June 25, 2013. http://eng.kremlin.ru/transcripts/5646.

³⁶ The Kremlin. "News conference following the working meeting of the Gas Exporting Countries Forum (GECF) summit." *President of Russia*. July 1, 2013. http://eng.kremlin.ru/transcripts/5666.

³⁷ Fyodorov, Boris. "Who is Putin?" *PBS*. Dec. 16, 2013. http://www.pbs.org/wgbh/pages/frontline/shows/yeltsin/putin/putin.html.

³⁸ The White House. "Daily Briefing by Press Secretary Jay Carney, 6/24/2013." *The White House of the United States*. June 24, 2013. http://www.whitehouse.gov/the-press-office/2013/06/24/daily-briefing-press-secretary-jay-carney-6242013.

³⁹ Mason, Jeff and Mark Felsenthal. "Obama jabs Russia, China on failure to extradite Snowden." *Reuters*. June 27, 2013. http://www.reuters.com/article/2013/06/27/us-usa-security-snowden-idUSBRE95Q0SW20130627.

⁴⁰ Cf. 5.36

⁴¹ Elder, Miriam. "Snowden applies for political asylum in Russia – and 20 other countries." *The Guardian*. July 1, 2013. http://www.theguardian.com/world/2013/jul/01/putin-snowden-remain-russia-offer.

⁴² The Guardian. "Ecuador's Correa says Biden asked him to deny Edward Snowden asylum." *The Guardian*. June 29, 2013. http://www.theguardian.com/world/2013/jun/29/edward-snowden-biden-correa-talks.

⁴³ Carroll, Rory. "Ecuador says it blundered over Snowden travel document." *The Guardian*. July 2, 2013. http://www.theguardian.com/world/2013/jul/02/ecuador-rafael-correa-snowden-mistake.

⁴⁴ Ningzhu, Zhu. "Brazil denies Snowden asylum." *XinhuaNet*. July 10, 2013. http://news.xinhuanet.com/english/world/2013-07/10/c_132526937.htm.

⁴⁵ Elder, Miriam. "Edward Snowden's options dwindle after political asylum rejections." *The Guardian*. July 2, 2013. http://www.theguardian.com/world/2013/jul/02/edward-snowden-asylum-rejections.

⁴⁶ CNN. "Tracking Snowden's asylum options." *CNN*. July 7, 2013. http://www.cnn.com/2013/07/06/world/snowden-asylum-options.

[47] WikiLeaks. Organization's Twitter account. *WikiLeaks*. July 5, 2013. https://twitter.com/wikileaks/status/353183588700798977.

[48] Herszenhorn, David and Randal Archibold. "Russian Official Says Venezuela Is the 'Best Solution' for Snowden." *The New York Times*. July 6, 2013. http://www.nytimes.com/2013/07/07/world/europe/russian-official-says-venezuela-is-the-best-solution-for-snowden.html?_r=0.

[49] Lam, Lana. "Snowden sought Booz Allen job to gather evidence on NSA surveillance." *South China Morning Post*. June 24, 2013. http://www.scmp.com/news/hong-kong/article/1268209/snowden-sought-booz-allen-job-gather-evidence-nsa-surveillance?page=all.

[50] Pincus, Walter. "Questions for Snowden." *The Washington Post*. July 8, 2013. http://www.washingtonpost.com/world/national-security/questions-for-snowden/2013/07/08/d06ee0f8-e428-11e2-80eb-3145e2994a55_story.html.

[51] Carmon, Irin. "How we broke the NSA story." *Salon*. June 10, 2013. http://www.salon.com/2013/06/10/qa_with_laura_poitras_the_woman_behind_the_nsa_scoops/.

[52] Greenwald, Glenn. Letter from Glenn Greenwald to Walter Pincus. *Economic Policy Journal*. July 9, 2013. http://www.economicpolicyjournal.com/2013/07/greenwald-goes-off-on-wapos-walter.html.

[53] Hosenball, Mark. "Snowden downloaded NSA secrets while working for Dell, sources say." *Reuters*. Aug. 15, 2013. http://www.reuters.com/article/2013/08/15/usa-security-snowden-dell-idUSL2N0GF11220130815.

[54] Walsh, Justin. "Edward Snowden Complete Press Conference - Moscow Airport - July 12th 2013." *YouTube*. July 12, 2013. https://www.youtube.com/watch?v=dukqMkTGEzU.

[55] AP, "Edward Snowden's cautious approach to Post reporter Barton Gellman." *Politico*. June 10, 2013. http://www.politico.com/story/2013/06/edward-snowden-barton-gellman-washington-post-92490.html.

[56] Cf. 5.12

[57] Lake, Eli. "Greenwald: Snowden's Files Are Out There if 'Anything Happens' to Him." *The Daily Beast*. June 25, 2013. http://www.thedailybeast.com/articles/2013/06/25/greenwald-snowden-s-files-are-out-there-if-anything-happens-to-him.html.

[58] Cf. 5.57

[59] Barrett, Devlin and Te-Ping Chen. "Snowden on the Run." *The Wall Street Journal*. June 24, 2013. http://online.wsj.com/article/SB10001424127887323683504578562852310273818.html.

[60] Maass, Peter. "How Laura Poitras Helped Snowden Spill His Secrets." *The New York Times*. Aug. 13, 2013. https://www.nytimes.com/2013/08/18/magazine/laura-poitras-snowden.html?pagewanted=all.

[61] RT. "UK spying on Germany's major data cable to US triggers media storm." *RT*. June 25, 2013. http://rt.com/news/uk-germany-wiretapping-criticism-201/.

[62] Goetz, Von, et al. "Briten schöpfen deutsches Internet ab." *Sueddeutsche*. June 24, 2013. http://www.sueddeutsche.de/politik/nachrichtendienst-gchq-briten-schoepfen-deutsches-internet-ab-1.1704670.

[63] Cf. 5.61

[64] Greenwald, Glenn and Spencer Ackerman. "How the NSA is still harvesting your online data." *The Guardian*. June 27, 2013. http://www.theguardian.com/world/2013/jun/27/nsa-online-metadata-collection.

[65] Greenwald, Glenn and Spencer Ackerman. "NSA collected US email records in bulk for more than two years under Obama." *The Guardian*. June 27, 2013. http://www.theguardian.com/world/2013/jun/27/nsa-data-mining-authorised-obama.

[66] Poitras, Laura. "The Program." *The New York Times*. Aug. 22, 2012. http://www.nytimes.com/2012/08/23/opinion/the-national-security-agencys-domestic-spying-program.html.

[67] Sanchez, Julian. "What the Ashcroft 'Hospital Showdown' on NSA spying was all about." *Ars Technica*. July 29, 2013. http://arstechnica.com/tech-policy/2013/07/what-the-ashcroft-hospital-showdown-on-nsa-spying-was-all-about/.

[68] The Guardian. NSA inspector general report on email and internet data collection under Stellar Wind – full document. *The Guardian*. June 27, 2013. http://www.theguardian.com/world/interactive/2013/jun/27/nsa-inspector-general-report-document-data-collection.

[69] The Guardian. Justice Department and NSA memos proposing broader powers for NSA to collect data. *The Guardian*. June 27, 2013. http://www.theguardian.com/world/interactive/2013/jun/27/nsa-data-collection-justice-department.

[70] Cf. 5.69

[71] Gallagher, Sean. "You may already be a winner in NSA's 'three-degrees' surveillance sweepstakes!." *Ars Technica*. July 18, 2013. http://arstechnica.com/information-technology/2013/07/you-may-already-be-a-winner-in-nsas-three-degrees-surveillance-sweepstakes/.

[72] Nixon, Ron. "Postal Service Confirms Photographing All U.S. Mail." *The New York Times*. Aug. 2, 2013. http://www.nytimes.com/2013/08/03/us/postal-service-confirms-photographing-all-us-mail.html?_r=0.

73 Gellman, Barton. "Is the FBI Up to the Job 10 Years After 9/11?" *Time*. May 12, 2011. http://content.time.com/time/magazine/article/ 0,9171,2068082,00.html.

74 Zetter, Kim. "New York Times' NSA Whistleblower Reveals Himself." *Wired*. Dec. 15, 2008. http://www.wired.com/threatlevel/2008/12/ny-times-nsa-wh/.

75 Cf. 5.60

76 Boadle, Anthony. "Glenn Greenwald: Snowden Gave Me 15-20,000 Classified Documents." *The Huffington Post*. Aug. 6, 2013. http:// www.huffingtonpost.com/2013/08/07/glenn-greenwald-edward-snowden-documents_n_3716424.html.

77 Harress, Christopher. "U.S Army Blocks Guardian Articles On Snowden N.S.A Leak." *International Business Times*. June 28, 2013. http:// www.ibtimes.com/us-army-blocks-guardian-articles-snowden-nsa-leak-1327925.

78 Poitras, Laura, et al. "Attacks from America: NSA Spied on European Union Offices." *Der Spiegel*. June 29, 2013. http://www.spiegel.de/ international/europe/nsa-spied-on-european-union-offices-a-908590.html.

79 Poitras, Laura, et al. "Codename 'Apalachee': How America Spies on Europe and the UN." *Der Spiegel*. Aug. 26, 2013. http:// www.spiegel.de/international/world/secret-nsa-documents-show-how-the-us-spies-on-europe-and-the-un-a-918625.html.

80 MacAskill, Ewen and Julian Borger. "New NSA leaks show how US is bugging its European allies." *The Guardian*. June 30, 2013. http:// www.theguardian.com/world/2013/jun/30/nsa-leaks-us-bugging-european-allies.

81 Poitras, Laura, et al. "Partner and Target: NSA Snoops on 500 Million German Data Connections." *Der Spiegel*. June 30, 2013. http:// www.spiegel.de/international/germany/nsa-spies-on-500-million-german-data-connections-a-908648.html.

82 Traynor, Ian, et al. "Key US-EU trade pact under threat after more NSA spying allegations." *The Guardian*. June 30, 2013. http:// www.theguardian.com/world/2013/jun/30/nsa-spying-europe-claims-us-eu-trade.

83 The Guardian. "G20 surveillance: why was Turkey targeted?" *The Guardian*. June 16, 2013. http://www.theguardian.com/world/2013/ jun/16/g20-surveillance-turkey-targeted-gchq.

84 Freedman, Richard. "Schulz on alleged bugging of EU office by the US authorities." *ABC*. June 29, 2013. http://abclocal.go.com/kgo/ story?section=news/national_world&id=9157195.

[85] Traynor, Ian. "Berlin accuses Washington of cold war tactics over snooping." *The Guardian.* June 30, 2013. http://www.theguardian.com/world/2013/jun/30/berlin-washington-cold-war.

[86] Tschampa, Dorothee. "Europe 'Shocked' by Spiegel Report of NSA Wiretappings." *Bloomberg.* June 30, 2013. http://www.bloomberg.com/news/2013-06-30/europe-shocked-by-spiegel-report-of-nsa-wiretappings.html.

[87] Lucas, Fred. "Obama on European Spying: 'That's How Intelligence Services Operate.'" *CNS News.* July 1, 2013. http://cnsnews.com/news/article/obama-european-spying-s-how-intelligence-services-operate.

[88] Wittrock, Phillip. "NSA Spying in Germany: How Much Did the Chancellor Know?" *Der Spiegel.* July 3, 2013. http://www.spiegel.de/international/germany/how-much-did-merkel-know-about-nsa-spying-in-germany-a-909174.html.

[89] Snowden, Edward. "Statement from Edward Snowden in Moscow." *WikiLeaks.* July 1, 2013. http://wikileaks.org/Statement-from-Edward-Snowden-in.html?snow.

[90] The United Nations. "Universal Declaration of Human Rights." *The United Nations.* Dec. 16, 2013. http://www.un.org/en/documents/udhr/index.shtml#a14.

[91] Elder, Miriam. "Edward Snowden withdraws Russian asylum request." *The Guardian.* July 2, 2013. http://www.theguardian.com/world/2013/jul/02/edward-snowden-nsa-withdraws-asylum-russia-putin.

[92] Roberts, Dan. "Edward Snowden given possible lifeline as Bolivia hints it would grant asylum." *The Guardian.* July 2, 2013. http://www.theguardian.com/world/2013/jul/02/edward-snowden-bolivia-lifeline-asylum.

[93] Emol. "Evo Morales se abre a ceder asilo a Edward Snowden si lo solicita." *Emol.* July 1, 2013. http://www.emol.com/noticias/internacional/2013/07/01/606824/evo-morales-se-abre-a-ceder-asilo-a-edward-snowden-si-lo-solicita.html.

[94] Fisher, Max. "Audio purportedly from inside the cockpit of Bolivian President Evo Morales's flight." *The Washington Post.* July 3, 2013. http://www.washingtonpost.com/blogs/worldviews/wp/2013/07/03/audio-purportedly-from-inside-the-cockpit-of-bolivian-president-evo-moraless-flight/.

[95] Shoichet, Catherine. "Bolivia: Presidential plane forced to land after false rumors of Snowden onboard." *CNN.* July 3, 2013. http://edition.cnn.com/2013/07/02/world/americas/bolivia-presidential-plane.

[96] Laughland, Oliver. "US admits contact with other countries over potential Snowden flights – as it happened." *The Guardian.* July 3, 2013.

http://www.theguardian.com/world/2013/jul/03/edward-snowden-asylum-live.

97 Taylor, Michael. *World Aircraft & Systems Directory*. 2nd ed. Sterling: Brassey's, 1999.

98 RT. "'Free from imperial persecution': Three Latin American countries offer shelter to Edward Snowden." *RT*. July 6, 2013. http://rt.com/news/maduro-snowden-asylum-venezuela-723/.

99 AP. "European states were told Snowden was on Morales plane, says Spain." *The Guardian*. July 5, 2013. http://www.theguardian.com/world/2013/jul/05/european-states-snowden-morales-plane-nsa.

100 BBC News Latin America & Caribbean. "Snowden case: France apologises in Bolivia plane row." *BBC*. July 3, 2013. http://www.bbc.co.uk/news/world-latin-america-23174874.

101 Payne, Ed and Catherine Shoichet. "Morales challenges U.S. after Snowden rumor holds up plane in Europe." *CNN*. July 5, 2013. http://www.cnn.com/2013/07/04/world/americas/bolivia-morales-snowden/.

102 Weissenstain, Michael and Angela Charlton. "Evo Morales' Snowden Plane Incident Infuriates Latin America." *The Huffington Post*. July 4, 2013. http://www.huffingtonpost.com/2013/07/04/bolivian-presidential-plane_n_3546460.html.

103 Davis, Carlo. "Bolivia Protest Descends On French Embassy To Express Anger Over Evo Morales Plane Diversion." *The Huffington Post*. July 3, 2013. http://www.huffingtonpost.com/2013/07/03/bolivia-protesters-descend-french-embassy_n_3541920.html.

104 Cf. 5.95

105 The Guardian. "Evo Morales threatens to close US embassy in Bolivia as leaders weigh in." *The Guardian*. July 4, 2013. http://www.theguardian.com/world/2013/jul/05/bolivia-morales-close-us-embassy.

106 Mallett-Outtrim, Ryan. "Venezuela's Maduro Condemns 'Violation of International Law' Against Morales, Reiterates Support for Snowden at UNASUR Summit." *Venezuelanalysis.com*. July 5, 2013. http://venezuelanalysis.com/news/9811.

107 Ramos, Daniel. "Morales back in Bolivia after Plane drama over Snowden." *Reuters*. July 4, 2013. http://www.reuters.com/article/2013/07/04/us-usa-security-snowden-idUSBRE9610C520130704.

108 Cf. 5.105

109 Reuters. "Latin American countries call summit over diversion of Evo Morales's plane." *Reuters*. July 4, 2013. http://www.telegraph.co.uk/news/worldnews/southamerica/bolivia/10158924/Latin-American-countries-call-summit-over-diversion-of-Evo-Moraless-plane.html.

[110] Cf. 5.106

[111] Cf. 5.106

[112] Macedonian International News Agency. "Bolivia considering closing US Embassy after plane incident." *Macedonian International News Agency.* July 5, 2013. http://macedoniaonline.eu/content/view/23624/53/.

[113] Cf. 5.106

[114] Cf. 5.105

[115] Kraul, Chris, et al. "Venezuela, Nicaragua open their doors to NSA leaker Snowden." *Los Angeles Times.* July 5, 2013. http://articles.latimes.com/2013/jul/05/world/la-fg-wn-venezuela-nicaragua-snowden-20130705.

[116] Watts, Jonathan. "Venezuela, Nicaragua and Bolivia offer asylum to Edward Snowden." *The Guardian.* July 6, 2013. http://www.theguardian.com/world/2013/jul/06/venezuela-nicaragua-offer-asylum-edward-snowden.

[117] Cf. 5.115

[118] Galeno, Luis. "Venezuela, Nicaragua offer asylum to NSA leaker Snowden." *NBC News.* July 5, 2013. http://worldnews.nbcnews.com/_news/2013/07/05/19309635-venezuela-nicaragua-offer-asylum-to-nsa-leaker-snowden?lite.

[119] Castillo, Mariano. "Bolivia latest country to offer asylum to Snowden." *CNN.* July 6, 2013. http://www.cnn.com/2013/07/06/world/americas/nsa-snowden-asylum.

[120] Kurmanaev, Anatoly and Nathan Crooks. "Venezuela Leads Latin American Shelter Offers to Snowden." *Bloomberg.* July 6, 2013. http://www.bloomberg.com/news/2013-07-06/venezuela-offers-asylum-to-u-s-fugitive-edward-snowden.html.

[121] Vyas, Kejal and Jose de Cordoba. "Snowden Is Offered Asylum by Venezuela." *The Wall Street Journal.* July 6, 2013. http://online.wsj.com/news/articles/SB10001424127887323899704578588351612234478.

[122] RT. "Kerry vows to put the screws to Venezuela over Snowden – report." *RT.* July 19, 2013. http://rt.com/news/kerry-threatens-venezuela-snowden-308/.

[123] Cf. 5.120

[124] A Customs Brokerage. "The Generalized System of Preferences Has Expired as of July 31, 2013." *A Customs Brokerage.* Aug. 19, 2013. http://www.acustomsbrokerage.com/uncategorized/the-generalized-system-of-preferences-has-expired-as-of-july-31-2013/.

[125] Ecuador Times. "Alvarado announces Ecuador's resignation of the ATPDEA with the U.S." *Ecuador Times.* June 27, 2013. http://

www.ecuadortimes.net/2013/06/27/alvarado-announces-ecuadors-resignation-of-the-atpdea-with-the-u-s/.

[126] Kumar, Nikhil. "NSA whistleblower Edward Snowden offered asylum by Venezuela, Nicaragua and now Bolivia." *The Independent*. July 6, 2013. http://www.independent.co.uk/news/world/americas/nsa-whistleblower-edward-snowden-offered-asylum-by-venezuela-nicaragua-and-now-bolivia-8691647.html.

[127] Cf. 5.121

[128] The Office of the United Nations High Commissioner for Refugees. "The 1951 Convention Relating to the Status of Refugees and its 1967 Protocol." *The Office of the United Nations High Commissioner for Refugees*. Dec. 16, 2013. http://www.unhcr.org/4ec262df9.html.

[129] Heritage, Timothy. "Analysis: Experts advise Snowden: fly commercial." *Reuters*. July 12, 2013. http://www.reuters.com/article/2013/07/12/us-usa-security-flights-options-analysis-idUSBRE96B0A820130712.

[130] Robertson, Geoffrey. "Edward Snowden's fear of flying is justified." *The Guardian*. July 23, 2013. http://www.theguardian.com/commentisfree/2013/jul/23/snowden-asylum-america-international-law.

[131] Wittmeyer, Alicia. "PassportMoscow to Caracas — the Scenic Route." *Foreign Policy*. July 7, 2013. http://blog.foreignpolicy.com/posts/2013/07/06/moscow_to_caracas_the_scenic_route.

[132] Cf. 5.60

[133] Greenwald, Glenn and Roberto Casado. "EUA espionaram milhões de e-mails e ligações de brasileiros." *OGlobo*. July 6, 2013. http://oglobo.globo.com/mundo/eua-espionaram-milhoes-de-mails-ligacoes-de-brasileiros-8940934.

[134] Greenwald, Glenn and Roberto Casado. "EUA expandem o aparato de vigilância continuamente." *OGlobo*. July 6, 2013. http://oglobo.globo.com/mundo/eua-expandem-aparato-de-vigilancia-continuamente-8941149.

[135] Guttman, Boaz. "La CIA y la NSA espiaron mediante satélites desde Brasil & Slides." *YouTube*. July 8, 2013. https://www.youtube.com/watch?v=kOAv7zbJkCk&hd=1.

[136] Internet archive. X-Keyscore slides. *DocumentCloud*. Dec. 16, 2013. http://s3.documentcloud.org/documents/743252/nsa-pdfs-redacted-ed.pdf.

[137] Ofuxico. "Rede Globo se torna a 2ª maior emissora do mundo." *DocumentCloud*. May, 11, 2012. http://www.ofuxico.com.br/noticias-sobre-famosos/rede-globo-se-torna-a-2-maior-emissora-do-mundo/2012/05/11-139187.html.

[138] Cf. 5.135

[139] Kloc, Joe. "Unpublished NSA slides air on Brazilian television." *Daily Dot*. July 25, 2013. http://www.dailydot.com/news/nsa-fairview-slides-brazil-spying/.

[140] Barnes, Taylor. "America spies on Brazil too, Snowden leaks." *Global Post*. July 8, 2013. http://www.globalpost.com/dispatch/news/regions/americas/brazil/130709/us-spying-brazil-snowden-leaks.

[141] Reuters. "Brazil seeks U.S. response to alleged spying on citizens." *Reuters*. July 7, 2013. http://www.reuters.com/article/2013/07/07/us-brazil-espionage-snowden-idUSBRE9660ER20130707.

[142] Greenwald, Glenn and Ewen MacAskill. "Boundless Informant: the NSA's secret tool to track global surveillance data." *The Guardian*. June (8) 11, 2013. http://www.theguardian.com/world/2013/jun/08/nsa-boundless-informant-global-datamining.

[143] Watts, Jonathan. "Brazil demands explanation from US over NSA spying." *The Guardian*. July 8, 2013. http://www.theguardian.com/world/2013/jul/08/brazil-demands-explanation-nsa-spying.

[144] BBC News Brazil. "EUA não responderão publicamente a Brasil sobre espionage." *BBC*. July 8, 2013. http://www.bbc.co.uk/portuguese/noticias/2013/07/130708_brasil_snowden_dg.shtml?ocid=socialflow_twitter_brasil.

[145] Cf. 5.60

[146] McCullagh, Declan. "Wikileaks editor skips NYC hacker event." *CNet*. July 17, 2010. http://news.cnet.com/8301-1009_3-20010866-83.html.

[147] McCullagh, Declan. "DOJ sends order to Twitter for WikiLeaks-related account info." *CNet*. Jan. 7, 2011. http://news.cnet.com/8301-31921_3-20027893-281.html.

[148] Rich, Nathaniel. "The American Wikileaks Hacker." *Rolling Stone*. Dec. 1, 2010. http://www.rollingstone.com/culture/news/meet-the-american-hacker-behind-wikileaks-20101201.

[149] Cf. 5.12

[150] Poitras, Laura and Jacob Appelbaum. "Edward Snowden Interview: The NSA and Its Willing Helpers." *Der Spiegel*. July 8, 2013. http://www.spiegel.de/international/world/interview-with-whistleblower-edward-snowden-on-global-spying-a-910006.html.

[151] Symantec. W32.Stuxnet profile. *Symantec*. July 13, 2010. http://www.symantec.com/security_response/writeup.jsp?docid=2010-071400-3123-99.

[152] Kiley, Sam. "Super Virus A Target For Cyber Terrorists." *Sky News*. Nov. 25, 2010. http://news.sky.com/story/820902/super-virus-a-target-for-cyber-terrorists.

[153] Pop, Valentina. "Germany defends intelligence co-operation with US." *EUObserver*. July 8, 2013. http://euobserver.com/foreign/120795.

[154] Cf. 5.153

[155] Poitras, Laura and Glenn Greenwald. "Edward Snowden: 'The US government will say I aided our enemies' – video interview." *The Guardian*. July 8, 2013. http://www.theguardian.com/world/video/2013/jul/08/edward-snowden-video-interview.

[156] Kaz, Roverto and Jose Casado. "NSA e CIA mantiveram em Brasília equipe para coleta de dados filtrados de satélite." *OGlobo*. July 8, 2013. http://oglobo.globo.com/mundo/nsa-cia-mantiveram-em-brasilia-equipe-para-coleta-de-dados-filtrados-de-satelite-8949723.

[157] Cf. 5.79

[158] Cf. 5.79

[159] Greenwald, Glenn and Roberto Casado. "Espionagem dos EUA se espalhou pela América Latina." *OGlobo*. July 9, 2013. http://oglobo.globo.com/mundo/espionagem-dos-eua-se-espalhou-pela-america-latina-8966619.

[160] RT. "NSA spied on Latin America for energy and military intel." *RT*. July 10, 2013. http://rt.com/news/nsa-latin-america-spying-867/.

[161] Forero, Juan. "Paper reveals NSA ops in Latin America." *The Washington Post*. July 9, 2013. http://www.washingtonpost.com/world/the_americas/paper-reveals-nsa-ops-in-latin-america/2013/07/09/eff0cc7e-e8e3-11e2-818e-aa29e855f3ab_print.html.

[162] Cf. 5.161

[163] Fisher, Max. "Here's the Russian official's now-deleted tweet saying Snowden accepted asylum in Venezuela." *The Washington Post*. July 9, 2010. http://www.washingtonpost.com/blogs/worldviews/wp/2013/07/09/heres-the-russian-officials-now-deleted-tweet-saying-snowden-accepted-asylum-in-venezuela/.

[164] Fitzpatrick, Alex. "Russian Lawmaker Deletes Snowden Asylum Tweet." *Mashable*. July 9, 2013. http://mashable.com/2013/07/09/russian-deletes-snowden-tweet/.

[165] RT. "Tweet delete: Russian MP 'Snowden to Venezuela' post adds to confusion." *RT*. July 9, 2013. http://rt.com/news/snowden-venezuela-asylum-request-844/.

[166] WikiLeaks. Organization's Twitter account. *Twitter*. July 9, 2013. https://twitter.com/wikileaks/status/354700693287870465.

[167] Microsoft Corporation. "Security features in Outlook.com." *Microsoft Corporation*. Dec. 16, 2013. http://www.microsoft.com/security/pc-security/webmail.aspx.

[168] Skype. "Skype Privacy Policy." *Skype.* Dec. 16, 2013. http://www.skype.com/en/legal/privacy/.

[169] Bamford, James. *The Puzzle Palace: Inside the National Security Agency, America's Most Secret Intelligence Organization.* New York: Penguin, 1983. 28-9.

[170] Cf. 5.60

[171] RT. "Snowden wants asylum in Russia, ready to meet condition not to damage US (VIDEO)." *RT.* July 12, 2013. http://rt.com/news/snowden-meets-rights-activists-013/.

[172] The Huffington Post. "Edward Snowden WikiLeaks Statement Sparks Doubts Of Authenticity On Twitter." *The Huffington Post.* July 1, 2013. http://www.huffingtonpost.com/2013/07/01/edward-snowden-wikileaks-statement_n_3530837.html.

[173] Black, Phil, et al. "Snowden meets with rights groups, seeks temporary asylum in Russia." *CNN.* July 13, 2013. http://www.cnn.com/2013/07/12/world/europe/russia-us-snowden/.

[174] Snowden, Edward. "Statement by Edward Snowden to human rights groups at Moscow's Sheremetyevo airport." *WikiLeaks.* July 12, 2013. http://wikileaks.org/Statement-by-Edward-Snowden-to.html.

[175] Cf. 5.54

[176] The Office of the United Nations High Commissioner for Refugees. *Handbook for Repatriation and Reintegration Activities.* Geneva: *The Office of the United Nations High Commissioner for Refugees,* 2004. http://www.unhcr.org/411786694.html.

[177] Owen, Paul and Tom McCarthy. "Edward Snowden appears at Moscow airport and renews asylum claim – as it happened." *The Guardian.* July 12, 2013. http://www.theguardian.com/world/2013/jul/12/edward-snowden-to-meet-amnesty-and-human-rights-watch-at-moscow-airport-live-coverag.

[178] Lewis, Paul. "Edward Snowden inflames US-Russian tensions with Moscow meeting." *The Guardian.* July 12, 2013. http://www.theguardian.com/world/2013/jul/12/edward-snowden-russian-moscow-meeting.

[179] Irvine, Chris. "Edward Snowden found – latest." *The Telegraph.* July 12, 2013. http://www.telegraph.co.uk/news/worldnews/northamerica/usa/10175540/Where-is-Edward-Snowden-live.html.

[180] Cf. 5.54

[181] Cf. 5.54

[182] Luhn, Alec. "Edward Snowden passed time in airport reading and surfing internet." *The Guardian.* Aug. 1, 2013. http://

www.theguardian.com/world/2013/aug/01/edward-snowden-airport-reading.

183 Felgenhauer, Pavel. "Russian Intelligence Intends to Gag Snowden and Keep Him in Russia." *The Jamestown Foundation*. July 18, 2013. http://www.jamestown.org/single/?no_cache=1&tx_ttnews%5Btt_news%5D=41139&tx_ttnews%5BbackPid%5D=7&cHash=ff9ec857407acb4097be21d8aeb7ae1b#.Ue9Y7o0wdT5.

184 Cf. 5.54

185 Cf. 5.183

186 Myers, Steven. "Snowden's Lawyer Comes With High Profile and Kremlin Ties." *The New York Times*. July 27, 2013. http://www.nytimes.com/2013/07/28/world/europe/snowdens-lawyer-comes-with-high-profile-and-kremlin-ties.html?pagewanted=all.

187 Cf. 5.182

188 United Press International. "Obama, Putin discuss Snowden in telephone conversation." *United Press International*. July 13, 2013. http://www.upi.com/Top_News/World-News/2013/07/13/Obama-Putin-discuss-Snowden-in-telephone-conversation/UPI-85231373736174/.

189 Luhn, Alec. "Edward Snowden plans to stay in Russia, says lawyer." *The Guardian*. July 24, 2013. http://www.theguardian.com/world/2013/jul/24/edward-snowden-stay-russia-lawyer.

190 Herszenhorn, David and Steven Myers. "Snowden Gets Novel and Change of Clothes, but No Clearance to Exit Airport." *The New York Times*. July 24, 2013. http://www.nytimes.com/2013/07/25/world/europe/snowden.html.

191 Zengerle, Patricia. "U.S. lawmakers want sanctions on any country taking in Snowden." *Reuters*. July 25, 2013. http://www.reuters.com/article/2013/07/25/us-usa-security-congress-idUSBRE96O18220130725.

192 Cf. 5.190

193 Stanglin, Doug and Kim Hjelmgaard. "Putin warns Snowden not to hurt U.S.-Russian relations." *USA Today*. July 17, 2013. http://www.usatoday.com/story/news/world/2013/07/17/putin-snowden-russia-asylum/2523763/.

CHAPTER 6

1 Trans. Constance Garnett. New York: Barnes & Noble Classics, 2007.

2 Der Spiegel. "'Prolific Partner': German Intelligence Used NSA Spy Program." *Der Spiegel*. July 20, 2013. http://www.spiegel.de/international/germany/german-intelligence-agencies-used-nsa-spying-program-a-912173.html.

[3] Gude, Hubert, et al. "Mass Data: Transfers from Germany Aid US Surveillance." *Der Spiegel*. Aug. 5, 2013. http://www.spiegel.de/international/world/german-intelligence-sends-massive-amounts-of-data-to-the-nsa-a-914821.html.

[4] Cf. 6.3

[5] Souza, Leonardo and Raphael Gomide. "Spies of the digital age." *Epoca*. July 27, 2013. http://epoca.globo.com/tempo/noticia/2013/07/spies-bdigital-ageb.html.

[6] Luhn, Alec. "Edward Snowden passed time in airport reading and surfing internet." *The Guardian*. Aug. 1, 2013. http://www.theguardian.com/world/2013/aug/01/edward-snowden-airport-reading.

[7] WikiLeaks. "Statement on Snowden's Successful Russian Asylum Bid." *WikiLeaks*. Aug. 1, 2013. http://wikileaks.org/Statement-on-Snowden-s-Successful.html.

[8] Mackey, Robert. "The Third Man on Snowden's Reading List." *The New York Times*. July 24, 2013. http://thelede.blogs.nytimes.com/2013/07/24/the-third-man-on-snowdens-reading-list/.

[9] Herszenhorn, David and Steven Myers. "Snowden Gets Novel and Change of Clothes, but No Clearance to Exit Airport." *The New York Times*. July 24, 2013. http://www.nytimes.com/2013/07/25/world/europe/snowden.html.

[10] Cf. 6.6

[11] Hayden, Michael. "Snowden — facts, fictions and fears." *CNN*. July 24, 2013. http://www.cnn.com/2013/07/24/opinion/hayden-snowden-reality/index.html?iid=article_sidebar.

[12] Acohido, Byron and Peter Eisle. "Snowden case: How low-level insider could steal from NSA." *USA Today*. June 12, 2013. http://www.usatoday.com/story/news/nation/2013/06/11/snowden-nsa-hacking-privileged-accounts/2412507/.

[13] RT. "NSA head: Replace would-be Snowdens with computers to stop future leaks." *RT*. Aug. 9, 2013. http://rt.com/usa/nsa-snowden-former-job-future-257/.

[14] Office of the Director of National Intelligence. Declassified Telephone Metadata Collection Documents. *Office of the Director of National Intelligence*. July 31, 2013. http://www.dni.gov/index.php/newsroom/press-releases/191-press-releases-2013/908-dni-clapper-declassifies-and-releases-telephone-metadata-collection-documents.

[15] Roberts, Dan, et al. "NSA surveillance: anger mounts in Congress at 'spying on Americans.'" *The Guardian*. June 11, 2013. http://

www.theguardian.com/world/2013/jun/12/anger-mounts-congress-telephone-surveillance-programmes.

[16] Savage, Charlie and David Sanger. "Senate Panel Presses N.S.A. on Phone Logs." *The New York Times*. July 31, 2013. http://www.nytimes.com/2013/08/01/us/nsa-surveillance.html?pagewanted=all.

[17] Mimoso, Michael. "NSA Director Defends Surveillance Activities During Tense Black Hat Keynote." *ThreatPost*. July 31, 2013. http://threatpost.com/nsa-director-defends-surveillance-activities-during-tense-black-hat-keynote.

[18] Greenwald, Glenn. "XKeyscore: NSA tool collects 'nearly everything a user does on the internet.'" *The Guardian*. July 31, 2013. http://www.theguardian.com/world/2013/jul/31/nsa-top-secret-program-online-data.

[19] Poitras, Laura. "Miranda Detention: 'Blatant Attack on Press Freedom.'" *Der Spiegel*. Aug. 26, 2013. http://www.spiegel.de/international/world/laura-poitras-on-british-attacks-on-press-freedom-and-the-nsa-affair-a-918592.html.

[20] C-SPAN. "Report Video Issue National Security Agency Data Collection Programs." *C-SPAN*. June 18, 2013. http://www.c-spanvideo.org/program/AgencyOp.

[21] Kiss, Jemima. "Edward Snowden should be put on kill list, joke US intelligence chiefs." *The Guardian*. Oct. 3, 2013. http://www.theguardian.com/world/2013/oct/03/edward-snowden-kill-list-joke-us-intelligence-chiefs.

[22] Greenwald, Glenn. "Edward Snowden: NSA whistleblower answers reader questions." *The Guardian*. June 17, 2013. http://www.theguardian.com/world/2013/jun/17/edward-snowden-nsa-files-whistleblower.

[23] Burnett, Erin. "Senators raise questions on NSA programs." *CNN*. July 31, 2013. http://www.cnn.com/video/data/2.0/video/bestoftv/2013/07/31/exp-erin-sot-nsa-collecting-phone-records.cnn.html.

[24] Fox News Test. "NSA leaker's father urges son to 'come home and face this.'" *YouTube*. June 17, 2013. http://www.youtube.com/watch?v=qzVVZOVK3jA.

[25] Goldman, T.R. "In the Snowden case, Bruce Fein finds the apex of a long Washington legal career." *The Washington Post*. Aug. 11, 2013. http://articles.washingtonpost.com/2013-08-11/lifestyle/41299734_1_edward-snowden-washington-times-lon-snowden.

[26] Fein, Bruce. Letter from Bruce Fein to Eric Holder. *CNN*. June 28, 2013. http://www.cnn.com/interactive/2013/06/us/snowden-holder-letter/.

[27] Kim, Eun. "Edward Snowden's father: My son is not a traitor." *Today*. June 28, 2013. http://www.today.com/news/edward-snowdens-father-my-son-not-traitor-6C10480514.

[28] AP. "Snowden's father praises son in open letter." *USA Today*. July 2, 2013. http://www.usatoday.com/story/news/nation/2013/07/02/snowdens-father-open-letter/2484251/.

[29] Calderone, Michael. "Edward Snowden Says Media Being Misled 'About My Situation.'" *The Huffington Post*. Aug. 19, 2013. http://www.huffingtonpost.com/2013/08/15/edward-snowden-media-misled_n_3764560.html.

[30] Fein, Bruce. Letter from Bruce Fein to Edward Snowden. *Scribd*. July 2, 2013. http://www.scribd.com/doc/151333544/Fein-Snowden-July-2.

[31] Gold, Hadas. "Edward Snowden dad letter: Son like Paul Revere." *Politico*. July 2, 2013. http://www.politico.com/story/2013/07/edward-snowden-dad-paul-revere-93667.html.

[32] Fein, Bruce. "Letter To Obama: Civil Disobedience, Edward J. Snowden, and the Constitution." *Popular Resistance*. July 26, 2013. http://www.popularresistance.org/letter-to-obama-civil-disobedience-edward-j-snowden-and-the-constitution/.

[33] NBC. "Edward Snowden's dad: 'This story is far from done.'" *Today*. July 26, 2013. http://www.today.com/video/today/52585686#52585686.

[34] Hallow, Ralph. "Edward Snowden's father suggests son's leaks may be protected by Constitution." *The Washington Times*. July 1, 2013. http://www.washingtontimes.com/news/2013/jul/1/father-fugitive/?page=all.

[35] Barakat, Matthew. "Snowden's father: Son better off now in Russia." *The Big Story*. July 26, 2013. http://bigstory.ap.org/article/snowdens-father-congress-trying-demonize-son.

[36] Cooper, Anderson. "Edward Snowden's father speaks." *CNN*. July 29, 2013. http://ac360.blogs.cnn.com/2013/07/29/edward-snowdens-father-speaks/.

[37] Post TV. "Snowden's father: Edward 'the brilliant one.'" *The Washington Post*. July 30, 2013. http://www.washingtonpost.com/posttv/video/thefold/snowdens-father-edward-the-brilliant-one/2013/07/30/091e3642-f964-11e2-8e84-c56731a202fb_video.html.

[38] Cf. 6.25

[39] Loiko, Sergei. "Edward Snowden's father thanks Putin for protecting son." *Los Angeles Times*. July 31, 2013. http://articles.latimes.com/2013/jul/31/world/la-fg-wn-snowden-father-thanks-putin-20130731.

[40] Cf. 6.39

[41] The White House. "Press Briefing by Press Secretary Jay Carney, 8/1/ 2013." *The White House of the United States.* Aug. 1, 2013. http:// www.whitehouse.gov/the-press-office/2013/08/01/press-briefing-press-secretary-jay-carney-812013.

[42] Luhn, Alec. "Edward Snowden plans to stay in Russia, says lawyer." *The Guardian.* July 24, 2013. http://www.theguardian.com/world/2013/jul/ 24/edward-snowden-stay-russia-lawyer.

[43] RT. "Russian official slams US for turning down Moscow's extradition requests." *RT.* July 22, 2013. http://rt.com/news/us-russia-extradition-snowden-418/.

[44] RT. "Edward Snowden will 'build a new life in Russia': lawyer." *RT.* Aug. 2, 2013. http://www.ndtv.com/article/world/edward-snowden-will-build-a-new-life-in-russia-lawyer-400240.

[45] The Kremlin. "Meeting with Gogland 2013 expedition participants." *President of Russia.* July 15, 2013. http://eng.kremlin.ru/transcripts/ 5731.

[46] Cf. 6.45

[47] CBS News. "Edward Snowden leaves airport after Russia grants asylum, says 'the law is winning.'" *CBS* News. Aug. 1, 2013. http:// www.cbsnews.com/8301-202_162-57596493/edward-snowden-leaves-airport-after-russia-grants-asylum-says-the-law-is-winning/.

[48] ITAR-TASS News Agency. "Snowden is in 'safe place' waiting for his father to discuss future." *ITAR-TASS News Agency.* Aug. 31, 2013. http:/ /www.itar-tass.com/en/c32/859415.html.

[49] Alpert, Lukas. "Putin Admits Early Snowden Contact." *The Wall Street Journal.* Sept. 4, 2013. http://online.wsj.com/news/articles/ SB10001424127887323623304579054890606102138.

[50] Risen, James. "Snowden Says He Took No Secret Files to Russia." *The New York Times.* Oct. 17, 2013. http://www.nytimes.com/2013/10/18/ world/snowden-says-he-took-no-secret-files-to-russia.html.

[51] Mackey, Robert. "Excerpts From Snowden's Letter Requesting Asylum in Ecuador." *The New York Times.* June 24, 2013. http:// thelede.blogs.nytimes.com/2013/06/24/excerpts-from-snowdens-letter-requesting-asylum-in-ecuador/?_r=0.

[52] Snowden, Edward. Letter from Edward Snowden to the Republic of Nicaragua. *Cdn.nuevaya.com.ni.* June 30, 2013. http:// cdn.nuevaya.com.ni/wp-content/uploads/2013/07/Snowden_letter.jpg.

[53] The Office of the United Nations High Commissioner for Refugees. "Chapter Six: Resettlement Categories." *The Office of the United Nations High Commissioner for Refugees.* Dec. 16, 2013. http://www.unhcr.org/ cgi-bin/texis/vtx/home/

opendocPDFViewer.html?docid=3d464e842&query
=threat%20of%20death%20asylum.

[54] Shane, Scott. "Ex-Contractor Is Charged in Leaks on N.S.A.
Surveillance." *The New York Times.* June 21, 2013. http://
www.nytimes.com/2013/06/22/us/snowden-espionage-
act.html?pagewanted=all.

[55] The Heritage Foundation. "Punishment of Treason." *The Heritage
Foundation.* Dec. 16, 2013. http://www.heritage.org/constitution/#!/
articles/3/essays/120/punishment-of-treason.

[56] Cf. 6.54

[57] Cf. 6.51

[58] Castillo, Mariano. "U.S. will not seek death penalty for Snowden,
attorney general says." *CNN.* July 27, 2013. http://www.cnn.com/
2013/07/26/us/nsa-snowden/.

[59] Holder, Eric. Letter from Eric Holder to Alexander Konovalov. *CBS
News.* July 23, 2013. http://www.cbsnews.com/htdocs/pdf/Attorney-
Genral-letter-to-Russian-Justice-Minister.pdf.

[60] Herszenhorn, David. "Leaker Files for Asylum to Remain in Russia."
The New York Times. July 16, 2013. http://www.nytimes.com/2013/07/
17/world/europe/snowden-submits-application-for-asylum-in-
russia.html?_r=3&.

[61] RT. "Snowden plans to settle and work in Russia – lawyer to RT." *RT.*
July 23, 2013. http://rt.com/news/snowden-work-russia-lawyer-482/.

[62] Bercovitch, Sascha. "Maduro: Venezuela Will Offer Snowden Political
Asylum." *Venezuelanalysis.com.* July 5, 2013. http://
venezuelanalysis.com/news/9812.

[63] Gabbatt, Adam. "US will not seek death penalty for Edward Snowden,
Holder tells Russia." *The Guardian.* July 26, 2013. http://
www.theguardian.com/world/2013/jul/26/us-no-death-penalty-
edward-snowden-russia.

[64] Cf. 6.9

[65] Cf. 6.42

[66] Cf. 6.42

[67] Owen, Paul and Adam Gabbatt. "Edward Snowden leaves airport: 'In the
end the law is winning' – as it happened." *The Guardian.* Aug. 1, 2013.
http://www.theguardian.com/world/2013/aug/01/edward-snowden-
leaves-moscow-airport-live.

[68] Gorst, Isabel and Joby Warrick. "Snowden granted asylum in Russia,
leaves Moscow airport." *The Washington Post.* Aug. 1, 2013. http://

articles.washingtonpost.com/2013-08-01/world/40934730_1_edward-snowden-moscow-airport-sheremetyevo-international-airport.

[69] Heritage, Timothy and Steve Holland. "Russia gives Snowden asylum, Obama-Putin summit in doubt." *Reuters*. Aug. 1, 2013. http://www.reuters.com/article/2013/08/01/us-usa-security-snowden-russia-idUSBRE9700N120130801.

[70] Alpert, Lukas. "Divisions Widen Among Snowden's Supporters." *The Wall Street Journal*. Aug. 15, 2013. http://online.wsj.com/article/SB10001424127887324823804579014611497378326.html.

[71] WikiLeaks. Organization's Twitter account. *Twitter*. Aug. 1, 2013. https://twitter.com/wikileaks/statuses/362906823411511296.

[72] WikiLeaks. Organization's Twitter account & Keyword Search results. *WikiLeaks*. Dec. 16, 2013. https://twitter.com/search?q=%22snowden%22%20from%3Awikileaks&src=typd.

[73] Cf. 6.7

[74] RT. "Snowden granted 1-year asylum in Russia, leaves airport (PHOTOS)." *RT*. Aug. 1, 2013. http://rt.com/news/snowden-entry-papers-russia-902/.

[75] Cf. 6.29

[76] Cf. 6.7

[77] Agence France Presse. "Snowden's Russian Lawyer: US Leaker Wears Disguises And 'I Am His Only Link With The Outside World.'" *Business Insider*. Sept. 23, 2013. http://www.businessinsider.com/snowdens-russian-lawyer-he-wears-disguises-2013-9.

CHAPTER 7

[1] Snowden, Edward. "Statement by Edward Snowden to human rights groups at Moscow's Sheremetyevo airport." *WikiLeaks*. July 12, 2013. http://wikileaks.org/Statement-by-Edward-Snowden-to.html.

[2] Baker, Peter. "Obama May Cancel Moscow Trip as Tensions Build Over Leaker." *The New York Times*. July 18, 2013. http://www.nytimes.com/2013/07/19/world/europe/moscow-trip-for-obama-may-be-off-as-snowden-tensions-build.html?pagewanted=all&_r=0.

[3] The White House. "Press Briefing by Press Secretary Jay Carney, 8/1/2013." *The White House of the United States*. Aug. 1, 2013. http://www.whitehouse.gov/the-press-office/2013/08/01/press-briefing-press-secretary-jay-carney-812013.

[4] Blake, Aaron. "Senators demand repercussions for Russia." *The Washington Post*. Aug. 1, 2013. http://www.washingtonpost.com/blogs/post-politics/wp/2013/08/01/senators-demand-repercussions-for-russia/.

5   Herszenhorn, David and Michael Gordon. "U.S. Cancels Part of Missile Defense That Russia Opposed." *The New York Times*. Mar. 16, 2013. http://www.nytimes.com/2013/03/17/world/europe/with-eye-on-north-korea-us-cancels-missile-defense-russia-opposed.html.

6   Cf. 7.2

7   Cf. 7.4

8   CNN. "Security worries trigger embassy closings." *CNN*. Aug. 1, 2013. http://security.blogs.cnn.com/2013/08/01/security-worries-trigger-embassy-closings/.

9   Starr, Barbara, et al. "Intercepted al Qaeda message led to shuttering embassies, consulates." *CNN*. Aug. 4, 2013. http://www.cnn.com/2013/08/04/politics/us-embassies-close/index.html?hpt=hp_t1.

10   Cf. 7.9

11   Bergen, Peter and Bailey Cahall. "What's behind timing of terror threat." *CNN*. Aug. 13, 2013. http://www.cnn.com/2013/08/02/opinion/bergen-terror-embassy/index.html?hpt=hp_t1.

12   Sturcke, James. "Nine killed as US consulate in Jeddah attacked." *The Guardian*. Dec. 6, 2004. http://www.theguardian.com/world/2004/dec/06/saudiarabia.usa.

13   Quinnipiac University. "Release Detail: August 1, 2013 - Snowden Is Whistle-Blower, Not Traitor, U.S. Voters Tell Quinnipiac University National Poll." *Quinnipiac University*. Aug. 1, 2013. http://www.quinnipiac.edu/institutes-and-centers/polling-institute/national/release-detail?ReleaseID=1930.

14   Swanson, Emily. "NSA Leaks Poll Finds Americans Divided Over Edward Snowden's Actions." *The Huffington Post*. June 13, 2013. http://www.huffingtonpost.com/2013/06/13/nsa-leaks-poll_n_3430506.html.

15   Calderone, Michael. "McClatchy Editor Defends Publishing Al Qaeda Detail CNN, NY Times Held Back." *The Huffington Post*. Aug. 6, 2013. http://www.huffingtonpost.com/michael-calderone/mcclatchy-editor-defends-al-qaeda-intercept_b_3713226.html.

16   Watkins, Ali, et al. "U.S. extends embassy closings; warnings renew debate over NSA data collection." *McClatchyDC*. Aug. 4, 2013. http://www.mcclatchydc.com/2013/08/04/198521/embassy-closings-travel-warning.html.

17   Starr, Barbara. "Source: al Qaeda leader urged affiliate to 'do something.'" *CNN*. Aug. 5, 2013. http://security.blogs.cnn.com/2013/08/05/source-al-qaeda-leader-urged-affiliate-to-do-something/?hpt=hp_t1.

18   Cf. 7.9

[19] Labott, Eliseand Mohammed Tawfeeq. "Drone strikes kill militants in Yemen; Americans urged to leave." *CNN*. Aug. 7, 2013. http://www.cnn.com/2013/08/05/world/yemen-us-drone-strike/index.html?hpt=hp_t2.

[20] Leno, Jay. "President Barack Obama ~ The Tonight Show with Jay Leno." *NBC*. Aug. 8, 2013. http://www.blinkx.com/watch-video/president-barack-obama-the-tonight-show-with-jay-leno/beChxKywGEWLC6lVDH8mqg.

[21] Yellin, Jessica, et al. "Obama cancels talks with Putin ahead of G-20 summit." *CNN*. Aug. 8, 2013. http://www.cnn.com/2013/08/07/politics/obama-putin/index.html?hpt=hp_t2.

[22] Cf. 7.21

[23] Cohen, Tom. "Response to terror threat scrutinized: Did U.S. go too far?" *CNN*. Aug. 8, 2013. http://edition.cnn.com/2013/08/08/politics/terror-threat/index.html?hpt=iaf_c2.

[24] Cf. 7.23

[25] Reuters. "Obama to hold news conference on Friday." *Reuters*. Aug. 8, 2013. http://www.reuters.com/article/2013/08/08/us-usa-obama-pressconference-idUSBRE97713E20130808.

[26] The White House. "Remarks by the President in a Press Conference." *The White House of the United States*. Aug. 9, 2013. http://www.whitehouse.gov/the-press-office/2013/08/09/remarks-president-press-conference.

[27] The Office of the Director of National Intelligence. "DNI Clapper Announces Review Group on Intelligence and Communications Technologies." *The Office of the Director of National Intelligence*. Aug. 12, 2013. http://www.dni.gov/index.php/newsroom/press-releases/191-press-releases-2013/909-dni-clapper-announces-review-group-on-intelligence-and-communications-technologies.

[28] United States Government. "The White Paper/The National Security Agency: Missions, Authorities, Oversight and Partnerships." *Cryptome*. Aug. 12, 2013. http://cryptome.org/2013/08/doj-13-0809.pdf.

[29] Holt, Rush. "H.R.2818." *The Library of Congress*. July 24, 2013. http://thomas.loc.gov/cgi-bin/bdquery/z?d113:h.r.02818:.

[30] Leahy, Patrick. "S.607." *The Library of Congress*. Mar. 19, 2013. http://thomas.loc.gov/cgi-bin/bdquery/z?d113:s.00607:.

[31] Leahy, Patrick. "S.1215." *The Library of Congress*. Apr. 25, 2013. http://thomas.loc.gov/cgi-bin/bdquery/z?d113:s.01215:.

[32] Merkley, Jeff. "S.1130." *The Library of Congress*. June 11, 2013. http://thomas.loc.gov/cgi-bin/bdquery/z?d113:s.1130:.

[33] Conyers, John. "H.R.2399." *The Library of Congress*. June 17, 2013. http://thomas.loc.gov/cgi-bin/bdquery/z?d113:h.r.02399:.

[34] Young, C. W. "H.R.2397." *The Library of Congress*. June 17, 2013. http://thomas.loc.gov/cgi-bin/query/z?c113:H.R.2397:.

[35] Cassata, Donna. "House debate gives new airing to NSA surveillance." *Yahoo*. July 24, 2013. http://news.yahoo.com/house-debate-gives-airing-nsa-surveillance-205624680.html.

[36] Sirota, David. "GOP insurrection heats up over surveillance." *Salon*. July 22, 2013. http://www.salon.com/2013/07/22/gop_civil_war_leaders_target_rising_star/.

[37] Gentilviso, Chris. "Justin Amash's NSA Surveillance Amendment Ruled In Order." *The Huffington Post*. July 22, 2013. http://www.huffingtonpost.com/2013/07/22/justin-amash-nsa-surveillance_n_3637462.html?utm_hp_ref=politics.

[38] The White House. "Statement by the Press Secretary on the Amash Amendment." *The White House of the United States*. July 23, 2013. http://www.whitehouse.gov/the-press-office/2013/07/23/statement-press-secretary-amash-amendment.

[39] RT. "White House denounces Amash amendment as dismantling of NSA." *RT*. July 24, 2013. http://rt.com/usa/white-house-amash-nsa-531/.

[40] Grim, Ryan and Matt Sledge. "NSA's Keith Alexander Calls Emergency Private Briefing To Lobby Against Justin Amash Amendment Curtailing Its Power." *The Huffington Post*. July 23, 2013. http://www.huffingtonpost.com/2013/07/23/keith-alexander-justin-amash_n_3639329.html.

[41] Cf. 7.36

[42] The Guardian. "Amash amendment: the full roll call." *The Guardian*. July 24, 2013. http://www.theguardian.com/world/2013/jul/25/amash-amendment-full-roll-call.

[43] Govtrack. "H.Amdt. 413 (Amash) to H.R. 2397." *GovTrack.us*. July 24, 2013. http://www.govtrack.us/congress/votes/113-2013/h412.

[44] Weisman, Jonathan. "House Defeats Effort to Rein In N.S.A. Data Gathering." *The New York Times*. July 24, 2013. http://www.nytimes.com/2013/07/25/us/politics/house-defeats-effort-to-rein-in-nsa-data-gathering.html?pagewanted=all.

[45] Maplight. "H. Amdt. 413." *MapLight*. July 24, 2013. http://maplight.org/us-congress/bill/113-hr-2397/1742215/contributions-by-vote?sort=asc&order=%24%20From%20Interest%20Groups%3Cbr%20%2F%3EThat%20Opposed&party[D]=D&party[R]=R&party[I]=I&vote[AYE]=AYE&vote[NOE]=NOE&vote[NV]=NV&voted_with[with]=with&voted_with[not-

with]=not-with&state=&custom_from=01%2F01%
2F2011&custom_to=12% 2F31%2F2012&all_pols=1&uid=44999&interests-
support=&interests-oppose=D2000-D3000-D5000-D9000-D4000-D0000-
D6000&from=01-01-2011&to=12-31-2012&source=pacs-
nonpacs&campaign=congressional.

46   The U.S. House of Representatives Committee on Appropriations. "H.R.
     2397–TheFiscal Year 2014 Defense Appropriations Act." *The U.S. House of
     Representatives Committee on Appropriations.* July 24, 2013. http://
     appropriations.house.gov/uploadedfiles/07.24.13_fy14_defense_bill_-
     _floor_adopted_amendments.pdf.

47   The U.S. House of Representatives Committee on Appropriations.
     "House Approves Fiscal Year 2014 Defense Appropriations Bill." *The U.S.
     House of Representatives Committee on Appropriations.* July 24, 2013. http:/
     /appropriations.house.gov/news/
     documentsingle.aspx?DocumentID=343918.

48   Howerton, Jason. "A Different Amendment Restricting NSA Spying Was
     Passed Overwhelmingly by the House – But 'No One Is Talking About
     It.'" *Yahoo.* July 25, 2013. http://news.yahoo.com/different-
     amendment-restricting-nsa-spying-passed-overwhelmingly-house-
     170036854.html.

49   Freire, J.P. "Pompeo Offers Amendment To Clarify NSA Programs."
     Official website of U.S. Representative Mike Pompeo. July 24, 2013. http://
     pompeo.house.gov/news/documentsingle.aspx?DocumentID=343908.

50   Congress.gov. "H.Amdt.412 to H.R.2397." *Congress. gov.* July 24, 2013.
     http://beta.congress.gov/amendment/113th-congress/house-
     amendment/412.

CHAPTER 8

1   Snowden, Edward. "An Open Letter to the People of Brazil." *Folha de S.
     Paulo.* December 16, 2013. http://www1.folha.uol.com.br/
     internacional/en/world/2013/12/1386296-an-open-letter-to-the-people-
     of-brazil.shtml.

2   Hopkins, Nick and Julian Borger. "NSA pays £100m in secret funding for
     GCHQ." *The Guardian.* Aug. 1, 2013. http://www.theguardian.com/uk-
     news/2013/aug/01/nsa-paid-gchq-spying-edward-snowden.

3   Baker, Al and William Rashbaum. "Police Find Car Bomb in Times
     Square." *The New York Times.* May 1, 2010. http://www.nytimes.com/
     2010/05/02/nyregion/02timessquare.html.

4   Hopkins, Nick, et al. "GCHQ: inside the top secret world of Britain's
     biggest spy agency." *The Guardian.* Aug. 1, 2013. http://
     www.theguardian.com/world/2013/aug/02/gchq-spy-agency-nsa-
     snowden.

5   Andrews, Wilson and Todd Lindeman. "$52.6 billion: The Black Budget."
     The Washington Post. Aug. 29, 2013. http://www.washingtonpost.com/
     wp-srv/special/national/black-budget/.

6   Goetz, John and Jan Lukas Strozyk. "Geheimdienste nutzen
     Firmendienste." *Tagesschau.de.* Aug. 1, 2013. http://
     www.tagesschau.de/ausland/geheimdienste114.html.

7   Goetz, John and Frederik Obermaier. "Snowden enthüllt Namen der
     spähenden Telekomfirmen." *Sueddeutsche.* Aug. 2, 2013. http://
     www.sueddeutsche.de/digital/internet-ueberwachung-snowden-
     enthuellt-namen-der-spaehenden-telekomfirmen-1.1736791.

8   Greenwald, Glenn, et al. "A carta em que o embaixador americano no
     Brasil agradece o apoio da NSA." *Epoca.* Aug. 2, 2013. http://
     epoca.globo.com/tempo/noticia/2013/08/carta-em-que-o-atual-
     bembaixadorb-americano-no-brasil-bagradece-o-apoio-da-nsab.html.

9   Gude, Hubert, et al. "Mass Data: Transfers from Germany Aid US
     Surveillance." *Der Spiegel.* Aug. 5, 2013. http://www.spiegel.de/
     international/world/german-intelligence-sends-massive-amounts-of-
     data-to-the-nsa-a-914821.html.

10   Duhigg, Charles. "How Companies Learn Your Secrets." *The New York
     Times.* Feb. 16, 2012. http://www.nytimes.com/2012/02/19/magazine/
     shopping-habits.html?pagewanted=1&_r=2&hp&.

11   Ball, James. "NSA's Prism surveillance program: how it works and what
     it can do." *The Guardian.* June 8, 2013. http://www.theguardian.com/
     world/2013/jun/08/nsa-prism-server-collection-facebook-google.

12   Timberg, Tim. "The NSA slide you haven't seen." *The Washington Post.*
     July 10, 2013. http://www.washingtonpost.com/business/economy/
     the-nsa-slide-you-havent-seen/2013/07/10/32801426-e8e6-11e2-aa9f-
     c03a72e2d342_story.html.

13   Cf. 8.12

14   Fantastico. "NSA Documents Show United States Spied Brazilian Oil
     Giant." *OGlobo.* Sept. 9, 2013. http://g1.globo.com/fantastico/noticia/
     2013/09/nsa-documents-show-united-states-spied-brazilian-oil-
     giant.html.

15   Greenwald, Glenn. "XKeyscore: NSA tool collects 'nearly everything a
     user does on the internet.'" *The Guardian.* July 31, 2013. http://
     www.theguardian.com/world/2013/jul/31/nsa-top-secret-program-
     online-data.

16   Jardin, Xeni. "Lavabit, email service Snowden reportedly used, abruptly
     shuts down." *BoingBoing.* Aug. 8, 2013. http://boingboing.net/2013/
     08/08/lavabit-email-service-snowden.html.

17 Lavabit. Official Lavabit homepage. *Lavabit*. Oct. 10, 2013. https://lavabit.com/.

18 Mullin, Joe. "Lavabit's appeal: We're actually not required to wiretap our own users." *Ars Technica*. Oct. 11, 2013. http://arstechnica.com/tech-policy/2013/10/lavabits-appeal-were-actually-not-required-to-wiretap-our-own-users/.

19 Poulsen, Kevin. "Edward Snowden's Email Provider Shuts Down Amid Secret Court Battle." *Wired*. Aug. 8, 2013. http://www.wired.com/threatlevel/2013/08/lavabit-snowden/.

20 GlobalPost. "Edward Snowden has applied for asylum in Russia: Russian media (LIVE BLOG)." *Global Post*. July 12, 2013. http://www.globalpost.com/dispatch/news/regions/europe/russia/130712/edward-snowden-meeting-moscow-airport.

21 Rushe, Dominic. "Lavabit reopens temporarily to allow customers to retrieve information." *The Guardian*. Oct. 15, 2013. http://www.theguardian.com/world/2013/oct/15/lavabit-reopens-temporarily-customers-information.

22 Rushe, Dominic. "Lavabit founder: 'My own tax dollars are being used to spy on me.'" *The Guardian*. Aug. 22, 2013. http://www.theguardian.com/world/2013/aug/22/lavabit-founder-us-surveillance-snowden.

23 Levison, Ladar. "The Story Continues." *Rally.org*. https://rally.org/lavabit.

24 Ball, James and Spencer Ackerman. "NSA loophole allows warrantless search for US citizens' emails and phone calls." *The Guardian*. Aug. 9, 2013. http://www.theguardian.com/world/2013/aug/09/nsa-loophole-warrantless-searches-email-calls#.

25 Feinstein, Dianne. "FAA Sunsets Extension Act of 2012." *Federation of American Scientists*. June 7, 2012. http://www.fas.org/irp/congress/2012_rpt/faa-extend.html.

26 Wyden, Ron and Mark Udall. Letter from Senators Ron Wyden and Mark Udall to General Keith Alexander. *Scribd*. June 24, 2013. http://www.scribd.com/doc/149791921/Wyden-and-Udall-Letter-to-General-Alexander-on-NSA-s-Section-702-Fact-Sheet-Inaccuracy.

27 National Security Agency. National Security Agency Section 702 of FISA and Section 215 of PATRIOT Act Fact Sheets. *Scribd*. Dec. 16, 2013. http://www.scribd.com/doc/149791922/National-Security-Agency-Section-702-of-FISA-and-Section-215-of-PATRIOT-Act-Fact-Sheets.

28 Lazare, Sarah. "NSA 'Disappears' Its Own Fact Sheet on Spying Program." *Common Dreams*. June 26, 2013. https://www.commondreams.org/headline/2013/06/26-3.

29 Nakashima, Ellen. "Obama administration had restrictions on NSA reversed in 2011." *The Washington Post*. Sept. 7, 2013. http://articles.washingtonpost.com/2013-09-07/world/41852332_1_obama-administration-americans-search-authority.

30 Ackerman, Spencer. "NSA surveillance: the long fight to close backdoor into US communications." *The Guardian*. Aug. 9, 2013. http://www.theguardian.com/world/2013/aug/09/senator-ron-wyden-mark-udall-nsa.

31 Poitras, Laura, et al. "Ally and Target: US Intelligence Watches Germany Closely." *Der Spiegel*. Aug. 12, 2013. http://www.spiegel.de/international/world/germany-is-a-both-a-partner-to-and-a-target-of-nsa-surveillance-a-916029.html.

32 Poitras, Laura, et al. "Codename 'Apalachee': How America Spies on Europe and the UN." *Der Spiegel*. Aug. 26, 2013. http://www.spiegel.de/international/world/secret-nsa-documents-show-how-the-us-spies-on-europe-and-the-un-a-918625.html.

33 Pilkington, Ed. "FBI directed my attacks on foreign government sites." *The Guardian*. Nov. 15, 2013. http://www.theguardian.com/world/2013/nov/15/jeremy-hammond-fbi-directed-attacks-foreign-government.

34 The Washington Post Editorial Board. "Plugging the leaks in the Edward Snowden case." *The Washington Post*. July 1, 2013. http://www.washingtonpost.com/opinions/how-to-keep-edward-snowden-from-leaking-more-nsa-secrets/2013/07/01/4e8bbe28-e278-11e2-a11e-c2ea876a8f30_story.html.

35 Greenwald, Glenn. Personal Twitter account. *Twitter*. July 2, 2013. https://twitter.com/ggreenwald/status/352108900495011840.

36 Sirota, David. "Meet the 'Journalists Against Journalism' club!" *Salon*. July 2, 2013. http://www.salon.com/2013/07/02/meet_the_journalists_against_journalism_club/.

37 Gellman, Barton. "NSA broke privacy rules thousands of times per year, audit finds.'" *The Washington Post*. Aug. 15, 2013. http://www.washingtonpost.com/world/national-security/nsa-broke-privacy-rules-thousands-of-times-per-year-audit-finds/2013/08/15/3310e554-05ca-11e3-a07f-49ddc7417125_story.html.

38 Gellman, Barton and Matt DeLong. "What to say, and not to say, to 'our overseers.'" *The Washington Post*. Aug. 15, 2013. http://apps.washingtonpost.com/g/page/national/what-to-say-and-not-to-say-to-our-overseers/390/#document/p1/a115520.

39 Gellman, Barton and Matt DeLong. "NSA report on privacy violations in the first quarter of 2012." *The Washington Post*. Aug. 15, 2013. http://

apps.washingtonpost.com/g/page/national/nsa-report-on-privacy-violations-in-the-first-quarter-of-2012/395/.

40 Der Spiegel. "'Follow the Money': NSA Spies on International Payments." *Der Spiegel*. Sept. 15, 2013. http://www.spiegel.de/international/world/spiegel-exclusive-nsa-spies-on-international-bank-transactions-a-922276.html.

41 Gellman, Barton and Matt DeLong. "First direct evidence of illegal surveillance found by the FISA court." *The Washington Post*. Aug. 15, 2013. http://apps.washingtonpost.com/g/page/national/first-direct-evidence-of-illegal-surveillance-found-by-the-fisa-court/393/.

42 Nakashima, Ellen. "NSA gathered thousands of Americans' e-mails before court ordered it to revise its tactics." *The Washington Post*. Aug. 21, 2013. http://www.washingtonpost.com/world/national-security/nsa-gathered-thousands-of-americans-e-mails-before-court-struck-down-program/2013/08/21/146ba4b6-0a90-11e3-b87c-476db8ac34cd_story.html.

43 Gellman, Barton and Matt DeLong. "NSA What's a 'violation'?" *The Washington Post*. Aug. 15, 2013. http://apps.washingtonpost.com/g/page/national/whats-a-violation/391/.

44 Auletta, Ken. "Freedom of Information." *The New Yorker*. Oct. 7, 2013. http://www.newyorker.com/reporting/2013/10/07/131007fa_fact_auletta?currentPage=all.

45 The Guardian. "Glenn Greenwald's partner detained at Heathrow airport for nine hours." *The Guardian*. Aug. 18, 2013. http://www.theguardian.com/world/2013/aug/18/glenn-greenwald-guardian-partner-detained-heathrow.

46 Rozenberg, Joshua. "David Miranda detention: schedule 7 of the Terrorism Act explained." *The Guardian*. Aug. 19, 2013. http://www.theguardian.com/law/2013/aug/19/david-miranda-detention-schedule-7-terrorism-act.

47 Cf. 8.46

48 Gov.uk. "Review of the Operation of Schedule 7: A Public Consultation." *Gov.uk*. Sept. 2012. https://www.gov.uk/government/uploads/system/uploads/attachment_data/file/157896/consultation-document.pdf.

49 Booth, Robert. "UK government given Tuesday deadline over David Miranda data." *The Guardian*. Aug. 23, 2013. http://www.theguardian.com/world/2013/aug/23/government-david-miranda-data.

50 Boadle, Anthony. "Glenn Greenwald: Snowden Gave Me 15-20,000 Classified Documents." *The Huffington Post*. Aug. 6, 2013. http://

www.huffingtonpost.com/2013/08/07/glenn-greenwald-edward-snowden-documents_n_3716424.html.

51 Logiurato, Brett. "Glenn Greenwald's Partner Was Carrying A Stunning Amount Of Sensitive Documents When He Was Detained." *Business Insider*. Aug. 30, 2013. http://www.businessinsider.com/david-miranda-glenn-greenwald-documents-national-security-2013-8.

52 Savage, Charlie and Scott Shane. "Justice Dept. Defends Seizure of Phone Records." *The New York Times*. May 14, 2013. http://www.nytimes.com/2013/05/15/us/politics/attorney-general-defends-seizure-of-journalists-phone-records.html?pagewanted=all&_r=1&.

53 AP. "U.S: CIA thwarts new al-Qaeda underwear bomb plot." *USA Today*. May 8, 2012. http://usatoday30.usatoday.com/news/washington/story/2012-05-07/al-qaeda-bomb-plot-foiled/54811054/1.

54 Ingram, David. "Associated Press says U.S. government seized journalists' phone records." *Reuters*. May 13, 2013. http://ca.reuters.com/article/topNews/idCABRE94C0ZW20130513.

55 White, Erin. "AP responds to latest DOJ letter." *Associated Press*. May 14, 2013. http://blog.ap.org/2013/05/13/ap-responds-to-intrusive-doj-seizure-of-journalists-phone-records/.

56 Marimow, Ann. "A rare peek into a Justice Department leak probe." *The Washington Post*. May 19, 2013. http://www.washingtonpost.com/local/a-rare-peek-into-a-justice-department-leak-probe/2013/05/19/0bc473de-be5e-11e2-97d4-a479289a31f9_story.html?tid=pm_pop.

57 Rosen, James. "North Korea Intends to Match U.N. Resolution With New Nuclear Test." *Fox News*. June 11, 2009. http://www.foxnews.com/politics/2009/06/11/north-korea-intends-match-resolution-new-nuclear-test/.

58 Savage, Charlie and Jonathan Weisman. "Holder Faces New Round of Criticism After Leak Inquiries." *The New York Times*. May 29, 2013. http://www.nytimes.com/2013/05/30/us/politics/holder-faces-a-new-round-of-criticism.html?pagewanted=all&_r=1&.

59 Richter, Greg. "Holder Personally OK'd Fox Reporter's Warrant." *NewsMax*. May 23, 2013. http://www.newsmax.com/Newsfront/holder-involved-fox-warrant/2013/05/23/id/506161.

60 Botelho, Greg and Laura Smith-Spark. "Glenn Greenwald's partner, David Miranda, 'afraid' during questioning." *CNN*. Aug. 21, 2013. http://www.cnn.com/2013/08/20/world/europe/greenwald-partner-detained/index.html?hpt=hp_t1.

61 Borger, Julian. "NSA files: why the Guardian in London destroyed hard drives of leaked files." *The Guardian*. Aug. 20, 2013. http://www.theguardian.com/world/2013/aug/20/nsa-snowden-files-drives-destroyed-london.

[62] Cf. 8.44

[63] Maass, Peter. "How Laura Poitras Helped Snowden Spill His Secrets." *The New York Times*. Aug. 13, 2013. http://www.nytimes.com/2013/08/18/magazine/laura-poitras-snowden.html?pagewanted=all.

[64] Cf. 8.44

[65] Cf. 8.61

[66] Cf. 8.44

[67] O'Carroll, Lisa. "Guardian partners with New York Times over Snowden GCHQ files." *The Guardian*. Aug. 23, 2013. http://www.theguardian.com/uk-news/2013/aug/23/guardian-news-york-times-partnership.

[68] Pilkington, Ed. "New York Times says UK tried to get it to hand over Snowden documents." *The Guardian*. Oct. 13, 2013. http://www.theguardian.com/world/2013/oct/13/new-york-times-snowden-nsa-files.

[69] Gorman, Siobhan and Jennifer Valentino-DeVries. "New Details Show Broader NSA Surveillance Reach." *The Wall Street Journal*. Aug. 20, 2013. http://online.wsj.com/article/SB10001424127887324108204579022874091732470.html.

[70] MacAskill, Ewen. "NSA paid millions to cover Prism compliance costs for tech companies." *The Guardian*. Aug. 22, 2013. http://www.theguardian.com/world/2013/aug/23/nsa-prism-costs-tech-companies-paid.

[71] Gorman, Siobhan. "NSA Officers Spy on Love Interests." *The Wall Street Journal*. Aug. 23, 2013. http://blogs.wsj.com/washwire/2013/08/23/nsa-officers-sometimes-spy-on-love-interests/.

[72] Cf. 8.37

[73] AP. "More NSA employees found to have spied on spouses, partners." *New York Post*. Sept. 27, 2013. http://nypost.com/2013/09/27/more-nsa-employees-found-to-have-spied-on-spouses-partners/.

[74] Ellard, George. Letter from George Ellard to Senator Charles Grassley. *Official website of U.S. Senator Charles Grassley*. Sept. 11, 2013. http://www.grassley.senate.gov/judiciary/upload/NSA-Surveillance-09-11-13-response-from-IG-to-intentional-misuse-of-NSA-authority.pdf.

[75] Campbell, Duncan, et al. "UK's secret Mid-East internet surveillance base is revealed in Edward Snowden leaks." *The Independent*. Aug. 23, 2013. http://www.independent.co.uk/news/uk/politics/exclusive-uks-secret-mideast-internet-surveillance-base-is-revealed-in-edward-snowden-leaks-8781082.html.

[76] Greenwald, Glenn. "Snowden: UK government now leaking documents about itself." *The Guardian*. Aug. 23, 2013. http://

www.theguardian.com/commentisfree/2013/aug/23/uk-government-independent-military-base.

77 Meyer, David. "UK newspapers clash over Snowden surveillance scoop claims." *PaidContent.org.* Aug. 23. 2013. http://paidcontent.org/2013/08/23/with-guardian-facing-reporting-restrictions-rival-uk-paper-outs-latest-snowden-scoop/.

78 Waterman, Shaun. "NSA trove in foreign hands: 58,000 'highly classified' documents, U.K. officials say." *The Washington Times.* Aug. 30, 2013. http://www.washingtontimes.com/news/2013/aug/30/snowden-trove-foreign-hands-includes-58000-highly-/.

79 Cf. 8.50

80 Blackhurst, Chris. "Edward Snowden's secrets may be dangerous. I would not have published them." *The Independent.* Oct. 13, 2013. http://www.independent.co.uk/voices/comment/edward-snowdens-secrets-may-be-dangerous-i-would-not-have-published-them-8877404.html.

81 Cf. 8.32

82 Goetz, John. "British Officials Have Far-Reaching Access To Internet And Telephone Communications." *Sueddeutsche.* Aug. 28, 2013. http://international.sueddeutsche.de/post/59603415442/british-officials-have-far-reaching-access-to-internet.

83 Esposito, Richard, et al. "Snowden impersonated NSA officials, sources say." *NBC News.* Aug. 29, 2013. http://investigations.nbcnews.com/_news/2013/08/29/20234171-snowden-impersonated-nsa-officials-sources-say.

84 Lake, Eli. "Greenwald: Snowden's Files Are Out There if 'Anything Happens' to Him." *The Daily Beast.* June 25, 2013. http://www.thedailybeast.com/articles/2013/06/25/greenwald-snowden-s-files-are-out-there-if-anything-happens-to-him.html.

85 Cf. 8.83

86 Miller, John. "Inside the NSA." *60 Minutes.* Dec. 15, 2013. http://www.cbsnews.com/news/nsa-speaks-out-on-snowden-spying/.

87 Hosenball, Mark. "Laptops Snowden took to Hong Kong, Russia were a 'diversion.'" *Reuters.* Oct. 11, 2013. http://www.reuters.com/article/2013/10/11/us-usa-security-snowden-idUSBRE99A0LK20131011.

88 Jennett, Greg. "Inquiry launched into claim of bugging Labor MP." *ABC.* Apr. 30, 2003. http://www.abc.net.au/lateline/content/2003/s844047.htm.

89 Veness, Peter. "Police raid home of Canberra Times journalist Philip Dorling." *The Herald Sun.* Sept. 23, 2008. http://www.heraldsun.com.au/story/0,21985,24389814-661,00.html.

[90] Personal correspondence with the author, October 7 and October 18, 2013.

[91] Dorling, Philip. "Australian spies in global deal to tap undersea cables." *The Age*. Aug. 29, 2013. http://www.theage.com.au/technology/technology-news/australian-spies-in-global-deal-to-tap-undersea-cables-20130828-2sr58.html.

[92] Timberg, Craig and Barton Gellman. "NSA paying U.S. companies for access to communications networks." *The Washington Post*. Aug. 29, 2013. http://www.washingtonpost.com/world/national-security/nsa-paying-us-companies-for-access-to-communications-networks/2013/08/29/5641a4b6-10c2-11e3-bdf6-e4fc677d94a1_story.html.

[93] DeLong, Matt. "Inside the 2013 U.S. intelligence 'black budget.'" *The Washington Post*. Aug. 29, 2013. http://apps.washingtonpost.com/g/page/national/inside-the-2013-us-intelligence-black-budget/420/.

[94] Poitras, Laura, et al. "How the NSA Targets Germany and Europe." *Der Spiegel*. July 1, 2013. http://www.spiegel.de/international/world/secret-documents-nsa-targeted-germany-and-eu-buildings-a-908609-3.html.

[95] Gellman, Barton and Greg Miller. "U.S. spy network's successes, failures and objectives detailed in 'black budget' summary." *The Washington Post*. Aug. 29, 2013. http://www.washingtonpost.com/world/national-security/black-budget-summary-details-us-spy-networks-successes-failures-and-objectives/2013/08/29/7e57bb78-10ab-11e3-8cdd-bcdc09410972_story.html.

[96] Cf. 8.5

[97] Broder, John and Scott Shane. "For Snowden, a Life of Ambition, Despite the Drifting." *The New York Times*. June 15, 2013. http://www.nytimes.com/2013/06/16/us/for-snowden-a-life-of-ambition-despite-the-drifting.html?pagewanted=all&_r=0.

[98] Gallagher, Sean. "As DefCon asks Feds to take 'time-out,' Black Hat welcomes NSA chief." *Ars Technica*. July 11, 2013. http://arstechnica.com/security/2013/07/as-defcon-asks-feds-to-take-time-out-black-hat-welcomes-nsa-chief/.

[99] Zaretsky, Staci. "Lawyers Rank Near the Top for Best-Paid Careers in America." *AboveTheLaw.com*. July 3, 2012. http://abovethelaw.com/2012/07/lawyers-rank-near-the-top-for-best-paid-careers-in-america/.

[100] Whitlock, Craig and Barton Gellman. "To hunt Osama bin Laden, satellites watched over Abbottabad, Pakistan, and Navy SEALs." *The Washington Post*. Aug. 29, 2013. http://www.washingtonpost.com/world/national-security/to-hunt-osama-bin-laden-satellites-watched-over-abbottabad-pakistan-and-navy-seals/2013/08/29/8d32c1d6-10d5-11e3-b4cb-fd7ce041d814_story.html.

[101] Gellman, Barton and Ellen Nakashima. "U.S. spy agencies mounted 231 offensive cyber-operations in 2011, documents show." *The Washington Post.* Aug. 30, 2013. http://www.washingtonpost.com/world/national-security/us-spy-agencies-mounted-231-offensive-cyber-operations-in-2011-documents-show/2013/08/30/d090a6ae-119e-11e3-b4cb-fd7ce041d814_story.html.

[102] Der Spiegel. "Snowden Document: NSA Spied On Al Jazeera Communications." *Der Spiegel.* Aug. 31, 2013. http://www.spiegel.de/international/world/nsa-spied-on-al-jazeera-communications-snowden-document-a-919681.html.

[103] Leonnig, Carol, et al. "U.S. intelligence agencies spend millions to hunt for insider threats, document shows." *The Washington Post.* Sept. 1, 2013. http://www.washingtonpost.com/politics/us-intelligence-agencies-spend-millions-to-hunt-for-insider-threats-document-shows/2013/09/01/c6ab6c74-0ffe-11e3-85b6-d27422650fd5_story.html.

[104] The White House. "Presidential Memorandum — National Insider Threat Policy and Minimum Standards for Executive Branch Insider Threat Programs." *The White House of the United States.* Nov. 21, 2012. http://www.whitehouse.gov/the-press-office/2012/11/21/presidential-memorandum-national-insider-threat-policy-and-minimum-stand.

[105] Whitlock, Craig and Barton Gellman. "U.S. documents detail al-Qaeda's efforts to fight back against drones." *The Washington Post.* Sept. 3, 2013. http://www.washingtonpost.com/world/national-security/us-documents-detail-al-qaedas-efforts-to-fight-back-against-drones/2013/09/03/b83e7654-11c0-11e3-b630-36617ca6640f_story.html.

[106] The Washington Post. "Tracking America's drone war." *The Washington Post.* Oct. 23, 2012. http://www.washingtonpost.com/world/tracking-americas-drone-war/2012/10/23/b16c0106-1d52-11e2-9cd5-b55c38388962_graphic.html.

[107] Miller, Greg, et al. "Top-secret U.S. intelligence files show new levels of distrust of Pakistan." *The Washington Post.* Sept. 2, 2013. http://www.washingtonpost.com/world/national-security/top-secret-us-intelligence-files-show-new-levels-of-distrust-of-pakistan/2013/09/02/e19d03c2-11bf-11e3-b630-36617ca6640f_story.html?wprss=rss_national-security.

[108] Der Spiegel. "'Success Story': NSA Targeted French Foreign Ministry." *Der Spiegel.* Sept. 1, 2013. http://www.spiegel.de/international/world/nsa-targeted-french-foreign-ministry-a-919693.html.

[109] Fantastico. "Documentos revelam esquema de agência dos EUA para espionar Dilma." *Fantastico.* Sept. 1, 2013. http://g1.globo.com/fantastico/noticia/2013/09/documentos-revelam-esquema-de-agencia-dos-eua-para-espionar-dilma-rousseff.html.

[110] Romero, Simon and Randal Archibold. "Brazil Angered Over Report N.S.A. Spied on President." *The New York Times*. Sept. 2, 2013. http://www.nytimes.com/2013/09/03/world/americas/brazil-angered-over-report-nsa-spied-on-president.html?_r=3&%20(http://cryptome.org/2013/09/nsa-spying-brazil.htm&.

[111] Kusnetz, Nicholas and Karen Weise. "A Reading List to Put the WikiLeaks 'War Logs' in Context." *ProPublica*. July 26, 2010. http://www.propublica.org/article/A-Reading-List-to-Put-the-WikiLeaks-War-Logs-in-Context.

[112] Kissane, Erin, et al. "ProPublica's Jeff Larson on the NSA Crypto Story." *Source*. Sept. 6, 2013. http://source.mozillaopennews.org/en-US/articles/propublicas-jeff-larson-nsa-crypto-story/.

[113] Ball, James, et al. "Revealed: how US and UK spy agencies defeat internet privacy and security." *The Guardian*. Sept. 5, 2013. http://www.theguardian.com/world/2013/sep/05/nsa-gchq-encryption-codes-security.

[114] McCullagh, Declan and Anne Broache. "Security firms on police spyware, in their own words." *CNet*. July 17, 2007. http://news.cnet.com/2100-7348_3-6196990.html.

[115] Internet archive. Man-in-the-Middle slide. *DocumentCloud*. Dec. 16, 2013. https://www.documentcloud.org/documents/785152-166819124-mitm-google.html.

[116] Peterson, Andrea. "Post reporter: Here's why we refused the NSA's demand to censor the names of PRISM companies." *The Washington Post*. Oct. 9, 2013. http://www.washingtonpost.com/blogs/the-switch/wp/2013/10/09/heres-why-we-refused-the-nsas-demand-to-censor-the-names-of-prism-companies/.

[117] Larson, Jeff, et al. "Revealed: The NSA's Secret Campaign to Crack, Undermine Internet Security." *ProPublica*. Sept. 5, 2013. http://www.propublica.org/article/the-nsas-secret-campaign-to-crack-undermine-internet-encryption.

[118] Perlroth, Nicole, et al. "N.S.A. Able to Foil Basic Safeguards of Privacy on Web." *The New York Times*. Sept. 5, 2013. http://www.nytimes.com/2013/09/06/us/nsa-foils-much-internet-encryption.html?_r=1&.

[119] Zetter, Kim. "Router Flaw Is a Ticking Bomb." *Wired*. Aug. 1, 2005. http://www.wired.com/politics/security/news/2005/08/68365?currentPage=all.

[120] Poitras, Laura and Jacob Appelbaum. "Edward Snowden Interview: The NSA and Its Willing Helpers." *Der Spiegel*. July 8, 2013. http://www.spiegel.de/international/world/interview-with-whistleblower-edward-snowden-on-global-spying-a-910006.html.

[121] Cf. 8.14

[122] Watts, Jonathan. "NSA accused of spying on Brazilian oil company Petrobras." *The Guardian*. Sept. 9, 2013. http://www.theguardian.com/world/2013/sep/09/nsa-spying-brazil-oil-petrobras.

[123] Cf. 8.122

[124] Cf. 8.115

[125] Lederman, Josh. "Obama talks with Mexico, Brazil leaders on NSA." *The Big Story*. Sept. 6, 2013. http://bigstory.ap.org/article/obama-talks-mexico-brazil-leaders-nsa.

[126] Reuters. "Obama and Rousseff meet in Russia after disclosure of alleged U.S. spying." *Reuters*. Sept. 6, 2013. http://www.reuters.com/article/2013/09/06/us-usa-security-snowden-brazil-idUSBRE98505220130906.

[127] Reuters. "Dilma Rousseff Cancels U.S. Trips Over Claims Of NSA Spying On Brazil's President." *Reuters*. Sept. 17, 2013. http://www.huffingtonpost.com/2013/09/17/rouseff-cancels-us-trip_n_3941973.html.

[128] Cf. 8.110

[129] Brooks, Bradley. "Rousseff wants Web servers to be housed in Brazil." *Yahoo*. Sept. 12, 2013. http://news.yahoo.com/rousseff-wants-servers-housed-brazil-235521587.html.

[130] Cf. 8.129

[131] Rosenbach, Marcel. "iSpy: How the NSA Accesses Smartphone Data." *Der Spiegel*. Sept. 9, 2013. http://www.spiegel.de/international/world/how-the-nsa-spies-on-smartphones-including-the-blackberry-a-921161.html.

[132] Svensson, Peter. "Smartphones now outsell 'dumb' phones." *3News*. Apr. 29, 2013. http://www.3news.co.nz/Smartphones-now-outsell-dumb-phones/tabid/412/articleID/295878/Default.aspx.

[133] Kravets, David. "Mobile 'Rootkit' Maker Tries to Silence Critical Android Dev." *Wired*. Nov. 22, 2011. http://www.wired.com/threatlevel/2011/11/rootkit-brouhaha/.

[134] Chen, Brian. "Programmer Raises Concerns About Phone-Monitoring Software." *The New York Times*. Dec. 1, 2011. http://bits.blogs.nytimes.com/2011/12/01/programmer-raises-concerns-about-phone-monitoring-software/.

[135] Priest, Dana. "NSA growth fueled by need to target terrorists." *The Washington Post*. July 21, 2013. http://www.washingtonpost.com/world/national-security/nsa-growth-fueled-by-need-to-target-terrorists/2013/07/21/24c93cf4-f0b1-11e2-bed3-b9b6fe264871_story.html.

136 Zetter, Kim. "Researcher: Middle East BlackBerry update spies on users." *Wired*. July 15, 2009. http://www.wired.co.uk/news/archive/2009-07/15/researcher-says-middle-east-blackberry-update-spies-on-users.

137 Kaplan, Lewis. Court opinion on United States District Court v. John Tomero, et al. *Politech: Politics & Technology*. Nov. 27, 2006. http://www.politechbot.com/docs/fbi.ardito.roving.bug.opinion.120106.txt.

138 Der Spiegel. Three NSA smartphone surveillance slides. *Der Spiegel*. Dec. 16, 2013. http://www.spiegel.de/fotostrecke/photo-gallery-spying-on-smartphones-fotostrecke-101201.html.

139 Rodriguez, Salvador. "Unlocking smartphones without permission illegal after Friday." *Los Angeles Times*. Jan. 25, 2013. http://articles.latimes.com/2013/jan/25/business/la-fi-tn-unlock-phone-illegal-20130125.

AFTERWORD

1 Ed. William Temple Franklin. Charleston: Nabu Press, 2010.

2 Lanchester, John. "The Snowden files: why the British public should be worried about GCHQ." *The Guardian*. Oct. 3, 2013. http://www.theguardian.com/world/2013/oct/03/edward-snowden-files-john-lanchester.

3 Cf. A.2

4 Department of Homeland Security. "Analyst's Desktop Binder." *Epic*. 2011. https://epic.org/foia/epic-v-dhs-media-monitoring/Analyst-Desktop-Binder-REDACTED.pdf.

5 The White House. "Daily Briefing by the Press Secretary, 9/30/13." *The White House of the United States*. Sept. 30, 2013. http://www.whitehouse.gov/the-press-office/2013/09/30/daily-briefing-press-secretary-93013.

6 Risen, James and Laura Poitras. "N.S.A. Gathers Data on Social Connections of U.S. Citizens." *The New York Times*. Sept. 28, 2013. http://www.nytimes.com/2013/09/29/us/nsa-examines-social-networks-of-us-citizens.html?_r=0&pagewanted=all.

7 Savage, Charlie. "In Test Project, N.S.A. Tracked Cellphone Locations." *The New York Times*. Oct. 2, 2013. http://www.nytimes.com/2013/10/03/us/nsa-experiment-traced-us-cellphone-locations.html?_r=1&.

8 Gellman, Barton and Matt DeLong. "The NSA's problem? Too much data." *The Washington Post*. Oct. 14, 2013. http://apps.washingtonpost.com/g/page/world/the-nsas-overcollection-problem/517/.

9 Ball, James. "Xbox Live among game services targeted by US and UK spy agencies." *The Guardian*. Dec. 9, 2013. http://

www.theguardian.com/world/2013/dec/09/nsa-spies-online-games-world-warcraft-second-life.

10 Education Database Online. "Videogame Statistics." *Education Online.* Dec. 16, 2013. http://www.onlineeducation.net/videogame.

11 The Washington Post. "Ecuador's foreign minister publicly reads Snowden asylum request letter." *The Washington Post.* June 24, 2013. http://articles.washingtonpost.com/2013-06-24/world/ 40157366_1_human-rights-universal-declaration-asylum-request.

12 Cassidy, John. "Demonizing Edward Snowden: Which Side Are You On?" *The New Yorker.* June 24, 2013. http://www.newyorker.com/ online/blogs/johncassidy/2013/06/demonizing-edward-snowden-which-side-are-you-on.html.

13 Privacy International. "Surveillance Monitor 2007 - International country rankings." *Privacy International.* Dec. 13, 2007. https:// www.privacyinternational.org/reports/surveillance-monitor-2007-international-country-rankings.

14 Cushing, Tim. "Former NSA Officer: Wikileaks Is A Front For Russian Intelligence And Snowden's (Probably) A Spy." *TechDirt.* Sept. 12, 2013. http://www.techdirt.com/articles/20130910/13145824474/former-nsa-officer-wikileaks-is-front-russian-intelligence-snowdens-probably-spy.shtml.

15 RT. "Obama administration drowning in lawsuits filed over NSA surveillance." *RT.* July 16, 2013. http://rt.com/usa/snowden-leaks-surveillance-suits-174/.

16 Bowe, Rebecca. "NSA surveillance: protesters stage Restore the Fourth rallies across US." *The Guardian.* July 5, 2013. http:// www.theguardian.com/world/2013/jul/04/restore-the-fourth-protesters-nsa-surveillance.

17 Newell, Jim. "Thousands gather in Washington for anti-NSA 'Stop Watching Us' rally." *The Guardian.* Oct. 26, 2013. http:// www.theguardian.com/world/2013/oct/26/nsa-rally-stop-watching-washington-snowden.

18 Lewis, Paul and Philip Oltermann. "NSA denies discussing Merkel phone surveillance with Obama." *The Guardian.* Oct. 27, 2013. http:// www.theguardian.com/world/2013/oct/27/barack-obama-nsa-angela-merkel-germany.

19 The White House. "Press Briefing by Press Secretary Jay Carney, 10/28/ 13." *The White House of the United States.* Oct. 28, 2013. http:// www.whitehouse.gov/the-press-office/2013/10/28/press-briefing-press-secretary-jay-carney-112813.

20 Washington's Blog. "Head of Congressional Intelligence Committee: 'You Can't Have Your Privacy Violated If You Don't KNOW Your

Privacy Is Violated.'" *Washington's Blog*. Oct. 30, 2013. http://
www.washingtonsblog.com/2013/10/head-of-congressional-
intelligence-committee-you-cant-have-your-privacy-violated-if-you-dont-
know-your-privacy-is-violated.html.

[21] Greenberg, Andy. "NSA Implementing 'Two-Person' Rule To Stop The
Next Edward Snowden." *Forbes*. June 18, 2013. http://
www.forbes.com/sites/andygreenberg/2013/06/18/nsa-director-says-
agency-implementing-two-person-rule-to-stop-the-next-edward-
snowden/.

[22] Bierman, Noah and Bryan Bender. "Leaks show US intelligence
vulnerability." *The Boston Globe*. June 11, 2013. http://
www.bostonglobe.com/news/nation/2013/06/10/surveillance-leaks-
point-hole-security-system-more-people-more-levels-gain-access/
d85USWewpmk5HiG72HZ9EO/story.html.

[23] Gjelten, Tom. "Officials: Edward Snowden's Leaks Were Masked By Job
Duties." *NPR*. Sept. 18, 2013. http://www.npr.org/2013/09/18/
223523622/officials-edward-snowdens-leaks-were-masked-by-job-duties.

[24] Leonnig, Carol, et al. "U.S. intelligence agencies spend millions to hunt
for insider threats, document shows." *The Washington Post*. Sept. 1, 2013.
http://www.washingtonpost.com/politics/us-intelligence-agencies-
spend-millions-to-hunt-for-insider-threats-document-shows/2013/09/
01/c6ab6c74-0ffe-11e3-85b6-d27422650fd5_story_1.html.

[25] Lawrence O'Donnell. "The Last Word with Lawrence O'Donnell (with
Glenn Greenwald)." *NBC News*. June 10, 2013. http://
www.nbcnews.com/id/45755883/ns/msnbc-the_last_word/vp/
52163467#52163467.

[26] Bamford, James. "The NSA Is Building the Country's Biggest Spy Center
(Watch What You Say)." *Wired*. Mar. 15, 2012. http://www.wired.com/
threatlevel/2012/03/ff_nsadatacenter/all/1.

[27] Cf. A.26

[28] Glüsing, Jens, et al. "Fresh Leak on US Spying: NSA Accessed Mexican
President's Email." *Der Spiegel*. Oct. 20, 2013. http://www.spiegel.de/
international/world/nsa-hacked-email-account-of-mexican-president-a-
928817.html.

[29] Wolverton, Joe. "NSA Surveillance in Germany May Threaten Merkel
Reelection." *The New American*. Aug. 29, 2013. http://
www.thenewamerican.com/world-news/europe/item/16423-nsa-
surveillance-in-germany-may-threaten-merkel-reelection.

[30] Ball, James. "NSA monitored calls of 35 world leaders after US official
handed over contacts." *The Guardian*. Oct. 24, 2013. http://
www.theguardian.com/world/2013/oct/24/nsa-surveillance-world-
leaders-calls.

[31] Saxena, Shobhan. "NSA planted bugs at Indian missions in D.C., U.N." *The Hindu*. Sept. 25, 2013. http://www.thehindu.com/news/ international/world/nsa-planted-bugs-at-indian-missions-in-dc-un/ article5164944.ece.

[32] Bedi, Rahul. "Indian High Commission returns to typewriters." *The Telegraph*. Sept. 27, 2013. http://www.telegraph.co.uk/news/ worldnews/asia/india/10339111/Indian-High-Commission-returns-to-typewriters.html.

[33] Follorou, Jacques and Glenn Greenwald. "France in the NSA's crosshair: phone networks under surveillance." *Le Monde*. Oct. 21, 2013. http:// www.lemonde.fr/technologies/article/2013/10/21/france-in-the-nsa-s-crosshair-phone-networks-under-surveillance_3499741_651865.html.

[34] The New York Times. "Oct. 22, 2013: European Union profile." *The New York Times*. Oct. 22, 2013. http://topics.nytimes.com/top/reference/ timestopics/organizations/e/european_union/.

[35] Schmitz, Gregor. "SWIFT Suspension? EU Parliament Furious about NSA Bank Spying." *Der Spiegel*. Sept. 18, 2013. http://www.spiegel.de/ international/europe/nsa-spying-european-parliamentarians-call-for-swift-suspension-a-922920.html.

[36] European Parliament. "MEPs call for suspension of EU-US bank data deal in response to NSA snooping." *The European Parliament*. Oct. 23, 2013. http://www.europarl.europa.eu/news/en/news-room/content/ 20131021IPR22725/html/MEPs-call-for-suspension-of-EU-US-bank-data-deal-in-response-to-NSA-snooping.

[37] Voice of America. "Obama to Meet With Chinese, French Presidents at G20." *Voice of America*. Sept. 5, 2013. http://www.voanews.com/ content/obama-to-meet-with-chinese-french-presidents-at-g20/ 1744252.html.

[38] Cunningham, Erin. "Edward Snowden the Focus of New Lingerie Ad." *The Daily Beast*. July 1, 2013. http://www.thedailybeast.com/articles/ 2013/07/01/blush-berlin-taps-snowden-nsa-scandal-for-lingerie-ads.html.

[39] Loveday, Eric. "Electric Vehicle Firm in Beijing Registers Snowden Name for its Top Secret Breakthrough Technology." *InsideEVs*. Aug. 20, 2013. http://insideevs.com/electric-vehicle-firm-in-beijing-registers-snowden-name-for-its-top-secret-breakthrough-technology/.

[40] Rosen, Jay. "The Snowden Effect: definition and examples." *PressThink*. July 5, 2013. http://pressthink.org/2013/07/the-snowden-effect-definition-and-examples/.

[41] Vlahos, Kelley. "The Right Rallies to Edward Snowden." *The American Conservative*. Aug. 8, 2013. http://www.theamericanconservative.com/ articles/the-right-rallies-to-edward-snowden/.

42 RT. "'Heroic effort at great personal cost': Edward Snowden nominated for Nobel Peace Prize." *RT*. July 15, 2013. http://rt.com/news/snowden-nominated-nobel-peace-099/.

43 Hibberd, James. "'South Park' NSA surveillance spoof gets big ratings." *Entertainment Weekly*. Sept. 26, 2013. http://insidetv.ew.com/2013/09/26/south-park-ratings-snowden/?hpt=hp_t3.

44 Maierbrugger, Arno. "Ready at last: Hong Kong director presents Snowden movie." *Investvine*. July 4, 2013. http://investvine.com/ready-at-last-hong-kong-director-presents-snowden-movie/.

45 Child, Ben. "Edward Snowden story on way to the big screen." *The Guardian*. June 14, 2013. http://www.theguardian.com/film/2013/jun/14/edward-snowden-story-nsa-whistleblower.

46 Kharpal, Arjun. "Filmmakers look to crowdfunding for Snowden movie." *CNBC*. Sept. 10, 2013. http://www.cnbc.com/id/101021408.

47 Perlman, Jake. "Maggie Gyllenhaal, John Cusack, Oliver Stone, and more tell NSA to 'Stop Watching Us' — VIDEO." *Entertainment Weekly*. Oct. 24, 2013. http://popwatch.ew.com/2013/10/24/stop-watching-us-video/?hpt=hp_t3.

48 Winter, Michael. "Sales of '1984' spike amid NSA spying scandal." *USA Today*. June 11, 2013. http://www.usatoday.com/story/news/nation/2013/06/11/1984-book-sales-jump-surveillance/2413433/.

49 Agence France Presse. "Snowden's Russian Lawyer: US Leaker Wears Disguises And 'I Am His Only Link With The Outside World.'" *Business Insider*. Sept. 23, 2013. http://www.businessinsider.com/snowdens-russian-lawyer-he-wears-disguises-2013-9.

50 BBC News Europe. "Snowden father 'meets son in Russia.'" *BBC*. Oct. 10, 2013. http://www.bbc.co.uk/news/world-europe-24470942.

51 Kim, Douglas. "Former National Security Whistleblowers Meet in Moscow and Award Sam Adams Prize to Snowden." *Whistleblower.org*. Oct. 10, 2013. http://www.whistleblower.org/blog/44-2013/3012-former-national-security-whistleblowers-meet-in-moscow-and-award-sam-adams-prize-to-snowden-.

52 Sheridan, Peter. "Are lover's enigmatic photos a secret message to 'traitor' Edward Snowden?" *Mail Online*. Oct. 19, 2013. http://www.dailymail.co.uk/news/article-2467914/Are-lovers-enigmatic-photos-secret-message-traitor-Edward-Snowden.html.

53 Black, Phil and Ben Brumfield. "NSA leaker Edward Snowden deserves a Nobel Prize, his father says." *CNN*. Oct. 10, 2013. http://www.cnn.com/2013/10/10/world/europe/moscow-snowden-nsa-leaks/.

[54] Eshchenko, Alla. "Edward Snowden gets website job in Russia, lawyer says." *CNN*. Oct. 31, 2013. http://www.cnn.com/2013/10/31/world/europe/russia-snowden-job/index.html?hpt=hp_t3.

[55] Snowden, Edward. "Letter from Edward Snowden to German Government." *The Guardian*. Nov. 1, 2013. http://www.theguardian.com/world/2013/nov/01/edward-snowden-letter-to-german-government-in-full-nsa.

[56] Snowden, Edward. "An Open Letter to the People of Brazil." *Folha de S. Paulo*. December 16, 2013. http://www1.folha.uol.com.br/internacional/en/world/2013/12/1386296-an-open-letter-to-the-people-of-brazil.shtml.

[57] Butler, Don. "Are we addicted to being watched?" *Canada.com*. Jan. 31, 2009. http://www2.canada.com/ottawacitizen/news/observer/story.html?id=ade6d795-4e7a-4ede-9fc1-f7bf929849c8&p=1.

[58] Clifford, Stephanie and Quentin Hardy. "Attention, Shoppers: Store Is Tracking Your Cell." *The New York Times*. July 14, 2013. http://www.nytimes.com/2013/07/15/business/attention-shopper-stores-are-tracking-your-cell.html.

[59] The Week. "Acxiom Corp: The 'faceless organization that knows everything about you.'" *The Week*. June 20, 2012. http://theweek.com/article/index/229508/acxiom-corp-the-faceless-organization-that-knows-everything-about-you.

[60] Gurnow, Michael. "Why Searching for Dog Toys Online Might Increase Your Home Insurance: The Importance of Internet Security." *Strike the Root*. July 1, 2013. http://strike-the-root.com/why-searching-for-dog-toys-online-might-increase-your-home-insurance-importance-of-internet-security.

[61] Cf. A.2

[62] Niznik, Steven. "How to Job Search Confidentially." *About.com*. Dec. 16, 2013. http://jobsearchtech.about.com/od/careerplanning/l/aa111102.htm.

[63] Cloud Security Alliance. "Government Access to Information." *Cloud Security Alliance*. July 2013. https://downloads.cloudsecurityalliance.org/initiatives/surveys/nsa_prism/CSA-govt-access-survey-July-2013.pdf.

[64] Castro, Daniel. "How Much Will PRISM Cost the U.S. Cloud Computing Industry?" *The Information Technology & Innovation Foundation*. Aug. 2013. http://www2.itif.org/2013-cloud-computing-costs.pdf.

[65] Arthur, Charles. "Fears over NSA surveillance revelations endanger US cloud computing industry." *The Guardian*. Aug. 8, 2013. http://www.theguardian.com/world/2013/aug/08/nsa-revelations-fears-cloud-computing.

[66] Strohm, Chris and Danielle Ivory. "Booz Allen to Lockheed Win Part of $6 Billion Cyber Award." *Bloomberg*. Aug. 13, 2013. http://www.bloomberg.com/news/2013-08-13/booz-allen-to-lockheed-win-part-of-6-billion-cyber-award.html.

[67] Gross, Grant. "People flock to anonymizing services after NSA snooping reports." *Computerworld*. Oct. 10, 2013. http://www.computerworld.co.nz/article/528833/people_flock_anonymizing_services_after_nsa_snooping_reports/?fp=16&fpid=1.

[68] Ball, James, et al. "NSA and GCHQ target Tor network that protects anonymity of web users." *The Guardian*. Oct. 4, 2013. http://www.theguardian.com/world/2013/oct/04/nsa-gchq-attack-tor-network-encryption.

[69] *Friends* magazine, 1970.

[70] Hackers News Bulletin. "NSA Fear: More than 11 Million users from U.S & U.K quitted Facebook." *HackersNewsBulletin*. Oct. 5, 2013. http://hackersnewsbulletin.com/2013/10/nsa-fear-11-million-users-u-s-u-k-quieted-facebook-accounts.html.

[71] Nakashima, Ellen. "NSA has made strides in thwarting encryption used to protect Internet communication." *The Washington Post*. Sept. 5, 2013. http://articles.washingtonpost.com/2013-09-05/world/41798759_1_encryption-nsa-internet.

[72] MacAskill, Ewen. "Edward Snowden, NSA files source: 'If they want to get you, in time they will.'" *The Guardian*. June 9, 2013. http://www.theguardian.com/world/2013/jun/09/nsa-whistleblower-edward-snowden-why.

[73] Rushe, Dominic. "Lavabit founder: 'My own tax dollars are being used to spy on me.'" *The Guardian*. Aug. 22, 2013. http://www.theguardian.com/world/2013/aug/22/lavabit-founder-us-surveillance-snowden.

[74] Daily Paul. "cc the DHS, NSA, CIA, and FBI on all of your emails." *Daily Paul*. May 21, 2012. http://www.dailypaul.com/235277/cc-the-nsa-nsa-cia-all-fbi-on-all-of-your-emails.

[75] Godlikeproductions. Online forum. *Godlikeproductions*. Aug. 16, 2013. http://www.godlikeproductions.com/forum1/message2322985/pg1.

[76] Riseup. Newsletter August 2013. *Riseup*. Aug. 2013. https://www.riseup.net/en/newsletter-2013-8.

[77] The Tor Project. Overview page. *The Tor Project*. Dec. 16, 2013. https://www.torproject.org/about/overview.html.en.

[78] Cf. A.76

[79] Gurnow, Michael. "Seated Between Pablo Escobar and Mahatma Gandhi: The Sticky Ethics of Anonymity Networks." *Dissident Voice*. June 28, 2013. http://dissidentvoice.org/2013/06/seated-between-pablo-escobar-and-mahatma-gandhi/.